GOLDENEYE

Also by Matthew Parker

The Battle of Britain

Monte Cassino

Panama Fever
(published in paperback as *Hell's Gorge)*

The Sugar Barons

GOLDENEYE

WHERE BOND WAS BORN:
IAN FLEMING'S JAMAICA

MATTHEW PARKER

PEGASUS BOOKS
NEW YORK LONDON

GOLDENEYE

Pegasus Books LLC
80 Broad Street, 5th Floor
New York, NY 10004

First Pegasus Books hardcover edition March 2015

ISBN: 978-1-60598-686-9

10 9 8 7 8 6 5 4 3 2 1

Printed in the United States of America
Distributed by W. W. Norton & Company, Inc.

For Anne and Paul Swain, with love and thanks
for the ever-generous enthusiasm

My own life has been turned upside down at, or perhaps even by, the small house named 'Goldeneye' I built on the north shore, and by my life in Jamaica.

Ian Fleming, 1963

Contents

Ian Fleming's Jamaica

Lucea

Montego Bay

Reading

ROSE HALL

Falmouth   Duncans   Runaway Bay

HANOVER

ST JAMES

Montpelier

TRELAWNEY

Cockpit Country

ST

Negril

WESTMORELAND

J

A

M

ST ELIZABETH

Black River

Christiana

Savanna-
la-Mar

MANCHESTER

Black River

Mandeville

Milk River

Alligator Pond

C a r i b b e a n
S e a

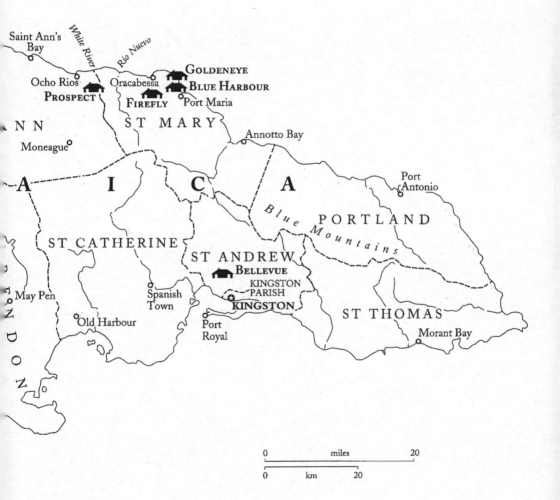

Saint Ann's
Bay

White River

Rio Nuevo

Ocho Rios   Oracabessa   **GOLDENEYE**
PROSPECT   **BLUE HARBOUR**
        FIREFLY   Port Maria

N N   S T   M A R Y

Moneague

A   I   C   A   Annotto Bay

Port
Antonio

Blue Mountains   P O R T L A N D

ST CATHERINE

ST ANDREW
BELLEVUE
KINGSTON
PARISH
   KINGSTON   S T   T H O M A S

May Pen

Spanish
Town

Old Harbour   Port
Royal   Morant Bay

R N D O N

0   miles   20

0   km   20

1943
Fleming and Jamaica
– First Contact

July 1943: a high-level Anglo-American naval conference in Kingston, Jamaica. German U-boats are causing havoc in the Caribbean, sinking vital shipping.

Assistant to the Director of Naval Intelligence Ian Fleming is sent to the island to help deal with the pressing problem. There are wild rumours that Axel Wenner-Gren, the millionaire Swede supposedly linked to Hermann Goering, has built a secret submarine base on Hog Island, his private paradise isle near Nassau. Urgent action is needed to prevent threats to the vital shipping route from the Gulf of Mexico to Europe and Africa.

Fleming brings along his boyhood friend Ivar Bryce, who also works in intelligence. Bryce is keen to show Fleming Jamaica, where his current wife has recently purchased a famous plantation 'Great House', Bellevue, perched 1,500 feet above Kingston. This is where the two men will stay.

Fleming and Bryce meet in New York and take the Silver Meteor to Miami – the very same journey that will one day be replicated by Bond and Solitaire in *Live and Let Die*. From there they fly to Kingston, to find Jamaica 'pelting with rain as well as quivering with the heat of a Turkish bath'. The five-day conference takes place at Kingston's waterside Myrtle Bank, one of the island's largest and best hotels. But thanks to Bryce, Fleming retreats each night from the sticky heat of the city up to the serenity of Bellevue.

It is at Bellevue that the story of Fleming in Jamaica begins. It is here that Fleming falls in love with the island that will give birth to his iconic creation: British intelligence officer James Bond.

Borrowing a car, Fleming and Bryce headed through the growing darkness and relentless downpour to Half Way Tree (then a village outside Kingston), before leaving the main road to climb a zigzagging track, the surface of which 'resembled a river bed'. After 'endless hairpin bends', requiring very careful driving, they reached Bellevue at last. It was dark, locked and had clearly seen better days. Shouting and knocking eventually produced Elizabeth, the old Jamaican caretaker, who let them in and rustled up a 'stringy, tasteless' chicken and some 'unaccustomed' yams for them to eat. There was no alcohol; only a bottle of grenadine, so that was what they drank that first night. Holding the pink glass, Fleming took a chair out on to the veranda, edging it as near the falling curtain of rain as possible. There he sat staring out into the streaming darkness, lost in thought.

For two hundred years, the Great House had served for visiting dignitaries and high-ranking colonial officials as a getaway from the heat and humidity of the city below. Nelson himself – a hero of Fleming – had lodged there. Bellevue had been through a large number of owners since Nelson's visits, and had operated as a small plantation, growing in different periods coffee, pimento, ginger, avocados and bananas. In Fleming's time it looked out over a huge green expanse of sugar cane at the feet of the red hills to the west. Around the house lay a rich tropical garden, including a nutmeg

J. B. Kidd's lithograph of Bellevue from 1835. Kidd specialised in idealised views of plantation life.

walk. Behind the estate to the east the mountains rose to their Blue Peak, 7,000 feet above sea level, and in front stretched an arresting view all the way across Kingston, the bay and the azure sea beyond.

Blanche Blackwell (née Lindo), who would become Fleming's lover and closest companion in Jamaica, visited Bellevue as a teenager in the late 1920s. For her, it was a special place, but menacing. She remembers 'lovely grounds around it', but also that the house had a 'very bad history'. The story went that a young woman had thrown herself off the cliff at the front of the property. 'It was definitely haunted,' says Blanche. She and her brothers had gone there with a Ouija board to make contact with the ghost.

Today, little of the original house remains, beside those bits made of stone – the kitchen, water butt, foundations and an outhouse. A house-sitter squats in a couple of the remaining rooms, and keeps the bush down immediately beside the heavily barred building. A dog

3

patrols the overgrown grounds, where fruits of all descriptions drip off the trees – ackee, jackfruit, cocoa, custard apple, naseberry. Few are collected and the fallen fruits are a riot of wasps, flies and crawling insects. The baking hot air carries a sweet, rotting smell. To the back of the property there is an ugly straggle of houses, some unfinished, as well as uncleared bush. The view across to Kingston is still there at the front, though. The current occupier, a scruffy-looking blue-eyed but black-skinned Jamaican, knows the story of the haunting, but declares he does not believe in ghosts, before adding, archly, 'How do you know I am not a ghost?'

For the next five days, Fleming and Bryce followed a routine of an early start down the mountain, the suppurating heat of the conference in the city, then the arduous climb in the dark back up to Bellevue, now equipped with the essential gin, 'foods with more variety, and baskets of gorgeous, unknown fruits'. But the weather never relented; Fleming wrote that 'it rained in rods'. Bryce remembered that 'little toadstools appeared in our leather shoes during the night'. He was depressed that Fleming had not been able to see the beauties of Bellevue or the island's other 'romantic' attractions, which he had described at length to his friend. 'I had hoped that Ian would love Jamaica and perhaps come and stay with us if the war ever ended,' he wrote. Sadly, Jamaica had been 'really dreadful'.

But as their plane climbed above Kingston, Fleming suddenly snapped his briefcase closed and turned to Bryce, announcing, 'Ivar, I have made a great decision. When we have won this blasted war, I am going to live in Jamaica. Just live in Jamaica and lap it up, and swim in the sea and write books.'

The successful opening ceremony of the 2012 London Olympic Games presented for the consumption of a huge worldwide television audience a tableau of Britain's past, present and future. It was overwhelmingly positive – no mention was made of empire or slavery

– and was clearly aimed at projecting an idea of Britishness – quirky, creative, tolerant – that we could all celebrate.

The undisputed climax of the show was, of course, the Queen – and James Bond. The two great British anachronisms. Bond has an audience with the Queen at Buckingham Palace, and then together they appear to parachute into the Olympic stadium to the accompaniment of what must be the most recognisable theme tune in movie history.

It was very funny, and very surprising, that the Queen would agree to appear with this particular fictional character in a scene that poked fun at her age, with her stunt double parachuting in clutching a handbag. When the laughter had died down, though, hastened on its way by the frowning expression of the real Queen, who now appeared in the stands, there was another 'double-take' head-scratching moment: how on earth had Ian Fleming's James Bond ascended to such heights of national iconography?

The first James Bond novel was published in 1953, the same year as the coronation of Elizabeth II. The books have now sold more than sixty million copies. Despite this, it might be argued that it is the films rather than the novels that have had the greater cultural impact. But as Fleming's friend and first biographer John Pearson noted in 2003, what surprised him about the Bond films 'is how much of Ian they retain … it is Ian's character that appears to have set the inescapable parameters for all the James Bond movies'.

The Queen aside, not much remains from Fleming's 1940s and 1950s, when Britain still had an empire. Much else has been discarded: popular music, art, film and, more importantly, attitudes to women, sexuality and race. But we keep Bond. What does that say about Fleming, and indeed about us?

Bond was created not only a long time ago, but also far away. For two months of every year, from 1946 to his death eighteen years later, Ian Fleming lived at the house he built on Jamaica's north coast on a point of high land overlooking a small white sand beach with a coral reef close by. All of his James Bond novels and stories were written here, at Goldeneye. This is the recurring birthplace of the patriotic imperial hero who puts Britain back on top and projects British power across the world.

Imperial, then post-imperial Jamaica contributes a vivid setting for three of these novels and a number of the short stories, as well as cropping up referenced in almost all of Fleming's other books. Indeed, Fleming's adventures underwater on his Goldeneye reef – a place of both beauty and danger – inspired some of the very best Bond scenes. More than that, the spirit of the island – its exotic beauty, its unpredictable danger, its melancholy, its love of exaggeration and gothic melodrama – infuses the stories.

In fact, many of the 'ingredients' that Fleming threw together in the warm bedroom of Goldeneye to create Bond – the high-end jet-set tourism world in which his hero moves, the relentless attention to race, the aching concern with the end of the Empire and national decline, the awkward new relationship with the United States, even the Cold War – all these roads lead back to Jamaica.

In 1965, a year after Fleming's death at just fifty-six, John Pearson visited Goldeneye for the first time. 'This really is Flemingland,' he scribbled in his notebook. 'It is the place where he wrote and the place he wrote about. His ghost is stronger here than anywhere else.' Pearson concluded that only in Jamaica could Fleming 'relax, be as much of himself as there was'. This echoes a comment made a decade earlier by the writer Peter Quennell, who was a frequent guest at Goldeneye in the fifties: 'In Jamaica Ian seemed perfectly at home,' he wrote, 'if he could be said ever to be really at home in any place he inhabited.'

To understand Fleming's relationship with the place so crucial to his creativity, we need to explore the huge changes occurring as the island, a microcosm for the wider empire, transformed itself and its relationship with Fleming's Britain. For it is Jamaica that offers the key to a fresh understanding of Fleming, Bond and our own strange relationship with this national icon.

Ian Fleming had found something in Jamaica that was irresistible, a combination of factors that made the island fit his awkward personality. In an interview close to the end of his life he described himself as 'rather melancholic and probably slightly maniacal as well ... Possibly it all began with an over-privileged childhood.' He was born on 28 May 1908, the second of four sons, and was a naughty, difficult, restless child. His background was contradictory and complex: both 'new money' and establishment, puritan and hedonistic. His grandfather Robert Fleming had risen from a humble background in Dundee to found a bank and accumulate a fortune investing in American railroads. Although he was famously parsimonious, never taking a taxi in his life, the family acquired a town house in London and rolling acres and a mansion in Oxfordshire. A shooting estate in Scotland was rented for 'country pursuits'. Ian's father Valentine attended Eton and Oxford, trained as a lawyer and became a country gentleman, with his own pack of beagles. In 1910 he was elected as a Conservative MP for the Henley division of Oxfordshire, becoming a close friend of Winston Churchill, a fellow MP and officer in the Oxfordshire Yeomanry.

In spite of his lack of enthusiasm for outdoor gentry pursuits, Ian seems to have been his father's favourite; Val called his second son 'Johnny' and spoiled him. The young Ian was endlessly curious about nature, from the highest birds to the lowest insects, but was not so keen on killing. He later wrote: 'If I have to make a choice, I would rather catch no salmon than shoot no grouse.' When he 'should have been out doors killing something', he preferred listening to Hawaiian guitar music, he later remembered, in particular the exotic tropical rhythms of the Royal Hawaiian Serenaders.

His mother Eve was a very different creature to her husband's austere Scottish family. A striking bohemian beauty, she was vain, self-centred and extravagant. Her two brothers were notorious womanisers and rakes. Eve was also domineering. Her granddaughter Lucy Williams remembers her as 'quite a frightening woman … beautiful and immaculate, she pierced you with beady eyes'. She had a tendency publicly to humiliate her sensitive second son. A picture of Eve Fleming with her boys shows them all smiling except Ian, who has his arm awkwardly wrapped around his mother's, with a posture half dependent and half resentful.

The Fleming boys, from left: Peter, Richard, Michael and Ian, with their mother Eve.

At the outbreak of war in 1914, Valentine Fleming immediately volunteered and was very soon on active service as a major in the Oxfordshire Hussars. When Ian was seven, he and his eight-year-old brother Peter were dispatched to Durnford School near Swanage in Dorset, a boarding establishment old-fashioned even for those times. Conditions were spartan and crowded, the food meagre and repulsive; there were no proper toilets. The routine included obligatory cold dips before breakfast and frequent punishments. Ian learned to avoid the extensive bullying by giving nothing of himself away. He also acquired a lifelong, almost neurotic craving for time on his own that some close to him later would find unnerving, fascinating or irritating. In *The Spy Who Loved Me*, Vivienne Michel echoes this desire for solitude, but worries about its basis: 'The fact that I was so much happier when I was alone was surely the sign of a faulty, a neurotic character.'

In May 1917, eight days before Ian's ninth birthday, his father's squadron was in Picardy, holding the outpost of Guillemont Farm. At 3 a.m. the Germans opened fire with artillery, the preparation for an infantry attack. 'Parties of the enemy got to within 50 yards of our frontline,' reads the squadron's report, 'but were driven off by rifle fire, leaving 2 prisoners in our hands. During the preliminary bombardment Maj. V. FLEMING, 2/Lt F. S. T. SILVERTOP and 3 O.R.s were killed.' Ian was hauled out of school, then sent back again sharply. His father received a posthumous Distinguished Service Order, and a glowing obituary written for *The Times* by his friend Churchill, a framed copy of which Ian would carry around with him for the rest of his life.

Ian made 'his inmost self strongly fortified', as a friend later commented, and followed his elder brother Peter to Eton in 1921. There, although he made lifelong friends, he acquired a reputation for being aloof, with a self-destructive streak. His close friend Robert Harling, writing near the end of Fleming's life, put the much-criticised violence and sadism of the Bond books down to 'the imprisonment of emotions' that came from upper-class boys of eight being sent to boarding school: 'the English upper crust wants and needs affection as deeply as any other crust, but impulses towards this important emotional release are frequently stifled for them … the boys grow up, professing to hate what they so need'. Eton schoolfriend Ivar Bryce remembered Ian as charming but moody. Another friend described him as 'self-consuming'.

Ian had first met Ivar Bryce, who would accompany him on that trip to Jamaica in 1943, on Bude beach in Cornwall in 1914, when Ian was six and Ivar eight. When they met again at Eton, Ivar was more a contemporary of Peter Fleming but got on better with Ian. Bryce was from an Anglo-Peruvian family who had made a fortune in the guano business. He put his good looks down to his Aztec or Inca blood. With his sensual face and laid-back manner, he also had a touch of the exotic and a rebellious streak that Fleming loved.

Bryce had laid his hands on a second-hand Douglas motorbike on which the two friends went on forays in search of excitement, or more exactly girls, round Windsor, Maidenhead and Bray. Thereby Ian lost his virginity on the floor of the box at the Royalty Kinema in Windsor, an episode replayed from the girl's point of view in *The Spy Who Loved Me* (the boy was an arrogant public-school type). On one occasion, when Ian was sixteen, they took the bike all the way to London to visit the British Empire Exhibition at Wembley.

But Eton was not a success. Although he was intelligent and did well at sports, Ian was always overshadowed by his brilliant and charismatic elder brother Peter. As he grew up, he increasingly chafed at the restrictions, and was unlucky enough to have a particularly sadistic housemaster. There were numerous warnings, then the latest trouble with some girls led to a looming expulsion. To avoid this embarrassment, his forceful mother intervened, taking Ian out of Eton a term early. She had decided that he should follow his martyred father into the army, and so he started at a special tutorial college to prepare for the Sandhurst military academy examination.

He worked hard and did well, his teacher writing to his mother, 'He ought to make an excellent soldier, provided always that the Ladies don't ruin him.' But the endless drill and strict discipline were not for Ian, and he bunked off as much as he could. When he missed a term having contracted gonorrhea from a London prostitute, he made up his mind not to return, resigning in August 1927.

His mother decided that he should instead try for the Foreign Office, but first Ian spent a year in the Austrian Tyrol, where he skied, learned languages, read a lot and conducted affairs ('having fun with the local Heidis and Lenis and Trudis', as his friend Cyril Connolly later described it). In his travel book *Thrilling Cities*, Fleming would report that Austrian girls 'have a powerful weakness for young Englishmen'. They certainly did for this one, who, as a fellow student recalled, was 'irresistible to women'. Another friend from that time later wrote that part of Ian's appeal was that he 'showed … a promise of something dashing or daring'.

After Austria, Fleming moved to Munich and then Geneva, studying for the rigorous Foreign Office entrance examination. In spite of working hard, he failed the test, and once more his mother swung into action, securing him a job at Reuters in London. Fleming would look back on his three years there, which included trips to Moscow and Berlin, with great fondness; but fed up with having to negotiate cash handouts from his manipulative mother, he now decided he wanted to earn serious money in the City. The last straw was the terms of the will of his grandfather Robert Fleming, who died in August 1933. The entire £3 million fortune went to his widow and surviving eldest son, with nothing for Eve or her family.

Ian's first appointment in a merchant bank was not a success, so he tried his hand at stockbroking at an old and established firm. Here he drew a generous salary of £2,000 a year, enough to set up his own house, but he was reportedly 'the world's worst stockbroker', and the huge fortune he dreamt of never materialised.

Meanwhile, in his private life he drifted between book-collecting, golf, bridge and women. He was notorious for his open-minded approach to sex, his obsessional interest in it and his direct manner of seduction. He had many affairs with women, young and old, single and married. One of his girlfriends from later in his life said that he was the best lover she had known. Ivar Bryce remembered from this time 'a series of appealing nymphs ... the lady's side followed a similar pattern composed of glamorous flirtation, abject slavery and fond nostalgia, in that order'.

So while his elder brother Peter went from triumph to triumph – publishing in 1933 one of the most brilliant travel books of the century, *Brazilian Adventure* – Ian languished, gaining a reputation for a 'cruel face', arrogant charm and a sophisticated manner but little accomplishment outside the bedroom.

He was rescued by the Second World War. As neurologist Sir James Maloney reflects in *You Only Live Twice*, 'countless neurotic patients had disappeared for ever from his consulting-rooms when the last war had broken out'. Thanks to recommendations from banking and stockbroking friends, Fleming was recruited by naval intelligence to work as the personal assistant to the Director, Admiral Sir John Godfrey, with the rank of commander (which Bond would share). Although his role left him guilty that his nerves and bravery had not been tested by combat action, it was the perfect job for his character and attributes – his fantastical imagination, his love of travel and gadgets, his curiosity and attention to detail.

'I couldn't have had a more interesting war,' Fleming told *Desert Island Discs* many years later. Indeed, Ivar Bryce described him during that time as 'happy and electrically alive'. But there was family tragedy repeated: his brother Michael was taken prisoner at Dunkirk and subsequently died of his wounds. In his travelogue *Thrilling Cities*,

Fleming broke his nose playing football at Eton but most agreed this augmented his 'piratical' good looks.

published fourteen years after the end of the war, Ian wrote: 'I left Berlin without regret. From this grim capital went forth the orders that in 1917 killed my father and in 1940 my youngest brother.' He also lost a devoted girlfriend, Muriel Wright, killed by a head wound in an air raid in 1944. He was called on to identify the body, and was reportedly full of remorse that he had not treated her better.

By the end of the war his romantic life had become complicated by an affair with a woman much more formidable than his usual casual conquests. He had first met Ann O'Neill, as she then was, in August 1935 by a swimming pool in the fashionable French resort of Le Touquet, subsequently the model for Royale-les-Eaux in *Casino Royale*. With her was a friend, Loelia, Duchess of Westminster, who described the twenty-seven-year-old Fleming as 'the most attractive man I've ever seen'. Ann, who had recently married, found him a 'handsome and moody creature', 'godlike but unapproachable'.

Ann, originally a Charteris, was five years younger than Ian, and connected through her Tennant mother to just about everyone in the British aristocracy. Her mother had died when she was eleven. She would later write that 'None of us had any affection in our tempestuous childhood and I have only seen its necessity very late.' Her marriage to Lord O'Neill produced two children, Raymond and Fionn, born in 1933 and 1936 respectively, but she remained a restless, bohemian spirit. A lifetime friend summed her up as 'a slim, dark, handsome, highly strung, iconoclastic creature with a fine pair of flashpoint eyes … [she] provokes extreme reactions as a wasp provokes panic'.

Ian had played golf with Ann's husband, who invited him to join them and their circle for bridge at the Dorchester, to which London elite society had retreated for the duration of the war. Here, among the dukes and duchesses, Ian and Ann got to know one another better. 'I thought Ian original and entertaining,' Ann recalled. 'He was immensely attractive and had enormous charm.' He was also 'unlike anyone else I had ever met. There was something defensive and untamed about him, like a wild animal.'

When Shane O'Neill left England for active service in Africa as a major in the North Irish Horse Guards, Ann and Ian began going for meals and to the cinema together. 'I never showed Ian I was in love with him,' Ann later wrote. 'I knew instinctively it would be fatal, but I did know he was becoming more and more dependent on me. He said I had the heart of a drum-majorette which off-set his melancholy.' With her husband away, she had several men pursuing her, but found herself drawn to Fleming's rakish insouciance and 'very dominant personality'. Sometime early in the war, she succumbed to his advances. In a throwaway remark to a friend, she once declared she could not understand why people took their emotions so seriously. She was attracted to 'cads and bounders', she declared.

O'Neill was killed in Italy in 1944, and Ann expected Ian to ask her to marry him. When this did not happen, in June 1945 she accepted the proposal of another lover, Esmond Harmsworth, Viscount Rothermere, proprietor of the *Daily Mail*. He had been having an affair with her since 1936. Ann later wrote: 'the night before I married Esmond I dined with Ian, and we walked and walked in the park. He said several times "I want to leave some kind of mark on you." If he had suggested marriage I would have accepted.'

Ann moved into Rothermere's lavish Warwick House on the border of Green Park, where she became London's society hostess par excellence. Before the end of 1946, Warwick House was operating in the 'affluent pre-War style', the first to do so. Her dinner parties brought together famous artists, authors and cabinet ministers. They were predominantly establishment and Tory, with guests including Princess Margaret and Winston Churchill, denouncing 'that little rat Attlee', but Ann herself was a 'stimulating *inspiratrice*' who liked 'a spirited contest, which she sometimes actively encouraged'.

Ann continued her affair with Fleming; if anything, her recent marriage added extra spice to their relationship, and she could not resist his strange combination of consideration and disdain. Fleming's close friend and fellow naval intelligence officer William Plomer described him as 'not a man of single aspect', with a 'private self, hidden or withdrawn'. To another friend he was 'a brilliant and witty talker, with ideas on everything', but others noticed how he 'conveyed the sense of being alone when not alone'. He was a man then of multiple, sometimes conflicting characteristics, the product of his age and background but somehow distanced, never fully at ease with either; someone in need of a place away from it all where he could at last be himself and whole. And so, when in 1943 he found himself in Jamaica, it seemed that he might finally – and unexpectedly – have discovered that home.

1946
Oracabessa and 'Old Jamaica'

> Mr Luttrell's house was left empty, shutters banging in the wind. Soon
> the black people said it was haunted, they wouldn't go near it.
>
> Jean Rhys, Wide Sargasso Sea

When Fleming announced his intention to build a house in Jamaica,
he begged Bryce to help him find the right site: 'Ten acres or so,
away from towns and on the coast ... There must be cliffs of some
sort and a secret bay and no roads between the house and the shore.
When you've fixed it for me I'll build a house and write and live
there.'

Bryce returned to Jamaica at the end of the war and had an enjoyable
time searching the island's 'by-roads and beaches'. But it was his letter
to a local land agent, 'an old gentleman ... mostly of white descent
called Reggie Aquart', that delivered the longed-for retreat to Fleming.
Aquart was from Martinique but lived in Highgate, near Port Maria.
According to him, Bryce had listed Fleming's requirements as 'a little
place with good swimming and an island'. Soon Aquart reported back
to Bryce that he had found the right spot, if 'the Commander' could
go to £2,000.

Bryce accompanied Aquart to the site, a fourteen-acre strip on the north coast in St Mary, about 500 yards long and 200 deep, alongside the village and harbour of Oracabessa. There was a sprinkling of big trees – banyan and silk cotton – but mostly rough grass, weeds and bush. There had been a racecourse here some years before, but now all that remained were a few fence posts and the ruins of a shack that had once been a kiosk selling banana dumplings to the racegoers. Out to sea lay a stunning view of a tranquil aquamarine bay protected by a broad and tangled reef some twenty yards from the coast. But here the land was high above the water, which lay at the bottom of a forty-foot cliff. Bryce and Aquart crawled forward carefully to look over the edge. Below, they discovered a strip of silver sand 'the length of a cricket pitch'. Bryce immediately envisaged stone steps descending to this private idyll. About ten feet out from the beach was a small rock, supporting a single *Portlandia grandiflora*, a Jamaican native with large bell-like white flowers. Presumably this qualified as Fleming's desired island. Tied to the plant was a dugout canoe, and swimming lazily towards the boat was a young naked girl. 'He will adore this place,' said Bryce. 'Tie it up tomorrow, Reggie.'

Bryce cabled Fleming in England and received a prompt and direct reply: 'Pray pause not Ian.' Fleming transferred £2,000 into the account of the land's owner, an Irish Jamaican called Christie Cousins, and the deal was done. Straight away Fleming started planning the house he would build in this idyllic-sounding spot, reading the area's history and poring over naval maps of his new domain.

There was something innocent and prelapsarian, magical even, in the location found by Bryce and Aquart. Of course, it was along this coast that Columbus first sailed when he 'discovered' Jamaica on his second voyage in 1494, reporting it to be 'a paradise', 'the fairest island that eyes have beheld; mountainous and the land seems to touch the sky'.

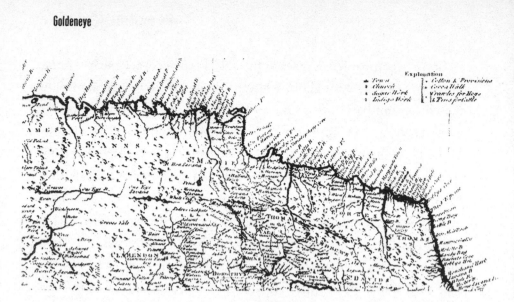

Detail of the area around Goldeneye from a map drawn by Emanuel Bowen and published in London in 1752 when Jamaica was at its height of prosperity.

Jamaica was at that time the most heavily populated of the Greater Antilles, the coastline thickly dotted with villages. The Taínos, whom Columbus called Arawaks, had been there for about 2,500 years, and what became Fleming's parish of St Mary was one of their first settlements. They had spread over the whole of the island – which they called 'Hamaika', 'land of wood and streams' – but most of their settlements were near the coast. There may have been as many as 50,000 Taínos at the time of European contact.

A peaceful, 'uncovetous' and gentle people, the Taíno 'Indians' were wiped out within two generations of Columbus landing on the island. The rigours and indignities of slavery, as the Spanish sent them mining in search of non-existent gold, together with the newly imported diseases, in particular smallpox, saw all but a handful perish. They left behind only a sprinkling of pottery and artefacts, and a 'handful of heartbreakingly relaxed sounding words' – hammock, barbecue, savannah, canoe.

The parish was also one of the first sections of the island to be occupied by the Spaniards. Port Maria, the capital of St Mary, just east of Oracabessa, was first recorded in world history in 1516, when the Spaniards built their second town on the north coast. (According to Bond's cover story in *Casino Royale*, this is where he lives.) It was close to here, too, that Spanish rule was finally ended 150 years later. The Spanish in Jamaica were few and weak; most had moved on in search of Eldorado, the fantastical city of gold. Nevertheless, following the invasion of Jamaica by a Cromwellian English force in 1655, the Spanish and their slaves took to the hills, fighting a bitter guerrilla war and landing occasional raiding parties on the north coast. In 1658 came the greatest effort at reconquest when nearly a thousand men from Cuba were put ashore just east of Oracabessa, where they quickly established a fort in a strong position on high ground protected by the deep Rio Nuevo.

Edward D'Oyley, the English governor of Jamaica at this time, was on the other side of the island. Rather than brave the guerrillas of the interior, he took a force of 750 by sea, landing a short distance from the Spanish position. By circling round through thick woods behind the fort, he managed to find a weak spot. With his vanguard throwing crude grenades into the palisade, scaling ladders were rushed up and the fort was breached. As D'Oyley reported, 'many of them made shift to run out of their Works, and ours followed their chase about three or four miles, doing execution'. Three hundred Spanish soldiers were killed, against some fifty English. Others fled down the cliff into the sea, where the offshore current carried them away. The English victory at Rio Nuevo saw the end of Spanish hopes of regaining the island. So, uniquely among the Greater Antilles, Jamaica would be British.

When Fleming touched down at the Palisadoes airport in early January 1946, the rain that had blighted his first visit two and a half years before was mercifully absent, and the drive from the airport, along the 'cactus-fringed road' in the darkness, was a pleasure. In *Dr No*,

Fleming describes the same journey, with its 'steady zing of the crickets, the rush of warm, scented air ... the necklace of yellow lights shimmering across the harbour'.

He was delighted with the site acquired for him by Bryce, and straight away set the construction in motion, securing the services of Reggie Aquart to manage the project, and appointing local architects Scovell and Barber to bring to life the sketches he had made back in London. For Fleming it was essential that the building should be 'simple' and that there should be 'no glass in the windows, only good old Jamaica jalousies'. He wanted it, he later wrote, 'so that the birds could fly through and so he could live as much inside as outside'. The cost of the build, which included a garage nearby with staff quarters, was another £2,000.

An early photograph of Goldeneye taken from the sea.

The design that emerged was indeed simple, even utilitarian, like Grant's villa in *From Russia, with Love*: 'modern – a squat elongated box without ornament'. Unusually for Jamaica, there were to be thick walls of local limestone rubble, unreinforced, with cut limestone facing. Another expatriate, American artist Marion Simmons, who had a house, Glory Be, built nearby soon after, described a typical construction scene: the 'native crew' is 'a small army of men, women, children, and donkeys. The men break big pieces of rock with sledge hammers, the children carry the pieces to the women, who sit with little hammers, breaking them into smaller pieces. The general effect is like a gypsy camp and very picturesque too. They build little fires and cook their meals, and the sun filters through the trees touching their bright clothing. They sing and laugh and fight and seem very much at home.'

The ceiling (now removed) was built low and of plain hardboard. As per Fleming's expressed wishes, the building was to be dominated by a large main room looking out over the sea, with only 'insignificant and small' bedrooms at the back. No cupboards were provided, just hooks for hanging clothes. The floor was painted navy blue (the naval theme was to be continued with blue towels and bedding) as were the push-out shutters. According to Bryce, 'They caused endless trouble, with the weight of their hanging, the hinges, the fastenings, but he loved them, and was rewarded on the sunny days when the whole room was open to the air.'

In everything, the emphasis was on simplicity and hardiness. There was no need for a large kitchen to fit fridges or other appliances. 'Surely you eat fruit in the tropics,' Fleming told Bryce, 'and fish of course. We shall catch our own fish, fresh. They [the staff] will just need a stove and a sink.' In the same vein, hot water seemed 'senselessly unnecessary', although he did relent on this after a few years. Nonetheless, the plumbing remained rudimentary. Fleming later admitted that the shower and lavatory 'often hiss like vipers or ululate like stricken bloodhounds'.

He also recruited a local carpenter to construct solid chairs and tables to his exact specifications. Bryce remembered the 'extremely uncomfortable dining table, made to his own deliberately Stoic design'. Reggie Aquart was instructed to hollow out an area twenty yards long and a dozen feet in width, stretching from the seaward doors of the main room to the clifftop, to make a sunken garden. 'That was a bit of a job,' he later reported. 'We had to cheat a bit. The rock started two feet down so we took soil and built up the sides slightly to give a better sensation of sinking.' Where it met the cliff, a strong timber rail was to be installed. Steps down to the cove were to be fashioned from cement and rocks, and the beach cleared of weed.

Inevitably there were delays and disappointments, but Fleming, a friend reported, was 'infinitely practical and direct, prompt and lucid'. He was also decisive about the name he wanted for his new abode. The spot had previously been known as 'Rock Edge' or 'Rotten Egg Bay'; clearly neither would do. Friends had suggested 'Shame Lady', after the green weed that covered the site (*Mimosa pudica*, which has a habit of folding up and shrinking at the slightest touch), and also 'Rum Cove'. But Fleming called his new house Goldeneye, after a wartime operation he had planned for the defence of Gibraltar, should Spain enter the war, and because of the happy coincidence that Oracabessa meant 'Golden Head' in Spanish. The name also contained a nod to the strange and dark 1941 Carson McCullers novel, *Reflections in a Golden Eye*.

During this trip of about two months, Fleming stayed most of the time at the house of his friend Sir William Stephenson. 'Little Bill', as he was known, was a millionaire Canadian who had headed British Secret Service operations in North America during the war. Fleming had met him in June 1941 on a trip to the US, and they had become firm friends. The Canadian and his wife Mary had recently bought Hillowtown, a Great House (the residence of the plantation owner) near Montego Bay. It had cost £7,000, and Stephenson considered it 'the finest house in the island'.

It was Stephenson who introduced Fleming to Jamaica's elite expatriate society. Also near to Montego Bay was Cromarty, the Jamaican mansion of the newspaper proprietor and wartime production and supply minister Lord Beaverbrook. Yet their first meeting was not a success. Fleming criticised as tasteless a recent article in Beaverbrook's *Daily Express*, then the largest-circulation newspaper in the world. 'That young whippersnapper!' Beaverbrook said of Fleming to Stephenson later. He strongly objected to being told at his own table how to run his newspapers. But at a subsequent dinner at Hillowtown, Fleming turned on the charm and peace was restored. The *Daily Express* owner would prove a very useful friend.

As had been the case since the days of the sugar barons, Jamaica provided a home for British eccentrics, second and third sons of the aristocracy and rich misfits. Lord Ronald Graham, the second son of the sixth Duke of Montrose, had left England in 1940 after his pre-war pro-Nazi views became an embarrassment. He set up a property agency in Jamaica and handled Fleming's purchase of the Goldeneye land from Christie Cousins (it was essential to get 'proper title' for land, Fleming would later warn). Lord Peregrine 'Perry' Brownlow, who had been lord-in-waiting to Edward VIII, and therefore at the pinnacle of the court, had also washed up on Jamaica's north shore. He had famously driven Mrs Simpson across France pursued by the press a week before the final abdication announcement. With his social standing thereafter much reduced, he was among those referred to as 'Gone with the Windsors'. Like most rich incomers, he had bought an old plantation Great House. His was at Roaring River, St Ann's Bay, just along the coast from Oracabessa past Ocho Rios.

Men like this, in their refurbished and lavishly staffed Great Houses, saw themselves as inheritors of the old plantocracy. On his walls at Hillowtown, Stephenson displayed a series of valuable J. B. Kidd prints, the famous 'Views in the Island of Jamaica'. They are classically imperialist in tone, depicting a tamed natural world and blacks, if at all, as tiny, inconsequential figures similar in status to draft animals. Nobel-prize-winning West Indian poet Derek Walcott recently described them and their like as drawn 'as if the sky were a glass ceiling under which a colonized vegetation is arranged for quiet walks and carriage rides'. Displaying such pictures was a statement of celebration of Jamaica's plantation past.

Millionaire businessman Sir Harold Mitchell, perhaps the north shore's most locally noted expatriate resident, created a plantation-style set-up pretty much from scratch. Having been a Conservative MP for fourteen years, as well as deputy chairman of the party, he had lost his seat in the Labour landslide of 1945. Thereafter he spent at least six months of the year in Jamaica, along with his family and half a dozen or so of his most important staff. As a child he had been told by an uncle who lived on the island 'stories of pirates and desperadoes … Elizabethan sea-rovers, of earthquakes and hummingbirds'. This had led him to buy, sight unseen, 1,200 acres on the high ground on the Oracabessa side of Ocho Rios.

On the land was a Great House of sorts, called Prospect. In fact it was a simple single-storey eighteenth-century stone fort, complete with firing slits to keep the French or the vengeful slaves at bay. Mitchell had ordered that another storey be built, in the plantation-house style. Inside, weathered cedar panelling was put up, and 'fine old mahogany furniture was installed in the principal rooms'. On the walls were hung portraits of Admirals Rodney and Vernon, both of whom made their names in the West Indies, and also such powerful sugar barons from the period of slavery as Rose Fuller and Peter Beckford. Along with more J. B. Kidd prints, there were also a number of prints originated from drawings by George Robertson, who specialised in depicting idealised Jamaican estates, far removed from the brutal reality of the sugar plantation. These can still be seen at Prospect, along with Mitchell's cricket bat, a 'Gradidge Imperial Driver'.

Mitchell grew coconuts, limes and pimento, kept a large herd of cattle and at one point dabbled in sugar. But he never made any money out of his 'modern-day plantation'. It was more a social experiment, an exercise in imperial nostalgia.

Of course, much of the attraction of Jamaica was as an escape from the cold of a London winter. In *Dr No*, Bond is delighted to leave behind 'hail and icy sleet', where 'people streamed miserably to work, their legs whipped by the wet hems of their macintoshes and their faces blotching with cold', and revels in the 'velvet heat' of Jamaica. In a much later short story, 'Octopussy', Bond takes a back seat while Fleming describes the appeal of Jamaica right after the war to his central character, Dexter Smythe, who has just emigrated: 'Prince's Club, in the foothills above Kingston, was indeed a paradise.' (This would become 'Queen's Club' in *Dr No*, and is based on a real establishment still in business, the Liguanea Club.) 'Pleasant enough members, wonderful servants, unlimited food and cheap drink, and all in the wonderful setting of the tropics.' Dexter Smythe and his wife enjoy 'one endless round of parties ... yes it was paradise all right, while, in their homeland, people munched their spam, fiddled in the black market, cursed the government and suffered the worst winter weather for thirty years'.

But Jamaica offered more than sunshine, rum and cheap servants. In his memoir, Mitchell remembered fondly an earlier time when 'those generously red-splashed maps which symbolized the power and influence of one small island' were 'a fact of life'. Others, including Fleming, shared this nostalgia for the 'years of greatness of the British Empire', which now seemed under threat. As Bond complains in *You Only Live Twice*, Britain had been 'bled pretty thin by a couple of World Wars'. In 1946, the country was bankrupt, rationing was getting even stricter and class relations seemed in worrying flux after the social upheaval of the war and the election of a Labour government in July 1945. This had led, Bond continues, to 'Welfare State politics

[that] have made us expect too much for free'. Furthermore, in 1941, Britain had signed up to the Atlantic Charter, committing herself in theory to decolonisation. The Labour administration looked as if it would follow through on this promise. In many parts of the Empire, most notably India, there were vociferous and growing movements for independence.

But Jamaica seemed, on the face of it, different, stuck in a comfortable time warp where imperial and social structures remained virtually unchanged from a hundred years previously. In *Dr No*, Bond drives with Quarrel across the island from Kingston to the north shore. On the way they see 'an occasional man going off to his precipitous smallholding on the flank of a hill, his three-foot steel cutlass dangling from his right hand, chewing at his breakfast, a foot of raw sugar cane'. Further along, they pass 'a woman sauntering up the road with a covered basket of fruit or vegetables for Stony Hill market, her shoes on her head, to be donned when she got near the village'. Bond reflects, with pleasure, that it 'was a savage, peaceful scene that had hardly changed, except for the surface of the road, for two hundred years or more'. Indeed, it could have been a scene from the slavery era.

In the same way, the people of Jamaica seemed to show the white English elite a deference that had been lost at home and elsewhere in the Empire. Ramsay Dacosta, who worked as a young man as a gardener for Fleming, says: 'We were scared, kind of shy of going near white people. If they say something to you harsh and so forth.' Schools taught British history and literature. Blanche Blackwell, who grew up in the Jamaica of the 1920s, remembers that they imbued people 'with the idea that England was the only place on earth'. Only a handful of non-whites attended secondary school, where, one later complained, 'We absorbed the doctrine that white was virtue, power, wisdom and that black was vice, weakness, stupidity.' For empire nostalgists, then, Jamaica seemed a delicious slice of the old imperial certainties, where their comparative wealth, Englishness and fair complexion gave them extra-special status.

As a writer on Jamaica's longest-established newspaper, the *Gleaner*, noted, the epicentre of 'the social life of the upper classes who either came from England, or liked to give the impression that they did' was King's House, the residence of the Governor and his family. In 1946 this was Sir John Huggins, a career colonial officer, viewed by Jamaicans as 'very reserved and even unfriendly'; 'an unimaginative man with no special intellectual tastes, no enthusiasms'. Huggins made little impact in Jamaica, but for his wife, Molly, it was a very different story.

Chris Blackwell, Blanche's son, who now owns Goldeneye, remembers Molly Huggins as 'very vivacious, a larger-than-life character. A big woman, tall, five foot ten or eleven. Nice-looking. Strong personality.' He doesn't recall meeting the Governor, but confirms that 'she was the one that really registered'. It was Molly who set the tone for the behaviour of the white society Fleming now engaged with, as well as its attitude to Jamaica and Jamaicans: in part well-meaning and affectionate, but hampered by ignorance, arrogance and double standards.

A child of the Empire, Molly was born in Singapore in 1907, so was just a year older than Fleming. While her father worked as a colonial resident in Malaya, she attended boarding school in England. After having had 'great fun' helping to break the General Strike and conducting a string of affairs, she was married in 1929 in Kuala Lumpur to John Huggins, then a colonial administrator in Malaya, who at thirty-seven was sixteen years her senior.

The couple, acquiring three daughters along the way, were posted to Trinidad, then Washington, then Jamaica in 1943, where Huggins became Governor. Here Molly's first task was to take King's House in hand. Apart from the central dining room, the residence had been destroyed in the 1907 earthquake, and rebuilt as what Molly called 'an ugly, squat, grey cement building'. Inside, 'immediate redecoration' was required, 'war or no war'. Her daughters were happy, however. They had a swimming pool, and 150 acres of grounds in which to ride their horses.

Amid a general refit, Molly had the silver from the West India Regiment polished up and displayed and the Joshua Reynolds portraits of George III and Queen Charlotte sent to England for restoration. Antique mahogany furniture was acquired locally, 'much of it brought out from England in the old days of the great sugar barons'. Soon everything was ready for the stream of visitors and functions. In this, Molly was determined to make a decisive change: 'We rather startled Jamaica in the early days by having coloured Jamaicans to play tennis, as this really had not been done very much in the past. But we had decided from the beginning that we would have no colour prejudices of any kind.'

'Lady Molly', as she was soon known across Jamaica, found the West Indies 'sadly neglected' and noted that 'there seemed to be a great deal of poverty, especially after the wealth of Malaya'. Although 'the Jamaican plantocracy (mostly of white background) had done a good deal in the field of social services', she writes, 'the sugar workers were very badly paid and, except on the very good estates, they lived under very poor conditions'. The demands from every parish, for better water and electricity supplies, housing and roads, were 'endless'. On arrival, she was immediately swamped with letters asking her to be chairman or president of organisations, 'and there were a great many pathetic ones asking for money, clothes, jobs, and in fact, help of any kind'. She immediately promised to be president of the Society for the Prevention of Cruelty to Animals (a particular bugbear of hers, and a concern she shared with Fleming) 'and of all the societies dealing with women and children … I intended to do a lot of work'. 'After I had seen much of the poverty and need for help,' she writes, 'I realized very quickly

From an empire family, Molly Huggins was raised by maiden aunts in Tunbridge Wells, seeing her parents 'every three or four years.' At Roedean boarding school she was captain of tennis, cricket and lacrosse.

that what Jamaican women needed was leadership.' So in 1944, Lady Huggins formed the Jamaican Federation of Women, with the motto: 'For our Homes and our Country'. The executive committee was dominated by the great and the good – Blanche Blackwell's sister-in-law, Pamela Lindo, as well as the wife of the editor of the *Gleaner* – but membership was open to all and was soon 25,000 strong, drawn from all parts of the population even if the middle classes dominated. Each member paid a penny a month, which was spent on school uniforms, books, girls' clubs and sewing, cooking and knitting lessons.

'I suppose I fell in love with Jamaica and its people almost as soon as I arrived,' Molly wrote in her memoir, backing up the sentiment always expressed in the many articles she wrote about herself. 'I gave a great deal of my heart, my mind and my energies to working for them. Their splendid response of love and gratitude has been one of the highlights of my life.'

Shortly after the war, *Life* magazine ran a profile of the Governor's wife, which begins: 'Nothing like Lady Molly Huggins ever happened before to Jamaica – or possibly to any other British colony.' Lady Molly, it reports alongside a picture of adoring black children holding a welcoming banner, 'steams about the island engaging in good works' and 'visits village markets, climbs onto tables and harangues her audiences on the importance of learning how to take better care of their children and homes'. We learn, however, that she still finds time for tennis – winning the Jamaica women's doubles championship – 'shoots golf in the low 80s' and had just organised her daughter's wedding, 'the social event of Jamaica's spring season'.

Unlike her husband, Lady Molly was extremely sociable. She unashamedly loved parties. 'The handsome young men simply swarm around her,' noted one local magazine journalist. She was often out on her own, as her husband had decided that to avoid charges of favouritism he should not attend dinners in private houses. A popular destination was the Craighton Estate Great House, high above Kingston beyond Irish Town. Here Bobby and Sybil Kirkwood gave lavish black-tie dinners for twelve or more, waited on by liveried servants.

Robert Kirkwood, an Englishman, was another pillar of elite Jamaican society and the most powerful businessman on the island. He had attended Harrow School and then taken a job at Tate & Lyle, thanks to his mother, who was a Lyle. At that time the company was involved with processing the sugar of Britain's heavily subsidised domestic beet crop. When they looked to expand in 1936, they sent Kirkwood, now a company director, to the West Indies. He recommended investing in cane sugar estates in Trinidad and in Jamaica's Westmoreland and Clarendon parishes. His suggestion that he take on the task of putting the largely derelict estates back into production was accepted.

The company bought cheap and then invested heavily in centralised factories: at an estate called Monymusk in Vere, Clarendon (previously owned by the Lindo family); and at Frome, Westmoreland. The latter was served by the port of Savanna-la-Mar on Jamaica's south-west coast, visited by Bond in *The Man with the Golden Gun*, where he comments on the 'drably respectable' villas built for the 'senior staff of the Frome sugar estates'.

Tate & Lyle formed a new subsidiary, the West Indies Sugar Company, known as WISCO, whose estates, run by expatriate British and white Jamaicans, accounted by the end of the war for about a third of the island's entire production.

In 1948, the irascible Kirkwood would fall out with his bosses and resign, to be replaced by Alan Walker, another Englishman. Kirkwood became chairman of the Sugar Manufacturers Association, a body representing all sugar producers, large and small, in their dealings with the government, suppliers and labour unions. This was a key position, as sugar remained Jamaica's biggest business and the largest employer – albeit seasonal – by a huge margin.

In spite of this relative importance, the sugar industry was a shadow of its former self, as the landscape of Jamaica at the time of Fleming's first visits amply testified. From almost the beginning of the eighteenth century, for a hundred years, Jamaica had been by far the richest and most important colony in the British Empire, thanks to its sugar crop. By 1774, average per capita wealth for a white man in Jamaica was £1,000, while in England it was around £42. This wealth built a large proportion of Britain's stately homes and contributed substantially to the capitalisation of the Industrial Revolution. So important was Jamaica to the Empire that its defence was prioritised over the suppression of the revolution in North America's Thirteen Colonies.

For 150 years after 1700, all the flat land around the future site of Goldeneye would have been planted in cane. The largest estate was Trinity, worked by over 1,000 slaves and consisting of about 5,000 acres around Port Maria. The area's reliable rainfall and proximity to the port made this 'one of the island's most desirable properties'. Adjacent to this estate was Frontier, with about 300 slaves working nearly 1,500 acres. To the west of Port Maria lay the plantation of Agualta Vale, owned by the eccentric Hibbert family. At its prime it consisted of 3,000 acres and nearly 1,000 slaves. In the late nineteenth century it would be sold to the Scottish physician Sir John Pringle.

On the high ground in the interior of Fleming's parish, near the border with St Catherine, Sir Charles Price, scion of one of Jamaica's richest sugar families, had built his retreat, Decoy. Price, who could trace his family back to one of Cromwell's invasion force, owned numerous properties, including Jamaica's most famous Great House, Rose Hall, as well as about 26,000 acres and some 1,300 slaves. Decoy, 2,000 feet up in the hills, provided an escape into cooler air. Here he entertained visitors from England, who could enjoy the surrounding park, grazed by imported fallow deer, in a fantastical imitation of the aristocracy at home. In front of the house was 'a very fine piece of water, which in winter is commonly stocked with wild-duck and teal', a visitor reported. Behind was an elegant garden, with numerous richly ornamented buildings and a triumphal arch.

In fact Price was already heavily in debt by the 1770s, and the family's fortune was gone by the next generation. The abolition of slavery, combined with natural disasters, endemic war and the planters' greed, corruption and decadence, saw the industry rapidly decline during the nineteenth century. As the sugar price fell, production in Jamaica slumped from 100,000 tons in 1805 to a low of 5,000 tons just over a hundred years later. In the last half of the century, the number of sugar plantations shrank from more than 500 to just 77. In common with the rest of the island, sugar production in Fleming's St Mary Parish collapsed after Emancipation. Trinity's output halved in the ten years after 1838.

This left the cane fields derelict and the countryside littered with decaying, squatted or abandoned Great Houses and sugar works, quickly reclaimed by vines and bush. Vandalism, hurricanes and fires contributed to the ruin, and almost every old house acquired its own ghost story. And each ruin acted as a visible, melancholy reminder that Jamaica's heyday was a hundred years in the past.

This romantic mood was memorably evoked at the beginning of Richard Hughes's 1929 *A High Wind in Jamaica*: 'ruined slaves' quarters, ruined sugar-grinding houses, ruined boiling houses', where 'two old Miss Parkers' had taken to their beds as their plantation house crumbled about them into 'half-vegetable gloom'. Of course, many other authors writing about Jamaica similarly employed this image of romanticised decay, Fleming included. The melodramatic melancholy suited his temperament to a T. It was also linked to his respect for Jamaica's 'aristocracy', the old families like the Havelocks, who are murdered for their property at the beginning of the short story 'For Your Eyes Only'. For Fleming, the Havelocks are exemplary white Anglo-Jamaicans: they are tolerant of the clumsiness of their servants, appreciative of nature and snooty about Americans. Their own lands – 20,000 acres given to 'an early Havelock' by Oliver Cromwell – are in good shape, having been maintained 'through three centuries, through earthquakes and hurricanes and through the boom and bust of cocoa, sugar, citrus and copra'. But a neighbouring estate, Belair, is in ruins, 'a thousand acres of cattle-tick and a house the red ants'll have down by Christmas!'

'Belair used to be a fine property. It could have been brought back if anyone in the family had cared,' complains Colonel Havelock.

'It was ten thousand acres in Bill's grandfather's day. It used to take the busher three days to ride the boundary,' adds his wife.

'That's one more of the old families gone,' continues the Colonel. 'Soon won't be anyone left of that lot but us.'

By Fleming's time, however, another crop had come to the rescue. Now planted all around the site of Goldeneye were bananas. This was the essential local business. Thanks to an American entrepreneur, what became known as the 'Green Gold Era' had started in Jamaica in the 1870s, and Oracabessa, just beyond Goldeneye's eastern border, had grown into an important hub from which the fruit was exported. By the 1930s, banana production had become a mainstay of the entire Jamaican economy.

In 1937, the island exported twenty-seven million stems, twice that of any other country. More than 70 per cent of the crop went to Britain. The business was particularly important for St Mary, where the landowning families – the Whites, McGregors, Marshes, Silveras, and in particular Blanche Blackwell's family, the Lindos – had grown rich from the crop. Leonora Rickets, local resident and granddaughter of a St Mary banana pioneer, remembers the plantation owners as 'vibrant, colourful characters', 'a happy-go-lucky lot, who drank a lot and had a lot of women'.

'Banana day', when the crop was loaded on to ships for export, 'was the highlight of the week. Everything revolved around green gold day.'

Whites Wharf, Oracabessa. A visitor to Fleming's house wandered down one banana-loading night to find 'sleazy, brilliantly lit wharves … Women lay asleep among the dried leaves. There was a smell of rum, a tinny whine of music.'

At the shallow port of Oracabessa, this involved the bananas being stacked on to red-painted barges, then rowed out to stocky white ships standing out in the bay. A writer on the *Gleaner* remembered the 'attractive sea-weedy-cum-banana-trash smell – a smell that holds all of the lush and potent Tropics'. Paddy Marsh, a local labourer, had a less romantic memory of having to walk a long way to the port, and then 'work night and day to make any money and the money was so small. We had to carry that banana on our head, sometimes we carry one, sometimes two, to the wharf.' At this point the 'tallyman' would tally the bunch as a 'six-hand, seven-hand, eight-hand' and so on. 'We had to sleep on the wharf, we take our bed. People cook down there,' recalled Marsh.

'You got a lot of exploitation,' conceded Rickets, 'but money was going round, people were employed.' The Second World War, however, hit the industry hard. No shipping could be spared or risked to take the fruit to its market in Britain. Nevertheless, some transports still called at St Mary's ports. Blanche Blackwell remembers that part of the local banana production was purchased by the British government, even though there was never any plan to ship the crop to England. Instead, the bananas were loaded on to the ships at Oracabessa and elsewhere on the island, everyone was paid, and then the fruit was carried out to sea and simply tipped over the side. Under this scheme, twelve million stems were purchased during the conflict at the pre-war price, but the rising cost of living and wages, as well as hurricanes and leaf-spot disease, saw many plantations abandoned nonetheless.

In 1946, production in Jamaica was at less than a fifth of the pre-war level. Although the end was still some years away, and tourists and expatriates, including Fleming and his friends, would enjoy viewing from the comfort of their verandas the picturesque spectacle of the banana-loading, the days of Oracabessa's prosperity were numbered, and the port – now overlooked by the rising outline of the new Goldeneye house – was in slow but melancholy decline.

1947
The Bachelor Party

He knew, deep down, that love from Mary Goodnight, or from any other woman, was not enough for him. It would be like taking a room with 'a view'. For James Bond the same view would always pall.

The Man with the Golden Gun

Early in 1947, Ramsay Dacosta, later Fleming's gardener, was among a group of small black boys who had swum round from Oracabessa to fish on the reef about twenty yards off the beach at Goldeneye. The beach, accessible only by sea, had been a favourite secret place for local children. Blanche Blackwell's brothers Frederick and Roy Lindo remembered using the small cave in the cliff as an arena for illegal cockfighting. But today Ramsay Dacosta and his friends could see steps leading down from the cliff above and a tall white man standing on the sand. It was now Fleming's beach. Dacosta remembers him waving to the boys in a friendly way.

Back in London, Fleming had secured a job at the *Sunday Times* as foreign news manager. The newspaper's proprietor, Lord Kemsley, was a bridge-playing friend of Ian's and had generously agreed to his new employee's stipulation that he have two months' paid leave every year to spend in Jamaica.

Goldeneye was completed in December 1946, a gently sloping roof now rising above Fleming's design of a 'squat, elongated box' with its large main room with huge open windows looking out over the sea. The following month Fleming was back in Jamaica to live in his new house for the first time. With him to stay for a few weeks were Ivar Bryce and another louche ex-Etonian friend, John Fox-Strangways. With the exception of a large Barringtonia tree that pre-dated the construction and still stands just outside the west-facing door, the

Ian with Ivar Bryce, who introduced him to Jamaica. Bond author Raymond Benson remembered Ivar as 'cool as hell and quite the playboy. I think there's a lot of him in Bond.'

new house was not yet softened by surrounding vegetation. Bryce found it 'a cubist arrangement of concrete surfaces ... a masterpiece of striking ugliness'.

The visit was something of a bachelor party. The three friends swam naked in the sea before breakfast every day and started drinking at 11 a.m. In letters to his lover Ann, Ian assured her that there was no female company, but one visitor remembered a 'beautiful married blonde from Bermuda' being part of the group at Goldeneye. By the rail at the end of the sunken garden there were now outdoor chairs and lilos, as well as a table pierced by a big sunshade. When the mood took them, the three men moved earth around to create a garden, and two paths were cut through the bush from the house to each frontier limit along the cliffs. Inside, they hung shelves and a set of French horse portraits. Ivar gave Ian a dog called Fox, the first of many mongrels that lazed around in the sun at Goldeneye. Another was Himmler, which acted as a guard for the property.

There was much exploring, from the mountains that rose behind the property to Negril at the farthest west of the island. In Falmouth, on the north coast west of Oracabessa, they admired the surviving Georgian buildings from the high point of empire and discovered a shop called Antonio's. Antonio was a 'Syrian' – Jamaican for anyone from the Levant. He was a merchant and shopkeeper who, Bryce later wrote, stocked 'a million fragments of damaged cotton goods from Manchester, printed in strange designs and bright and jarring tints for the West African markets. These prints are unobtainable in Manchester, but when stitched together into shirts, give great pleasure to the connoisseur of early Jamaican touristiana.' Bryce purchased one in mauve and puce, depicting Winston Churchill holding up his fingers in the V sign. 'Ian had many trouvailles from Antonio,' he reported, 'which all lent colour and character to the Goldeneye scene.'

On one occasion, travelling along the north coast road on his own, Fleming noticed a substantial building on the crest of the hills near

Fleming with assorted mongrels at the door of the back bedroom of Goldeneye, where later Bond stories would be written.

Duncans, a village perched above the road just east of Falmouth. He assumed it was a Great House and was intrigued. Turning up the hill, he drove up a narrow winding drive until he reached the gates. He rang the bell pull, which was answered by a picturesque old butler with crinkly silver hair and a majestic smile. 'The Colonel will be delighted to receive you, sir,' he intoned. Fleming was shown into a large, dimly lit room containing an old couple who, from appearances, seldom left the house. The butler soon reappeared bearing a silver salver with three full glasses. 'Vespers are served,' he announced. The drink turned out to be a curious mix of frozen rum, fruit and herbs, which his hosts were accustomed to imbibe most ceremoniously at six o'clock. 'Ian was delighted by the scene,' remembered Bryce, 'and left the great house in great good humour ... he never returned, but this gracious visit acquired a romantic aura of unreality which pleased him greatly.' Back at Goldeneye, with Bryce's help, he did his best to recreate the cocktail.

Fleming's favourite thing of all, though, was the reef, where he would spend hours floating, observing or hunting, enjoying the coolness of the water, his body's natural buoyancy and the exciting other-worldliness of it all. He had been introduced to underwater swimming by his wartime boss, Admiral Godfrey, and Goldeneye soon acquired a rubber dinghy, flippers, snorkels and masks, as well as spear guns and steel tridents. The target was lobsters, or anything else that could be eaten. The hazards included sharp coral, barracudas and sharks.

For Fleming, being out in the bay was the perfect combination of action and sensuality that would become James Bond. The reef would also provide a milieu for Bond's most vivid and exciting challenges, and fuel for Fleming's best writing. Kingsley Amis, looking back on the Bond books, would comment: 'All writers possessed of any energy annex some corner of the world to themselves, and the pelagic jungle roamed by ray and barracuda is Mr Fleming's.'

Fleming's companions were enthusiastic collaborators. 'Every exploration and every dive results in some fresh incident worth the telling,' remembered Bryce. 'And even when you don't come back with any booty for the kitchen, you have a fascinating story to recount. There are as many stories of the reef as there are fish in the sea. At Goldeneye, the doings on the reef filled the whole day with interest and pleasure.' Soon the shelves in the house were cluttered with collected shells.

Fleming was enchanted. On 26 January he wrote to Ann that she would love it too. 'There are so many things which would make you giggle here ... The weather is beautiful and you would feel a different person and you would get small freckles under your eyes which would annoy you but which I would like. And you wouldn't be able to dance about like a dragon-fly because there is no point in it here.' The butterflies were wonderful, he wrote, 'and when you bathe in the dark there are fireflies which drift about and disappear. We never wear any clothes when we bathe and it is just a question of walking out of bed and down the steps into the warm sea.'

In his accounts of the early days of Goldeneye, Fleming reported 'small blackamore troubles which arise the whole time', and later wrote that he spent much effort in the early years 'coping with staff'. 'They require exact instructions, constant reminders, exhortation and a sense of humour, which the majority appreciate,' he noted later that year. Nonetheless, in *The Man with the Golden Gun* we are told that 'Jamaican servants, for all their charm and willingness', are not of very high 'calibre'.

On this visit, however, Fleming made one tremendously successful appointment in the form of Violet Cummings. Introduced by Reggie Aquart, she was a local thirty-one-year-old woman, who had never travelled far from her home near Oracabessa. She would work for Fleming as Goldeneye's housekeeper for the rest of his life. Frequent visitor Ivar Bryce called her 'One of those superlative human beings who distribute comfort and well-being continuously among ordinary and lesser mortals. The whole establishment runs like clockwork with Violet as the mainspring.' Her great-niece, Olivia Grange-Walker (a Jamaican Member of Parliament and until recently a government minister) remembers her as 'calm, confident and self-assured … a strict no-nonsense person'. She cleaned, washed, shopped and cooked, cared for Fleming's and his guests' clothes, performed errands, and kept the spear-fishing equipment in trim. She could also, Bryce wrote, 'conjure up any number from one to five of slim and jungly assistants within the hour, if needed'.

To visitors, Violet became an intrinsic part of Goldeneye, though she never read a Bond book. She and Fleming clearly had a very good relationship. After his death, Violet spoke about him in an interview with the *Gleaner*: 'The Commander was the best man I ever met, better than all the men in Jamaica, and in the rest of the world, too.' She adored him. According to Blanche Blackwell, Ian for his part was 'devoted' to Violet and fiercely protective, worried all the time that she would be poached by someone else. To Violet's delight, he was also a fan of her Jamaican cooking, which most other English visitors considered 'a culinary disaster'. Saltfish and ackee was her speciality, but Ian also enjoyed her shrimp, oxtail, black crab soup and liver. 'He also like real Jamaican goat fish and not many English people like that,' Violet told John Pearson in 1965. Very special guests were given conch gumbo and fried octopus tentacles with tartare sauce.

In his relations with Violet, Fleming made a point of never arguing or raising his voice. (In his travelogue, *Thrilling Cities*, Fleming would complain that: 'Too many of the English and American wives had no idea how to treat good servants. They would clap their hands and shout "Boy!" to cover their lack of confidence. This sort of behaviour was out of fashion and brought the Westerner into disrepute.') She, in turn, gave 'the Commander', as Fleming is still known to everybody around Goldeneye, a good reputation locally and helped with further recruitment. By the end of his first stay, he had lined up Daisy the cook, Holmes the gardener, Hall the houseboy, Stewart the fisherman, and an old lady, Ann, a cleaner. He paid them between three and four shillings a day.

Pearl Flynn, a veteran resident of Oracabessa who can remember the arrival of Fleming in the locality, admits that there was suspicion at first: 'Some of them didn't like him, you understand, white man come dis.' But, she continues, 'when they employ them and give them work, it made a difference'.

In *Dr No*, Bond's assistant Quarrel was useful as 'a passport into the lower strata of coloured life which would otherwise be closed to Bond'. It seems Violet did the same for Fleming. After this visit, he wrote of Goldeneye: 'My neighbours, both coloured and white, are charming and varied.'

On 24 January, before the end of their bachelor sojourn, Fleming, Bryce and Fox-Strangways motored down to Montego Bay on the north-west coast of the island for the opening of the Sunset Lodge

Fleming urged visitors to 'embrace' all aspects of Jamaica, including dangerous-looking food.

Club. This is now seen as a seminal moment: the birth of what would become the 'North Coast Jet Set'.

The hotel's creator was Carmen Pringle, a charismatic and well-connected local figure. She was originally a de Lisser, a long-established white Jamaican family, but had married Kenneth Pringle, one of the sons of the Sir John Pringle who had bought the Hibbert estate in St Mary and subsequently became the island's biggest landowner, with 100,000 acres of sugar, banana, citrus and cattle lands throughout the parishes of St Ann, St Mary and Portland. The marriage had produced a son, John Pringle, born in 1925, but had ended in separation. According to Molly Huggins, Carmen 'really preferred women to men'.

The new hotel boasted offering 'the last word in comfort and luxury without for one moment losing the charm and simplicity which is Jamaica'. A key selling point was 'the only private beach in Montego Bay'. Sports on offer included golf, tennis, croquet and badminton; 'Alligator shooting and polo can be easily arranged.'

Carmen Pringle had the idea of inviting the great and good of Britain and America to come to the beachfront hotel free of charge – with the exception of their bar bill – in return for telling their friends about the place. Fleming reported back to Ann that there was a 'huge bonfire on the beach, and a lot of expensive people and two superb local bands playing the sort of Rum and Cococola tunes you like'.

The experiment was a great success. According to Blanche Blackwell, it was the moment when Jamaica was discovered by the international rich who had previously holidayed in the South of France. 'When they found Jamaica, they found it so beautiful it wasn't true,' she says. 'People arrived in Jamaica and just fell in love with it. Never wanted to leave it. It's what made Jamaica come alive.'

Tourism in Jamaica dated back to the late 1870s, when Lorenzo Dow Baker, the boss of Boston Fruit, began ferrying Americans to the island in his banana boats. To cater for them, a small number of high-class hotels, including Myrtle Bank in Kingston, were constructed in the late 1880s, and in the 1900s Baker himself built the lavish 400-room Titchfield Hotel near Port Antonio. During the winter months, wealthy East Coast Americans would arrive on the banana boats from the US and stay for a few weeks enjoying balls and bridge evenings.

In 1918, Baker purchased Myrtle Bank as well, reconstructed after suffering in the earthquake of 1907. The 1920s and 1930s saw development starting around Montego Bay, centred on Doctor's Cave Beach, where a natural spring offered health benefits. In 1931, the world-famous American aviator Charles Lindbergh, in a four-engined Sikorsky S40, landed smoothly in Kingston Harbour, to the delight of many spectators; thereafter a regular Pan Am service was established from Miami to Kingston and, soon after, Montego Bay, where the graceful seaplanes landed off Doctor's Cave Beach, an event that become a popular focus of Sunday outings for local Jamaicans. By 1938, visitor numbers had grown in a decade from 14,000 to more than 62,000.

By the time of the opening of Sunset Lodge, runways on the Palisadoes opposite Kingston and at Montego Bay, both built during the war for military purposes, were now in action, ferrying far more passengers than the seaplanes had coped with. At the beginning of 1948 the *Gleaner* would report, under the title 'Here they come': 'Now the pace has become so fast and furious that it needs a strong man-about-town to survive it.' Noting 'dukes, duchesses, lords and ladies ... wanting change from austerity and winter cold', the reporter applauded the 'variety that brings welcome colour and change to the monotony of our lives'. A new world of extreme luxury, a world that James Bond would make his own, was now being born in Jamaica.

One of the great attractions of the Bond stories is that Fleming takes his readers to faraway locations, which in the days before cheap air travel were beyond the reach of most. The only novel not to feature foreign adventure is *Moonraker*, and this would lead to complaints, including a letter to Fleming from an elderly couple: 'We want taking out of ourselves, not sitting on the beach in Dover.'

Often Bond is simply a tourist, or, more exactly, engages with the world he is defending in a touristic way. For one thing, he loves travelling, particularly by air, the experience of which he feels almost sensually. Indeed, at the beginning of the short story 'Quantum of Solace', he announces that 'I've always thought that if I ever married I would marry an air hostess.' Bond enjoys journeying by train as well, particularly the 'melancholy' rhythmic sound of the wheels on the tracks, and many climactic scenes in the novels occur in the glamorous but precarious carriages and cabins of trains or airliners.

Fleming was to become an accomplished travel writer, and he was not shy of inserting large chunks of travelogue into the novels and stories. His touristic eye takes in details of restaurants, beaches, hotels and bars, even commentating, often in a grudging way, on value for money and standards of decor and service.

Furthermore, where he sends Bond – and where he doesn't – is an important part of the success of the books. Fleming knew that his readers didn't want 'taking out of themselves' to some gritty impoverished destination. Writing in 1963, he pointed out that the 'sun is always shining in my books – a state of affairs which minutely lifts the spirits of the English reader [taking] him out of his dull surroundings into a warmer, more colourful, more luxurious world'. Apart from a flying visit to Sierra Leone on the last four pages of *Diamonds are Forever*, Bond never goes to Africa or South America – both at the time associated with poverty. Three of the novels are set largely in the United States (*Diamonds are Forever, Goldfinger, The Spy Who Loved Me*), an acknowledgement of the mystique that American wealth and modernity held for his readers, as well as a nod to the US market for his books. In another three the main action occurs in Jamaica (*Live and Let Die, Dr No, The Man with the Golden Gun*), with the Caribbean again making an appearance in *Thunderball* (allowing Fleming to indulge once more his love of underwater scenes inspired by Goldeneye). The short stories also feature Bermuda, the Seychelles, and Jamaica again twice. Fleming, sitting at his typewriter in Goldeneye, frequently delights in comparing the sunshine enjoyed by Bond in the Caribbean with the miserable weather back in England.

But his attitude to tourism is more than simply escapist, and in the course of his time in Jamaica it would alter, shaped by his experience of the rapidly expanding tourist scene on the island and his changing relationship with it.

The success of Sunset Lodge and everything that came in its wake owed a great deal to a storm off the coast of Jamaica in mid 1946. In its midst, on board his yacht the *Zaca*, was Hollywood superstar Errol Flynn.

'After four days of storm I could not make out the nature of a curious body of land that rose from the sea,' wrote Flynn in his autobiography, *My Wicked, Wicked Ways*. 'What was it? Where were we? Suddenly the

Errol Flynn, 'discoverer' of the attractions of Jamaica, aboard his latest yacht, 1941.

sky cleared sharply. Winds howled the clouds out, and a powerful sun illuminated the greenest hills I'd ever seen.' The *Zaca* was steered to safety, and Flynn, who had made his name in the film *Captain Blood*, set in Jamaica, was ashore on the island for the first time. It was, he said, a 'paradise' more beautiful than any woman he had ever known. According to his widow, Patrice, it was Jamaica's similarity to New Guinea, where Flynn had lived as a teenager, that was the secret of the attraction. Flynn quickly decided that 'here I would buy property and settle. Here I would salvage myself.' Within a year he had purchased land near Port Antonio and built a house. Whenever he 'drew a big pay cheque', he invested it in land and livestock in Jamaica and soon had over 2,000 acres.

'I cut an imperial figure along the north shore of Jamaica,' he later wrote (an interesting choice of adjective), describing how each day he would ride over his land on horseback. 'Then perhaps a trip in my motor boat around Navy Island or down the coast. At night, a stroll in the market place of Port Antonio. You get the feeling you have gone back 150 years ... Everywhere there is rum and calypso music.' Flynn was loud in his praise of Jamaica, and following in his wake came other Hollywood stars, including Bette Davis, Grace Kelly, Ginger Rogers and Claudette Colbert.

Soon after Flynn's arrival in Jamaica, he received a letter from Joseph Blackwell, an ex-Irish Guards officer who in 1936 had married Blanche Lindo. Flynn and Blackwell had a mutual friend in Ireland. 'Joe took me to his house to meet his wife,' said Flynn. 'She hadn't wanted to see me, for she was ill. But when I arrived and met this palefaced girl with dark, intense eyes and beautiful teeth, and a laugh like the sound of water tinkling over a waterfall, we fell into the most animated conversation.' Blanche and Flynn quickly became so close that he thought about proposing, even though they were both still married, Flynn to his second wife Nora Eddington. But he feared rejection and that he would spoil their friendship. Instead, he writes,

'Blanche and I formed an enduring friendship amazingly platonic.' Blanche would later describe Flynn as a 'gorgeous god … he was the most handsome man I've ever seen in my entire life. He had a wonderful physique.'

Blanche Blackwell, to whom Ann Fleming would later refer as 'Ian's Jamaican wife', had been born in 1912. Her family, the Lindos, were originally Sephardic Jews, forced to flee Spain during the time of the Inquisition. After Venice, Amsterdam and Bordeaux, the family ended up in Jamaica in the mid eighteenth century. There they made and lost fortunes as traders, including in slaves. At the end of the nineteenth century, Blanche's branch of the family decamped to Costa Rica, where they pioneered growing bananas and coffee, developing highly profitable plantations. In 1915, the banana lands were sold to United Fruit for $5 million, and the family returned to Jamaica, where they invested the huge sum in sugar and acquired Jamaica's leading rum producer, J. Wray and Nephew. Blanche's father Percy also bought a lot of the old sugar estates near Oracabessa. These were by now planted with bananas and coconuts.

The Lindos were probably the richest family in Jamaica. This meant that no one was quite good enough to be friends with Blanche, and she remembers a solitary, lonely childhood. She was tutored at home by a seventy-year-old Englishman and had little opportunity to make friends. 'I just wasn't allowed to know any black people,' she remembers. 'Which was a pity.'

Her mother did not bother to conceal her preference for her sons; Blanche's favourite childhood memories are of her father, and riding with him to inspect the plantations. She would remain a keen horsewoman, energetic and down-to-earth – very different from Ann Fleming.

When she was sixteen, Blanche was sent to school in England, then to finishing school in Paris. She was presented at the British court in 1933 and met Joseph Blackwell on one of her family's frequent

49

trips to England. Shortly afterwards, he appeared in Jamaica as part of the entourage of the visiting Duke of Kent. On Blanche's next trip to London, the pair were married. According to their son Chris, Joe was 'a very handsome man. He loved women and women loved him.' Chris was born in 1937, a year after his parents' wedding. Joseph was given a job on one of the St Mary estates, but the family lived in a lavish mansion in Kingston, Terra Nova.

Shortly before the end of the war, Blanche travelled to England to put Chris into a boarding school. At first based at the Grosvenor Hotel, she then lived at a house in a village outside Newbury, Berkshire. Trips back to Jamaica continued but she looked to make her life in England. She would divorce Joe in 1949 and it would be another six years before she returned to Jamaica and met Ian.

In spite of their shared enthusiasms for drinking and womanising, Errol Flynn and Ian Fleming never got on, and they avoided each other as much as possible in the goldfish-bowl social life of Jamaica's north coast. According to Flynn's widow Patrice, Errol found Ian 'pretentious and full of himself'. For Ian, perhaps Flynn was just too Hollywood. In *From Russia, with Love*, Bond is offended when Tatiana says he looks like an American film star: 'For God's sake! That's the worst insult you can pay a man.'

Ian was fast coming to rival Flynn as Jamaica's most noted expatriate lothario, even though Ann had promised fidelity to him, apart from what was strictly necessary with her husband. During both the 1947 visit and his first extended trip the year before, Fleming was carrying out a high-profile affair with Millicent Huttleston Rogers, a wealthy socialite who was heiress to part of the immense Standard Oil fortune and a regular visitor to Jamaica. A dark-haired beauty in her mid forties, Rogers was energetic, outgoing and an exhibitionist, with a penchant for appearing in fancy dress costumes. She was also even more obsessed with sex than Ian. Fleming biographer Andrew Lycett tells the story of how she once turned up to a party in Jamaica with two Navajo Indians, informing anyone who asked, and even those who didn't: 'Yes, I'm fucking them both.'

Ian ended the relationship before he left Jamaica, and wrote to Ann that he had been having a 'botched affair', where 'everything starts wrong and goes on wrong and getting wronger'. But still, other women had been invited back to Goldeneye to sample the snorkelling on the reef, including 'an admiring sugar planter's daughter', who repaid the favour by donating two smart chairs to the house's meagre and uncomfortable furniture collection.

Ian also acquired a canasta table for Goldeneye from Molly Huggins, the wife of the Governor, who was still in the process of upgrading King's House. Molly and Ian had met through Bill Stephenson on his visit the year before. 'His days of fame … were still to come,' she later wrote of Ian. 'But even then, what a brilliant, clever person he was! He was so good-looking in a rugged way.' Visiting him at Goldeneye, she found the house 'rather austere', but the beach 'beautiful'. The two became 'firm friends'. Ian taught her to 'swim under water and spear fish', which she enjoyed in spite of cutting her foot so badly on a piece of coral that she almost had to miss the finals of the Montego Bay tennis tournament the next day. The following summer, Ian lent her Goldeneye for her mother and two eldest daughters to stay in.

Molly now had a spectacular new project. To blame for Jamaica's poverty and its attendant family breakdown, she had decided, was the high proportion of children born illegitimate. 'If the moral standard of the women can be raised,' she declared, 'the whole island will benefit.' The answer was to encourage marriage. But no Jamaican, she was told, would marry without a gold ring to hand over, which most could not afford. So Molly did a deal to buy wholesale from a London jeweller 2,000 gold rings, to be passed on at five shillings each, rather than the two or three pounds' going rate in Kingston. She then organised a string of mass weddings, with fifteen couples at a time, who 'came in cars, on mules, donkeys and horses'. These weddings were graced by

The 'moralising mission': Lady Molly, centre, presides over a mass wedding of black Jamaicans. Many Jamaican women were less than happy with the legal and property implications of marriage and the experiment was not a success.

an appearance from Lady Molly herself, with tea and cakes provided by the Women's Federation.

Her attitude to her own marriage was somewhat different, however. For her own conduct, she preferred 'the Continental attitude'. 'I didn't quite see how two people could be expected to be physically faithful for all their lives, however fond of each other they might be ... I saw no harm in occasional love affairs by either party,' she wrote in her memoir, in which she is very frank about her sex life and her sexual appetite. Blanche Blackwell, who remembers her vividly, went as far as to describe her as a 'nymphomaniac'. Even before she had arrived in Jamaica, Molly writes, the difference in age with her husband had begun to tell. One source of conflict, apparently, was that he was jealous of 'the love of the people of Jamaica for me'. Soon after taking up residence in King's House, she began a long-running affair with

Bobby Kirkwood, Tate & Lyle's man in Jamaica. Little effort was made to keep it under wraps. Nor was Kirkwood the sole beneficiary of her affections; there were a number of other men who became 'firm friends'.

Fleming returned to England in March 1947 in love with the Jamaica he had discovered. It would be the subject of his first substantial piece of writing, for Cyril Connolly's *Horizon* magazine. What seems to have made the biggest impression on him was the spectacular beauty and range of the island's flora and fauna. He writes of the '2,000 different varieties of flowers' (in fact, there are more than three thousand, of which a thousand are endemic), as well as 'innumerable butterflies and humming-birds and, at night, fireflies of many kinds'. Although he was a lover of nature from an early age, Jamaica brought out the ornithologist in Fleming. We learn of the 'frigate birds, black and white, with beautifully forked tails, and dark blue kingfishers' that 'hang over the reef', and the 'clumsy pelicans and white or slate grey egrets' that 'fish at the river mouths'.

This passion for the natural world, in part inspired by the beauty of Jamaican wildlife, would become a recurring theme of the Bond stories. The short story 'For Your Eyes Only' opens with the declaration that 'The most beautiful bird in Jamaica, and some say the most beautiful bird in the world, is the streamer-tail or doctor humming-bird.' James Bond never kills a bird or a mammal – except humans – and rarely kills a fish except to eat. Anyone who does kill a bird in a Bond story invites Bond's fiercest anger and always ends up deservedly dead: Mr Big's associate 'the Robber' in *Live and Let Die*, who shoots a pelican for fun; Von Hammerstein in 'For Your Eyes Only', who blasts an innocent kingfisher; Scaramanga in *The Man with the Golden Gun*, who shows off his shooting skills by killing two kling-kling birds. (Bond even criticizes Gala Brand in *Moonraker* for picking a flower.) And if cruelty to nature is a sure sign of villainy, an appreciation and knowledge of the natural world, such as are shown by fictional Jamaicans Honeychile Rider and Quarrel, are a certain indication of good character.

In *Live and Let Die,* Fleming describes Jamaica as having 'some of the most beautiful scenery in the world'. Elsewhere he calls it 'the most beautiful large island in the world'. Best of all was the variety of landscape. On the cooler uplands lay meadows that reminded Fleming of Ireland or the Tyrol; then, he continues in his *Horizon* article, 'you drop down, often through a cathedral of bamboo or a deep-cut gully of ferns', into the tropical jungle, rich in palms, cotton trees and hardwood; after valleys of sugar cane and bananas, there is the sea, 'breaking in silver on the reef' – a description that Fleming would reuse in *Live and Let Die,* when Bond and Quarrel are driving across the island.

Other Jamaican attractions outlined in the 1947 article are the Great Houses, including 'Prospect, belonging to Sir Harold Mitchell' and 'Bellevue Plantation, belongs to the Bryces', and the hot springs at Bath and Milk River, the latter boasting 'the highest radio-activity of any mineral bath in the world', useful for 'curing your rheumatism or sciatica (or just having an aphrodisiac binge)'.

The food was plentiful and exciting. Fleming details a mouth-watering menu that includes black crab, roast stuffed suckling pig, and guavas (as Quarrel would make for Bond and Solitaire in *Live and Let Die*). Here in Jamaica you could gorge yourself on treats unavailable at home, just as Bond would do. There were 'Unbounded drinks of all sorts'. He also recommends the local weather, the *Daily Gleaner* – 'my favourite newspaper above all others in the world' – the 'electric rhythms' of the music, and swimming in a bay after dark, shining 'like an Oscar, because of the phosphorus'. He was a man clearly passionate about his Jamaica.

The only real shortcomings of the island for Fleming were 'the mosquitoes, sandflies, grass-ticks and politics. None of these are virulent hazards.' Having dismissed it as a mere irritation, however, he then goes on to describe his views of the politics of the island in some detail.

Like other incomers, Fleming initially knew little about the political undercurrents on the island, although he does refer in his article to 'recent disturbances'. Jamaica had been a Crown colony, ruled directly from London, since the 1860s, although twenty years later a very limited form of representative government was introduced. Nevertheless, by the 1930s, only a twelfth of the population was entitled to vote, and real power was still in the hands of the British Governor and the Colonial Office. One Caribbean historian has recently described the politics of this period as a 'dictatorship of white supremacy'.

The first real challenge to this came from New York. Then, as now, the city played host to a large Jamaican community. New York, with its 'Harlem Renaissance', gave West Indians an opportunity that they did not enjoy at home to engage in political activity, and a context in which to assert themselves. In 1936, W. Adolphe Roberts, Wilfred Domingo and the Reverend Ethelred Brown launched the Jamaica Progressive League, committed to 'work for the attainment of self-government for Jamaica'. Soon the organisation was sending activists from New York to Jamaica.

What they found there was atrocious poverty, squalor and governmental neglect. Where tourists and visiting expatriates saw picturesque scenes of time stood still or romantic decline, they saw urgent social and economic problems. Disease and malnourishment were everywhere, and few places off the beaten track had electricity or piped water. A book about Jamaica published in 1938 described the hill dwellers as a 'lost people': 'the children have yaws on their legs, or are blown with midget elephantiasis ... there is no doctor here but the Obeah man'. Roads, hospitals and poorhouses were in a disgraceful condition. Education provision was amongst the worst in the Empire, with most children only attending school three times a week, and then in classes of seventy or more. Only 3 per cent of the population was educated beyond the age of ten, and as much as half the black population was illiterate.

Unemployment was rife and the global depression had pushed down wages in the key sugar business to levels not much higher than in 1830. There was growing protest about poor pay and working conditions, including, in 1935, strikes and riots among the banana workers at Oracabessa. This came to a climax in May 1938, when Kirkwood's new Tate & Lyle sugar factory at Frome advertised for workers. Thousands turned up, and when there was not nearly enough work to go round, riots broke out that claimed the lives of eight men and led to a declaration of martial law. Strikes and rioting spread across the island.

The disturbances saw the emergence of new unions under the leadership of the flamboyant and energetic Alexander Bustamante, and, more widely, a new Jamaican nationalism spearheaded by Norman Manley, a Rhodes scholar and the island's leading barrister. Manley had fought for the Empire during the First World War as an artilleryman, experiencing violent racial prejudice from his comrades. (His brother Roy was killed near Ypres in 1917, aged twenty-one). His sculptress wife Edna Manley had already started a movement of anti-colonial Jamaican art.

In the same year as these disturbances, Manley launched the socialist People's National Party (PNP), pledging to 'raise the standard of living and security of the masses of the people' and to 'develop national spirit'. While empire nostalgists like Fleming looked back fondly on the old Jamaica of the Great House, Manley saw the island's 'ugly' past as a ruinous curse that had created a 'culture of dependency', making people 'turgid and lethargic'. 'We are still a colonial people. The values of the plantation still prevail,' he lamented. Manley was fond of quoting a British colonial official who had admitted: 'The

Norman Manley addressing a crowd during the 1962 election campaign. Intellectually brilliant, hard-working and both tough and sensitive when required, Manley should have led Jamaica to independence. Although he was a fine public speaker, critics say he was too erudite for the 'ordinary' Jamaican.

Empire and British rule rest on a carefully nurtured sense of inferiority in the governed.'

Public Opinion newspaper, founded in 1937 to take on the establishment views of the *Daily Gleaner*, saw neglect of education in Jamaica as the result of a 'social oligarchy' deliberately aiming to 'nurture a sense of inferiority in the masses', who as a result 'are embittered with a feeling of frustration'. 'Each Jamaican is a smoldering little volcano of resentment,' warned one magazine writer. Another predicted a 'revolution because of class resentment', which 'would be suppressed by British bayonets and boycotted by Yankee capital'.

During the Second World War, the British Governor of the time, Sir Arthur Richards, used the cover of imperial security to enhance his own powers and harass and arrest his opponents, earning himself the nickname 'the Repressor'.

But the authorities in London conceded that change had to come. At the Foreign Office, Anthony Eden, who would later, famously, stay at Goldeneye, urged that due to their proximity to the United

States, it was essential to 'make our Colonies in the Caribbean good examples of our Imperial work'. Richards was replaced by Huggins, and in February 1943 a new constitution was proposed that allowed for a House of Representatives on the island, elected by universal adult suffrage. In July 1943, Bustamante, who had been imprisoned for seventeen months for sedition, formed his own political party, the Jamaican Labour Party (JLP), to rival his cousin Norman Manley's PNP. The election was to be held in December of the following year.

Bustamante, for now, was unsure about self-government, not just because he thought it unaffordable, but because he saw the inevitable outcome as the control of the black masses by the 'brown' middle class; what he called 'a new slavery'. Bustamante was inherently conservative but also a shrewd and opportunistic populist and a stunning orator. To one cheering crowd he declared: 'We want bread! B-R-E-D bread!' When the election came, he managed to secure far greater funding

than the PNP and to garner the votes of both the elite whites and the poorest blacks, winning twenty-two of the thirty-two seats in the House of Representatives. A disappointed Edna Manley wrote in her diary that 'I shall never forget the rich people rolling in in their hundreds to vote Labour' so

Alexander Bustamante, with St. William Grant, being freed from prison after arrest for inciting unlawful assembly during the unrest of May 1938. Along with other Jamaican nationalists and trade unionists, he would be arrested again during the first year of World War Two.

as 'to keep Manley out'. This victory made Bustamante the unofficial government leader, under the title of Minister of Communication. But real power and responsibility resided with the Executive Council, made up of five elected members, or ministers, and five men appointed by the Governor, who himself sat in the chair and therefore kept control.

Nonetheless, the chance to vote for the first time had given ordinary Jamaicans new confidence that their interests and opinions mattered. As a consequence, support for self-government and involvement in politics grew. From 1945 onwards, this sometimes manifested itself in political violence, with the victims more often innocent bystanders, rival trade-union or party groups rather than the colonial authorities.

Even the wife of the Governor was no longer immune from criticism. Molly's mass marriages 'had caused more harm than good. A number of happy homes have come to grief,' Adolphe Roberts would complain. 'Lady Huggins,' wrote *Public Opinion*, 'must have been sent out by the Colonial Office to sell British Imperialism. The salesmanship was good but the article for sale was shoddy.' According to leaders of the PNP, her Women's Federation constituted 'political activities'. The Governor, they argued, should 'put a restraining hand upon her'. There were also hints that her personal conduct was bringing the Governor's office into disrepute; that he should not 'let his attractive wife roam at large and, from all appearances, do very much as she liked'.

Molly's lover, Kirkwood, was furious, and at a party given at King's House defended her from attacks by the PNP leaders. Edna Manley, who was at the party, noted in her diary that night that 'Kirkwood had "too many" and went all over the crowd saying "the PNP" is a pack of crooks, bastards and anti-British. He and Lady Huggins are pretty matey. It's funny because when she came to see me she said she didn't like him, he was all "I – I – I." So is she, poor darling.'

In his 1947 *Horizon* article, Fleming summed up local politics as 'the usual picture – education bringing a desire for self-government, for riches, for blacker coats and whiter collars, for a greater share (or all) of the prizes which England gets from the colony'. He saw the independence movement as materialistic – an urge to own 'all the desirable claptrap of the whites' such as cars and racehorses. 'Two men are fighting each other to take over the chaperonage of Jamaica,' he reported, before describing Bustamante as 'a gorgeous flamboyant rabble-rouser' and Manley as 'the local Cripps and white hope of the Harlem communists'. The latter, he declared, has 'the right wife to help him'. Of the two leaders, Fleming wrote, 'you would like both of these citizens although they would both say that they want to kick you out'. Fortunately, he concluded, 'holding wise and successful sway is the Governor, Sir John Huggins', assisted by Hugh Foot as Colonial Secretary and Lady Molly Huggins, 'a blonde and much-loved bombshell'. 'Heaven knows what the island would do without her,' he added.

Local politics for Fleming, reporting in 1947, was picturesque, populated by 'zany' characters, reassuringly old-fashioned rather than a 'grave danger'. He was confident that the 'edge' would be kept off the rising political 'passions' by 'the liberality and wisdom of our present policy'. Pax Britannica, it seemed, still ruled in Jamaica.

1948
Lady Rothermere

Bond knew that he was very close to being in love with her.

Diamonds are Forever

Fleming had written frequently to Ann Rothermere during his 1947 stay at Goldeneye, extolling the wonders of his Jamaica. Later that spring, back in England, their relationship became much more passionate and intense. Fleming stayed close to the Rothermere circle, taking advantage of any absence of Ann's husband to steal some time with her. Often this was spent in furious argument. On one occasion they were surprised by Ann's sister-in-law Virginia, who reported: 'They'd just had the mother and father of all rows. Clearly they thrived on it. They liked hurting each other.'

In late August, the pair met up for a secret rendezvous in Dublin. Afterwards Ann wrote to Ian, 'I loved being whipped by you and I don't think I have ever loved like this before … I love being hurt by you and kissed afterwards.' If they could not be alone, Fleming tagged along with the Rothermere party. They all saw New Year in together at the Chelsea Arts Club, but in January came what Ian and Ann had been most looking forward to: Ann's first visit to Jamaica.

Considering that she was married to a newspaperman, Ann was incredibly indiscreet when she arrived at Kingston. On page 12 of the *Gleaner* from 13 January 1948 is a photograph of Ian and Ann standing next to one another, just off the aeroplane from Miami, saying how pleased they were to be there – Ian 'happy to be home' – and that

Lady Rothermere with Lady Huggins in the dining room at King's House. Ann's aristocratic background added to Ian's cachet in Jamaica.

they would be staying together at Goldeneye. (The same page carries a large notice of a public meeting with a photograph of Bustamante in full oratorical flow and the appeal: 'Come in your Thousands!') With them, as a sort of chaperone, was mutual friend (and a previous lover of Fleming) Loelia, Duchess of Westminster, whose marriage to the Duke had been dissolved the year before after many years of separation. The party was met by the Bryces and conveyed to Bellevue above Kingston, now much refurbished. After a couple of days there, which included lunch with the Governor and Lady Huggins at King's House, the three headed for Oracabessa.

They arrived at Goldeneye 'at typical tropical sunset hour'. Violet, Holmes the gardener and two other maids were lined up outside to 'welcome "Commander" with much grinning'. Ian was 'ecstatically excited' to be back, Ann reported.

It was very quickly dark, and the night full of the noise of frogs and crickets. Ann suddenly felt a bit depressed, although she hid it from Ian. The house seemed to her to be extremely rudimentary. In fact, Ian's mother and half-sister Amaryllis had visited the previous month and been so put off that they had moved out to stay in a hotel. 'The house is scarcely furnished ...' Ann complained. There was a dining alcove with hard wooden benches but nowhere to sit in comfort. At dinner Ian made it clear that his position was 'facing the window and staring at the night'.

The next morning, Ann woke early. Ian and Loelia were still asleep. She wandered round the outside of the property, noting sea grapes and orange, lemon and grapefruit trees, along with much miscellaneous bush. Then she ventured down the steep stone steps to the small white sand beach directly below the house and plunged in, finding the water 'warm transparent shallow'. It was dreamy. 'Depression totally gone,' she noted. 'Only Ian could devise this manner of life.' Climbing back up the steps, she came across him awake, and furious that she had not waited for him to show her everything. 'Too full of wellbeing

Ann's first visit, gamely posing for Loelia's camera. Fleming's girlfriends in Jamaica who didn't love the reef were given short shrift. But Ann loved snorkelling.

to be troubled by this,' Ann noted. 'Breakfast of paw paw, black [*sic*] mountain coffee, scrambled eggs and bacon.'

After breakfast, Ian ceased sulking and the two spent 'a wonderful day of birds, flowers and above all fish'. Masks and snorkels were employed and Ann found the 'tropical underwater more beautiful than land, strange alarming canyons of coral rock'.

Ann noted that Ian now 'devised a halcyon way of life': a swim at sunrise, then Violet brought his shaving water and received instruction on how his eggs should be cooked for breakfast. Fleming was as meticulous about breakfast as Bond would be. After eating, he liked to read in the sunken garden, then go for a potter in his rubber dinghy or march around with Holmes the gardener making plans. The idea was to plant more flowers to attract hummingbirds. In England, Ian always complained that flowers gave him headaches, but not here. Ann noted dramatically that 'Each rose has a large black beetle eating its heart out.' There was also a plan to plant an avenue of palms from the house to the gate on the road. 'Little will come of this,' Ann predicted, 'as it is clear no work will be done in Ian's absence.'

There was then a martini before lunch, which would be resolutely local fare, such as silk fish or snapper 'grilled in butter and served with a great deal of rice'. They also had curried goat, or steak. Ann's favourite was kidneys or liver grilled over charcoal. Any leftovers were taken away by the staff to share with their large families.

Ian was rapidly accumulating reference books on Jamaican shells, birds, fish, flora and the stars to be seen from Goldeneye. Among these was the 1947 edition of *Field Guide to Birds of the West Indies* by ornithologist James Bond. Loelia was uninterested, but Ann, who had inherited from her father Guy Charteris a keen interest in birds, started using the book as a guide to the specimens found around Goldeneye, which included beautiful rarities such as the tiny vervain hummingbird, or 'little doctor bird', and the unique Jamaican woodpecker.

For now, though, the fish were the biggest draw. There was much to admire – butterfly-, angel- and parrotfish, rock beauties and fairy basslets – and there were delicious lobsters to be hunted with trident forks.

Loelia, who described Ian as 'a curious and complex person, and immensely attractive to women … both clever and conceited', would usually be left behind as Fleming and Ann went adventuring together. 'I cannot say I enjoyed my Goldeneye days,' she later complained. 'I soon discovered that the reason I had been asked was to spread a thin aura of respectability as chaperone for Ann.' She and Ian 'were madly in love', Loelia wrote, and 'used to leave in a small boat to fish or study the reef and not return until dusk. I was left on this stick of coral to wander about among the blackamores in the village.'

According to Ann's daughter Fionn, Ian and her mother loved teasing Loelia. Bond has a go too, in *Moonraker*, where Loelia Ponsonby (the Duchess's maiden name) is the secretary he shares with two other

Ian and Ann, Goldeneye 1948: 'Madly in love.'

members of the 00 section. Bond and his colleagues have all made 'determined assaults on her virtue'. 'I'll never call you Loelia,' he says to her. 'It sounds like somebody in an indecent limerick.'

After dinner, a ritual was established of leaning over the railing at the end of the sunken garden and watching the 'spray of the reef or the high bright large stars'. As Ann reported in her diary, 'the air is so clear of dirt or dust there is an illusion of vast universe and the sea horizon is very round. Ian remains longer than us, smoking and wallowing in the melancholy.'

Loelia found the evenings equally as trying as the days. The problem for her were the huge open windows, which 'in daytime was fine, but at night, when the lamps were lit, every insect known to man seemed to pour in from the darkness outside'. In general, she found the house 'strangely uncomfortable'. The concrete floor, originally painted navy blue and cleaned with oranges, had for an unknown reason been covered in a layer of black boot polish, which created a condition known as 'Goldeneye foot' as it wore off on people's bare soles. There was no proper bathroom and only one cold tap. She found it a very masculine and austere place. Ian suggested to Ann that she and Loelia might help with furnishing. Ann thought that curtains might be a good idea, a suggestion Ian found appalling and ignored entirely, along with any other attempts to feminise the house.

Boasting a duchess and a lady, the Fleming party was much in demand at the island's smartest addresses. On 26 January, there was a lunch with Lady Huggins and the Duke and Duchess of Sutherland. Four days later came a trip to the Stephensons' lavish Hillowtown mansion near Montego Bay. Guests included both Lord Lyle and Mr and Mrs Tate, out in Jamaica inspecting their new fiefdoms.

Still, Fleming's two lady companions found some of these gatherings dull, while he blamed them for indulging in 'Mayfair talk' to pass the time, later writing: 'If you burden yourself with the big-town malaises you came here to escape – the telephone, gin and canasta jitters, gossip and how to keep up with the procession – those will be the serpents in this Eden. But if you can leave this *triste* baggage behind, you will find Jamaica has everything you need.'

On Thursday, 5 March, Ann and Loelia left for Miami and New York en route home. From the RMS *Queen Mary* Ann wrote to Ian: 'I did love it all and please take me back again next year. I shall like it even better because I shall have tiny roots there.'

In fact, this first visit would turn out to be the happiest time Ann ever had at Goldeneye. In high-end circles in Jamaica her affair with Fleming had been pretty much common knowledge, although one American gossip columnist – 'Cholly Knickerbocker' – got the wrong end of the stick and wrote that his lover was Loelia, describing Fleming as 'a sort of Beau Brummel of the islands'.

Ian had a further month on his own in Jamaica before returning to London. A highlight was his first shark hunt, with Aubyn Cousins, the son of the man who had sold him the Goldeneye land. John Pearson,

Fleming's first biographer, met Cousins in 1965, noticing that, like Bond's Jamaica sidekick Quarrel, he had grey eyes. Cousins claimed to be part Irish – 'My great great grandfather was captain of a schooner out of Dublin' – and spoke very fondly of 'the Commander'.

Fleming and Cousins dragged out to the deep water beyond the reef a pair of stinking animal corpses – a donkey and a cow – in order to lure ocean predators. It was clearly an inspirational episode. In *Live and Let Die*, Mr Big similarly throws blood and offal into the sea, causing 'frenzy' among the sharks and barracuda, 'whirling and snapping in the water like hysterical dogs'. Here, the effect was almost as dramatic. Straight away two huge sharks appeared, the first biting the head off the cow with a sound Fleming uses for the death of Robber in *Live and Let Die* – a 'terrible snuffling grunt as if a great pig was getting its mouth full. He knew it for the grunt that a shark makes as its hideous flat nose comes up out of the water and its sickle-shaped mouth closes on a floating carcass' – and for that of Mr Big himself – 'a horrible grunting scrunch'.

At that moment Cousins slipped a nylon noose over the nose of the shark and held on as the enraged animal struggled and thrashed. According to Cousins, Ian loved the danger of this moment, as the small vessel tipped violently, threatening to hurl them both into the sea. Fleming described this first hunt to Ann as 'the most thrilling thing' he had done in his life. But once the shark was 'tied up good and firm', said Cousins, 'it seemed like he lost interest. And he never let me kill a shark. "Cousins," he'd say, "cut the damn thing loose. We've had our fun for the day."'

Ann was a little anxious about Ian being on his own, writing from America: 'I do hope the remoteness of Goldeneye won't force you to collect some sordid female to replace me.' In a subsequent letter, she continued, 'It would be an interesting feat to be faithful to someone for three weeks, you have never done it before and it might make you feel very happy.' Ian assured her that he had been 'steadfast as a rock' and that there 'had been little temptation to stick my umbrella into anything except the sea'. But with Ann away, there were a number of female visitors, including the society writer Elsa Maxwell, and the stunningly attractive novelist Rosamond Lehmann, who had read Fleming's *Horizon* article and told him he was a good writer and should do more. Ian assured Ann that their relationship was 'spiritual'.

Also staying for a couple of days was the travel writer Patrick Leigh Fermor, who was researching what would become his successful book *The Traveller's Tree*. Leigh Fermor took the opposite view to Loelia on the subject of the Goldeneye windows, declaring that Fleming's design 'might serve as a model for new houses in the tropics ... great windows capture every breeze, to cool, even on the hottest day, the large white rooms'. Even better, the 'enormous quadrilaterals' framed a 'prospect of sea and cloud and sky, and tamed the elements, as it were'. Fleming would return the compliment

The garden and sea from inside Goldeneye.

when in *Live and Let Die* Bond reads Fermor's 'extraordinary book' after a recommendation from M: "'It's by a chap who knows what he is talking about.'"

Before going home after two months on the island, Fleming spent a weekend with the Stephensons and then a night with Molly and Sir John Huggins. He also penned a short article for the *Gleaner* under the heading 'Commander Fleming Gives Modest, Practical Suggestions For Island's Development'. And modest they were: better postcards and guidebooks for the tourists, and homespun wisdom about using more seafood and planting two new trees when you cut one down. What is perhaps most interesting is what it says about Jamaica at the time that a visiting Englishman with no particular expertise should be asked to comment in the national newspaper.

Back in London, Fleming resumed his usual life of leisurely work at the *Sunday Times*, bridge or dinners in the evening and golf at the weekend. But soon after his return, he and Ann found out that she was pregnant. In a letter to Evelyn Waugh, Ann mentioned her 'sad condition' and 'sorry state', but said that she was 'resigned' and 'accepting her duties cheerfully'. Because of the timing of their Jamaican sojourn, it had to be Ian's child.

Fleming had asked Loelia to use her stay in New York to try to find some rich American to rent Goldeneye in his absence. On 3 March, she was at a cocktail party in Manhattan given by the Broadway producer Gilbert Miller and his wife Kitty. There she met Noël Coward, and in spite of her grumbles gave him a favourable report of Goldeneye, making it sound 'marvelous'. Coward was in need of a break after a demoralising flop on Broadway, and had visited Jamaica before, in 1944. Like Fleming, he had stayed at Bellevue and fallen in love with the country: 'The spell was cast and held, and I knew I should come back.' He arranged to meet up with Fleming when he was passing through New York a few days later.

Coward had encountered Fleming during the war but did not know him well. Ian's brilliant brother Peter was married to Celia Johnson, star of the recent Coward-written *Brief Encounter*. In the previous three years, Coward had occasionally come across Ian at parties given by the Rothermeres, where Fleming was usually in attendance. Coward knew Ann, in society hostess mode, much better. In New York, he and Ian haggled over the price, with the latter claiming he had high-paying Americans already lined up, but the deal was soon done. Two weeks later, Coward became Goldeneye's first paying guest, at £50 a week. This included the services of Violet and two other staff.

Coward, together with his companion Graham Payn, reached Jamaica on 22 March 1948. 'Ship arrived five hours late and rammed the pier,' he noted drily. They were met by an aide-de-camp (ADC) from the Governor, who arranged the necessary paperwork, and the pair arrived at Oracabessa just before dusk. 'It is quite perfect,' Coward wrote in his diary that night. The house seemed fine, the staff friendly, and there was 'a small private coral beach with lint white sand and warm clear water. The beach is unbelievable.' After a delicious dinner from Violet, they swam, then lay on the sand, perfectly warm under a full moon. 'So far,' Coward wrote, 'it all seems far too good to be true.' Two days later, having spent the time painting, swimming, sunbathing and rowing the rubber dinghy, he was already musing on the possibility of himself 'building a shack somewhere isolated on this island … an idyllic bolt-hole to return to when life became too frustrating'.

Coward would enjoy teasing Ian Fleming about Goldeneye's drawbacks. He reckoned the stark, modern new building looked like a medical clinic, and christened it 'Goldeneye, nose and throat'. He complained about the 'plague of ants', the loose shutters, the odd rat, the uncomfortable iron beds and the 'hordes of ageing shells' everywhere. Violet's Jamaican food palled and had misses as well as hits. One meal of salt fish and ackee, followed by guavas with coconut cream, 'all tasted of armpits'. As for the spacious sitting room, Coward bemoaned that it faced so as to miss the sunset, and that 'the long window-sills had been so cunningly designed that they entirely cut off the view as you sank into the sofa upholstered with iron shavings … All you Flemings revel in discomfort.'

But he loved wading out to look at fish through glass-bottomed buckets, and enjoyed the surrounding scenes inland: 'Behind the house are banana plantations and then green covered hills and blue mountains in the distance.' At the end of this stay he would write in the guest book that it had been 'The happiest two months I have ever spent.' Coward was so won over that by the time he left he had purchased not one but two plots of land nearby, and was already building his own house. Before half their stay was over, he and Graham Payn had found a property five miles along the coast east of Oracabessa on the brow of the hill before it made its descent to Port Maria. Sufficiently secluded to be hidden but open to the sea and protected by a reef, the spot was populated by 'blue-green lizards splashed with red, electric-blue butterflies and beelike hummingbirds, with ominous John Crow black vultures wheeling above'. On the three acres grew oranges, limes, breadfruit, avocado pears, pimentos, 'and all sorts of tropical deliciousness'. On 25 April, Coward wrote in his diary: 'I am now a property owner in Jamaica and it is jolly fine.' It was to be called Blue Harbour.

Straight away Coward employed an expatriate Englishman as a builder and Fleming's architects Scovell and Barber, with Reggie Aquart again acting as overseer. The plans included a saltwater swimming pool overlooking the secluded bay. Two weeks later, with the design of the new house under way, Coward and Payn drove up to a high point above Blue Harbour called the Look-Out. Here were the ruins, 'grown over with orchids', of an old stone house, reputedly an observation post used by Jamaican legend Sir Henry Morgan. Coward loved the spot, in particular its view, and finding that Blanche

Blackwell's brother Roy Lindo was selling the land at only £10 an acre, he bought the site for £150, with the idea of building a separate writing retreat.

Coward would spend much of the rest of his life in Jamaica, and so began what might in some respects be considered an unlikely close friendship between him and Fleming. It was, at its heart, a friendship made in Jamaica. The first time the two men met in London after Coward's visit, they ignored the rest of the party and chatted furiously about the island. Through all Fleming's adventures at Goldeneye over the next fifteen years, Coward would be a continual presence. For his part, Coward was so fascinated by Fleming-in-Jamaica that he would make him a recurring character in his writing.

Much of their relationship revolved around leg-pulling and friendly rivalry over their respective Jamaican homes. In 'For Your Eyes Only', for instance, we hear that 'Somebody's suddenly gone and bought that ghastly Blue Harbour hotel.' Peter Quennell, who knew both men and made three visits to Goldeneye, in 1954, 1955 and 1962, reckoned that Coward played up to Fleming, 'who was himself resolutely, even at times aggressively heterosexual'. Coward apparently treated him 'as if he were a distinguished member of the opposite sex, almost a prima donna; and Ian, oddly enough, responded and dropped some of his masculine defenses. He enjoyed being admired and teased, and having a bouquet or two thrown at his feet.' Coward's attitude to Ian's 'dark moods and passionate prejudices', Quennell later wrote, 'was always subtly understanding. He humoured, scolded, occasionally derided, yet somehow never did the smallest damage to Ian's ticklish *amour propre*. His victim, indeed, seemed positively to enjoy being teased or even ridiculed.'

In fact, in some respects the two men were very alike. Coward shared Fleming's love of the Royal Navy, distaste for intellectuals, fondness and nostalgia for a romantic version of empire, and horror at the diminished post-war power of his country. In August the previous year India had become independent, removing at a stroke three-quarters of the Empire's subjects. When Gandhi was assassinated in January 1948, Coward wrote in his diary: 'a bloody good thing but far too late'. Like Fleming, he believed that the post-war Labour government had damaged the 'psyche of the kingdom' and that Britain was now a place where, as Fleming wrote, 'taxation, controls and certain features of the Welfare State have turned the majority of us into petty criminals, liars and work-dodgers'.

It is striking that two such influential defenders of the Britain of its empire days were close neighbours and friends in Jamaica in the 1950s and early 1960s as the country moved from imperial throwback all the way to independence. The crucial difference between them, however, was that Coward, once a rebel of sorts, was in the process of losing his touch, his ability to communicate with his public through his plays and films. His formula of imperial pride thinly disguised with light self-mockery was beginning to seem, some said, 'an irrelevant survival from a bygone era'. Fleming, however, would show that there was still huge appetite for patriotic stories. As historian David Cannadine wrote, Bond was 'a reaffirmation of Britain's continued great-power status and imperial amplitude ... an action-man British hero, flying the flag, confounding the enemy, committed to queen and country and empire'. In 1970, French theorist Raymond Durgnat called Bond 'a one-man Suez task force'. But to get away with this, Fleming's stories would need an altogether more modern flavour than Coward's.

Esmond Rothermere, although described by Quennell as benevolent to the point of indifference, must have known about, or at least doubted, the paternity of his wife's forthcoming child. Nevertheless, he stuck with her through the difficult pregnancy, and in mid July, the family, including Ann's two children from her first marriage, Raymond and Fionn, went on a golfing holiday at Gleneagles Hotel in Scotland. Tagging along were Loelia and Fleming. During the holiday, while the four were playing bridge, it suddenly became apparent that Ann was going into labour a month early. She was rushed to hospital in Edinburgh, but the premature little girl only survived a few hours. Rothermere was at her bedside, whilst Ian wrote furious letters from the hotel, sneaking a fleeting visit as soon as he could.

A few days later, Ann sent a letter to Ian from the hospital in Edinburgh: 'My darling, there was morphia and pain and then you were here and now you've gone and there's nothing except the realisation of what happened in the last ten days ... I have cried all day ... I am very bruised and bewildered.' The little girl was christened Mary, and put in the family vault at Aberlady, 'while I was lying in a haze of morphia and you were playing golf'. Ann went on to implore Ian: 'I do love you; please help me over this. I am muddled and distressed.' The next day she wrote again, apologising for the 'self-indulgent' letter, writing: 'It was cruel to take it out on you during your golf week.'

Shortly afterwards she was writing to thank him for sending magazines and 'making a fuss' of her, which made her 'want to purr'. 'I think any man would be a frightful bore after you,' she went on. 'I should miss the infinite variety of wall-gazing, pointless bullying so harsh and then so gentle when I cry ... You beast, you must write your book.'

1949
Noël and Ian, Samolo and Jamaica

a new set of people
arrive
to lie bare-assed in the sun
wanting gold on their bodies
cane-rows in their hair
with beads – even bells

So I serving them

Olive Senior, 'Meditation on Yellow'

In what turned out to be a rather feeble effort to put on a respectable front, when Ann Rothermere arrived in Jamaica with Ian Fleming on 6 January, she claimed she was staying with the island's new celebrity resident, Noël Coward – a confirmed bachelor, as everyone knew. Still, the *Gleaner* cheerfully went on to report that after a visit to the Bryces at Bellevue, they were both heading for Goldeneye. Coward wasn't even in Jamaica at the time.

The spur for the discretion came in part because of Esmond Rothermere's growing impatience with his wife's affair with Fleming. In the autumn, after Mary's death and perhaps hoping to activate some sort of newspaper proprietors' union, Rothermere had complained to Ian's boss Lord Kemsley about his employee's behaviour. Kemsley, described by Ann as standing for 'Empire, family life and the Conservative Party', gave Ian a severe dressing-down, though he stopped short of firing his old bridge-playing friend. But for Ian and Ann, there was a feeling that big decisions about their future had to be made.

Coward did arrive in Jamaica on 3 February, accompanied by his partner Graham Payn. He surveyed his now completed property, then they raced round to see Ann and Ian, who were 'welcoming and sweet'. Blue Harbour had not been built quite as Coward had intended, layered into the hillside, but he was nonetheless delighted. 'The house is entrancing. I can't believe it's mine,' he wrote in his diary that night. When they got back from Goldeneye, he and Graham 'sat on the verandah on rockers, looking out over the fabulous view, and almost burst into tears of sheer pleasure'.

The pleasure would continue, much of it in the company of Ian and Ann for dinners, drinks, cards or trips. It was not only that Coward needed an audience; he was also intrigued by their relationship. They in turn were invigorated by his and Graham's desire to explore and experience Jamaica. Two weeks into Coward's trip, they all went rafting on the nearby Rio Grande, a tourist highlight first popularised by Errol Flynn. The narrow wooden rafts were intended for carrying bananas down from the highlands to Port Antonio, and Flynn had asked for a ride. It was a wonderful experience: 'As you glide down this river you look up on either side to the most magnificent skyline that God or Nature had created,' Flynn later wrote. The trip took four hours, which included fishing and stops for swimming. Fleming later described the experience for readers of the *Sunday Times* as an

Rafting on the Rio Grande. One of the highlights for Fleming was his favourite boatman's 'Strong Bak Soup – a ridiculous cauldron brew of langoustines and exotic roots.'

'enchantingly languid … elegant and delicately romantic adventure'. On either side of the river were hills 'befeathered with bamboo and bright with flowers'. Afterwards Ian drove Noël and Graham home 'and was vastly entertaining all the way'.

Coward was finding in Jamaica, and in Ian Fleming in particular, excellent source material. On 6 April, while rereading Evelyn Waugh's *Vile Bodies*, he had his first idea for the play *Home and Colonial*, to be set on a fictional colonial island called Samolo. Ostensibly in the South Pacific, Samolo in fact became Coward's take on Jamaica. There should be a 'scandal with a local Bustamante … It's a heaven-sent opportunity to get in a lot of Jamaican stuff,' he confided to his diary on 6 April. The Jamaican material continued to come, and he would revisit Samolo a number of times, in a novel, *Pomp and Circumstance*; in short stories; and in other plays. Although of course fiction, Coward's Samolo provides a fascinating take on tourism, empire, race and other Jamaica-inspired concerns that would similarly become so important to his friend Fleming's Bond novels.

The expatriate white community of Coward's Samolo is cliquey, claustrophobic and, as Bond would also be, libertarian with regard to sex and alcohol consumption. Almost all of the characters are recognisably drawn from real people in Jamaica during his time there. For example, a lesbian couple in *Pomp and Circumstance* are inspired by painters Marion Simmons and Rhoda Jackson, fixtures in the north-coast artistic circle and friends of Coward. Carmen Pringle, grande dame of Sunset Lodge, makes an appearance as hotel owner Juanita, with a 'buccaneer quality' and 'a personality like a battering ram'.

Coward's Samolan-Jamaicans are guileless, engaging and friendly: 'They sing from morning till night ... and never stop having scores of entrancing children.' Although the most racist attitudes are given to unsympathetic characters, the consensus attitude of the expatriate British whites to the locals is still one of affectionate condescension. Craftsmen are 'industrious and enthusiastic, but ... incapable of making identical pairs of anything'. The Samolans are a sweet and cheerful people, 'too young' yet for the 'brave experiment of independence'. Education is deemed unnecessary, as when locals are hungry they can simply 'nip a breadfruit off a tree or snatch a yam out of the ground'.

(When *Pomp and Circumstance* was eventually published in 1960, the *Evening Standard* wrote: 'If there is anywhere on earth where the old Coward world still credibly lingers on, it is probably a fairly peaceful tropical colony ruled over by a British Governor General.' A more typical reviewer called it 'stuffy and stale'.)

Samolans are also depicted by Noël Coward as innocently and spontaneously sexy. Fleming took a similar line about Jamaicans in his *Horizon* article: '"Will you do me a rudeness?" means "Will you sleep with me?",' he explained. 'To which a brazen girl will reply "You better hang on grass, I goin' move so much."' Both Fleming and Coward's depictions chimed with long-held empirical views of the sensuality and eroticism of the West Indies. In 1948, a dance performance in London, *A Caribbean Rhapsody*, had attracted huge press interest. 'With that race, that place, that title, audiences know what to expect. They are not disappointed,' wrote the reviewer for *Picture Post*. 'Enthusiasts praised the pace and excitement of it all, the exoticism, the sexiness, what they call the "animal primitivism" of the dancing.' The *Daily Mail* gushed: 'There spills on to the audience the hot, throbbing swamps of the West Indies.'

Noël Coward notes in his Samolo novel, 'There is a great deal of sex which goes on all the time with a winsom disregard of gender.' 'I do like the Jamaicans,' he wrote in his diary on 3 May 1949. 'Fortunately they like me too and I couldn't be more pleased that they do.'

According to Molly Huggins, 'The people of Jamaica loved Noël and he did a great deal to help them, especially the poor and needy in the villages and towns near him.' A small portion of the Look-Out land was given over as a community sports pitch, and Coward's numerous visitors kept local grocers busy. At Blue Harbour, he employed a staff of at least six. Molly had met Coward before in Singapore, where she had come across him, in a story almost too perfect, shopping for silk pyjamas. 'What a fascinating and brilliant man he is!' she exclaimed in her memoir. On this visit he descended on King's House, where he sat at the piano, 'with his lean figure and fascinating versatile face, and sang songs', including making up a 'most amusing rhyme about my second daughter, Cherry'.

The central character of Coward's *Home and Colonial* is Sandra, who, like Molly, is the English Governor's wife. Sandra is the object of a crush from a local 'native' politician (who 'hilariously' mixes up his English idioms). What pressure there is for self-government comes from a tiny minority of Samolans and left-wing politicians from Britain. The vast majority of Samolans, Coward tells us, are 'empire minded'; most so 'happy and contented under British rule for so many years that they just don't understand when they're suddenly told that it's been nothing but a corrupt capitalistic racket from the word go'.

In fact, while many Jamaicans, particularly from the 'brown' middle class, remained Anglophile and committed to the Empire, as Coward suggested of the Samolans, others felt very differently. A local writer in *Public Opinion* early the following year declared the Empire to be based 'nakedly on force and autocracy', commenting that 'After the last war British imperialism was too weak to hold its Indian Ocean Empire: India, Burma and Ceylon have gone. Only the old-fashioned imperialist barbarity still preserves a precarious foothold in Malay and Hong Kong. It can hardly be disputed that the British Empire, dear to old-fashioned Tories, is on the way out.'

The main part in *Home and Colonial* was written for actress Gertrude Lawrence; when she unexpectedly died, it was offered to Vivien Leigh. Coward was surprised by the reaction. Both Leigh and her partner Laurence Olivier violently disliked the play, warning, as Coward put it, that it was 'old fashioned Noël Coward and would do me great harm'. In the end, renamed *Island Fling*, it was briefly staged in 1951 with Claudette Colbert in the lead. Coward subsequently reworked it, and it was restaged (with some popular though little critical success) in 1955 as *South Sea Bubble*, with the increasingly erratic Leigh now in the lead role after all.

In *Pomp and Circumstance*, we learn from the narrator that 'Tourism has brought the island undreamed of prosperity and set our hitherto rather insecure economy on a firm basis.' As early as 1949, Coward had noted in a letter that 'This coast is being bought up like mad', change that only gathered pace over the next few years, leading to the 'rash of millionaire hotels' that Bond, with mixed feelings, notices as he flies in over Jamaica's north coast in *Dr No*. Coward uses the same expression to describe the sudden development, from five or six private beach houses, owned by 'the wealthier members of the plantocracy whose plantations lay back in the hills', to 'no less than nine American-style hotels, three motels, and a rash of erratically designed beach bungalows which are rented for astronomical prices

for the winter season'. Enjoying the slipstream created by Sunset
Lodge in Montego Bay, still 'undoubtedly the most fashionable
resort in the West Indies', were Shaw Park, above Ocho Rios, 'In a
cool elevation overlooking the sea', Silver Seas Hotel, and the Ruins
restaurant, which became a favourite of Katharine Hepburn and her
partner Irene Selznick, and would much later be a location for the
filming of *Live and Let Die*. Sans Souci hotel opened at the same time,
'on top of the cliff, with a breath-taking view of the Caribbean ...
terraced gardens take one down the hillside to a circular swimming
pool which is fed by a mineral spring'. It too would serve as a location
for Roger Moore's adventures in Jamaica, as well as for Connery's in
Dr No.

Indeed, in 1951, the *Gleaner* reported that thanks to the pioneers
Coward and Fleming – described as 'of England's powerful Kemsley
Press' – 'all along the coast a remarkable development is going on',
now stretching from 'Frenchman's Cove and San San estate in the east
to Tryall in the west'. As contemporary advertisements demonstrate,
a private beach, from which local Jamaicans were excluded, was a key
selling point; and those built first got the pick of the best north-coast
beaches.

Amongst them was the famous, small but exclusive Jamaica Inn
at Ocho Rios, first opened in 1950 by Canadian entrepreneur Cy
Elkins. Like a lot of the construction along the north coast, it was
built by the firm of Maffissanti and Fillisetti, led by Italians who had
formed part of Jamaica's POW population during the war. (Several
thousand Italian and German captives – mainly from merchant ships
– had spent time during the war on the island, along with some 1,500
Gibraltarians evacuated from their threatened home, and a number
of Jewish refugees.) According to American artist Marion Simmons,
whose house, Glory Be, was built by the same firm, 'Mr F., being
Italian, has excellent manners, and all the airs and graces of the Old
World.' When he passed a customer in his truck, 'he would sweep off

Marilyn Monroe and Arthur Miller on their honeymoon at the Jamaica Inn, January 1957.

his straw hat from his red head in a wide circular gesture as if it has plumes on it'.

Marilyn Monroe and Winston Churchill – who described the appeal of the tropics as 'soft breezes and hard liquor' – would be amongst Jamaica Inn's most famous guests, and it quickly gained a reputation for its lively costume parties. It was also famous for its food: a Graeco-French-Italian chef employed during the key winter season dazzled guests with his fabulous buffet lunch each day. Highlights were cold tongue, ham, roast beef, marinated beef fillet, conch salad and heart of palm. A Jamaican, Teddy Tucker, who worked as the beach-barman during the 1950s and still works there today, remembers serving endless planter's punch and bullshots – vodka and beef bouillon – to a lot of smartly dressed guests, while a five-piece band – Byron Lee and the Dragonaires – kept the dancing going. The very same band would feature in the film of *Dr No*.

A clearer pointer to the future, though, was already in operation just west of Jamaica Inn. Tower Isle hotel opened in 1949, a huge eighty-room art deco construction, raised in record time for the 1949–50 winter season. Costing a quarter of a million pounds, it required new roads, five miles of piping for water, and the importation of tiles from Britain and Belgium, kitchen equipment from Canada and furniture from the United States. It was straight away hailed as 'the finest and largest hotel in the British West Indies' and 'immediately became the centre of life in the area'. Tower Isle was the brainchild of Abe Issa, the owner since 1943 of the Myrtle Bank hotel in Kingston, itself now enjoying a 'golden age', with regular celebrity guests including Joan Crawford, Ann Miller and Walt Disney. Issa was from a Palestinian family who had come to Jamaica in the 1880s. They quickly amassed a fortune as importers of dry goods, then as owners of the country's biggest and best retail emporia. In the election of 1944, Issa had headed a political party, the Jamaica Democratic Party, representing business, but did not win a single seat. Nonetheless, he would remain for many years the key mover in the new Jamaica tourism industry.

'Turn your back to the Jamaican mountain scenery, and at Tower Isle you could imagine yourself at Miami Beach,' wrote a local Jamaican. At night, guests would dance under the stars on the roof terrace to a local band, who always began their playlist with the hotel's theme song, 'Tower Island Magic'. Errol Flynn, who had been befriended by Issa, was an early patron. Noël Coward, visiting early one morning with Lord Beaverbrook, caused a stir by ordering champagne for breakfast.

In 1951, Jamaica played host to nearly 100,000 visitors, the majority from the United States. This was nearly three times the 1946 figure. Inspired by Errol Flynn's lead were other Hollywood giants, the cream of British aristocracy, and the brightest and richest of the United States' and Europe's business, theatre, literature and secret service elites. You weren't a proper Hollywood star until you had been photographed in Jamaica. In the Bond short story 'For Your Eyes Only', as the Cuban hit men escape Jamaica in a 'twin-dieseled Chriscraft motorboat', the 'fishermen and wharfingers ashore watched her go, and went on with their argument as to which of the filmstars holidaying in Jamaica this could have been'.

Stories from this time of the drinking, bed-hopping and luxurious excess in Jamaica recall the antics of the British in Happy Valley, Kenya. Noël Coward contributed to the atmosphere with a string of theatre friends coming to stay at Blue Harbour, where he had several small cottages built in the grounds. Guests included Laurence Olivier, Vivien

Noël Coward in Jamaica, with Port Maria bay in the background. Coward was Fleming's closest friend and constant companion on the island.

Leigh, Charlie Chaplin, Alec Guinness, Audrey Hepburn, Michael Redgrave, Peter O'Toole, Peter Sellers and many others. Coward had a rule that swimming in his pool could only be in the nude. Indeed, when John Pringle visited Blue Harbour with his wife Liz, they found the Oliviers 'naked on Noël's terrace, Vivien draped over Larry's cock. It was some introduction!' Olivier was also an enthusiastic consumer of the local ganja, although Coward himself didn't indulge. Blanche Blackwell remembers that visitors were 'completely different when they got into the tropics. They let go.' Veteran *Gleaner* journalist Morris Cargill concurred: 'For a brief spell, which ended in 1960, certain very rich and certain rather poor upper-class English people drank, idled and committed adultery in the sunshine.' In the languid heat of Jamaica, the morality of home was forgotten. Cargill himself complains he lost his girlfriend to his father's mistress.

It wasn't to everyone's taste. Alec Waugh (brother of Evelyn), who would make his name with his novel *Island in the Sun*, wrote in his *Notes from the Sugar Islands* that the Jamaican tourist scene was now astronomically expensive, as well as torpid. 'By day you idle on a beach; in the evening you sip cocktails on a veranda. One day becomes the next.' Patrick Leigh Fermor expressed the same sentiment in his *Traveller's Tree*, describing the jet-set thus: 'The atmosphere is a compound of Wall Street, the *Tatler*, *Vogue*, Tout Paris and the *Wiener Salonblatt* anomalously transplanted in a background of palm trees and blazing sunlight … Ice clatters in shakers and poker dice are thrown unceasingly on the bars of this Jamaican Nineveh, and, for the uninitiated visitor, the chasms of tedium yawn deeper every second.'

In 1950, the growing expatriate circle was joined by Ivor Novello, who bought a house near Montego Bay. Lord Beaverbrook took Coward to see it: 'Quite quite horrid … exactly like a suburban villa,' was Coward's verdict. Novello was part of a burgeoning and highly visible north-coast homosexual community, led by Coward and wealthy fashion designer Edward Molyneux. Established gay and lesbian white couples feature in Coward's Samolo stories as par for the course; clearly Jamaica gave them the freedom to be themselves denied at home in Britain.

Ian Fleming, although of course an enthusiastic adulterer and drinker, was ambivalent about this invasion of the decadent jet-set. In this he had much in common with a number of Jamaicans watching with despair the rapid changes happening to their island. For one thing, whatever Coward said about his Samolans' 'winsome disregard for gender' in their sexual behaviour, most Jamaicans were religious, strait-laced and strongly opposed to homosexual activity. Even before the post-war explosion of tourism, there were furious complaints that Montego Bay was besieged by 'an epidemic of homosexuality'.

This was part of wider concerns about a great expansion of prostitution, something conceded by Coward in his *Pomp and Circumstance*, where, corrupted by the 'Almighty Dollar', 'there is hardly a lissom chambermaid or a muscular beach boy who is not daily prepared to make the supreme sacrifice for suitable remuneration'. More generally, some locals argued, the 'evil example' of the wealthy and idle tourists was threatening to 'de-Jamaicanize' the population. Tourism, critics contended, brought to the island the 'standardized fripperies of Palm Beach' and cheapened the morals of Jamaican youth, who mimicked the observed behaviour of the tourists with drinking, smoking and public 'necking'. In turn the tourists, lying like 'fleshy lobsters' on the beach or 'turning their eyeballs inwards' at the nearest cocktail bar, showed little interest in Jamaica or Jamaicans, preferring 'sybaritic torpor'.

Black Jamaican journalist Evon Blake wrote that tourism had turned Jamaican youth into touts, beggars and parasites. 'The labourers will not work for economical wages; life is more exciting for men who lounge and hang round trippers and tourists with pockets filled with pound and dollar notes, and from whom they can get fat tips rather than spend their days in tilling the soil.' Other critics

Although a forceful campaigner for self-government and racial equality, like many Jamaicans Evon Blake remained a passionate monarchist.

contended that it would make Jamaica 'a nation of waiters. We will become more servile and be further away from self-government.' While the economic benefits of tourism were meant to mitigate the problems of Jamaica's colonial past, it was argued that the industry actually shored up many core features of that original condition and trapped the island in the grip of neocolonialism. For some, it was a trade-off between dignity and much-needed dollars.

Perhaps most serious was the concern that tourism, with its segregationist structure of closed enclaves and private beaches, was 'sharpening colour prejudice'. Leigh Fermor noted of Jamaica that 'a colour bar that is non-existent in law [is] in social practice violently alive'. This was most apparent at the smart hotels. Morris Cargill, a white Jamaican, tells of how he was offered a season ticket by the manager of Myrtle Bank hotel. But why was it necessary? he asked. 'That's how we keep out the niggers,' came the reply. Black Jamaican journalists reported how in the grandest hotels, particularly those catering for American tourists, they were made to feel unwelcome and 'in some barred by means of adroit subterfuges'.

Evon Blake had lived in Panama in the US Canal Zone, so knew all about racial segregation. In the summer of 1948, as tourists and local whites lounged by the side of Kingston's Myrtle Bank hotel pool, Blake suddenly burst on the scene, stripped to his swimming trunks and plunged into the pool. The white swimmers immediately clambered out. The staff quickly gathered at the edges, shouting threats at the intruder. From the middle of the pool, Blake defiantly challenged: 'Call the police. Call the army. Call the owner. Call God. And let's have one helluva big story.' Although the *Gleaner* declined to report the incident, news of the protest quickly spread all over the island. The hotel's owner, Abe Issa, made loud noises about how everyone was welcome, but in photos of the hotel from the late forties and fifties, the only black faces are the staff. After Blake's plunge, the pool was drained and refilled.

There was, of course, another side to the story. Although ownership of the hotels was largely in the hands of foreigners or a tiny elite of brown or white Jamaicans, the development provided work for thousands, as well as stimulating construction and infrastructure improvements. Douglas Waite, who worked his entire life as a policeman in Oracabessa, remembered the huge boon that the new hotels brought to his town, suffering so badly with the decline of sugar and the banana business. 'Tourists were people with money. Everybody rushed to get a job in the hotel,' he says. 'The salaries were very low, but in those days they get good tips. Out of what they get from the hotel a lot of people were able to buy bicycle, buy motor car, build lovely houses and send their children to school.' The alternative was 'work on the plantation: banana, coconut and chop the field all day'.

For Ramsay Dacosta, who would go on to work for Fleming as a gardener, the arrival of the jet-set opened up another world. 'We saw water, electricity, motor cars and wanted these things and were stirred to work towards them,' he says. 'People gathered good knowledge of things from that time. Jamaica start to get up. Come up.'

Furthermore, many felt that the arrival of famous tourists, as well as expatriate residents, had put Jamaica on the map. In 1949, the *Gleaner* gave a warm welcome to Jamaica's established regular visitors 'with homes of their own' who 'make an impressive contribution. Noël

Coward, Ian Fleming, Ivor Novello, Lord Beaverbrook, Sir William Stephenson – people like these are the focusing points for a number of little eddies of social and cultural activity, and confer upon this island a lasting benefit.'

Late in February, Ann, Ian, Noël and Graham decided to motor along the coast to Montego Bay for a stay at Carmen Pringle's Sunset Lodge, now filled with American millionaires and British aristocrats. Ian made a point of being photographed with Babe Paley, the glamorous wife of CBS chief Bill Paley, and the young and curvaceous Diana Huggins, daughter of the Governor. Ann stayed out of the picture. But the effect was somewhat ruined by Ian and Ann breakfasting together the next morning in full view on the balcony of their room. Coward stormed round to give them a stern lecture on discretion. 'I must say they are very sweet,' he wrote in his diary, 'but I have grave fears for the *avenir*.'

At the heart of Coward's Samolo novel *Pomp and Circumstance* is a very thinly fictionalised account of Ian and Ann in Jamaica in early 1949. The novel is narrated by a friend of the Governor's wife called Grizel, married to an English banana planter. A smart, beautiful and aristocratic woman – Eloise – is coming out to the island to conduct an affair, and Grizel has to weave a web of lies to pretend to the public and extremely interested press that Eloise is staying with her rather than with her lover, Bunny, who lives part of the year in a house nearby.

Like the Duchess Eloise in the novel, Ann, Lady Rothermere, had arrived 'in a blaze of Jamaican publicity and announced she was going to stay with me', as Coward wrote in his diary. But when a photographer from *Life* magazine arrived unexpectedly, the houseboy had to be dispatched 'hot foot' to Goldeneye to fetch her. Coward later remembered: 'There then began a very natty high comedy scene in which she kept forgetting she was a house guest and asking what we had been doing all the morning, etc.'

In the character of Bunny, Eloise's lover, we have a remarkably unflinching portrait of Ian Fleming's time on the island in 1949–51, the years immediately preceding his marriage to Ann and the simultaneous launch of James Bond.

Bunny, after a war spent in 'cloak-and-dagger activities', comes out to Samolo/Jamaica for two or three months a year and 'spends all his time doing underwater fishing with an Aqua Lung and a spear gun and green rubber flippers on his feet'. He has a succession of different lovers to stay with him, sometimes chaperoned, sometimes not. If these women are interested in 'barracuda, lettuce coral, blowfish, and other wonders of the deep, so much the better for them'. If not, they get foisted off on Grizel, the narrator. As well as these 'ill-starred romances', Bunny also 'managed to have a few local flings'.

It's astonishing how little Coward bothered to make up. If Fleming 'reveled in discomfort', Bunny is 'allergic to all forms of physical comfort'. The teasing about Goldeneye continues. Bunny's 'beach villa' is a 'bleak, overmasculine barrack' with nasty pictures of horses on the wall and grubby shells everywhere. Even Fleming's precious Violet appears, in the form of Cynthia, Bunny's housekeeper, characterised by 'amiable nonchalance'. There is a row about Eloise not eating the maid's simple local food: she is 'far too luxury-loving and thoroughly spoilt'.

Like Fleming, Bunny is 'a partner, not a very active one', in a publishing firm. In London he too lives in 'the all-pervading atmosphere of solid, sleek bachelorhood'.

And here was the rub for Coward, whose female narrator describes Bunny as an 'irrepressible dilettante'. 'It seemed inconceivable that he should seriously contemplate giving all that up and settling down with an ex-duchess whose spiritual home was the Oliver Messel suite at the Dorchester,' she concludes of the doomed Eloise–Bunny affair. If Coward had 'grave fears' for Ian and Ann's future, it was because, like Grizel's fears for Bunny, Ian would 'find himself caught up in an over-social marriage for which he was temperamentally unsuited and probably be utterly miserable'.

Ann left Jamaica before Ian that year, and under a cloud. On 20 February, Fleming wrote to her at her stopover in New York: 'I've funked everything these last few days and almost purposely tried to squabble with you and vex you so that the melancholy should keep away.' In fact both Ann and Ian were contemplating taking serious decisions about their relationship. 'We will be brave one way or another before the end of the year,' Ann wrote back. 'I would like to look after you forever … and you should know this when talking to Esmond,' replied Ian, although he was worried that his 'difficulties' might be too irritating for her, and there was also the question of how Ann was 'accustomed to money'. 'If we have enough money for gin and cigarettes I think I might be very happy,' she replied.

When she reached Southampton, she was met by an emissary of her husband, who handed her a sealed envelope. Inside were curt orders that she should desist from seeing Fleming or face divorce.

This message did not end the affair, but some further effort was made at discretion. Noël Coward had purchased a line of small cottages at St Margaret's Bay in Kent, right beside the iconic white cliffs. One, previously rented by spy-thriller writer Eric Ambler, was made available as a 'nest' to Ian and Ann. Coward himself was frequently next door, and in an echo of their Jamaican sojourns, they shared many evenings of canasta and high-spirited charades. But in spite of the bonhomie, and Coward's abetting of the relationship, he wrote in his diary on 10 July 1949: 'I have doubts about their happiness if she and Ian were to be married. I think they would both miss many things they enjoy now.'

1950
Doctor Jamaica

'Up to forty, girls cost nothing. After that you have to pay money, or tell a story. Of the two it's the story that hurts most.' He smiled into her eyes. 'Anyway, I'm not forty yet!'

Bond to Tiffany Chase, *Diamonds are Forever*

Just before Christmas 1949, Fleming flew out to Jamaica on his own. By this time there were two London to Kingston routes: one via New York and Miami with Pan Am; the other with BOAC via Lisbon, the Azores, Bermuda and Nassau. Fleming used the former route more. They cost the same, £235 return, about a half of his gross monthly salary. Both airlines used Boeing's Stratocruiser, a direct descendant of the wartime B-29 Superfortress bomber. The four-engined plane had two decks, a bar and sleeping berths, and typically carried only sixty or seventy passengers, with half fewer on long-haul, where most would have berths.

Fleming, now forty years old, felt in need of Jamaica, where, he later wrote, he enjoyed 'the most healthy life I could wish to live'. Three years previously, unbeknownst to Ann or anyone else, he had visited a New York cardiac specialist while passing through the city. He had been suffering from a 'constricting pain in the heart'. The doctor reported: 'The patient admits to smoking seventy cigarettes a day and drinking at least a quarter of a bottle of gin'. But he found no evidence of heart weakness, and Fleming came away reassured, though firmly instructed to stop smoking and reduce his alcohol intake, advice he entirely ignored.

In late 1949, he suffered painful kidney stones; then the tightness in his chest returned. He went to see his bridge-playing friend Dr Beal; Beal referred him to Sir John Parkinson, a leading Harley Street heart specialist, who repeated the urgings of the New York doctor. This time Fleming took some notice, for a while cutting down the huge gin martinis he usually enjoyed before dinner, and avoiding the brandy, port and liqueurs afterwards. But he still kept up his weekly 300-cigarette order from Morlands in Grosvenor Street, a supply often further replenished. Soon afterwards, the kidney trouble returned with a vengeance, bringing on a painful attack while he was eating dinner with a young lady at the Etoile restaurant in Soho. He had to be helped back to his flat in excruciating agony. Dr Beal arrived and straightaway gave the patient a strong dose of morphine.

For Fleming, Jamaica would always provide a place of recovery. So too for Bond: in *Live and Let Die*, he undertakes a fitness regime there combined with abstemious living; in both *Dr No* and *The Man with the Golden Gun*, he is sent by M to Jamaica in part to recover from a previous physical and mental trauma – in the former after near-death by poisoning at the end of *From Russia, with Love*; in the latter after he has been brainwashed by the KGB following a harrowing battle with Blofeld in *You Only Live Twice*.

Fleming found Jamaica immensely soothing, both physically and mentally. American artist Marion Simmons – whose clifftop house Glory Be was now completed just down the coast from Goldeneye – was the same, enjoying scuba diving in particular for its therapeutic benefits. In Simmons' friend Noël Coward's *Pomp and Circumstance*, the Bunny/Fleming character when miserable and tense is advised: 'On with your Aqua Lung and go and have a look at a few nice barracuda … You know it always cheers you up.' Coward himself called the island 'Dr Jamaica'. One friend, when asked if Coward had an analyst replied, 'If Noël has a problem, he flies to Jamaica.'

Coward had come out on 15 December to find that 'Everything is unbelievably lovely.' The garden at Blue Harbour had grown quickly, and the sea and air were both warm. 'I have fallen in love with the place all over again,' he wrote. On Christmas Eve, he dined with Fleming and a few other friends, including society photographer Cecil Beaton and actor Alec Guinness. After dinner they all played canasta.

As well as finding a trip to Jamaica hugely restorative, Coward also found it creatively invigorating. After one visit he wrote in his diary that 'It has been a lovely holiday – I feel well and full of ideas and, as usual, I am grateful to dear Jamaica.' On another occasion, he noted: 'this place has a strange and very potent magic for me. I also seem to be able to do more work here in less time than anywhere else.' Ann, too, recommended Jamaica to her aspiring novelist brother Hugo as 'healing, beneficial and inspiring'. Fleming agreed. 'Here there is peace and that wonderful vacuum of days that makes one work,' he noted while writing *Goldfinger*. Not only Coward, but 'other still more famous writers, let alone painters, have been stimulated by Jamaica', he later wrote. 'I suppose it is the peace and silence and cut-offness from the madding world that urges people to create here.'

It all contributed to making Fleming a different person in Jamaica from how he was in Britain. Peter Quennell, who knew him well in both places, wrote that he 'Always took life strangely hard, except in Jamaica.' The island smoothed Fleming's rough edges; instead of coming across as tense and aloof, he was unassuming, diffident, relaxed. His friend Robert Harling, a frequent visitor, wrote that in Jamaica 'Fleming is at his mellow best.' Jamaican friends from all walks of life remember him as a 'very charming, attractive character, warm even'.

A life-giving plant, the Traveller's Tree is so named because its leaves have large sheathes at their base in which water collects in such quantity as to provide a welcome draught to thirsty by-passers.

Fleming was determined to throw himself into exploring his reef, and before his late 1949 trip had bought a naturalist's notebook and had it bound in black leather by Sangorski and Sutcliffe of London. Picked out in gold on the cover was 'Sea Fauna or the Finny Tribe of Goldeneye'.

One of his earliest notes was the spotting of two 'Hunt class barracudas', which he christened Bicester and Beaufort. On Christmas Eve, he 'declared war on them' because they were 'getting too big and frighten the customers', the other fish. That afternoon, he descended the stone steps with a Champion spear gun and went after Beaufort. 'As usual he examines me with wary curiosity and a pronounced but possibly forced sneer,' Fleming noted. 'He allows me, moving very slowly and softly, to come within six feet, at which range I shoot and miss, probably low. Beaufort travels twelve feet like a bullet then stops dead, broadside on.' Fleming moved closer, but the fish 'merged silently away into the grey mists of deeper water'. He made up for it by taking it 'out on a half pound lobster, shot through the head'. The day after Christmas at Blue Harbour, Fleming was back on the Goldeneye reef, where he encountered Beaufort again. This time he managed to gash him behind the head with his trident, concluding that 'the parasites will have him within a day or two'.

Like the shark-hunting episode with Aubyn Cousins the previous year, this watery peril would be poured into the novels. In *Thunderball*, Bond is on a dive at night when a barracuda approaches: 'The gold and black tiger's eye was on him, watchfully incurious, and the long mouth was half open an inch so that the moonlight glittered on the sharpest row of teeth in the ocean – teeth that don't bite at the flesh, teeth that tear out and chunk then hit and scythe again.' Bond's insider knowledge of Caribbean waters meant that 'his stomach crawled with the ants of fear and his skin tightened at his groin'.

For Fleming the danger was the grit in the oyster, the spicy seasoning to the mellow sensuality of the reef. All of Jamaica should be 'embraced', he would shortly write. 'It is easy to enjoy the orchids and the hummingbirds, but here is much that is very strange.' Visitors should also be able to marvel at the 'fruits that are sometimes deadly poison … the hideous vultures, the ants' nests like brown goiters on the trees, the blood thirst of shark and barracuda …'

Ann joined Ian for a couple of weeks halfway through January. She would encounter the dangers of the reef at first hand when she stood on a spiny puffer fish. Other smart visitors suffered exotic injuries. When Laurence Olivier was staying with Coward, he was 'lightly stroked across the shoulders by a stingray tail' and had to lie on his front for two days. 'I am still grateful for the gentle ministrations of Noël's black maids, who periodically laid cool slices of melon, papaya and mango all over my back,' he later wrote. David Niven, friend of Errol Flynn as well as Coward, who visited in 1955, was nearly attacked by a scorpion and then, he reports, suffered an infestation of grass ticks in his crotch.

Ann's short visit ended acrimoniously. In mid February, she wrote to Ian from New York alluding to the pain of leaving him 'and the lobsters' but also to a furious row – 'Do you know that when you said that to me if I'd had a revolver I should have shot you? Damn you … You're a selfish thoughtless bastard, but we love each other.'

Ian had promised that he would accompany her to New York to spend a few days together there, but when the time came, he suddenly decided that he'd rather stay in Jamaica than go to what he would call the 'stressed-concrete jungle' of the American city.

Britain's uneasy and changing relationship with the new imperial power of the United States is of central concern to Fleming and his Bond stories. In fact, his takes on the Anglo-American relationship are some of the most sparky and deeply felt sections of the novels.

Fleming knew that for policymakers in Whitehall, the greatest threat to the British Empire lay in American support for the rising nationalist movements among colonised people. After all, self-determination was one of the founding principles of the United States. Following the signing of the Atlantic Charter, Roosevelt had kept constant pressure on Churchill to address the issue of Indian independence.

At the same time, Britain could not afford a breakdown of relations with the US, who after the war had lent London money and put its troops on the ground to help prop up British interests in the Middle East, the Mediterranean and elsewhere. This dependence of the Empire on the upstart Yankees, who drove a hard bargain with Britain before, during and after the war, was not to the liking of those, such as Fleming, who looked back fondly on the days of British supremacy.

Both Fleming and Bond made frequent visits to the United States.

Certainly Fleming loved the country's speed, its scale, its service and its food. He had huge admiration for its technical know-how and muscle. In *From Russia, with Love*, for instance, we learn that the Americans, in 'such matters as radio and weapons and equipment, are the best'. Even the Russians use American knives of 'excellent' manufacture and American Zippo lighters. But at the same time, Fleming despaired of what he called, in a letter to Ann in 1947, 'their total unpreparedness to rule the world that is now theirs'.

Scottish novelist Candia McWilliam identifies as part of the appeal of the Bond books their 'continual homeopathic doses of Anti-Americanism'. It is striking how, with the exception of Felix Leiter, almost all the Americans Bond meets are surly, uncooperative and jealous of his success and panache. In *From Russia, with Love*, praise of American technical skill is countered by the criticism that 'they have no understanding of the [espionage] work … they try to do everything with money'. And quickly acquired wealth has poisoned the country. In *Diamonds are Forever*, the Chief of Staff briefs an incredulous Bond on America's appalling murder rate and 'ten million' drug addicts, and how gambling, controlled by the Mafia, is the biggest business, 'bigger than steel. Bigger than motor cars.' In his travelogue *Thrilling Cities*, having beaten the 'syndicates' of Las Vegas, Fleming goes to bed 'after washing the filth of the United States currency off my hands'.

Elsewhere, we learn that Las Vegas is 'ghastly', New York is obsessed with 'the hysterical pursuit of money', and Chicago has 'one of the grimmest suburbs in the world'. In all, the country is crime-ridden and in crisis, thanks to consumerism and the breakdown of the traditional family in a 'society that fails to establish a clear moral definition of right and wrong'.

Fleming's attitudes to the United States were shaped not only by his own experiences there, but also by the situation in Jamaica. One of the reasons Bond loves the country on his earlier trips is that it is British space, where, for once, he is not dependent on American resources or approval. In *Live and Let Die*, the FBI's surly Captain Dexter tells him that Jamaica is 'your territory'. In *Dr No*, M is given the Jamaica case after nagging from the Americans 'because the place is British territory'. When Bond comes to Jamaica from the United States in *Live and Let Die*, it is a blessed relief for him, an escape to a space uncontaminated by American materialism: 'Bond was glad to be on his way to the soft green flanks of Jamaica and to be leaving behind the great hard continent of Eldollarado.'

But in subtle ways Jamaica is also shown to be under threat of American colonisation. In *Live and Let Die*, the Harlem gangster Mr Big has taken control of Surprise Island, just off the coast. Strangways, station commander in Jamaica, explains to Bond that this involves complications: 'You see, it belongs to an American now ... with pretty good protection in Washington.' Dr No, who has colonised another Jamaican island, has 'a trace of an American accent', and his men call Bond a 'Limey' in the American manner. More obviously, both Fleming and Coward saw the preponderance of Americans among Jamaica's hotel owners and tourists – 'millionaires in beach clothes' – as cause for regret and a threat to Jamaica's integrity.

The Spanish-American war at the end of the nineteenth century had left the United States as the dominant power in the Caribbean, further enhanced by the completion of the Panama Canal in 1914. In 1911, *The Times* newspaper had predicted that the 'islands of the West Indies ... will gravitate in due course to amalgamation with the Great Republic of the North'. But while the US intervened freely in Central America and what had been the Spanish Antilles, the British islands remained part of the Empire, albeit a neglected one.

This had all changed with an agreement signed in March 1941: in return for much-needed destroyers, Britain gave the US long leases on eleven military bases in the area. For London, the deal represented

The Lend-Lease agreement of March 1941 saw the 'American invasion' – the deployment of US military power across the British West Indies.

the abdication of exclusive authority over the British Caribbean and, at the same time, the very beginning of the 'Special Relationship'. The Caribbean and the deals done there, such as at the naval conference attended by Fleming in 1943, formed a bridge between Britain and the United States.

The American aim was threefold: to secure the islands, should Britain surrender in Europe; to counter the serious submarine threat; and to maintain order in the region lest it cause trouble for their national interest. In 1942, as anti-colonial winds blew in from Asia, US troops were used to suppress revolt in St Lucia and the Bahamas, in the latter case after a personal request from the Duke of Windsor, the recently abdicated Edward VIII.

On the islands, it was called 'the American invasion'. In Jamaica, there were two large bases: an airfield at Vernamfield, Clarendon, and a naval station at Goat Island in Old Harbour Bay. For almost all Jamaicans, this was their first contact with North Americans. Lower classes largely welcomed the free-spending incomers. Sweets were handed out to children. Operators of popular nightclubs like downtown Kingston's famous Glass Bucket prospered. In Trinidad, a new calypso swept all before it: 'Working for the Yankee Dollar'.

But employers saw their control of wages and the labour market challenged, and political activists found themselves in a dilemma. Although historically Americans had seemed pro-self-government, the lack of local consultation on the destroyers-for-bases agreement pointed in the opposite direction. Jamaican nationalists were uneasy that the deal might be the sharp point of a wedge that would presently see the ownership of the colonies simply shift from Britain to the United States. For them, then, the much-expanded American influence in the region offered both threat and promise. The fear of being subsumed within a new US colonial system was weighed against the opportunity to exploit American anti-colonial rhetoric to reinforce opposition to British rule.

The issue of race was similarly complicated. During the wartime rule of Governor Richards, black trade unionists and nationalists, including Bustamante, were rounded up and imprisoned. But when in 1941 Wilfred Domingo, founding member in New York of the Jamaica Progressive Party, was arrested on his arrival on the island, there were vigorous protests from the National Association for the Advancement of Colored People (NAACP), based in New York. Worried that New York blacks were going to cause trouble, the US government complained about the arrest. In 1942, Domingo was released, and Richards replaced. The conceding of the universal franchise soon afterwards was also hastened by American pressure.

By the end of the war, however, the power of Harlem and the NAACP had faded, and American influence started to be viewed rather differently by black nationalists in Jamaica. The precedent of racial segregation in the Panama Canal Zone was worrying, as were the examples of how tourism was developing in the British colonies of Bermuda and the Bahamas, where US dominance in hotel ownership and in visitors was even greater than in Jamaica. The American-owned British Colonial Hotel in Nassau refused entry to a number of distinguished Jamaicans, even Bustamante, for fear of upsetting its white patrons. Evon Blake, in his *Spotlight* magazine, highlighted these cases to show the possible effect of expanded American influence in Jamaica, writing that the attitudes in Nassau towards negroes 'were equalled only in the most sociologically retarded of Dixie backwaters'. In late 1952, Blake urged the Colonial Secretary, Oliver Lyttelton, to outlaw such 'Jim Crow' practices. But in the House of Commons, Lyttelton announced that he was 'advised that [the maintenance of the colour bar in Bermuda] is essential to the tourist trade on which people of the colony as a whole depend for their livelihood'. In Blake's estimation, Lyttelton was presented with a choice between 'US dollars and democracy', and 'by excusing racial discrimination as a modus operandi of tourism, had unapologetically chosen the former'. It was a decision, according to Blake, that 'threatened the undoing of the British Empire'.

Nonetheless, for Blake, the Empire, however indifferent, remained preferable to the active racism of the Americans. Writing in *Spotlight* in August 1950, he urged locals to buy bonds to help 'the present and future welfare of this great little island of ours', and added the warning: 'The Yanks would love to own it, you know.'

But Jamaica still needed American dollars. In 1950, the Jamaican government lifted restrictions on foreign capital investment and on taking the profits of such investment out of the country. It was very much the dollar, rather than the pound, that was being targeted. A delegation from the Chambers of Commerce of Kingston and Montego Bay toured the US the same year looking for investors. According to a US official report, 'the delegation made it plain that the position of these Islands places them fully within the sphere of North American influence. There was no question of less than complete allegiance to Britain, but Britain's "many problems" made that country unable to offer immediate major economic assistance.'

Jamaicans also hoped to play on British fears of an American takeover to get what they could from the mother country. 'I was in New York. It's only good to make money,' Bustamante told the British press while on a visit to London in late 1948. 'Jamaica stays with Britain,' he announced, thereby highlighting the alternative. By 1951, frustrated by trade restrictions that forced Jamaicans to buy expensive British imports, he was threatening to switch allegiance away from Britain and towards the US.

By now, however, the United States offered little succour to Jamaican nationalists. For one thing, much of its anti-colonial rhetoric had been more about business interests than concern for oppressed people. During the 1930s, Europeans had attempted to re-establish mercantilism across their empires, shutting out US investment and access to markets and resources. But as these restrictions were swept away, American anti-colonialism lost a lot of its impetus. As early as 1942, the US airline Pan Am received a promise that it could develop a route to Jamaica on a level commercial playing field. The following year, the State Department successfully lent its active support to the US-based Reynolds Metals Company to acquire concessions to exploit bauxite resources in Jamaica. (Thus Fleming would regretfully write in 1952, as the bauxite market took off: 'Jamaica has the largest bauxite deposits in the world, being exploited by Americans, of course.')

The other new factor was the Cold War, which began in earnest with the formation of NATO and the Warsaw Pact in 1949. United States foreign policy was now dominated by the idea of 'containment' – influencing and policing the perimeters of the non-communist world. This made the British Empire and Commonwealth, whose mandate spread across scattered swathes of this space, a pillar of American security. Unrest in the colonies, it was thought, would only benefit the Soviet Union. Reform was still needed, then, to prevent this, but only if those empowered showed no risk of going over to the 'other side', as a number of Jamaican nationalists would soon discover.

*

With or without the Americans, Jamaica was changing, and colonial culture was about to change as well.

Fleming in his 1947 *Horizon* article identified two great worries about 'social ambience' that an emigrant from Britain to the Empire might have. 'You fear the moral "dégringolade" of the tropics, the slow disintegration ... In your imagination you hear the hypnotic whisper of the palm trees stooping too gracefully over that blue lagoon. You feel the scruffy stubble sprouting on your chin. The cracked mirror behind Red's Bar reflects the bloodhound gloom of those ruined features...' (Bond, with his weakness for the sensual, erotic and intoxicating, is constantly tempted by this 'tropical sloth'.)

'On the other hand,' Fleming continues, 'you are appalled by the tea-and-tennis set atmosphere in many of the most blessed corners of our Empire. You smell boiled shirts, cucumber sandwiches and the L-shaped life of expatriate Kensingtonia.' Bond himself, in *Dr No*, 'wanted to get the hell away from King's House, and the tennis, and the kings and queens'. But what Jamaica offered, Fleming wrote in 1947, was a balance of the two: 'A middle way between the lethe of the tropics and a life of fork-lunches with the District Commissioner's wife can be achieved and I believe you will achieve it in Jamaica.'

But the world of Molly Huggins, tennis and grateful 'natives' was coming to an end. In September 1947, King's House had played host to Arthur Creech Jones, Labour Secretary of State for the Colonies. Molly wrote that she liked Jones, 'though our political views differed'. She also liked his wife, Vi, 'though I don't think she really approved of me. Perhaps she thought I was too gay ... I think she felt it was democratic to go about in rather an old cotton dress and no stockings and flat shoes. I tried to explain to her that the people of Jamaica really expected one to dress up for them, as otherwise they felt they were being insulted. I think I got the message over to her, at last.'

In fact, the Joneses were much more interested in meeting Jamaican nationalists Norman and Edna Manley than in any of the King's House flummery. Jones was in Jamaica for a conference at Montego Bay to discuss the British West Indies being formed at some point in the future into a federation, a political union of the English-speaking islands. This new entity then could be granted dominion status in a body that, with the large and small islands together, would absolve the British of responsibility for what were in most cases uneconomic entities. It turned out to be a half-baked plan, but it did signal a more rapid journey towards self-government than had previously been thought possible.

In January 1948, Burma followed India and Pakistan to independence, with Sri Lanka joining them a month later. At a conference on African affairs the same year, Jones issued a memorandum on local government in the colonies, which confirmed the intention to bring in responsible government. It was not all about high ideals. There were problems in the Gold Coast, Kenya, Malaya, Iran, Egypt and elsewhere in the Empire that the British government could simply not afford to cope with. In September 1949, the Chancellor of the Exchequer was forced to announce a humiliating devaluation of the pound.

In Jamaica, the election of 1949 saw a return to power of Bustamante's JLP, once again garnering the funding of the wealthy elite and the support of the illiterate peasantry. Still, it wasn't quite business as usual. Bustamante was coming round to the idea of self-government, and Manley's fiercely pro-independence PNP had gained much ground, actually polling more votes than the JLP and reducing Bustamante's majority in the House of Representatives to just four. A much larger turnout than before signified greater involvement of the ordinary Jamaican in politics.

In January 1950, Governor Huggins was booed at the opening of the Legislature, something that had never happened before, and the following month he was jeered by a crowd, causing Molly to exclaim tersely, 'I'll be damned.' It was clearly time for a new governor; Huggins was retired, and the family left Jamaica in September that year. (The story of the Huggins has a surprising coda: back in England Molly continued her 'continental' approach to her marriage, then in early 1958 her dry old stick of a husband Sir John suddenly ran off to Italy with a married woman. The story was covered in the *Express*. At the time Molly was trying to get selected as a prospective Tory MP in a constituency thought to favour a female candidate. According to Molly, the scandal ruined her chances; instead the party in Finchley chose Margaret Thatcher.)

The new Governor was very different from the staid and uninspiring Huggins. Hugh Foot was the son of a Liberal Party MP, Isaac Foot. His brothers included Sir Dingle Foot, a Liberal MP who later switched to Labour and served in Wilson's cabinet; Lord John Foot, who became a Liberal peer and fierce defender of colonial peoples; and Michael, who would become leader of the Labour Party. 'We were proud to be nonconformists and Roundheads,' Hugh once wrote of his family. 'Oliver Cromwell was our hero and John Milton our poet.' By 1950, he and his wife Sylvia had three children. The eldest, fourteen-year-old Paul, would become a campaigning journalist.

Foot had done his national service in Jamaica in the 1920s and had returned in 1945 as Colonial Secretary. Locals found him 'dapper' and 'well-bred', but also 'conscientious'. Standing in for the absent Governor in 1946, he had dealt skilfully with an outbreak of political violence, then 'travelled the island extensively, learned conditions and displayed a genuineness' that showed 'his desire to play ball with Jamaicans without seeming to work wholly for the Colonial Office'. Edna Manley found him a 'charming, likable, infinitely clever person'.

In 1947, he had been posted to Nigeria, where he had narrowly survived assassination, and was delighted now to be returning to Jamaica as Governor. He loved the island – 'nowhere I know in the world is there such a variety of people in such a small compass or such

Governor Sir Hugh Foot addressing the Jamaican House of Representatives. After a distinguished career in the twilight of empire, Foot dubbed himself 'the colonial governor who ran out of colonies'.

a mixture' – was a great fan of West Indian cricket and was excited by the changes taking place.

Both Coward's novel *Pomp and Circumstance* and the earlier play *South Sea Bubble* feature Samolo's governor, Sir George Shotter, 'a cheerful man of about fifty', who closely resembles Sir Hugh Foot. The previous incumbent is described in *South Sea Bubble* as 'Quite nice, really, but a bit sticky'. In *Pomp and Circumstance*, he is 'true-blue conservative' and 'aloof'. Shotter is entirely different, having been 'an ardent socialist in his earlier years'.

In *South Sea Bubble*, Shotter's support for the more left-wing and independence-leaning of the two local parties in Samolo (Manley's PNP in Jamaica) causes distress for the island's white 'die-hards', and also confusion for the supposedly 'empire-minded' majority of Samolans. Certainly Foot arrived with a new attitude to empire, determined to act on behalf of the island. As he later wrote, 'When

I was governor of Jamaica I did not regard myself as the agent of London, but as the advocate of Jamaica.' For him, it was a 'critical time', 'refreshing and absorbing': Jamaica was 'advancing at an accelerating rate towards her coming of age in independence'.

In Britain, the Labour Party had fought and narrowly won the February 1950 election on a platform that included the pledge: 'In the Colonial territories our purpose is to help in creating the economic and social basis for democratic self-government.' Clearly Foot's brief from his superiors was to make democratically elected Jamaicans responsible for the island's domestic government. The days of the colonial backwater, much loved by Coward and Fleming, were numbered.

In *Pomp and Circumstance*, Coward's English colonials react to the changes fast approaching them with a sort of inward-looking exhausted languor. Fleming's reaction to the end of empire in Jamaica and in the wider world as evidenced in James Bond would be very different.

1951
'Disciplined Exoticism'

What I endeavour to aim at is a certain disciplined exoticism.

Ian Fleming, 'How to Write a Thriller'

Ann and Ian continued their correspondence during the spring and summer of 1950, although their meetings were, for discretion's sake, few and snatched. Ian professed his love for her 'more than any other woman', but also his misgivings about her divorcing and their marrying. He was a solitary man, but she was at the centre of family, home and friends. He felt bad about Esmond – 'there is no evil in him and neither of us wishes him harm' – and the children, Fionn and Raymond, who had got used to their Rothermere stepfather and 'shouldn't be shaken up again'. 'I know all the other side,' he wrote in February 1950, 'our basic love and faith in each other and in our stars. They would be enough to sail our ship if it weren't for the harm we would do.'

Ann found herself in what she described to her brother Hugo as a 'static emotional state'. She loved Ian – Rothermere was very much 'second-best' – but lacked the 'courage to leap from the merry-go-round'. This was partly because she liked the excitement of her social life at Warwick House, and her ever more frequent meddling in the running of the *Daily Mail*. Ian, Ann reported to her brother, 'rightly says he cannot offer the public life and in fact hates social gatherings, and so I hesitate to take the step'. For his part, Esmond had by now 'deserted – for an American blonde – but I don't think it's serious'.

In November, she wrote to her brother again: 'Christmas without Ian seems a bleak affair, he was always there at Christmas, long before Esmond, and he gave the children presents about which he had taken trouble.' (This included jazz records bought in New York for Raymond.) But Ian was no longer welcome at Warwick House, and then there was the whole issue of Jamaica. The arrival of winter also made Ann think of 'the last two years when I was able to anticipate sunshine and an Eden shared with an Adam, who though he may not be the solution to all things at least [watched] me colour fish and lizards with sympathetic enthusiasm'.

Somehow, by pretending once more to be staying with Noël Coward, Ann managed to snatch two weeks in February with Ian at Goldeneye. Tactfully, her letters to friends were addressed from 'Blue Harbour, Port Maria'. In one, she gleefully recounted teaching snorkelling to Coward's guests Cecil Beaton and Oliver Messel, the theatrical designer: 'Cecil was tremendously brave and seeing a sneering dangerous barracuda chased it "because it looked like a disagreeable dowager". Oliver appeared unable to swim a stroke and constantly sank in bubbling ecstasies…'

To Ann's displeasure, Ivar Bryce was also in attendance. Ivar, who admitted to being 'indolent and forgetful', was considered by Ann to be a gold-digger and a bad influence on Ian. Ann's daughter Fionn remembers 'something reptilian about him'. Bryce had separated from his wife Sheila and married for the third time, to a hugely rich American, Marie-Josephine Hartford, granddaughter of George Huntingdon Hartford, founder of the A&P supermarket chain. The newly-weds were honeymooning on a luxury yacht with their

A photograph taken on the first floor veranda of Blue Harbour by Cecil Beaton (with a self-timer) showing from left Ann, Graham Payn, Beaton, Coward, Natasha Wilson and Ian.

American friends the Leiters, as well as the new Mrs Bryce's daughter and son-in-law. Their only firm plan was to dock at Oracabessa and visit Goldeneye.

Having reached Jamaica's north coast, the captain left the ship to do some shopping. In his absence, the crew hit the liquor store and as a result were in no fit shape to prevent the yacht slipping its anchor in a sudden storm and smashing against the reef. According to Ann, who described the event in a letter to her friend Lady Diana Cooper, it was 'a genuine coral reef 18th century-print wreck, and only a hair's breadth that no lives were lost'. She, Ian and Coward were 'swigging martinis' when the 'door broke open and four of the USA's richest citizens fell into the room snow white and dripping water … from then on it was a blissful blissful night – Noël was able to play "In Which We Serve", Ian was Masterman Ready and I was "Admirable Crichton". Noël and Ian rescued the crew while I poured disinfectant into … wounds and handed out rum to dull the pain, and then Noël took the prettiest sailors to the nearest hotel and rubbed them down with brandy – it was a small Mafeking night for the British.'

Less amusing for Ann was the sudden appearance of Rosamond Lehmann. Described by Stephen Spender as 'one of the most beautiful women of her generation', Lehmann had just finished a long romance with the poet Cecil Day-Lewis. According to Noël Coward, she now had her sights set on Fleming, who had invited her to Goldeneye clearly in the hope that she would arrive when he was alone there. But with Ann in residence, all hell broke loose, and eventually Fleming had to bribe Coward with his Leica camera to take Lehmann off his hands. Noël agreed as long as the tripod was thrown in as well. (Lehmann would later comment that Fleming 'got off with women because he could not get on with them'. Coward similarly berated him for 'the extremely unfeeling use to which he put his great attractions', even going so far as to call him a 'c***tease'.)

Ian had about two weeks on his own following Ann's departure. By now he had explored most of the island and one of the places that most seized his imagination was Port Royal, which lay on an outcrop at the end of a narrow sand spit stretching nearly all the way across the mouth of Kingston Harbour. Here the English had built a fort within a year of their 1655 invasion of Jamaica. The deep, well-sheltered water on its landward side was perfect for a harbour and anchorage. Thus Port Royal became the home base of the Royal Navy in the West

A view of Port Royal and Kingston Harbour, published in 1782. Fort Charles can be seen in the foreground.

Indies and the centre of naval operations in the region for the next two hundred years.

Fleming loved the navy for its clubbishness, the heroes of its exciting history, and its central role in British 'greatness' and the story of the Empire. It was a romantic passion that he would pass on to James Bond. In *On Her Majesty's Secret Service*, Bond reflects that he could listen to M's yarns about the navy all day, 'stories of battles, tornados, bizarre happenings, courts-martial, eccentric officers, neatly worded signals'. Fleming almost always dresses Bond in navy blue, and litters his books with naval references. In *Goldfinger*, Secret Service headquarters at night 'gave you the impression of being in a battleship in harbour'. M has 'a keen sailor's face, with the clear, sharp sailor's eyes' and a 'jaw [that] stuck out like the prow of a ship'. For

Bond, a naval association is a sure sign of someone with courage and integrity. In *Moonraker*, the heroine Gala Brand is trusted all the more for being named after a Royal Navy cruiser, *Galatea*, captained by her father. Similarly, in *Live and Let Die*, we know Bond likes and respects Jamaica station chief Strangways because he has 'the sort of aquiline good looks that are associated with the bridges of destroyers'.

Fleming, who loved being called 'the Commander' by his Goldeneye staff, enjoyed the rich naval history of Jamaica and the West Indies, where sea power was absolutely critical. The heroic version of this history includes Admirals Benbow, who died in Port Royal after being wounded in naval action against the French in 1702, Vernon, who in November 1739 had captured Porto Bello in Panama, and Rodney, whose victory at the Battle of the Saints in April 1782 saved Jamaica from invasion.

But it is the ghost of Nelson that Fleming would have most enjoyed imagining at Port Royal. Nelson had been on the Jamaica station from 1777 to 1783 fighting the French, Spanish and Americans. In 1779, he was briefly in command of Port Royal's Fort Charles, which still stands overlooking the entrance to Kingston Harbour, and boasts a plaque that reads: 'In this place dwelt Horatio Nelson. You who tread his footprints remember his glory.' Nelson returned again from 1784 to 1787, and was lucky to leave alive as disease wiped out many of his men. Fleming was very moved to see the memorial in St Peter's Church in Port Royal to the twenty-five midshipmen who died there of yellow fever in 1787. Nelson returned to the West Indies for the last time in June 1805, chasing the French fleet that he would destroy at Trafalgar four months later.

Fleming idolised Nelson. A miniature of the Admiral he had owned since he was a boy was amongst his most treasured possessions. When M, writing Bond's obituary at the beginning of *You Only Live Twice*, credits him with 'what almost amounted to the "Nelson Touch" in moments of high emergency', we know there can be no higher praise.

Fleming was even teased about his obsession: guests at Goldeneye nicknamed Violet 'Hardy' to Ian's Nelson.

Port Royal is perhaps most famous, though, for Sir Henry Morgan, a figure frequently referenced in the Bond novels. Alongside the naval base grew a substantial town, at that time the second most populous in British America after Boston, and the busiest port. The English rulers of Jamaica sponsored privateers to harass enemy shipping. Greatest of these was Morgan, who in 1670 famously, with 'divers barbarous acts', looted and destroyed Panama City, one of the jewels of the Spanish empire. Prize cargoes enriched the Jamaican town along with copious smuggling and outright piracy, and soon there were 800 buildings crowded on to just sixty acres, much of it little more than sand. The streets were full of 'debauched wild blades' drinking, whoring and gambling. Half the premises were bars or brothels. One visitor described it as 'now more rude and antic than e'er was Sodom'.

Then, on 7 June 1692, divine vengeance came in the form of a huge earthquake that liquefied the sand on which much of Port Royal stood. Within three minutes half the town had been plunged into the harbour. Two subsequent shocks left most buildings underwater, with only the tops of houses and the masts of sunken vessels showing above the surface. The next day, the harbour was choked with a thousand bodies.

So the Port Royal of Fleming's time was much smaller than in its heyday, and he was fascinated by the idea of the houses, brothels and bars of the buccaneers lying like buried treasure under the water nearby. On one visit he brought his snorkel, mask and flippers and swam down to inspect the old brickwork. He was a keen supporter of archaeological efforts, which had produced a mass of pewter plates and goblets, as well as pub signs such as Black Dogg, Catt & Fiddle and Sign of Bacchus.

It was his uncle's stories of 'the buccaneers of Port Royal, the most wicked city in the world' that had first interested Sir Harold Mitchell in Jamaica. Their story had been told in Hollywood swashbucklers (including Errol Flynn's breakthrough *Captain Blood*) and provided fuel for the 'four-penny horrors' that Fleming said he was raised on. Writing about Jamaica in 1947, Fleming told his readers with relish that the caverns and sinkholes on the island were 'doubtless stuffed with pirate treasure including Sir Henry Morgan's hoard'. Of course, the plot for his second Bond novel, *Live and Let Die*, would turn on the discovery of Morgan's treasure trove on an island based on Cabritta Island in Port Maria Bay. But almost all of his stories would be riddled with references to pirates. They appealed to the Tory part of Fleming's imagination: they were devil-take-the-hindmost, self-reliant and vigorous. Bond would have this spirit, of course. In *On Her Majesty's Secret Service*, Tracy tells him, 'I wouldn't love you if you weren't a pirate.' In *Casino Royale*, we learn that the scar on Bond's cheek makes him look 'piratical'. (Several women in Fleming's life would note 'the slightly piratical air given him by his broken nose'.) In the short story 'Risico', Bond's underworld ally Enrico Colombo is a 'greedy boisterous pirate'. Kerim Bey, Bond's much-admired helper in *From Russia, with Love*, is described as an 'exuberant shrewd pirate'. Kerim goes on to say about his fellow Turks: 'All this pretence of democracy is killing them. They want some sultans and wars and rape and fun.'

Fleming would later pronounce that: 'All history is sex and violence.' For him, Jamaican history was exciting, colourful and exotic – elements epitomised by the exploits of the Maroons. The Maroons are descendants of a much-debated mixture of runaway slaves from the Spanish period, possible Taíno survivors, and escaped slaves from the British plantations. The mountainous interior where they built their villages proved excellent defensive territory. They fought two wars against British soldiers, in the 1730s and 1790s, both ending in bruised stalemate. In 1739, a deal was struck that the British would leave them alone in return for the Maroons handing back any future slave escapees and assisting the white militia if threatened by invasion or slave revolt.

Fleming's telling of the Maroon story, in a passage that would be omitted when he republished the *Horizon* article fifteen years later, was full of naïve wonder. In 'a curious part of the island', he writes, is the Cockpit Country, 'known, the map says, by the name of Look Behind'. 'The terrain has never been surveyed and, if you look at the map you will see a large white patch.' Here are the Maroons, 'Spanish negro inhabitants of this province'. Redcoats were sent to quell them, Fleming relates, but they were repulsed, and the Maroons set up their

A Jamaican Maroon from the end of the eighteenth century. Fleming's view of Jamaican history as exciting and glamorous was in sharp contrast to the heavy psychological burden Jamaican nationalists felt it imposed on the people.

LEONARD PARKINSON, a Captain of MAROONS,
taken from the life.

own government, refusing allegiance to the Crown. 'They still refuse it,' he continues, 'the only corner of the British Empire to do so.'

(As Fleming doesn't seem to have been aware, there was a still a small Maroon community living on high ground at Scott's Hall in Fleming's parish of St Mary, only a few miles from Oracabessa.)

If this was all a bit Rider Haggard, then that was because Fleming's Jamaica, or at least his first impressions of it, with the pirates, redcoats and admirals, machetes and ghost stories, awoke in him the adventure stories of his childhood. One of the few respites at Durnford prep school was on Sunday evenings, when the whole school would assemble in the hall to hear the headmaster's wife read tales of exploration and derring-do. Her favourite for a long time was John Meade Falkner's *Moonfleet*, a story of diamonds, smuggling, phantoms and shipwreck. Also enjoyed by the boys were *The Prisoner of Zenda*, and the Bulldog Drummond stories. Best of all for Fleming were Sax Rohmer's novels, with fast-paced plots featuring the 'Yellow Peril' archetype of the Chinese criminal genius. Fleming later told Raymond Chandler that he 'was brought up on Dr Fu Manchu'.

Fleming's own reading included John Buchan, Erskine Childers and E. Phillips Oppenheim, as well as Poe, Verne, Rider Haggard and Robert Louis Stevenson – influences that would soon become clear in Fleming's own writing. Right from the beginning, his Bond books were seen as a modernisation of the 'Clubland Heroes' of the 1930s: a reviewer would christen his first novel, *Casino Royale*, 'supersonic John Buchan'.

But according to his friend John Pearson, Fleming's all-time favourite author was the now-forgotten 1930s novelist Hugh Edwards. In 1963, Fleming tried to persuade his publisher Jonathan Cape to reissue Edwards' *All Night at Mr Staneyhursts*, a story set in the eighteenth century involving treasure, shipwreck and castaways. Cape only agreed on the condition that Fleming, by then at the height of his fame, write an introduction. In this, he outlined the appeal of Edwards' novels:

their 'romantic sexuality and the background of high life'. Edwards had served in the West India Regiment before the First World War, and Fleming suggested that his inspiration came from 'seeing the West Indies in their last rip-roaring days, and his memories of the barbaric splendour – a compound of blood, champagne and pretty quadroons'.

Fleming's other favourite Edwards novel was *Sangoree*, set in Barbados during the time of slavery, published in 1932 and never reprinted. A garish take on West Indies history, it is full of cruelty and melancholy. Edwards depicts planters feasting for breakfast on black-crab pepper-pot washed down with claret, hock and rum; there is widespread gambling on faro, hazard and macao; slave girls dance naked and much else for the men; nature is 'edenic' and society characterised by 'luxury and licence'.

When he wrote about Jamaica's 'literary associations', Fleming championed the dark and violent gothic novelists 'Monk' Lewis and William Beckford, author of *Vathek*, a fantastical novel full of exotic locations, rapid action and exaggerated passions. Fleming would later conclude from his own plotting and characters, particularly the villains, that he enjoyed 'exaggeration and things larger than life', key elements of local Jamaican writing and storytelling and of European West Indian travelogues, as well as this gothic tradition.

Most highly recommended by Fleming in his *Horizon* article on Jamaica was Herbert de Lisser's *White Witch of Rosehall*, a story of 'hot-blooded sadism and slaves set in the 1850s'. This is the account (actually set during slavery) of a newcomer from England being at first appalled by the slave society, and then becoming corrupted by it. He works for a woman at Rosehall called Annee Palmer, who had dabbled in witchcraft, murdered four husbands and had countless lovers. She is finally hacked to pieces by the slaves she had terrorised.

Fleming was later famously accused of writing 'Sex, Snobbery and Sadism'. Certainly de Lisser's story has sex and sadism, but it is above all about the appalling cruelty of the plantation system. Jamaica was the most brutal of all the British slave colonies, and this left a legacy of violence and resentment that Fleming could not have missed. The vicious tyranny of slavery was met by continual resistance, and Fleming's parish was the epicentre of the island's biggest slave rebellion of the eighteenth century. On Easter Sunday in 1760, fifty slaves on the Frontier plantation near Port Maria, then owned by Ballard Beckford, a scion of one of Jamaica's most famous and notorious families, rose up under the leadership of an enslaved African called Tacky. They marched on Port Maria and captured the fort that guarded the harbour. Other slaves at the neighbouring plantation, Trinity, also rebelled, and soon much of the island was in uproar, with enslaved men and women burning cane fields and sugar works and destroying the hated Great Houses. Their aim was the 'entire extirpation of the white inhabitants.' Although outnumbered and ill equipped, Tacky's followers held Port Maria and kept the British at bay for more than a month before the rebellion could be subdued, with help from the Maroons at nearby Scott's Hall. Sixty whites and about three hundred blacks were killed. Fifty further slaves were subsequently executed in the main by being slowly burnt alive.

Modern Jamaica had a dark side for Fleming. In many of his stories the Caribbean functions as a lawless space, somewhere to hide for criminals, misfits and ex-Nazis. And in Jamaica itself, there is danger among the beauty, just as there is on the reef. In a newspaper article, he recommends avoiding 'the stews of Kingston' – 'a tough town – tough and dirty'; in a later piece, he mentions wild stories about 'naked black men, their bodies glistening with coconut oil, who roam abroad at night to thieve and rape'. When Fleming first arrived in Jamaica, Ivanhoe 'Rhyging' Martin, an outlaw and folk hero who inspired the film *The Harder They Come*, was still at large. He was finally tracked down and killed in a shootout at Lime Key in 1948.

In her writings, American artist Marion Simmons – a friend of Coward's – is almost always upbeat about Jamaica and complimentary

– if patronising – about 'the natives', as she calls them. But, as Fleming also experienced, a more hostile aspect sometimes asserted itself. 'Some things have happened recently that make me wonder what possessed me to settle in this barbaric place,' she wrote in 1951. She was driving her car when someone threw a stone, hitting and damaging the windscreen. Then 'a black man' yelled 'White Bitch!' at her. 'On top of this some (to me) fairly large sums of money have been taken from my purse ... we have started locking up the house at night and suddenly everything is horrid.'

A friend, Val, tells her she must get a pistol, and a second-hand one is found for her – 'an evil looking thing which I have no idea how to shoot, and indeed am loath to touch'. She got a licence from the police, then took the gun home and shut it in a drawer, 'where it will no doubt rust and rot – but Val says everyone knows when you have one, whether you shoot it or not, and that it's a sound idea'.

Fleming's mother Eve, who moved to the Bahamas in 1950, also kept a gun – writing to Ian, 'The thing is to let the blacks know I *have* a pistol' – as did Fleming himself in Jamaica. In all, he owned three guns: a twelve-bore shotgun kept permanently at Holland & Holland gunsmiths; a Colt .38 given him by General Donovan of the US secret services; and a Browning .25 issued to him during the war, which he took with him each year 'for defence against the Blackamoors'. (In his Jamaican short story 'For Your Eyes Only', it is no surprise that Havelock has a gun in his desk drawer.)

Writing about Jamaica, Fleming also conceded that 'there will always be racial simmering and occasional clashes between coloured and white vanities', and explained that Friday and Saturday nights saw 'plenty of heavy drinking' and 'ganja' smoking. But on the whole he reported that he had found Jamaicans 'most law abiding and God-fearing', with 'a strictness of behavior and manners which will surprise you and charm you'. 'Bad or indecent language' was 'almost absent', and 'law and the church are a great counterweight to the human extravagance which the hot sun breeds. I think you will appreciate the fairly solid civic framework which contains this tropic luxury.' In fact, Jamaica seemed to Fleming the perfect mix of British old-fashioned imperial influence and law and the dangerous and sensual, of reassuring conservatism and the exciting exotic: in effect, the same curious combination that would make the Bond novels so appealing and successful. Candia McWilliam admires this dichotomy in the novels' 'luscious clash of ostentation and restraint' (a succinct summary, too, of Fleming's character). When late in his life Fleming was asked the secret of his best-selling formula, he too was clear on this contrast: 'What I endeavour to aim at is a certain disciplined exoticism.'

Fleming later described how during the six years between building Goldeneye and the start of his first book, he had had 'plenty to do exploring Jamaica, coping with staff and getting to know the locals, and minutely examining the underwater terrain within my reef'. But by the sixth year, he had done all this and was looking for a new challenge.

Now he was acclimatised. And each year, Jamaica had soaked into him, with its creative spirit and cocktail of luxury, melancholy, imperialism, fantasy, sensuality, danger and violence. Now, at last, it seemed he was ready to fulfil his Jamaican home's original purpose as pronounced to Ivar Bryce on the aeroplane in 1943 – to write that book.

1952
Casino Royale

Then he slept, and with the warmth and humour of his eyes
extinguished, his features relapsed into a taciturn mask, ironical,
brutal, and cold.

Bond, described in *Casino Royale*

Fleming's trip to Jamaica at the beginning of 1952 was the pivotal
moment of his life. By the time he left in late March, he was both an
author and a married man.

Much had changed since the previous visit in October 1951.
Esmond Rothermere and Ann had agreed to a divorce, and by January
Ann knew she was pregnant again.

Although many of his friends advised against it, Ian had decided
this time to 'do the right thing' and marry her. The wedding was to
be in Jamaica – 'the easiest way', according to Ann – just as soon as
the divorce papers came through. Ann's brother Hugo, although he
disliked Ian, sent him a letter of support, to which Fleming replied:
'We are of course totally unsuited ... I'm a non-communicator, a
symmetrist, of a bilious and melancholic temperament ... Ann is a
sanguine anarchist/traditionalist. So china will fly and there will be

rage and tears. But I think we will survive as there is no bitterness in either of us and we are both optimists – and I shall never hurt her except with slipper.'

But Fleming, the 'sleek' bachelor of forty-four years of age, was worried by the marriage, or 'this dangerous transmogrification', as he put it. Would his 'difficulties', he wrote to Ann, still be tolerated when she was no longer in love with him but instead settled into 'the usual married friendship'? 'You might get too irritated, I don't know,' he wondered.

For her part, Ann was aware that Ian liked his own company and that the change would be 'quite a step for him after 43 years of solitude'. 'I fear Ian's martyrdom is imminent,' she wrote to her brother and his wife, 'with intrusion of talking parrot, saxophone, R. [Raymond], F. [Fionn], and self to his perfectly run bachelor establishment … the immediate future looks rather chaotic'.

Because of the difficulties of her first pregnancy, Ann took it easy after their arrival at Goldeneye at the end of January, passing the time sitting under a large straw hat in the sunken garden, painting birds, fish and flowers. Although most of her friends considered her entirely 'London', she had inherited from her naturalist father a love of wildlife, and like Coward found Jamaica conducive to creativity. Not that the north-coast social scene was entirely ignored. Soon after her arrival on 29 January, the *Gleaner* reported that Ann had been seen with local aristocrat Lady Brownlow on the Montego Bay cocktail party circuit. The north coast from Port Antonio to Montego Bay was christened by the paper 'Jamaica's Gold Coast'. In the sky above, they reported, the British Overseas Airways Corporation, 'BOAC, with its Stratocruiser is bringing down the tourists in luxurious comfort from way above the clouds'. By this time, more than 80 per cent of tourists arrived by air, the majority still to the Kingston Palisadoes airport (later named after Norman Manley), rather than the north coast. Pan Am, however, were planning a direct route from New York to Montego

The Sunken Garden. Ian's step-son Raymond remembered, 'Humming birds buzzing all around you – it was absolute paradise.'

Bay, described the same year by an American newspaper as 'the best resort in the British Empire'.

For Ann and Ian, there was also a trip across the Blue Mountains to the south coast. 'I watched the banks for new flowers,' wrote Ann in her diary. 'Ian stopped whenever I shrieked for it was marvelous new territory. Two day lilies with stems inches thick.' With a machete brought for the purpose, Ann dug these out to replant at Goldeneye. After a picnic of 'iced limeade, bottle of gin, hard boiled eggs, marmalade, sandwiches and fruit', followed by a siesta, there were more flowers to be found – 'amaryllis lilies, smaller and far more appealing than the hothouse variety ... a very delicate pale salmon colour, or else salmon and white stripes. Presently green valleys of lemon orchards in flower, then baked fields with vast watermelons ripening upon them.'

Their destination was a spa hotel on the Milk River. When they reached it, they found a small eighteenth-century sugar planter's house, its paint flaking and a 'closed' sign on the door. Nearby lay a dead alligator. It was just the sort of ramshackle Jamaican scene that Ian loved. Eventually he managed to rouse the proprietress and charmed her into letting them stay and even provide them with a dinner of lobsters straight out of the sea.

The spa itself, consisting of a large rocky excavation just below the hotel, seems to have been something of a disappointment, and the beach nearby was punishingly hot. But retreating from the scorching sand, they came across a deep pool of ice-cold fresh water. Ian dived in and speared three mackerel-like fish, which they enjoyed for supper. The planned crocodile hunt, though, was rained off.

On 7 February, Ann's divorce was finalised, and she and Ian could start planning their wedding, now set for the end of March. On the 16th, Noël Coward arrived in Jamaica and once again rushed round to Goldeneye the same evening. 'Dine with Ian and Annie,' he wrote in his diary that night. (Previously they had always been referred to as Annie and Ian). 'I sensed that Annie was not entirely happy.'

Ann reported of the visit in an undated diary fragment that Noël had 'told all our favourite jokes', but she was beginning to tire of 'The Master'. A fortnight later, she complained in a letter to Cecil Beaton that Noël 'should be used as a cabaret and not as a guest, he does not understand the give and take of talk and the deserts of pomposity between the oases of wit are too vast'. This new mood put a strain on the usual Goldeneye dynamic.

As the wedding loomed, and without the distraction of guests, Ann noted that it was 'rather a tense period in our lives'. She had become enthused by her painting, but Ian seemed at a loose end. According to Ann, she suggested that he should write something just to amuse himself. And so, in the same undated diary fragment that tells of the Milk River trip, we find the following from Ann: 'This morning Ian started to type a book. Very good thing. He says he cannot be idle while I screw up my face trying to draw fish.'

Perhaps Ann takes too much credit. Ian had packed his twenty-year-old 'Imperial portable' typewriter, and on passing through New York ten days earlier had purchased a ream of best-quality folio writing paper from a shop on Madison Avenue. The intention to write was already there.

On around 17 February, he sat down at his desk in Goldeneye's main room, plucked a name from the author of *Birds of the West Indies*, whose book sat on his shelf, lined up his ream of smart paper and started to write. So began Bond, with the claustrophobic first line of *Casino Royale*: 'The scent and smoke and sweat of a casino are nauseating at three in the morning.'

When later asked what inspired him to create James Bond, Fleming's stock answer – much to the annoyance of Ann – was that he started writing to take his mind off the 'hideous spectre of matrimony'. It fact, that was only part of a wider crisis for Ian that included concerns about money, his health, and the state of his country and empire.

The Conservatives, led by Winston Churchill, had returned to power at the end of 1951 on a platform that included a more assertive and independent foreign policy and a 'strengthening of the resources of the Empire in order to close the dollar gap'. But their mandate was small – a majority of sixteen seats, with less of the vote than Labour – and there was no promise to roll back the Welfare State so disliked by Fleming. Churchill was a much-diminished figure from the wartime colossus, and some felt he should have given way to the next generation of Eden, Macmillan and Butler.

In the meantime, a series of blows had fallen on the Empire. The Anglo-Iranian Oil Company, owner of the world's biggest oil refinery, at Abadan, was taken over by the Iranian government; in Egypt, nationalists were attacking British troops in the Canal Zone; Cyprus made a bid for independence; nationalists were victorious in elections in the Gold Coast; in recognition of Britain's declining reach, Australia and New Zealand made a security pact with the United States.

Worst for Fleming, though, was the seismic shock delivered to the British intelligence services and the country as a whole by the disappearance in the summer of 1951 of two British spies, Guy Burgess and Donald Maclean, who had been tipped off by a mysterious 'Third Man' (correctly identified by the Americans as Kim Philby, British intelligence's liaison man in Washington). There were strong suspicions – later proven correct – that Burgess and Maclean were traitors and had fled to Moscow. British intelligence was in crisis.

On a more personal level, Fleming's impending change from bachelor to husband and father threw up a number of challenges. Ann had secured a £100,000 divorce settlement from Rothermere, but nonetheless, Fleming was presented with the need to provide for a wife with expensive tastes, and, of course, a child. His salary from the *Sunday Times* was generous, but so had been his bachelor expenditure. For his lifestyle to be maintained, along with these new drains on money, a fresh source of income was required.

Over the previous two years, Ian had made strenuous efforts to rent out Goldeneye during the ten months he was not there. In this he had had some success, but barely enough to cover the costs of the place, as 'the house runs away with money all through the year'. So as well as everything else, he needed Bond to pay for Goldeneye.

Also under threat was his personal space, the aloof loneliness he had wallowed in for so long. From the very first, Fleming established a routine for his writing at Goldeneye. Retreating inside, he closed the large wooden jalousies, shutting out the noisy colour of the garden, the views of sea and sky, the calls of birds and the crash of the surf on the reef. He didn't discuss what he was writing with Ann, nor did she ask to see any of it. Thereby he managed to maintain a private, self-regarding space, even when his bachelor pad in Jamaica was being thoroughly invaded by the looming proximity of marriage and fatherhood.

The maleness of that space he created at Goldeneye is, of course, in black and white on the pages of the books, starting with *Casino Royale*. 'These blithering women, who thought they could do man's work,' Bond exclaims at one point. In *Casino Royale*, we learn too from Bond about the nature of relationships for men like him: 'the lengthy approaches to a seduction bored him almost as much as the subsequent mess of disentanglement'. Women are for 'entertainment' only, although preferably with a violent twist – 'brutally ravaged'. In fact, in his detachment Bond is outdone by his lover Vesper, who is given the line: 'People are islands. They don't really touch. However close they are, they're really quite separate. Even if they've been married for fifty years.'

It all came out very fast, poured on to the page. Ann later commented that Ian 'wasn't very anxious to start, but once he'd begun, of course, he found himself enjoying it, and he finished the book in a great burst of enthusiasm'. This first novel was finished at the latest on 18 March, possibly even earlier, which meant an average of more than 2,000 words a day. Out of reach of the delicious cooling sea breeze, it must have become very hot inside shuttered Goldeneye. But the prospect of a refreshing dip in the bay would have been a great reward for a target reached – just another thousand words! Fleming later declared that the 'main thing is to write fast and cursively in order to get narrative speed'. It was fatal to start criticising what you had just written, he advised. Instead, you just had to keep going. Awful bits could always be corrected later. (In fact, the manuscript of *Casino Royale* shows more subsequent changes than any other of his books.)

Almost all the Bond books would be written at a similar rate, and sometimes it shows. For *Casino Royale*, however, Fleming clearly had key scenes well thought out before he sat down in front of his typewriter. The card game between Bond and Le Chiffre would remain, many books later, one of his finest creations. Le Chiffre is the secret paymaster of a communist-controlled union in north-west France, 'an important fifth column in the event of war with Redland'. (It was a time when dissent in the unions and in the colonies was often blamed on 'communist influence'.)

But Le Chiffre has lost the union's funds in a private venture and needs to recover the money promptly or face retribution from SMERSH, the 'efficient organ of Soviet vengeance'. He has elected to do this by playing high-stakes baccarat. To prevent him winning, and thereby cause his destruction, M, the head of the British Secret Service, sends his organisation's best card player, James Bond, to take him on at the casino of Royale-les-Eaux, a high-end resort on the French Channel coast. Bond is to be supported by a French agent, Mathis, as well as by the CIA.

Bond's cover in France is as a 'Jamaican plantocrat whose father had made his pile in tobacco and sugar and whose son chose to play it away on the stock markets and casinos'. He signs his name in the hotel register as 'James Bond, Port Maria, Jamaica'. He is also to be controlled from the island, receiving instructions via a 'taciturn man who was head of the picture desk on the *Daily Gleaner*, the famous newspaper of the Caribbean'. A friend of Bond's from Jamaica, 'Charles DaSilva of Chaffery's, Kingston', has agreed to pretend to be his attorney, 'if inquiries were made'.

It is assumed by the Frenchman Mathis that part of Bond's Jamaican cover should be 'hot blood' (a persistent stereotype of West Indian Creoles) and thus the companionship of an attractive escort. 'What is more natural than that you should pick up a pretty girl here?' he asks. 'As a Jamaican millionaire what with your hot blood and all, you would look naked without one.' Enter Vesper Lynd, named after the drink Fleming had enjoyed at the strange Great House at Duncans. Vesper is assistant to the head of Station S (Soviet Union), and Bond, although preferring to work alone, is immediately 'intrigued by her composure' and 'excited by her beauty' – particularly her 'fine breasts'.

In spite of all precautions, Bond's cover is already blown. His hotel room is bugged, and he must survive an assassination attempt by a pair of Bulgarians ('"They're stupid, but obedient. The Russians use them for simple killings"'), as well as a gun in his back during the game itself.

Nonetheless, he takes on Le Chiffre, who watches him during the game 'like an octopus under a rock'. Afterwards, Vesper is kidnapped and Bond himself is captured trying to rescue her. In one of Fleming's most explicit scenes, Bond is then tortured by having his testicles beaten. He survives to consummate his flirtation with Vesper, but is left at the end with a desire for vengeance against SMERSH, and a broken heart belied by the savage last line of the book: 'The bitch is dead now.' (We learn in *On Her Majesty's Secret Service*, written ten years later, that he still makes an annual pilgrimage to Royale-les-Eaux to visit Vesper's grave.) With heartbreak and vengeful anger fuelling the tank, James Bond is launched.

The Bond who emerges from Fleming's first take on his hero is at once old-fashioned and modern, austere and decadent. He is highly professional and expert, but an aficionado of sensual enjoyment, taking 'a ridiculous pleasure in what I eat and drink'. His name, anonymous and sleek, differentiates him from his Clubland Hero predecessors, all the Carruthers, Berties and Algernons, though he, like them, thinks and talks in sporting analogies such as 'bowled out'. When, years later, Fleming was asked about the influence of Buchan and Bulldog Drummond, he declared that 'the old days of the hero getting a crack over the head with a cricket stump have rather gone out'. It was 'ridiculous', he said, to go on writing thrillers in the old way 'when life has come on so fast beside us'. But in *Casino Royale*, Bond very nearly meets his nemesis from a gun hidden inside a walking stick, which is not so far removed from the cricket stump.

Kingsley Amis said that Bond wasn't an aristocrat because he didn't drink port or sherry. Neither are his vodka martinis a pint down the pub. Bond doesn't hunt or sail, but he's also uninterested in a working-class sport like football. His are the consumer sports – skiing, golf, gambling – open only to those with money but relatively free of old class assumptions.

Like the sunseekers of Jamaica's 'Gold Coast', Bond moves in spaces that are rich, for sure, but becoming increasingly classless. Outnumbering the lords and maharajas at the casino table in Royale are a Belgian who has made a fortune in colonial Congo, a Greek shipowner, sundry rich Americans, including a flaky film star, and a young Italian 'who had probably had plenty of money from rackrents in Milan'. It is the new jet-set, classless, always abroad, detached from where they are, feeding their appetites. It is Bond's milieu: he is a new hero for the jet age.

Detachment is an important part of Bond's charm. His power and charisma come from his combination of style and isolation; he treats women with 'a mixture of taciturnity and passion'. His character has coldness, cynicism and ruthlessness, but he is constantly trying to control and conceal his emotions and suppress his appetites. Mathis says, 'I don't think Bond has ever been melted.' But Fleming reveals of his hero that, 'like all harsh, cold men, he was easily tipped over into sentiment'.

Above all, though, Bond is soaked in a disconcerting psychological unease, his face 'ironical, brutal and cold'. Like Fleming, he enjoys staring out to sea, 'lost in his thoughts'.

Like Fleming also, Bond loves cars, and smokes Morland cigarettes in the same quantity – 'Bond lit his seventieth cigarette of the day.' He also matches Fleming's own prodigious alcohol consumption, although without the attendant health problems beginning to bother his creator. Peter Quennell reckoned that James Bond incorporated Fleming's 'passion for speed, his taste for mechanical devices, his masculine hedonism and restless energy'.

Aside from the character of the hero, other distinctive elements of the Bond novels to come are laid out in *Casino Royale* for the first time. The villain is of mixed race, 'probably a mixture of Mediterranean with Prussian or Polish strains', as they almost all would be. Le Chiffre, like many of Bond's adversaries, is also physically unusual and repulsive, with overlarge false teeth and ear lobes, and moist yellowish skin, a 'flagellant' with a 'large sexual appetite'.

Then there are the detailed, lip-smacking descriptions of conspicuous luxury consumption and lifestyle – cars, hotels, wine and food, including caviar, lobster and foie gras. We learn about Bond's special self-authored cocktail: 'three measures of Gordon's, one of vodka, half a measure of Kina Lillet. Shake it very well until it's ice-cold, then add a large thin slice of lemon peel.' The bar staff are honoured to follow these expert instructions; then Bond helpfully advises that grain-based rather than potato-based vodka would make the recipe better. For 1953's rationed and skinflint Austerity Britain, this was pure delicious escapism, just as Fleming's sojourns in Jamaica were for him.

But while *Casino Royale* launches a recognisable Bond, and a recognisable style, it remains somehow different from the rest of the novels. It is at times clunky in its exposition, and has an unsatisfactory structure, with an overlong coda after the gruesome climax of the action. But it also has a claustrophobic tension not experienced again until the much later books. It is rawer and less polished than later Bond novels, as perhaps we should expect of a first attempt, but at the same time it seems more nuanced and subtle than much of what would follow. (For Raymond Carver, it would remain the best Bond novel.)

The shadow of the real-life Burgess–Maclean treachery that hangs over *Casino Royale* makes it perhaps the closest Fleming came to a Le Carré-style spy story. The plot addresses the disastrous infiltration of MI5, with the twist in the tail being the exposure of a mole at the heart of the Secret Service's Station S. We also have the American view on the newly revealed unreliability of the British Secret Service. When Bond meets Felix Leiter for the first time, he senses a certain reserve behind the American agent's charm: 'Although he seemed to talk quite openly about his duties in Paris, Bond soon noticed that he never spoke of his American colleagues in Europe or in Washington and he guessed that Leiter held the interests of his own organization far above the mutual concern of the North Atlantic Allies. Bond sympathized with him.'

More widely, *Casino Royale* tries to reflect these changed times of diminished British power. Bond needs to be bailed out by Leiter, his CIA contact, when the gambling goes astray. Leiter slips him an envelope containing thirty-two million francs, labelled 'Marshall Aid'. Bond is able to return the money later, but comments, 'That envelope was the most wonderful thing that ever happened to me ... talk about a friend in need.' Similarly, Bond is in fact saved by a Russian *deus ex machina*, rather than by his own efforts (as would almost always be the case in later books).

But however diminished the status of Britain, and its intelligence services, *Casino Royale* still depicts Britain in general and Bond in particular as being in the front line of the Cold War against the Russians, just as Buchan's Richard Hannay had once been against the Germans. Even though the action takes place in France, French operative Mathis is clearly subservient to Bond. The American Felix Leiter is also 'under the orders' of the British. As Leiter confides, 'Washington's pretty sick we're not running the show ...'

Felix Leiter is a combination of two of Ian's friends. Felix was Ivar Bryce's middle name, and Leiter came from Tommy Leiter, a mutual friend from a rich Chicago family. Tommy was a hopeless drunk, but his wife Marion, known as 'Oatsie', was a spirited Southern lady who struck up a strong and lasting friendship with Ian that would have important consequences. The Leiters had a house in Jamaica at Reading, in the hills overlooking Montego Bay, near the Stephensons.

Leiter appeared as Bond's American sidekick in five of the novels, and would be played, somewhat confusingly, by eight different actors in the later Bond films. His close and friendly relationship with Bond represents an optimistic, or even fantastic, model for Britain's relationship with the United States. Leiter's role is to supply Bond with technical support, hardware and muscle, as well as money. Bond – and by implication Britain – provides the leadership, intelligence and daring.

But as he recovers from his torture, Bond experiences a mini-crisis, complaining that 'History is moving pretty quickly these days and the heroes and villains keep on changing places.' We are fighting communism, he tells Mathis, but fifty years ago the 'brand of Conservatism we have today would have been damn near called Communism and we should have been told to go and fight that'. He even goes as far as to pronounce: 'this country right or wrong business is getting a little out of date', a subversive doubt never expressed by Bond again.

But it is only a brief glimpse into the Le Carré-ish world of complicated disloyalties and the Cambridge spies. Although the plot is about a traitor in the British Secret Service, there is nothing political or ambiguous about Vesper's motives for betraying her country. Instead she is trapped by love and by the sheer nastiness of the opposition, who have tortured her Polish lover – an RAF wartime hero – and threatened him with retribution if she does not cooperate.

Le Chiffre himself, because of his extreme cruelty, simplifies the murky moral landscape of the Cold War (so different to the certainties of Britain's fight in the Second World War), and thereby resolves

Bond's doubts about his career, as he explains: Le Chiffre 'was serving a wonderful purpose, a really vital purpose,' Bond concludes. 'By his evil existence ... he was creating a norm of badness by which, and by which alone, an opposite norm of goodness could exist'. It's a manifesto for the Bond villain figure, who would become over time far more outlandish and extreme, and therefore fulfil the 'vital purpose' of clarifying right from wrong even more effectively. So although *Casino Royale* has a moral landscape with more 'grey areas' than any other Bond book, it ultimately hopes to reassure its British readers about their country's rectitude as well as its status and role in the world.

In spite of Ian's writing, and Ann's pregnancy, their involvement in the burgeoning north-coast social life continued. On 27 February there was another cocktail party at Sir Harold and Lady Mitchell's Prospect Great House in Ocho Rios, 'one of the highlights of the north coast season', as the *Gleaner* reported. Lady Mitchell, 'in vivid red, was a busy hostess', welcoming among her guests Ann ('wearing a cream creation') and Ian, the Brownlows, Lord and Lady Graham and Lord and Lady Mansfield. The last, the paper continued, 'in strawberry pink was obviously delighted to be back in Jamaica ... Guests had a glimpse of the garden, gay with roses, scarlet salvias and hibiscuses of every shade. Bowls of flowers gilded the rooms, blending easily with the old cedar paneling.'

When not partying, Ann and Ian were 'asleep by 10.30 and bathing at sunrise, writing, painting, shooting, eating and snoozing for the rest for the day', as Ann wrote to her brother Hugo 'from the Lotus Islands'. 'It is frighteningly agreeable.' Ian described it as 'a marvelous honeymoon among the hummingbirds and barracudas'.

Ann's divorce became absolute on Monday 24 March. She and Ian married the same day at Port Maria town hall. There were only two witnesses: Noël Coward, and his secretary Cole Lesley. Coward had warned Violet, 'I shall wear long elbow gloves and give the bride away. I may even cry a little at the sheer beauty of it all.' In fact, according to Lesley, 'We took our duties very seriously; wore ties (unheard of for Noël in Jamaica) with formal white suits, our pockets full of rice, and got to the Town Hall early. We attracted a crowd of six and a smiling though toothless black crone who entertained us with some extremely improper calypsos, including one called "Belly Lick".' (Lyrics include the line: 'Drop your pants and lie down'. Fleming refers to the song in his Jamaica novel, *The Man with the Golden Gun.*)

Coward, who saw himself as the matchmaker, having assisted during Ann's previous adulterous trips to Jamaica, remembered Ann and Ian at their wedding as 'surprisingly timorous'. Fleming wore his usual nautical belted blue linen shirt with blue trousers. Ann, four months pregnant and beginning to show, was in a silk dress copied from a Dior design by a local Port Maria seamstress. Coward noticed that she was shaking so much the dress fluttered. 'It was an entirely hysterical affair,' he later wrote.

Inside the parochial office, the first thing they all saw was 'an enormous oleograph of Churchill scowling down on us with bulldog hatred'. Once married by the registrar, Mr L. A. Robinson, they headed for Blue Harbour for strong martinis, then back to Goldeneye for a special wedding supper prepared by Violet. Coward remembered it as particularly bad: the black crab, which 'can be wonderful to eat if you have a good cook, but Ian didn't have a good cook', 'tasted just like eating cigarette ash'. To make things worse, Violet then brought out 'a slimy green wedding cake, and dusky heads peered round the door to make sure we ate it. Ian had to because he was directly in line of sight, but later we took the cake outside and buried it so as not to hurt anyone's feelings.' The evening ended with a punch of Fleming's own creation – white rum poured on citrus peel then ignited.

The next day, the newly-weds motored to Montego Bay to stay a night at Sunset Lodge before flying to Nassau, then on to New York.

Heavily pushed by Ian's brother Peter and his friend William Plomer, the finished manuscript for *Casino Royale* was accepted for publication by Jonathan Cape, for whom Plomer worked as a scout. Ian had wanted to dedicate the book to Ann, but she replied, 'Surely one doesn't dedicate books of this sort to people.' The space for the dedication remained empty.

On 12 August, Ann gave birth, after a difficult Caesarean, to a 9lb 4oz baby boy, Caspar. She spent the next two weeks in hospital, with 'tubes performing every physical function'. Her doctors advised her to have no more babies, 'rather strongly, which is depressing'. 'You have been wonderfully brave and I am very proud of you,' Ian wrote to her. 'I do hope darling Caspar has made it up to you a little. He is the most

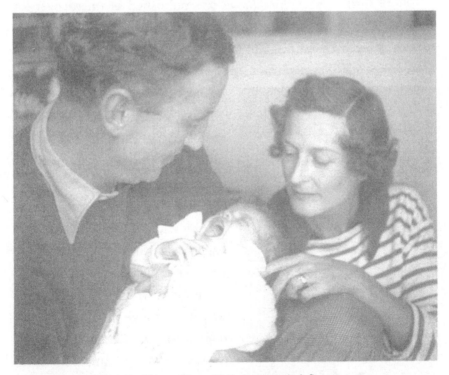

Cecil Beaton's photograph of Ian and Ann with their new arrival, Caspar.

heavenly child and I know he will grow up to be something wonderful because you have paid for him with so much pain. Goodnight my brave sweetheart.' A month later, Ann was still having nightmares about long red rubber tubes, and was weeping continuously.

Caspar's godparents were to be Cecil Beaton, Anthony Eden's wife Clarissa (a close friend of Ann's), Ian's brother Peter, and Noël Coward. Ann explained in a letter to a friend that they thought Noël would be offended if not asked, 'as he considers himself responsible for the whole thing'. She soon regretted it, writing to Beaton in September about a visit from Coward: 'He was quite delightful for the first hour ... and then he suddenly became so vulgar and dull that I longed to cancel the G-parent arrangement and be frightfully rude to him; my only false relationships are with him and Rosamond Lehmann and I cannot extricate myself from either.'

On 13 April 1953, *Casino Royale* was published as a hardcover for 10s. 6d. The first print run of just over 4,700 copies sold out in a month. A second print run also sold out, as did a third of 8,000 copies. It was respectable enough for Cape quickly to offer Fleming a deal for a further three books.

The jacket of *Casino Royale*, designed by Fleming himself, is noticeably restrained, particularly in comparison with the garish girl-straddling-gun covers that would feature on the later Pan paperbacks. Indeed, *Casino Royale* was marketed as quality 'literary' spy fiction, which explains why it was given notices in places like the highbrow *Times Literary Supplement*. Most reviewers assumed the novel was for the 'knowing reader' who would pick up the parodic elements. During the climactic moment, Le Chiffre tells Bond that 'The game of Red Indians is over ... This is not a romantic adventure story in which the villain is finally routed and the hero is given a medal and marries the girl. Unfortunately these things don't happen in real life.'

This is one of a number of curious moments, repeated at least once in all the novels, when Fleming suddenly gives the reader a 'knowing look'. In *Dr No*, the villain tells Bond that he has 'been reading too many novels of suspense. Your little speech reeked of grease-paint and card-board.' In *Diamonds are Forever*, Fleming's minor villain Pissaro 'looked like a gangster in a horror-comic'. The heroine of *The Spy Who Loved Me*, on hearing of Bond's latest adventure, exclaims: 'I could hardly believe it. It was like something out of a thriller.' In 'Quantum of Solace', by which time Fleming's stories were appearing as a cartoon strip in the *Daily Express*, Bond ponders that his duties are 'the stuff of an adventure-strip in a cheap newspaper'. And there are many other examples. This self-awareness and self-deprecation are central to the Bond novels and to the wider Bond phenomenon. In a copy of one of his books sent to his novelist friend Paul Gallico, Fleming wrote: 'To Paul, who has always seen the joke.' Perhaps this self-consciousness prevents Fleming from being considered a truly great thriller writer, but it has ensured his longevity.

As a journalist, Fleming was well placed to encourage reviews of the book. His own newspaper, the *Sunday Times*, declared him 'the best new thriller writer since Eric Ambler'. Although there were complaints about the graphic torture scene, most reviews were favourable. In the *Daily Telegraph*, John Betjeman declared that 'Ian Fleming has discovered the secret of narrative art ... the reader had to go on reading.' Alan Ross in the *TLS* called the novel 'an extremely engaging affair', with his greatest praise for the 'high poetry with which he invests the green baize lagoons of the casino tables'. The *Manchester Guardian* called it 'a first rate thriller … with a breathtaking plot'.

Ann's brother Hugo, who had ambitions as a novelist himself, was unimpressed, telling his sister Mary Rose that 'Ian's thriller starts well but ends as the most disgusting thing I've ever seen in print – torture such as Japs and Huns eschewed as not cricket. I always knew he was neurotic and tangled.'

After a heavy Christmas, Ian was longing for Jamaica, telling his friend Cyril Connolly that 'the Doctor Birds are waiting in the Crown of Thorns bushes and the Butterfly fish on the reef'. Having parked Caspar with his nanny in London, Ann and Ian flew out to New York, staying for one night before heading on to Florida, where Ian wanted to do some research on his next book. Most of the action, though, he planned to take place in his beloved Jamaica.

1953

The First Jamaica Novel – Live and Let Die

Carribean reality resembles the wildest imagination.

Gabriel García Márquez

At the end of 1952, it was learnt that British Prime Minister Winston Churchill was shortly to visit Jamaica for a two-week holiday. He'd be arriving after a trip to the United States to meet President Truman and President-Elect Eisenhower as part of his strenuous efforts to stoke more life into the 'Special Relationship'. The *Gleaner* was in ecstasy at the news. 'This island is no stranger to distinguished visitors – To royalty, statesmen, film stars, literati, millionaires … Jamaica takes most such visitors in its stride,' the paper opined. But Churchill deserved extra 'reverent affection'. The announcement of his visit had, the paper reported, 'stirred the patriot emotion of all the people of Jamaica'.

The Governor, Sir Hugh Foot, in a white suit, was standing at the bottom of the steps on 9 January as Churchill climbed out of the US presidential jet, lent to take him on his holiday. With Foot at Montego

Churchill's impending holiday in Jamaica trumps the Queen's first Christmas broadcast to lead the front page of the *Gleaner* on 27 December 1952.

Bay airport was Sir Harold Mitchell, at whose Prospect Great House Churchill was to stay. Churchill inspected his guard of honour lined up in white pith helmets and was then introduced to Bustamante, who presented him with Jamaican cigars.

At Prospect, the road to the main gates had been resurfaced by the government and telephones installed in every room, with a special exchange on the first floor. The Mitchells had already moved out of the main house into one of their cottages to make room for Churchill's wife, daughter and son-in-law, who arrived on separate flights, as well as two secretaries, two detectives, a maid and a valet. The secretaries were to deal with mail and cables from London and to 'work on his memoirs'. A police camp of forty men was established in a citrus grove near the house.

Churchill spent much of his time on the veranda, which had been converted into a studio for his painting. Mitchell's staff kept the whisky and sodas flowing. 'The doctors have advised me not to swim,' Churchill declared when he arrived; 'I intend to swim every day.' 'And indeed he did,' Mitchell remembered, 'even when it was quite rough.' Where the Prospect land met the sea was Frankfort beach. Here, while the Prime Minister swam, a mounted policeman kept a lookout at the gate and two plain-clothes detectives concealed themselves in the bushes at either end of the tiny strip of sand.

To commemorate the visit, Mitchell asked his guest to plant a mahogany tree in front of the house. Churchill 'selected the exact spot and went to work with a spade in a business-like manner'. 'When the ceremony was over he called for champagne, his favourite Pol Roger' and he and Mitchell 'toasted the tree'. The mahogany is still there, now grown to a huge size.

Although he was on holiday, there were still some official duties for the Prime Minister to perform. On 17 January, there was a tour through Kingston followed by a reception for a thousand guests at King's House. Churchill's speech at the occasion tellingly celebrated the unity and importance of the 'Great British Empire'. The following day he visited the new University College of the West Indies and then Spanish Town, where he admired the lavish memorial to Admiral Rodney.

The Pathé News footage of the visit is extraordinary. It was created by the Jamaican Film Unit, which had recently been established with a policy to 'produce films for Jamaicans, by Jamaicans, with Jamaicans, designed to assist in the solution of Jamaica's problems – educational, social, cultural, and economical'. But in the reel, the elderly British imperialist politician is filmed at the centre of every scene, surrounded by adoring, cheering homogenous black crowds. In spite of the current moves towards self-representation and autonomy within Jamaica, as evidenced in ongoing political and artistic agitation, the film shows a very traditional image of Jamaica and its relationship to Britain, as if all Jamaicans were unified in support of the Empire.

Enthusiasm for Churchill was also surprising in the context of his well-known objection to Jamaican emigration to Britain. The *Empire*

Windrush had docked at Tilbury in June 1948 with 492 passengers from the West Indies; it was the birth of multicultural life in Britain. As Evon Blake wrote in 1950: 'Britons made them feel like the uninvited they were ... Nipped and gnawed by starvation, many begged to be (and were) repatriated ... Bitter stories by sadder and wiser returnees did not deter more travelling to the Land of Unwelcome.' In 1952, some 2,000 Jamaicans migrated to Britain. It was still a trickle rather than a flood – in 1955, the figure would reach 17,000 – but it was still too many for Churchill's liking. He told Sir Hugh Foot that he feared Jamaican migration would produce a 'magpie society and that would never do', and tried to get his cabinet to legislate to stop it. He would also suggest that for the 1955 election campaign the Conservatives stand on the slogan 'Keep Britain White'.

But it does seem that Churchill's 'star quality' won over some doubters. Every time his car left Prospect – for instance to visit Beaverbrook at Cromarty – crowds would line the streets to catch a glimpse of the old man, who gamely gave his famous V sign. Foot himself was overwhelmed by the enthusiasm of Kingstonians as he accompanied the Prime Minister through the city. He had been slightly anxious that Churchill would be suspicious of his family's politics, particularly those of his brother Michael. But for the whole visit, Churchill 'made no reference whatever to any of my political relatives' until they were both standing surveying the cheering throng in Kingston, when the Prime Minister turned to Foot, and only just audibly above the 'din of acclamation' asked: 'I wonder what Michael would say about all this?'

It all strikes a rather unreal note. Ironically, the day before Churchill's arrival, the Governor had announced through the *Gleaner* that he was acceding to demands for greater democratic reform in Jamaica. What was agreed was the establishment of proper ministries, headed by elected officials, who now also achieved a majority on the Executive Council. By the approval of the House of Representatives,

Seventy-eight-year-old Winston Churchill greets crowds at Montego Bay.

Bustamante became Jamaica's first Chief Minister. Defence, foreign affairs, justice and finance to a large measure remained under the control of the Colonial Service officials on the spot, but it was nonetheless an undoubted diminution of the power of the British Governor and a significant lurch towards Jamaican self-government.

Although Foot differed politically from Churchill, and certainly had very much more liberal views on race, somewhat surprisingly he did share the Prime Minister's strident anti-communism. In August that year, he made a speech alleging that 'the Communist movement in Jamaica' was being financed by a 'supply of foreign Communist money'. Suspected communists had their whereabouts tracked and post opened. Foot's particular bugbear was the Chinese community on the island, which he saw as a Maoist vanguard. He ordered that all Chinese incomers be fingerprinted and photographed, and even suggested that previously naturalised citizens have their Jamaican nationality revoked.

A lot of it now looks like overreaction, but Foot's fear of communist infiltration was shared by many, particularly in the United States, then in the throes of McCarthyism. By now, the spread of American influence and the start of the Cold War had made the 'red menace' an international issue.

In February 1952, Bustamante, on Jamaican government business, was detained in the US colony of Puerto Rico, on suspicion of being a communist. He demanded an apology, which was hardly surprising as in fact, according to Foot, he was a 'fanatical opponent of communism'. In November the same year, Bustamante called for it to be banned by law in Jamaica, and for many years he had been using anti-communist rhetoric to attack the PNP, in which 'red communism', he said, was 'rampant'. On several occasions Norman Manley's party had been forced to declare publicly that it was not communist.

Despite these denials, American anti-communist interest was also focused on the PNP. As early as 1948, an American from the consulate met Manley to discuss 'communist accusations'. As the Cold War stepped up, so American security policy towards Latin America and the Caribbean was increasingly directed against the spread of communism. It became ever clearer that the United States would simply not tolerate 'communist' regimes popping up in their back yard. For example, in 1953, elections in Guyana saw victory for the People's Progressive Party, which the American State Department considered too supportive of communism. The colonial authorities in London were unconcerned, but American pressure saw the constitution suspended, a state of emergency declared and the colony occupied by British troops. The following year, following arm-twisting, a majority of the Organisation of American States foreign ministers supported a US resolution declaring communism incompatible with the inter-American system.

In January 1952, Governor Foot launched an attack on Kenneth Hill, who was a founder member of the PNP, the mayor of Kingston and the most popular leader of the PNP's left wing. Foot described him as 'an extremist who cares nothing for the disruption which he causes to industrial development in Jamaica and if he is eliminated from the trade union field Jamaica will certainly be better for it'. Later the same year, the party was forced to set up a committee to investigate charges that the left had been engaged in communist teaching. The result was the expulsion from the party of the 'Four H's': Hill, his brother Frank, Richard Hart and Arthur Henry. The event, which sent shock waves across the Caribbean, was accompanied, according to *Public Opinion*, by 'shouts, screams and threats, followed by bottles and chairs hurled by Communist observers'. In June, Edna Manley wrote in her diary, 'The political world seethes and boils and it's too, too much.'

In *Live and Let Die*, written at Goldeneye in February and March 1953, the action takes place in the context of this fear of communist infiltration in the Caribbean. If the fantastical elements of the story are stripped away, effectively Bond's mission is to defeat a communist agent established in Jamaica. But, interestingly, Fleming seems rather half-hearted about this fear. In the novel, we are told that Bond had been on a 'long assignment' in Jamaica just after the war, 'when the Communist headquarters in Cuba was trying to infiltrate the Jamaican labour unions'. We are given no more details except a very curious comment from Bond that 'It had been an untidy and inconclusive job.' This is immediately followed by the reader learning that he was very pleased to be back in Jamaica. Earlier, we hear from the heroine Solitaire that Cuban and communist agents are actually controlled out of US territory – Florida and Harlem. As will emerge in the later novels, sometimes Fleming's anti-Americanism even trumps his anti-communism. The greatest threat to his Jamaica was not the Soviet Union, but Uncle Sam.

Ann and Ian arrived in Jamaica the day Churchill left, 22 January 1953. On the way, they had taken the train from New York to Florida, the same journey that Solitaire and Bond (under the name of Bryce) would travel in *Live and Let Die*. It was all research for this next book. In Florida, Fleming visited a live worm warehouse at St Petersburg, which would soon inspire the Ourobourus Worm and Bait Company, the setting of Bond's discovery of fish tanks containing gold, and his fight with Robber, the villain's local agent.

Goldeneye was looking fine, its harsh outlines now slightly softened by 'a cloak of verdure'. To sort out the paying of bills, repairs and other problems, as well as to help Violet ready the house if it was to be rented, Fleming had employed a local 'attorney', Anthony Lahoud.

In a letter to the author Evelyn Waugh, Ann did not mention Ian's ongoing writing, describing their 1953 trip to Goldeneye as 'two months of freedom from care, there was constant sunshine, black slaves, and solitude save for occasional intrusions from celebrities'. Most 'shocking' was an encounter with Katharine Hepburn: 'She was wearing brief shorts from which protruded an immense length of bone and old skin knitted together by vast purple varicose veins, she must be the oldest gamine in the world.'

Hepburn, along with other Hollywood celebrities, was staying at the Titchfield Hotel in Port Antonio, which in 1951 had been purchased by Errol Flynn. (His ghost-writer later criticised Flynn for the way he treated locals around the Titchfield Hotel and his Boston Estate. He spoke to them in pidgin English, they were very badly paid, and he 'seemed to derive pleasure out of seeing them bow and scrape whenever he appeared on the scene'. It was also claimed that he used local pimps to procure underage girls.) Flynn, now married to his third wife Patrice Wymore, was also trying to build an airfield at Port Antonio, which was currently missing out to booming Montego Bay. He had artist Olga Lehman paint a large mural in the reception of his hotel depicting 'Bloody Morgan' and other infamous pirates.

Angus Wilson, an orchid enthusiast, and his partner Odo Cross invited Ian and Ann for dinner at their new house in Ocho Rios, and in turn visited Goldeneye. The usual party fare from Violet was 'suckling pig – big one roast in the oven'. There was also a special drink wheeled out on every celebratory occasion. As Violet explained: 'Where there is a party, the Commander make his Poor Man's Thing.' It sounds like the concoction Fleming served on his wedding night. 'You have a dish,' said Violet. 'You have skin of orange, skin of lemon. Pour rum on top. Put sugar in dish. Put on oven, keeping stirring. Set light when coming to the boil. Put lid on the dish, then turn out all the light in the house when carry it in to the guests.' This spectacular concoction, plus Ian's combination of martinis and other cocktails, saw Odo Cross pass out and have to be carried to a bed to recover.

Noël Coward at nearby Blue Harbour had a string of visitors, including actor Michael Redgrave and his partner, and later the novelist Joyce Cary. Coward held a series of parties up on his land on Look-Out Hill, and was confirmed in his decision to build another house for himself there. Returning from a Coward party one night, Ian and his companions were surprised by the noise of insistent drumming and singing. Leaving their car, they found they had stumbled on a local variation of the voodoo funeral. Ian was fascinated and fairly baffled, as the contents of *Live and Let Die* would show.

Due to visit Goldeneye at the beginning of March were Ann's father Guy Charteris and his second wife Violet, together with the artist Lucian Freud. Freud had painted Ann in 1950, portraying her with hard pursed red lips, a tiara on her head, with her chin jutting forward purposefully. 'She asked me to one of those marvelous parties, semi-royal, quite a lot of them were,' Freud later remembered. Ann had enjoyed showing off the young wunderkind at her soirées.

Ann and Ian went to meet them all at Kingston harbour, and made a trip of it, having dinner with the Foots at King's House, and then spending a night with Charles and Mildred D'Costa, described by Ann in a letter to her brother as 'rich influential Portuguese Jews'. (D'Costa provided the model for the Jamaican businessman lined up to vouch for Bond in *Casino Royale*.) Charles had been tutored in Jamaica by a young Cyril Connolly, who remembered him as 'the world's bloodiest boy … incredibly selfish, greedy and conceited'. The D'Costas had managed to secure special passes at the port for the Flemings and their guests and had offered to put them up for the night. According to Ann, breakfast at the D'Costas' luxury house in Kingston consisted of 'three black slaves', 'ebony black in starched shocking pink' livery, arriving not with trays but a with a 'vast mahogany table' which they then spread with linen and silver. 'The first course was exquisitely prepared grapefruit, pawpaw, pineapple slices and peeled banana; Ian grew very excited and said "a nabob's breakfast" but alas, the silver coffee pot was half full and the scrambled eggs a grey mush.' When they met the boat, Fleming had to go on board to vouch for Lucian Freud, who only had ten shillings with him.

Ian disliked Freud intensely, partly because he wrongly suspected that he was having an affair with Ann. For Freud, the feeling was mutual; he described Fleming as 'ghastly'. Ann's friend Peter Quennell wrote to her from London imagining the scene: 'Palms wave – waves ripple – tarantulas crawl – barracudas undulate … The Commander groans quietly under the horrors of his unwanted guests.' Fortunately for Ian, he could always retreat inside to write.

Freud spent a lot of his time at Goldeneye painting in a nearby banana grove: 'I am still sitting in almost the same place and am now such a fixture there that birds sit on me and spiders use my head to hold up their new webs,' he wrote. The result was a series of oil paintings that focus on the exotic lushness of the banana plant's leaves and fruit. He did, however, accompany Ann and Ian on a mission to dig out author Graham Greene, who was staying with his mistress Lady Catherine Walston at the Tower Isle Hotel in Ocho Rios. Ann had 'bombarded' Greene with invitations with no success, but now they found the pair at Number One Bungalow at the hotel, and dry martinis and peanuts ensued. However, to Ann's frustration, the 'evening was totally ruined' by the arrival of the boorish Lord Brownlow and a coterie of his friends.

Meanwhile, Ann's father Guy Charteris, a keen naturalist and birds' egg collector, was loving Jamaica: 'Papa is very happy and Vi a faithful sweating follower, he has found 50 birds and tomorrow we camp in the wilderness,' wrote Ann to her brother. Guy kept a naturalist's diary of his time at Goldeneye. He found the place 'wonderful and bewildering', noting the moths, the fireflies and the chorus of tree frogs. He was particularly taken with the rare Solitaire bird, with its outer tail feathers conspicuously tipped with white and its unhurried and flutelike song. Ian, of course, borrowed the name for his new heroine.

The novel that emerged from this time on the island is possibly Fleming's best. Certainly it is the book that establishes the winning formula. *Live and Let Die* is tightly plotted and well paced, with the end of each short chapter dragging the reader on to the next. Raymond Carver would call it 'forceful and driving'. Fleming's experiences of the Goldeneye reef provide inspiration for Bond's first underwater sequence, superbly done. The book's climactic scene is thriller writing of the highest order: Mr Big, inspired by Henry Morgan's way of dealing with enemies, undertakes Bond's destruction by dragging him and Solitaire behind a boat across the razor-sharp tropical reef.

The story is framed by the Cold War and contains a nod to modern Jamaica with the mention of the strategic importance of bauxite. But with its lost pirate treasure, sharks and killer centipedes and black magic, it is really an old-fashioned *Boy's Own* adventure story. One American reviewer would call it a 'lurid meller contrived by mixing equal parts of Oppenheim and Spillane'. Fleming concedes this with his soon-to-be customary knowing looks to the reader: Bond describes his mission as an 'adventure'; one villain looks 'like the bad man in a film about poker-players and gold mines'; Bond's Jamaica colleague

Strangways, on hearing that the heroine needs rescuing, exclaims, 'Sort of damsel in distress? Good show!'

The villain is Mr Big, a 'half negro and half French' Harlem gangster and SMERSH operative with a grotesquely enormous head, whose skin is 'grey-black, taut and shining like the face of a week-old corpse in the river'. Literally larger than life, he is the model for all the classic Bond villains – a 'raving megalomaniac' hoping 'to ultimately win recognition in the history of our times'. Mr Big is smuggling seventeenth-century gold coins from Jamaica to the US to fund Soviet spy activities there and clearly make a lot of money for his organisation. The gold is from 'one of the most valuable treasure troves in history', belonging to 'Bloody Morgan, the pirate', the fruits, Fleming delights in mentioning, 'of countless raids on Hispaniola, of the capture of innumerable treasure-ships sailing for The Plate, of the sacking of Panama and the looting of Maracaibo'.

Mr Big runs a huge 'black network' in the United States and the Caribbean, keeping order through terror tactics. The heroine, Solitaire, is a white Haitian Creole beauty with 'a face born to command. The face of the daughter of a French Colonial slave owner.' Bond, betraying his weakness for romantic West Indian stereotypes, vividly imagines her past: 'a lonely childhood on some great decaying plantation, an echoing "Great House" slowly falling into disrepair and being encouraged on by the luxuriance of the tropics'.

Uniquely for the Bond novels, *Live and Let Die* contains supernatural elements. Solitaire says that Mr Big has 'great psychic power'. He had been 'initiated into Voodoo as a child' and has 'originated an underground Voodoo temple in Harlem'. Now he is the head of the Black Widow cult and believed by that cult to be the Zombie of Baron Samedi, 'the most dreadful spirit in the whole of Voodooism' – impossible to kill because he is dead already. Briefing Bond about the cult, M tells him that it will 'frighten the daylights out of you'.

Bond takes this seriously, reading up on Haitian voodoo in Patrick Leigh Fermor's *The Traveller's Tree*. When he is interrupted, 'it took him minutes to forget the atmosphere, heavy with terror and the occult, that had surrounded him as he read'.

Mr Big's voodoo is shown to be a sham employed to keep local Jamaicans away from his island and to terrify his American black network into obedience. (François Duvalier, who became president of Haiti four years later, would also claim to be linked to Baron Samedi for similar motives.) However, in the case of the novel's heroine, Solitaire, Fleming is more equivocal. Solitaire had been kept by Mr Big as he believes she has the power of telepathy, and can tell when one of his enemies is lying. As they flee south on the train, Bond asks her if she really does have 'second sight'. 'Yes, I have. Or something very like it,' she replies. Though she criticises Haiti for being 'riddled with Voodoo superstitions', she also admits to her 'half-belief in them'. For his part, Bond learns to respect 'the extraordinary power of her intuitions'.

In his 1947 *Horizon* article, Fleming had been dismissive: 'Local black magic (obea) is scarce and dull but credited by most. It consists largely of brewing love potions and putting on hoodoos. If you find a white chicken with its head cut off lying on your doorstep you have, or should have, had it.' But five years later, writing about Jamaica in the *Spectator*, he seems to have changed his mind, describing how, compared to Europeans, black Jamaicans' 'extra-sensory perception, their sixth sense, is more highly developed'. Of course Fleming uses voodoo in the novel to impart a sense of exotic dread, what Solitaire describes as 'the secret heart of the tropics, at the mercy of their anger and stealth and poison … the mystery of the drums…' But at the same time, he had developed a surprising respect for these 'dark' practices and was fascinated by English occultist Aleister Crowley. He later wrote that he was 'rather intrigued by fortune-telling and all matters connected with extra-sensory perception'.

In Jamaica, belief in the supernatural, in obeah and ghosts, known locally as 'duppies', was widespread. Blanche Blackwell recounts several incidents where the spirits of dead people intervened in her life beneficially, on one occasion causing a car to stop in time to avoid a collapsed bridge. Her son Chris, as well as seeing the same Bellevue ghost as his mother, talks about Jamaica's 'strong feel of the supernatural in the air'. Even the firmly English Molly Huggins believed she had seen the ghost at Bellevue: 'the shadowy form of a woman' wearing 'the tight-waisted dress of the Edwardians, full puffed sleeves and long skirts'.

So the supernatural strain in *Live and Let Die* is a reflection of the atmosphere of Jamaica. But it is also shown to affect some people rather more than others. Bond declares that he has 'read most of the books on Voodoo and I believe that it works'. But not on him, as he 'stopped being afraid of the dark when I was a child and I'm not a good subject for suggestion or hypnotism'. Indeed, Solitaire fears the power of voodoo will be difficult to explain to someone like Bond, with such 'certainty of spirit, with that background of common sense, brought up with clothes and shoes among the warm houses and the lighted streets'. In contrast, it is, Bond notes, 'accepted through all the lower strata of the negro world … still deeply, primevally ingrained in the negro subconscious'.

Whatever Fleming's sympathies with and interest in the occult, in *Live and Let Die* it also functions to reflect his views on race. Writing in 1952 about black Jamaicans, he notes: 'their physical strength is often undermined by weak nerves, and this makes them an easy prey to sickness or fear'. He balances this with what he would have thought was a compliment – 'their organs of sight and hearing are keener than ours' – but which ends up implying that black people are more 'animal' than whites, a racist cliché that goes back to the days of slavery. Solitaire at one point muses on 'the sixth sense of fish, of birds, of negroes'.

So in *Live and Let Die*, Mr Big's henchmen are 'clumsy black apes'. The villain himself has 'animal eyes, not human'. Harlem, where the smell of 'negro bodies' is 'feral', is several times referred to as a 'jungle'.

The novel has none of what writer Simon Winder called 'the crazily distasteful black-hands-on-white-flesh scenario' of the 1973 film. But it still produces problems for modern or liberal readers and perhaps for anyone on whose behalf Bond has been adopted as a national icon. In 1968, Eldridge Cleaver, an early leader of the Black Panthers, attacked Bond as an example of a white 'fantasy world': 'The "paper tiger" hero, James Bond, offered the whites a triumphant image of themselves, saying what many whites want desperately to be reaffirmed: I am still the White Man, Lord of the land, licensed to kill, and the world is still an empire at my feet.' Today, Ian's niece Lucy Williams almost squirms in embarrassment when talking about the 'obvious racism' of *Live and Let Die*, in particular the naming of the Harlem chapter: 'Nigger Heaven'. Fleming's American publisher changed the chapter title to 'Seventh Heaven'. Jonathan Cape kept it in, presumably assuming their readership would recognise it as the title of an anti-racist novel from the 1920s by Carl Van Vechten about the Harlem Renaissance.

It is also important to note that Fleming – and Bond – looked down on pretty much *everyone* who was not British and perceived people of all colours in terms of negative stereotypes of race and nationality. In *Moonraker*, Bond comments on 'the usual German chip on the shoulder'. The Japanese, Bond tells us in *You Only Live Twice*, have 'an unquenchable thirst for the bizarre, the cruel and the terrible'. In *Diamonds are Forever*, he describes Italians as 'bums with monogrammed shirts who spend the day eating spaghetti and meatballs and squirting scent over themselves'. Afrikaners, we learn in the same book, are 'a bastard race, sly, stupid and ill-bred'. In *Dr No*, the Chinese are 'hysterical'. And so on, across every nationality Bond encounters. No villain in the Bond novels is ever British. Even when they are British citizens, such as Goldfinger or *Moonraker*'s Sir Hugo Drax, they turn out to be of foreign racial origin. In a letter to Ann in 1956, having complained about Americans, Ian declared that 'all foreigners are pestilential'.

But with black Jamaicans and even black Americans, Fleming's viewpoint seems slightly different. In fact, there is more affection towards these individuals in the novels than is offered towards almost any of the other non-British characters.

When, in *Live and Let Die*, Bond and Leiter go uptown to Harlem to check out Mr Big's home turf, Bond feels they are 'trespassing. They just weren't wanted', and he experiences the 'same uneasiness of when he was operating behind enemy lines in the war'. He and Leiter receive contemptuous or hostile looks and several men spit in the gutter as they pass. Nonetheless, Leiter tells Bond: 'Fortunately I like the negroes and they know it somehow … I admire the way they're getting on in the world.' His affection – albeit patronising – is based on music, the sort of jazz that Fleming was by now in the habit of buying in New York for his stepson Raymond. Leiter even uses this link to talk himself out of a severe beating later on.

In his fourth novel, *Diamonds are Forever*, Fleming tells us that, like Leiter, 'Bond had a natural affection for coloured people.' For Fleming, it is a sign of a 'good sort'. Just as shooting birds or hurting animals is a sure sign of villainy, if a character in a Bond novel is cruel to a black person, they can expect a prompt comeuppance. In *Diamonds are Forever*, the corrupt jockey Tingaling, 'cocky' and with a 'sharp weasely face', arrives at the Saratoga mud baths and addresses the black man working there with 'Hey, you black bastard!' before trying unsuccessfully to trip him up as he passes with a pail of mud. Tingaling gets his just rewards in the form of boiling mud on his head when hooded hitmen arrive who work for the diamond-smuggling Spang gangsters. One of the hoods, for no apparent reason, 'lashed his revolver into the centre of the negro's huge belly'. This then provides Bond with his motivation. 'I've suddenly taken against the brothers Spang,' he later tells Leiter. 'I didn't like those two men in hoods. The way the man hit that fat negro.'

Despite feeling unwanted and out of place, Bond loves Harlem in *Live and Let Die*. He is 'spellbound' by the Savoy Ballroom: 'He found many of the girls very beautiful. The music hammered its way into his pulse until he almost forgot what he was there for.' Early on, he eavesdrops on a conversation between two young blacks, and tells Leiter that it 'Seems they're interested in much the same things as everyone else – sex, having fun … Thank God they're not genteel about it.' As with Coward's Samolans, and Fleming's Jamaicans asking directly 'Will you do me a rudeness?', Bond admires these characters' lack of hypocrisy. As the night progresses, the music gets even louder, a stripper appears to the backing of voodoo drums and the air fills with the 'sour sweet smell' of marijuana. Bond loves the spontaneity, the physicality and what he would see as the sexy exoticism of it all. His affection is genuine, then, but based on what we would now see as racist clichés.

Similarly, there are good intentions in the well-known passage near the beginning of *Live and Let Die* when Bond and M discuss the 'progress of the negro race'.

Bond, told by M that Mr Big is 'probably the most powerful negro criminal in the world', replies, 'I don't think I've ever heard of a great negro criminal before … plenty of negroes mixed up in diamonds and gold in Africa, but always in a small way. They don't seem to take to big business. Pretty law-abiding chaps I should have thought except when they've drunk too much.'

M, who can do no wrong in Fleming's eyes, and is always described in terms of 'remarkable' and 'shrewd', continues: 'The negro races are just beginning to throw up geniuses in all the professions – scientists, doctors, writers. It's about time they turned out a great criminal. After all there are 250,000,000 in the world. Nearly a third of the white population. They've plenty of brains and ability and guts. And now

Moscow's taught one of them the technique.' Mr Big himself says almost exactly the same thing to Bond near the end of the novel: 'In the history of negro emancipation there have already appeared great athletes, great musicians, great writers, great doctors and scientists. In due course, as in the developing history of other races, there will appear negroes great and famous in every other walk of life … It is unfortunate for you that you have encountered the first of the great negro criminals.'

Live and Let Die was reviewed by the Jamaica *Gleaner* when it came out in hardback the following year. The paper's regular reviewer found it 'a taut, exciting, intelligent and extremely sophisticated whodunnit'. But two years later, a paperback was picked up by George Panton, a black writer for the paper. Noting that Fleming's house on the north coast 'ranked high among the fabulous dwellings there', but that he himself did not 'in the normal course of events meet the glitter set from our Golden Coast', he went on to express his dismay and disgust at the book, and in particular the exchange quoted above. 'Surely one is not being over-sensitive at the implied condescension,' he asked, before describing M's comments as 'provocative'. Not that these attitudes surprised him: 'There is a special West Indian touch that many of us will find all too familiar,' he wrote. So, for this reader, Fleming's attempt at 'affection' misfires.

Writing about his time in Jamaica right at the end of his life, Fleming's proudest boast was that he had 'learned about living amongst, and appreciating, coloured people – two very different lessons I would never have absorbed if my life had continued in its pre-Jamaican metropolitan rut'. The *Gleaner* journalist, and friend of Fleming, Morris Cargill, writing in the same book, *Ian Fleming Introduces Jamaica*, set out the manifesto of the work as aiming to 'tell about the things he saw and experienced, and to tell them from the Jamaican point of view – a point of view he had been increasingly adopting as year by year Jamaica worked her magic on him'.

Fleming, newly-landed at Kingston airport, signs a James Bond novel for a local fan.

But what did the 'Jamaican point of view' and 'living amongst, and appreciating, coloured people' actually mean to Fleming? Cargill, who disliked Ann, criticised her for not wanting to see anyone in Jamaica except friends from England, 'whereas Ian was a gregarious person and liked to meet all the local tradespeople and that sort of thing'. There's no doubt that Ian did genuinely like Jamaicans, whom he saw as 'full of goodwill and cheerfulness and humour'. According to Violet's great-niece Olivia, Fleming was 'integrated' into Oracabessa life by Violet, who in his absence allowed people onto the property and the local revivalist church to use the beach for baptisms. But, like almost all white expatriates, most white Jamaicans and certainly all tourists, Fleming did not have any real, equal-status black Jamaican friends. All his relationships were, in the end, with 'tradespeople and that sort of thing'. Chris Blackwell explains that this was not about racism, but class: 'It was like the South of France, which the British pretty much invented. They would all go there and wouldn't mix with the French. It was the same thing in Jamaica. It's not a racial thing, it's just you don't have anything to say to anybody.'

At the time of writing *Live and Let Die*, Fleming's ideal black person – and the one for whom Bond has the greatest 'natural affection', even 'love' – was Quarrel.

When Bond arrives in Jamaica from Florida, he is brought up to date by the station head Strangways about Mr Big's Isle of Surprise, and filled in on the arrangements made for him. Strangways has organised a house opposite the island called Beau Desert (situated, it seems, very close to Coward's Blue Harbour); there's also a car, and 'a good man to act as your factotum. A Cayman Islander called Quarrel. Best swimmer and fisherman in the Caribbean. Terribly keen. Nice chap.'

When Bond and Quarrel meet the next morning, 'Bond liked him immediately.' Usually being mixed race is a sure sign of devilry for Fleming, but for Quarrel he makes an exception, as 'There was the blood of Cromwellian soldiers and buccaneers in him.' Quarrel reappears in Fleming's second Jamaica novel, *Dr No*, in which we are told that he is descended from a 'pirate of Morgan's time'. This is of course highly commendable in the Fleming universe, and also means that only his 'spatulate nose and the pale palms of his hands were negroid', he is 'brown-skinned' and, like Aubyn Cousins, has 'warm grey eyes'. (Writing about the Cayman Islands in 1957 in the *Sunday Times*, Fleming notes approvingly that Caymanians 'have somehow managed to keep their bloodstream free of negroid strains'.)

Quarrel ticks all the Fleming boxes. As well as having pirate and old English blood, he comes from 'the most famous race of seamen in the world' and, it is soon made clear, is knowledgeable and sympathetic to nature, as well as an aficionado of the reef. He calls Bond 'Captain', just as Fleming loved being called 'the Commander'. He also has, to Fleming and Bond, the endearing and disarming characteristics they associated with 'coloured people': 'innocence'; 'simple lusts and desires'; 'reverence for superstition and instincts, and childish faults'.

When Quarrel first meets Bond, 'there was no desire to please, or humility in his voice. He was speaking as mate of the ship and his manner was straightforward and candid. That moment defined their relationship. It remained that of a Scots laird with his head stalker; authority was unspoken and there was no room for servility.'

So here we have Fleming's ideal colonial relationship. There is no challenge to Bond's superiority – rank, as on a ship, is taken as read; Quarrel is unmistakably 'staff'. But with mutual respect established and power relations solidified by history and custom, there is no need for coercion. Quarrel will 'follow Bond unquestioningly'. He therefore almost embodies the frustrations of Norman Manley – 'We are still a colonial people.' He is also the closest Bond is going to get to a real black friend.

Part of Quarrel's job as 'factotum', or servant to Bond, is to get him in shape for his underwater adventures to come. For almost all the novel's duration, Bond is in jeopardy, his whereabouts known to his enemies. This is, of course, a big part of the excitement of the book. But two-thirds of the way through, Fleming gives Bond and the reader a wonderful moment of stillness when he and Quarrel retreat to Negril on the far western coast of Jamaica.

Here Fleming relishes taking his readers to the idyllic, touristic Jamaica, where 'nothing has happened since Columbus'. It is, for Bond, 'the most beautiful beach he had ever seen, five miles of white sand sloping easily into the breakers and, behind, the palm trees marching in graceful disarray to the horizon'. Jamaican fishermen with 'grey canoes pulled up beside pink mounds of discarded conch shells' have taken the place of the 'Arawak Indians', but otherwise 'there is the impression that time has stood still'.

Here Bond runs, swims and sails and is taught the ways of the reef by Quarrel (although his knowledge of the dangerous West Indian fish in the tanks in Florida, and the attack habits of sharks and barracuda, indicates that he already has substantial underwater expertise). In the evenings they enjoy the 'quick melancholy' of the tropical twilight, then hear the 'zing and tinkle' of the crickets and tree frogs. Bond's Man Friday, Quarrel, gives him a massage, then cooks for him 'succulent meals of fish and eggs and vegetables'.

A village by the shore at Negril. Unspoilt in Fleming's day, it is now home to a number of hotels, nightclubs and a golf course.

By the end of the week, 'Bond was sunburned and hard. He had cut his cigarettes down to ten a day and had not had a single drink … all the scales of big city life had fallen away from him.' Quarrel deems him ready for the challenge ahead.

Fleming's love of his version of Jamaica is unmissable; and the contrast with the United States Bond had recently left could not be clearer. Arriving on the island, Bond had been immensely 'glad to be back' amongst its 'staunch, humorous people', its 'beautiful old plantations' with 'romantic' names and its old-fashioned imperial culture. As well as feeling a long way from the troubles besetting the Empire – the Mau Mau uprising in Kenya, or the 'emergency' in Malaya – there is nothing here of America's 'women at the wheel, their menfolk docilely beside them', the shouty notices and 'the thick rash of television aerials and the impact of TV on hoardings and shop windows'. In the place of the 'grim suburbs of Philadelphia showing their sores, like beggars' and the 'gloomy silent withered forests of Florida' there are the 'gleaming moonlit foothills of the Blue Mountains', the 'beautiful little banana port of Oracabessa' and the 'soft green flanks' of Jamaica. Instead of 'melted butterscotch' and 'Ham-n-Eggs', Bond enjoys 'paw-paw with a slice of green lime, a dish piled with red bananas, purple star-apples and tangerines, scrambled eggs and bacon, Blue Mountain coffee – the most delicious in the world – Jamaican marmalade, almost black, and guava jelly'. Surveying the view of Kingston and Port Royal from Strangways' veranda up on Stony Hill, 'he thought how lucky he was and what wonderful moments of consolation there were for the darkness and danger of his profession'. The result is that Bond, like Fleming, is at his most relaxed and warm in Jamaica.

With the successful completion of his mission, Bond clears the American/Soviet Mr Big out of British Jamaica at the same time as doing the United States a huge favour by closing down the funding of an enemy spy network on their territory and allowing them to move at last against the Harlem gangsters on gold-smuggling charges. American Leiter is a fine friend for Bond, but he is little help. The only time he tries to take the initiative, when he goes off to investigate the worm factory in Florida, he ends up badly injured with an arm and a leg missing and a note attached: 'He disagreed with something that ate him.' (Fleming's original intention was to kill Leiter off, but protests from his literary agent in New York saved him.) There may be plenty of 'Anglo-American snarls to disentangle' at the end, but there is no doubt that it is Bond, Britain's imperial hero, who has triumphed.

Live and Let Die was published on 5 April 1954, with a first printing of 7,500 quickly followed by a 2,000-copy reprint. As with *Casino Royale*, it carried an austere, type-led cover designed by Fleming. Because of the book's sexual content, it was banned in Ireland, which gave it some welcome extra publicity.

Reviews were favourable again, with Fleming's *Sunday Times* exclaiming, 'How wincingly well Mr Fleming writes.' The *TLS* was largely supportive, calling Fleming 'the most interesting recent recruit among thriller-writers', but warning that 'Mr Fleming works often on the edge of flippancy, rather in the spirit of a highbrow having fun writing a parody of "Sapper".' In contrast, the *Daily Telegraph* considered this a strength, that the book 'is more entertaining because Mr Fleming does not take it all too seriously himself'.

Perhaps in the hope that it would evoke fond memories of his trip to Jamaica, on publication Fleming sent a copy of *Live and Let Die* to Winston Churchill. He attached a note: 'It is an unashamed thriller and its only merit is that it makes no demands on the minds of the reader.'

1954-5
Moonraker; Diamonds are Forever

'Most marriages don't add two people together. They subtract one from the other.'

Bond to Tiffany Case, *Diamonds are Forever*

Only two years after their wedding at Port Maria, Ian and Ann's marriage was showing signs of strain. The sexual side of the relationship had diminished after Ann was left with great scars after her second Caesarean, and fears that they had both expressed of their incompatibility – with her sociable and him not – had been realised. On their return to London from Jamaica in March 1953, they had moved into a house in Victoria Square, near the station, and here Ann continued her role as society hostess. According to Cecil Beaton, a regular visitor, 'She now corrals the people she finds interesting in her small but congenial house ... This she has made into an oasis for people who are creative in some field ... all her friends agree that her parties are more amusing than they were at Warwick House.'

But Ian hated the parties. He found the seemingly ever-present 'creative people' – including Lucian Freud, Alastair Forbes, Malcolm

Muggeridge, Stephen Spender, Frederick Ashton and James Lee-Milne – gossipy and full of themselves. He started calling Ann's soirées 'gab-fests'. Mary Crickmere, who lived in the basement and cooked the meals – her husband lived there too, and worked as valet, driver and waiter – remembered the racket the intellectuals made: 'The noise in there! They all talked, nobody listened.' Ann's daughter Fionn, who was fifteen when her mother married Ian, remembers how stuffy and claustrophobic the house became when full to the brim. She called Victoria Square Ian's 'gilded cage'. Loelia Westminster, much more a friend of Ann than Ian, later wrote that 'The Flemings' life together deteriorated ... Ann's friends did not listen to him and he grew sulky. Finally he refused to go to her parties.' Indeed, few of Ann's friends thought much of Ian. Malcolm Muggeridge wrote in his diary after one evening at Victoria Square that he couldn't understand why Ann had fallen for him.

Each weekend Ann and Ian would drive down to their cottage at St Margaret's Bay, where Caspar lived full time with his nanny, Joan Sillick. Now in her forties, she had performed the same role for Raymond and Fionn O'Neill. Yet even at St Margaret's, Caspar would see little of his parents, only being brought down from his playroom to meet them for a brief moment before dinner and then taken back upstairs. At times, Ian would get a bee in his bonnet about his son – on one occasion he became obsessed with Spock's book, *Baby and Childcare*; on another he was appalled when Sillick took Caspar on a bus. But generally he tried to make up for his absence by being overprotective. Sillick told Fleming biographer Andrew Lycett that, like many men of his generation and class, Ian wasn't much of a father. 'He couldn't cope at all,' she remembered.

Before Ann and Ian's next trip to Goldeneye, Jamaica paid host to the new Queen, Elizabeth II, and her consort Prince Philip, who were on their first Commonwealth tour. The visit, in November 1953, was of great importance to the Governor, Sir Hugh Foot: the monarch was key to his vision of Jamaica's future. Although, as he wrote to London the following year, he believed 'whole-heartedly in West Indian self-government' (within a federation), he did not see this as an inevitable jettisoning of British interest and influence in the region.

The Whig historian Thomas Macaulay famously declared that the day the Raj ended would be 'the proudest day in English history', not because the Empire had failed, but because it had given way to a new transcendent realm: 'the imperishable empire of our arts and our morals, our literature and our laws', just as the civilisation of ancient Rome had survived the passing of the Caesars. Like other liberals and progressives, Foot hoped that the end of empire would not really be the end at all, that people would still willingly embrace British institutions of government under self-rule. In 1955, he made a broadcast to the Jamaican people, declaring: 'I as an Englishman know very well how many faults and failures there have been in England's long history. But some of the finest things that the world has ever known have come from England. We see them here in our religious life and our judicial processes and our education and our form of government.' (Foot later wrote: 'We may have been accused of having been paternalistic. Perhaps in a sense we were.')

The key to this was the idea of the Commonwealth, seen by optimists not as a 'mere afterglow following sunset, ending in night', but 'a rebirth, an empire transforming itself into a free Commonwealth family'. In this family, the strong would help the weak, and British influence would be sustained without the 'mother country' having to 'bear the burdens of command'. Of course, this could not be maintained through loyalty to the government of Great Britain. Instead, it would be the 'apolitical' monarch who would unite the Commonwealth through an emotional bond. Churchill was fond of quoting the old aphorism: 'There are two ways to rule men – by bamboozle or bamboo.' The cult of the royals, with its costumes, march-pasts and salutes, would, it was hoped, fascinate the former subject peoples.

In the West Indies, there was fertile ground, thanks in part to the popular but entirely incorrect impression that Queen Victoria had been personally responsible for Emancipation. In fact, emotional loyalty to the British monarch was one of the very few things that almost all sections of the Jamaican population could agree on. Bustamante, who had been sent to meet George VI in London in 1948 and come back 'a most loyal supporter of the Crown', welcomed the Queen's visit as the 'occasion when theories of Majesty and Royalty become real and alive'. Pearl Flynn, then a young woman living in Oracabessa, remembers, 'The Queen was like Lord you know. We would line up for hours.' Another black Jamaican recalled that 'There was total respect for the head of state. We stood up in Montego Bay and cheered. It was fun.'

Every second of the Queen's schedule was accounted for: opening roads, greeting endless parish officials and parochial boards, with everyone wearing 'all Orders and Decorations'. Villages in which the royal cavalcade was to slow down were listed so that the crowds could be prepared. Guards of honour and military parades were frequent. It was all a very untropical rush, and with no space or time given to spontaneity, the young Queen struggled to project any sort of personality.

Norman Manley was ill, so his place at official events was taken by his wife Edna, sparking rumours that he was snubbing the British monarch. Edna found that the young Queen had 'the character and stability to carry the role she was born into, and that is saying a great deal. But there is no sparkle, as indeed there never could be.' 'How odd and unreal the Royal procedure is,' she wrote in her diary. 'You curtsey here, you curtsey there – in fact you curtsey everywhere. Give me the new democracies, where a friendly handshake is all that is necessary,

The Queen and Prince Philip greeted at Sabina Park cricket ground by 20,000 Jamaican schoolchildren.

with or without gloves.' But even years later she had to concede that British royalty could 'rouse a storm of loyalty and excitement, exactly the same way that Queen Victoria would have been felt to be the repository of all wisdom, all power'.

Ann and Ian's trip out to the island in early 1954 began badly: Ian was ill and they suffered twelve days of guests they had tired of after two. They also found themselves less enamoured with the north-coast party scene they had once so energetically been a part of.

The seventh of January had seen the opening of Round Hill, a milestone in the history of Jamaica tourism. It was the brainchild of John Pringle, the son of Carmen Pringle who ran Sunset Lodge. His idea was to set up a 'cottage colony for the very rich or beautiful'. Individual villas would be sold to those who wanted a house in

Jamaica but without the trouble of absentee ownership. They could also have a share in hotel profits if their cottage was rented out. It was an entirely new way of running a resort.

The year before, on a flight to New York to raise money for the venture, Pringle had found himself sitting next to Noël Coward. 'He was a great friend of my mother's but I'd never met him before,' remembered Pringle. 'I started to tell him about Round Hill and went into a lot of detail and showed him some photographs I had. And with his hand tightly clasping my knee, he said, "If you stop boring me, I'll buy one of your fucking cottages!"' Coward introduced Pringle to Adele Astaire, who also bought a cottage, as well as five or six other people. Coward also performed at the launch party in January 1954.

Pringle imported two French chefs from the George V hotel in Paris, and Round Hill fast became the destination of choice for the biggest celebrities of the day, including Bing Crosby, Clark Gable, Paul Newman, Alfred Hitchcock, Leonard Bernstein, Cole Porter and John and Jackie Kennedy. Its model was widely copied around the world.

John Pringle would also later go on to become a successful minister for tourism, but there is something slightly ironic about him having such a key role in the Jamaica tourist business. In 1938, his father Kenneth had published a book called *Waters of the West*. In this he describes the effects of tourism in Jamaica as 'positively evil', believing that visitors, 'with their mimic high life and imbecile deportment … have sown habits of discontent in the fertile imaginations of the natives of the shores which they have honoured'. Montego Bay, where his son and his estranged wife Carmen Pringle now ran their hotels, was 'a hundred yards of sand on which several hundred rich and roseate wrecks are lying like strange fish'. At night the moon had never shone 'on a more fantastic assembly of ghosts'.

In 1946, there had been 229 hotel rooms in Montego Bay. By 1956, there were 1,350. With so many hotels, the north coast now saw polo matches, balls and bonfire beach parties every night.

Ian was not an enthusiast of Montego Bay. According to Ivar Bryce, he 'regarded it as a tourist trap'. Coward, who had paid £40,000 for his Round Hill cottage, sold it two years later for a substantial profit. 'Montego was horrible as usual,' he wrote in his diary soon after. 'Roundhill is full, packed with all the soi-disant gratin of New York … there is no doubt about it, the idle rich are, always have been, and always will be, boring … I would rather live in a shack on a deserted sandbank than be stuck in Roundhill with all those shrill dullards.'

For the austere Scot part of Fleming's make-up, it was all a bit too much, and in his Atticus column for the *Sunday Times* in March 1954 he expressed his regret at Jamaica's 'crazily inflated tourist boom' and castigated Jamaican hoteliers ('most of them "plantocrats" who have gravitated to the hotel business since the war') for their high prices. Even the *Gleaner*, usually a cheerleader for tourist development in the country, reflected that it was 'Rather odd that in Jamaica, we pay our own people, the labourers, less than anywhere else in the world, and charge the visitor more!' Jet-set characters in Fleming's books – Count Lippe, Count Vicenzo – tend to be worthless sorts. In *On Her Majesty's Secret Service*, Bond's father-in-law Marc-Ange speaks disparagingly of the 'fast international set', and in *Moonraker*, M voices his suspicion of 'sunburned men in England'. 'Either they've not got a job of work to do or they put it on with a sun-lamp.'

By now, the new Jamaica Tourist Board, under the leadership of the hugely energetic Abe Issa, was also targeting the less wealthy in the United States as potential tourists. The aim was to encourage visitors during the summer months, when up until now almost all the hotels shut down. (It was also hoped that less wealthy visitors would be more 'interested in Jamaica and Jamaicans' than the 'playboy' variety of winter visitor, who spent the time in 'sybaritic' torpor.) The campaign was a great success, with obliging American journalists praising Jamaica's sunshine, music and 'British atmosphere'. The *Charleston*

Gazette also helpfully noted that 'There are no "America. Go Home!" signs on this island. The Jamaican knows which side his tourist bread is buttered on, and he is prone to kill Americans with kindness.' In August 1955, Pan Am flew 2,400 travel agents and their wives to stay in Jamaica, which they claimed as the 'biggest peacetime human airlift ever attempted'.

The following month, the *Gleaner* reported that the 'success stories in the tourist industry of Jamaica' were not just the big hotel owners and travel agents, but also the 'barefoot boys from country villages in Jamaica who today are respected, well paid, well-shod members of the industry [which] has brought a new life and a new standard of living to the thousands of Jamaican waiters, bartenders, cooks, laundresses'. As well as providing new prosperity, tourism was believed to have 'widened the horizons' of the 'village boys'.

With visitor numbers growing rapidly – doubling between 1951 and 1959 to nearly 200,000, spending an estimated £11 million during the year – tourism was an increasingly vital part of Jamaica's economy, now second only to sugar in terms of foreign currency. But how the island was marketed – what Kenneth Pringle back in 1938 called 'fantastic absurdity and make-believe' – caused concern for some. Evon Blake had for a long time argued that advertising showing beaches empty of local people (except as waiters) or postcards portraying blacks as 'picturesque' peasants – barefoot boys climbing palm trees, donkeys and women with loads on their heads – fostered American racist perceptions of the black population of Jamaica. 'The American who comes here for the first time,' he wrote, 'is surprised when he walks out of a hotel and sees ... we are a civilized people and not savages.'

Fleming, whose version of Jamaica in *Live and Let Die* also stressed its 'pre-lapsarian' side, considered himself different from the run-of-the-mill tourists. In *The Diamond Smugglers*, he speaks favourably of his interviewee in Sierra Leone who has 'invested in local property' and as such 'had a genuine stake in the country'. But he and Coward were also tiring of the winter-sun expatriate set, and their interminable cocktail parties, 'usually three or four a week and frequently more and the same groups of people foregather, wearing more or less the same clothes and discussing more or less the same things. The same drinks and same canapés are served.' Now they both preferred to meet and play canasta in the evenings or just spent the time with their guests from England.

In February, Peter Quennell arrived to stay for three weeks at Goldeneye. His passage had been paid for by Ann, who wanted company while Ian wrote. Originally a poet, Quennell had become a literary historian and essayist as well as a founder editor of *History Today* and editor of the conservative *Cornhill Magazine* from 1951. He was the first of Ann's literary friends. He adored her and became known as 'Lady Rothermere's Fan'. He was also a great favourite of her daughter.

Quennell was unusual among Ann's circle in that he got on with Ian too. He put this down to the fact that he was 'neither a wild bohemian nor a rampant homosexual'. 'I must admit,' he later wrote, 'I could not take to James Bond. But Ian himself I liked.' The difference between them, he thought, was that Fleming altogether lacked Bond's 'self-esteem and unquestioning self-assurance'. He saw Ian as 'a natural melancholic, subject to bouts of gloom … puritan, too, at heart perhaps an ingrained Calvinist'. (In *Moonraker*, Fleming approvingly comments on part of M's character: 'The Puritan and the Jesuit who live in all leaders of men'.)

The author or editor of sixty-two books, Quennell was sometimes accused of over-flowery language. Nonetheless, his is the most lyrical account we have of the charms of Goldeneye and its surrounds. As with other visitors, there is little in his descriptions about the politics of Jamaica or its people – a sight of some road sweepers evokes for him scenes from a French novel – but plenty about the wildlife and the beauties of the reef.

In his book, *The Sign of the Fish*, published in 1960 and dedicated to 'my friends at Goldeneye', Quennell described how arriving late at Montego Bay airport, he reached the house just as dawn was breaking: 'dew was glittering on my friends' garden; and the immense arch of a nearly perfect rainbow spanned the Caribbean Sea. Against a backdrop of big expansive flowers, a humming bird perched by the kitchen-door; and at the end of the garden, below a rocky cliff, tufted with palms and festooned with pendulous tree-roots, the transparent wind-ruffled lagoon thrust up gentle glassy waves, which lapped into the rosy mouth of a conch lying half-buried at the edge of the water.'

In the 'romantic half-tamed garden' he found the tropical flowers not to his liking: 'huge papery, obtrusive blossoms that often suggest the showy merchandise of some prodigious bargain-basement'. But he enjoyed the birds, including the kling-klings and the doctor birds, which would drop down towards him 'in a celestial spark of metallic brilliance'.

Fleming with his gardener, Felix Barriffe. The garage and staff quarters can be seen on the right.

Although a timid and inexperienced swimmer, Quennell found the lagoon off the Goldeneye beach 'a country in itself'. 'As one lies face down on the warm resilient water and turns one's glass-fronted helmet from side to side, the surface, viewed from below, becomes a sheet of wrinkled quicksilver, shedding a silvery-soft light that ripples and trembles across the sandy floor. Large fish move like planets; shoals hang like constellations, suspended in the blue-grey distance.' Among the forests of coral and weed, he admires the angelfish, 'orange and heliotrope: youthful Parrot Fish, blue and grass-green, with wavering rosy touches around their scales: Butterfly Fish striped black and yellow; and a fish that, having a large peacock's eye near the tail-fin, seems perpetually to be swimming backwards. There are other, more menacing presences – a miniature Barracuda, pencil-thin and torpedo-straight, which hovers alongside the swimmer and fixes him with its flat malevolent gaze, and, now and then, the speckled ribbon of a fierce Moray Eel, nosing and undulating through a bed of sea-grass.' He soon became an 'intrepid swimmer', unruffled as a 'shark sailed by'. At the end of the day, he wrote, 'The Caribbean night falls with a weight and density from which it is difficult to believe that day will ever recover.'

For three 'calm and unusually happy weeks', Quennell corrected the proofs of his new book while Ann 'painted flowers and fishes and shells, and Ian hammered out his latest story'.

Like others, Quennell noticed that Fleming 'worked and played according to a prearranged schedule that nobody might interrupt'. Ian was furious when Quennell, on his way for a morning swim, crossed his view as he lay in bed observing 'the morning freshness of his garden'. 'Ann was therefore instructed to suggest that I should change my irritating habit and, so as to remain invisible from Ian's bedroom, take a longer path behind the house.'

'Another peculiarity of the place,' Quennell explained, 'was that it was always rather hard to get a drink when you wanted it. The

Fleming strikes a meditative pose looking out of the large main window.

Commander tended to drink in the American way. Vodka martinis
or very brown whisky sodas would appear late in the day, and he
would drink rather heavily then. But at dinner itself there was seldom
anything to drink; and I had usually to ask Ian if I could have some
beer; at which Ian would order "A bottle of beer for Mr Quennell,
Violet!" in sepulchral and reproving tones, and Violet would throw up
her hands and eyes, muttering "Lordie, Lordie!", and you would feel
that you were upsetting the routine of the entire place.'

Fleming biographer John Pearson makes the point that readers
of the Bond novels might have imagined Goldeneye as some sort of
tropical Shangri-La, with luxurious decadence everywhere, but as
Ian's friend Robert Harling, who visited on at least two occasions,
commented, Fleming was more like a 'genial Caribbean squire'.
His routine, Pearson wrote, was 'far closer to the life of some self-
absorbed eighteenth-century original than to the glamour of the

international millionaire smart-set who build their summer houses along this coast'.

By now the familiar routine – Violet and the shaving water, the instructions for his breakfast, the swimming, writing, drinking – was set in stone, and 'traditions' established for Goldeneye that could not be broken. Although Ian was far less defensive and prickly with other people in Jamaica than he was in England, if his routine was disturbed, it 'awoke the authoritarian' in him, as Ann recounted. Violet remembered that 'Everybody understood that his work came first. They respected his schedule.' Ian himself said on *Desert Island Discs* in 1963 that unless he stuck to a routine, 'if I just wait for genius to arrive from the sky, it just doesn't arrive'.

Quennell remembered that during his visit in 1954, Fleming 'evidently enjoyed his work', writing every day from an early breakfast until nearly one o'clock, 'shut into his bedroom and protected from the outer world by wooden blinds, through which the rattle of his typewriter, like a burst of machine-gun fire, regularly swept across the terrace'. He worked at Goldeneye 'with a fierce intensity'.

By 24 February, he had written 30,000 words of his third novel, *Moonraker*. *Moonraker* is unique in the Bond adventures in that it is set entirely in England. The threat that Bond has to deal with is to Britain alone, rather than, in the two previous books, France and the United States.

The villain, Sir Hugo Drax, 'a raving paranoiac', is named after the old sugar estate just down the coast from Goldeneye. Drax Hall was once owned by William Beckford, the gothic novelist recommended by Fleming in his *Horizon* article on the island. In the novel, Drax is one of Britain's leading businessmen, having made a fortune cornering the market in 'columbite', essential for missile technology. Although a bit 'loud-mouthed and ostentatious', he is now a national hero, having offered to produce a missile, the Moonraker, designed to give Britain 'an independent say in world affairs'.

But M's suspicions about Drax are aroused by his cheating at cards, and after Drax is bested by Bond in a game of bridge, M sends in his operative to investigate Drax's establishment on the white cliffs of the south coast of England.

Bond eventually discovers that Drax is an 'enemy within', a Nazi set on achieving revenge for Britain's victory in the war by destroying London, with the help of a Soviet-supplied nuclear warhead.

With only days to save millions of lives and 'British civilization', the plot is exciting and fast-moving, but the doomsday scenario, so inflated compared to the previous books, strains believability. The home setting doesn't help. In the exotic badlands of the Caribbean, anything seemed possible, but the familiar ground here adds to the reader's incredulity. The setting also contributes to a feeling of imperial contraction. The British, or at least the part of the population that included Fleming, had believed they were a great people because they had an empire. Now, in *Moonraker*, that empire seems to be on the wane. Drax tells Bond that the British are 'Useless, idle, decadent fools, hiding behind your bloody white cliffs while other people fight your battles. Too weak to defend your colonies, toadying to America with your hat in your hands.' The details of defence establishments in Kent, both modern and ancient, are a reminder of threats very close to home. At Manston, previously the forward aerodrome of the Battle of Britain, it is American jets writing 'white scribbles in the sky'.

In the place of empire, *Moonraker* is a hymn to England. Even Krebs, Drax's Nazi sidekick, is moved by the sight of the Kentish countryside, and Bond and his heroine Gala Brand are brought together by a shared appreciation of the view from the iconic white cliffs: 'where Caesar had first landed two thousand years before … a panorama full of colour and excitement and romance'. Bond even calls English cooking 'the best in the world'. Under threat from the Moonraker rocket is 'the Palace. The nursemaids in the park … the softly beating heart of London.' In an essay for the *Spectator*, Fleming later wrote that 'of course I have the affectionate reverence for Sir Winston Churchill that most of us share'. The icon of Britain's moment of glory in 1940 is similarly idolised by Gala Brand as the voice of every important moment in her life, even though – at the time of writing – Prime Minister Churchill, after several strokes, was doing his best to hide the collapse in his health and vitality.

Much later, Fleming would describe Bond as having only two virtues, patriotism and courage. In *Moonraker*, this patriotism has a distinctly naval feel: nowhere else are we reminded so many times of Bond's preference for navy blue clothes. When Bond contemplates a suicide effort to stop the atomic bomb hitting London, he declares, 'The boy stood on the burning deck. I've wanted to copy him since I was five.' But it is clear from the story that the power of the Royal Navy, the bedrock of British imperial glory, is a thing of the past, and not just because of wartime losses and budget cuts. Missiles such as the Moonraker have made ships obsolete. What's more, the atomic age has produced a new threat against which no destroyer can operate: 'the most deadly saboteur in the history of the world – the little man with the heavy suitcase'. It is a melancholy picture for Fleming's England.

Moonraker is also unique in that, for once, Bond doesn't get the girl. Before he meets Gala Brand, he knows her 'vital statistics': 'Height: 5ft 7. Weight: 9 Stone. Hips 38. Waist: 26. Bust: 38. Distinguishing marks: Mole on upper curvature of right breast. Hm! Thought Bond.' Ian had asked Ann for the 'perfect measurements' for Gala Brand, but apparently she got it wrong. 'Fortunately,' Ann wrote to her brother from Jamaica, 'Noël brought a Mainbocher [couture] saleswoman for a cocktail and all is well.' Even in this least Caribbean of the books, Bond and his heroine come closest to union while swimming: 'At once nothing else mattered but the velvet ice of the sea and the beauty of the patches of sand between the waving hair of the seaweed.' Bond even catches a lobster on the English coastline. But there is a new sourness to his relations with women: we learn that he spends his evenings 'making love, with a rather cold passion, to one of three similarly disposed married women', and that 'Marriage and children and a home were out of the question if [he was] to be of any use "in the field".' In fact, while attempting to make Bond a less 'cardboard character' than in the previous books, what emerges is a distinct portrait of the 'sleek bachelor' of Fleming's pre-wedding days.

Bond triumphs over Drax, of course, but what results is a huge cover-up of the whole episode. 'What's the alternative? ... War with Russia? Lots of people on both sides of the Atlantic would be only too glad of an excuse,' says M, worried about the current bellicosity of the Americans. In the summer of the previous year, Fleming had been in the United States and had found, seemingly, the whole country, led by Senator Joe McCarthy, obsessed by 'anti-American activities'. In November 1953, in one of his first columns for the *Sunday Times'* Atticus, Fleming had written that this 'prairie fire of fear, intolerance and hatred [and] atmosphere of purge and persecution' were ridiculous. There is even a suggestion that the Cold War had made the United States as dangerous as the Soviet Union. For his next novel, *Diamonds are Forever*, Fleming would step back from both the apocalyptic threat of *Moonraker* and from the Cold War.

Unlike all the other 1950s Bond novels, the villains of *Diamonds are Forever* are not working directly or indirectly for the Soviets, as Bond acknowledges: 'What's [M] so worried about?' he asks. 'It's not as if this was Iron Curtain business.'

Instead, Bond's mission is a rather grubby one. Diamond smuggling from the British colony of Sierra Leone is causing a fall in income for the Treasury in London. M outlines the issue: 'Seems that most of what they call "gem" diamonds are mined on British territory and that ninety per cent of all diamond sales are carried out in London.' It's the 'biggest dollar-earner we've got. So when something goes wrong with it, the Government gets worried.' So Bond is sent, effectively, on an economic mission for hard-pressed Britain, a need Fleming acknowledges when he writes in his *Spectator* article that 'we cannot afford to eat forever on borrowed money'. M seems almost embarrassed by the profit extracted by his country, telling Bond: 'Don't ask me why. The British got hold of the business at the beginning of the century and we've managed to hold on to it.' The unspoken coda is 'for now'. By 1955, Sierra Leone was well on the way to self-government and independence. By the time Fleming was writing *Diamonds are Forever*, there was nothing 'forever' about the Empire in Africa (the Gold Coast would lead the way, achieving independence as Ghana in 1957).

There is also an implication in M's comment that Britain has no real right to these riches. In *The Diamond Smugglers*, a collection of essays for the *Sunday Times* that would be published as a book in 1957, Fleming is similarly shamefaced at the situation in Sierra Leone, describing the colony as underfinanced and 'pretty near the bottom of the pile' of British priorities. The British local expert he interviews even declares that 'One's almost ashamed of it being an English possession.' The root of the problem of smuggling, he explains, is 'the general idea among the illicit miners that the soil of Sierra Leone belongs to the Sierra Leoneans'.

There's nothing so subversive in the novel itself; but the plot does highlight Britain's parlous economic situation, and the lack of sympathy forthcoming from the United States, where the smuggled diamonds are being sold. For the Americans, this is only a very small part of the fight against the Mafia, so the FBI, M confirms, 'won't be much help to us, I'm afraid'. Moreover, M doesn't want to hand the case over to the FBI and have the Americans 'pick Britain's chestnuts out of the fire'.

Bond's journey to the US, as he infiltrates the diamond smuggling pipeline, gives Fleming the chance for plenty more sneering about

America and Americans. Local smoked salmon is 'a poor substitute for the product of Scotland'. The scenery around Las Vegas is 'a blasted Martian landscape' where the heat 'hit Bond's face like a fist' (the heat in Jamaica, in contrast, is described as 'sticky fingers' that 'brush Bond's face'). The mountains, unlike Jamaica's 'soft green', are 'streaked with red like gums bleeding over rotten teeth'. (Recovering from a beating at the hands – or, more exactly, feet – of Spang's heavies, Bond wishfully dreams he is back in Jamaica.) The strip is 'ghastly glitter'. And Leiter, conveniently now privately employed by Pinkerton's detective agency so he can help Bond without official involvement, tells him that the country is utterly crime-ridden: 'Now the hoodlums don't run liquor. They run governments. State governments like Nevada.' The villains have protection from corrupt politicians and officials in Washington. Once again, it takes Englishman Bond to sort it all out: 'Maybe you can strike a blow for Freedom, Home and Beauty with that old rusty equalizer of yours,' says Leiter. Bond has no respect for American gangsters, 'only contempt and dislike', and feels huge relief when he boards the *Queen Elizabeth*, the (actually much-subsidised) symbol of British maritime excellence, and 'the great safe black British belly' of the ship.

There are some excellent set pieces in *Diamonds Are Forever* – the drive-in, the mud-baths, the racetrack at Saratoga (where Bond appreciates 'the extra exotic touch of the negroes'), but the story misses the crazy central megalomania of the villains of the previous two books. The 'knowing looks' to the reader – 'He had been a stage-gangster, surrounded by stage properties'; 'Mike Hammer routine. These American gangsters were too obvious'; 'That was quite an exit. Like something out of an old Buster Keaton film' – feel more tired than arch. 'For Bond it was just the end of another adventure,' Fleming concludes, his weariness palpable.

Fleming would later explain his annual cycle of writing in Jamaica, editing and checking proofs in England in the spring and then, in the autumn, beginning the hunt for ideas for the next book. For him, this was the most difficult, often 'heart-sinking' moment. After *Diamonds are Forever*, he felt wiped out, writing to his friend Hilary Bray: 'I baked a fresh cake in Jamaica this year which I think has finally exhausted my inventiveness as it contains every single method of escape and every variety of suspenseful action that I had omitted from my previous books – in fact everything except the kitchen sink, and if you can think up a good plot involving kitchen sinks, please send it along speedily.' Peter Quennell, who was in Jamaica for the creation of the last two novels, believed that, 'As early as 1955 [Ian] was already growing tired of Bond.'

Meanwhile, *Moonraker* had been published to a number of good reviews, the *New Statesman* commenting: 'Mr Fleming is splendid, he stops at nothing.' In the *Spectator*, John Metcalfe wrote: 'It is utterly disgraceful – and highly enjoyable,' but also said that it was not Fleming's best. The *TLS* called it a 'disappointment'. *Diamonds are Forever* had a similarly mixed reception when it was published in April 1956; the ability of the British Fleming to write convincingly about America was much praised, but the *TLS* called it Fleming's 'weakest book, a heavily padded story'. By then Fleming had completed his next novel to first draft and was seriously considering killing off his hero.

Apart from the somewhat guilty colonial exploitation and the 'therapeutic anti-Americanism', perhaps what is most interesting about *Diamonds are Forever* is the love interest, Tiffany Chase.

She is gorgeous, of course, her 'brazen sexiness' introduced when Bond first sees her, sitting half naked astride a chair like the famous Keeler picture taken by Lewis Morley seven years later. It gets better when Bond discovers she is an accomplished card sharp and a heavy drinker and smoker – abstinence, like that of Rufus B. Saye in this novel, is a sure sign of villainy in the Fleming universe. She and Bond seem made for each other.

The book ends with a long coda aboard the *Queen Elizabeth* that is more than anything a discussion of marriage. Earlier Bond had felt 'they had all the time in the world' (a favourite expression of Fleming's that is also used during the torture scene with Le Chiffre), and that 'they both knew the answer to the big question'. By the end of the novel, 'Bond knew that he was very close to being in love with her'.

But Bond's bachelordom is, in the end, unassailable. He says he can handle life better on his own and tells Tiffany that marriage subtracts rather than adds to two people. He doesn't want to be in the role of 'healer', dealing with a 'patient'. If he married, it would involve the horror of 'handing round canapés in an L-shaped drawing-room. And there'd be all those ghastly "Yes, you did – no I didn't" rows that seem to go with marriage. It wouldn't last. I'd get claustrophobia and run out.' After that, he changes the subject. It's hard not to wonder what Ann made of this, although she claimed not to have read the book.

The troubles of their marriage had a lot to do with the self-centred personalities of both Ann and Ian, which made them, as Noël Coward had accurately predicted, unsuitable for matrimony and monogamy, but also with Goldeneye – Ian's bachelor space – and with Bond. Ann originally thought she had married a newspaperman, as she done before, but now found herself partnered to a popular genre novelist. Ian had written to Ivar Bryce in late 1954: '*Live and Let Die* has the wind under its tail and Annie is horrified that I may be becoming famous which has upset all her calculations.' For Ann, Bond was an embarrassment. To her friends, she now referred to Ian's books as 'horror comics' and 'pornography'. In public she would decry 'these dreadful Bond books'.

When Coward read *Moonraker*, he noted in his diary: 'It is the best he has done yet, very exciting and, although as usual too far-fetched, not quite so much so as the last two and there are fewer purple sex passages. His observation is extraordinary and his talent for description vivid. I wish he would try a non-thriller for a change; I would so love him to triumph over the sneers of Annie's intellectual friends.'

Ian's patience with Ann's circle, so often packed round the dining table at their Victoria Square house, was now running out. Peter Quennell remembered one occasion at dinner where 'the Commander was suffering greatly' sitting next to a duchess. Quennell noted him looking 'very Bond-ish, his handsome Aztec mask deeply scored with lines of pain, weariness and disgust'. Now Fleming much preferred going out to his club to play bridge in the evenings. But it was impossible when he returned home to avoid the 'gab-fest', as to get to his bedroom he had to go through the crowded dining room. There is a story, possibly apocryphal, that he came back one night to hear Ann's friends mockingly reading aloud from *Live and Let Die*.

In the summer of 1954, Ann and Ian had separate holidays – Ian with the Bryces in Vermont, Ann with Fionn in Greece to stay with Patrick Leigh Fermor and his wife. The winter trip to Goldeneye, previously the scene of their happiest times together, now caused rows. Ann wanted to take Caspar, but Ian would not hear of it, arguing somewhat unconvincingly that it was far too dangerous for a two-year-old.

Ann acquiesced, but then insisted that they travel separately so that an accident, such as occurred to a BOAC Stratocruiser just before Christmas 1954, in which twenty-eight people died, would not leave Caspar an orphan. The result was that Ann arrived after Ian and, deciding to get a boat home, left two weeks before him.

While Ian's love for Jamaica was entirely undiminished, for Ann the novelty seems to have worn off. Her letters that year show she left England 'with great reluctance' and was missing Caspar.

This year also saw them meeting and getting to know the *Gleaner* columnist Morris Cargill. He became a close friend of Ian, and would appear as a *Gleaner* journalist in *Dr No* and as a Justice of the Supreme Court in *The Man with the Golden Gun*. Cargill described Fleming as 'a very interesting man. A very nice man.' Ann was 'highly intelligent and beautiful, but very strange. She loved men but disliked other women intensely.' The Fleming marriage, said Cargill, was 'armed neutrality'. Fleming told his new friend that 'he felt totally trapped by the whole thing'.

To keep her company while Ian was, as Ann put it, 'polishing up horror comic number four' – *Diamonds are Forever* – Evelyn Waugh and Peter Quennell came to stay at Goldeneye. Quennell came first and was his usual mellow and accommodating self, 'a peaceful and appreciative guest', alternating 'pursuing humming-birds' with correcting his latest proofs.

Waugh's mother had died in December 1954, and friends recommended he go somewhere warm to get over it. He stayed first with the Brownlows for two weeks but found it, he later told Ann, 'a great intellectual strain to find words simple enough to converse with them – they are indeed a grisly household, gin from ten-thirty on'. Perry Brownlow had 'troubles' and drank far too much whisky, Waugh reported. 'The women concentrate on a smooth sunburn and hairless bronzed shanks, the men lounge and yawn or play cards … There was a lady here went to sleep on a mattress in a red bathing dress and all the vultures thought she was dead and bloody and tried to eat her.'

Waugh sought early refuge with the Flemings, which he much preferred, writing to Ann afterwards: 'Goldeneye was delightful, I should not have believed that a modern house could be so congenial.' He and Quennell reportedly 'hated each other', but here they were forced to put aside their differences. On one occasion they both went rafting on the Rio Grande with Ann, while Ian pressed on with his writing. 'Evelyn wore blue silk pyjamas and a pink-ribboned Panama hat,' Ann wrote to Patrick Leigh Fermor. 'He ordered a stupendous lunch from the Titchfield Hotel – wine packed in ice in biscuit tins, cold roast fowls and legions of hard boiled eggs – he treated Peter as a native bearer and we rode ahead on the first raft, Peter and the biscuit tins behind us; whenever we shot a tiny rapid he roared over his shoulder "Stop looking so poetical and mind the lunch" but alas it was Peter's victory for the river was in spate, our punter inexperienced for he lost balance and fell overboard, we cannoned into the rocks and subsided slowly into the river – Peter said it was like watching an old-fashioned carriage accident … We swam for the shore, Evelyn doing a slow breaststroke, blue eyes blazing and mood much improved, for he liked things to go wrong.'

Waugh struggled with the snorkelling, and according to Quennell was 'entirely unappreciative of nature': 'I have watched him, a cigar in his mouth and a large straw hat crammed on his angry head, wearing a striped suit that increased his resemblance to a rich plantation owner of the last century, stumping ponderously along a Caribbean beach without a glance for the spectacle of sky and sea, despite the humming birds that played through the hedge or the liquid aquamarine of glassy wavelets that slid up against the blanched sand.'

Waugh was also unusual among Goldeneye guests in noticing, or more exactly commenting on, Jamaica beyond the beauties of sea and garden. 'Jamaica is an odd island,' he wrote in a letter to his son, Bron. 'The whole north coast has quite lately become the resort of millionaires, mostly American. Ten years ago the coast was an empty coral strand with a few negro fishing villages. Now it is all Hollywood style villas and huge hotels charging 40 dollars a day for their smallest rooms and the poor negroes cannot find a yard of beach to paddle in … Land on the coast which ten years ago could be bought for £20 an acre now costs £2,000. Great fortunes have been made in land speculation but no benefit goes to the people. Perhaps they will massacre the whites one day. At present they seem too lethargic.'

Waugh was prone to hyperbole in his letters, but it is still an arresting statement. For his part, the Governor, Sir Hugh Foot, remained vigilant against what he saw as the communist threat. Labour leaders suspected of communist links were harassed and arrested. 'The Moscow Trojan horse has arrived in Jamaica,' he declared in 1954. 'It is foreign to every good tradition which has grown up in the island ... it depends on foreign money.' In fact, the entire Latin America region occupied the last place in the Soviet leadership's system of priorities. Small amounts of money were, in the late fifties, passed by the KGB to communist parties in South America, but the Caribbean was ignored. In the event, Foot's personal friendship with and respect for the Manleys, Norman and Edna, and the previous purging of the PNP made him relaxed about the expected victory of Manley's party in the election of January 1955.

Those expelled from the PNP in 1952 had founded their own party, the National Labour Party, and ran three candidates in the 1955 election. Also running was the new Farmers' Party, established by Robert Kirkwood to represent the interests of the landowning class. Neither won a seat at the election, in which the PNP garnered over 50 per cent of the vote and achieved a majority over Bustamante's JLP for the first time.

Manley's victory triggered huge celebrations. 'Massive crowds jammed Duke Street,' Edna wrote in her diary. 'People climbed trees, clung to fences.' A 'huge emotional throng' sang the rousing lines of 'Jamaica Arise'. ('The trumpet has sounded ... so awake from your slumber...')

Norman Manley's speech on winning showed a new leader desperate to look and move forward, unlike some of Jamaica's white semi-residents. 'I am now stripped of the rancor or remembrance of hurt in the past,' he declared, 'and offer to one and all to go forward from here for a better Jamaica.'

There were, indeed, grounds for hope that Jamaica's appalling poverty and inequality might at last be surmountable. It was an optimistic time. Both major parties supported the establishment of the West Indies Federation, the fast-track to dominion status. Bauxite mining had started in earnest in 1952, even if its extraction was in the hands of North American companies. Manley renegotiated the contracts so Jamaica got a bigger royalty from the money made by the foreign companies. As a result, by 1957 it was one of the country's biggest foreign exchange earners.

Sugar had revived a little, driven in part by the activities of Tate & Lyle. Although Manley was amongst those concerned that tourism would 'spoil' Jamaica and Jamaicans, the business was expanding rapidly, and the mass emigration of Jamaicans to Britain, which had risen from 2,000 in 1952 to nearly 20,000 in 1955, was now bringing in hefty remittances. The new government also set about land reform, founded the Jamaica Broadcasting Corporation, widened the intake of children to the best schools and centrally planned industrial development.

Morris Cargill, in an article in late 1954, had described Manley as 'always more skillful as a national psychiatrist than as a politician'. For Manley, Jamaica's biggest challenge was overcoming the psychological legacy of its past. He believed that it was the colonial relationship going back to slavery that had made black Jamaicans 'lethargic', to quote Waugh, and had created a culture of passive victimhood and dependency. 'We have to stop being colonials and start being Jamaicans,' he frequently declared. He saw the 'natural' subservience and 'childishness' of the likes of Fleming's Quarrel character as holding Jamaica back.

Pearl Flynn, long-time resident of Oracabessa, sees this time as a watershed. She was working at the famous Shaw Park Hotel near Ocho Rios, owned by an Englishman. There was a huge staff, with thirty employed just to do laundry, but in the office, it was all 'white girls' apart from her and one other woman. The two black staff had to eat separately from their fellow office workers and Pearl protested:

'I don't see why me and the telephone operator from St Mary, we should sit with the gardeners, who come out of the sun and sweat. So I said I don't eat.' Her stand was successful and she and her friend were 'promoted' to the smarter restaurant: 'We were satisfied,' she says. She also tells the story, amid much gleeful laughter from her listening friends, of how 'Mr [Frank] Pringle, who was the ADC to the Governor, came up one night. A taxi driver by the name of John Pottinger drove up and parked somewhere. And he came out and said, "You are not supposed to park there!" So this taxi man said, "I'm not going to move."

'Pringle said, "Do you know who I am? I am the ADC to the Governor!"

'And the man said, "You could be the ADC to Jesus Christ himself, but I'm not moving."'

It seems a trivial incident, but not to Jamaicans who remember the unthinking subservience of former times. 'From then things began to get a bit better,' Pearl remembers, 'because they see the natives were getting, you know, different … getting hostile, becoming themselves.'

This was a change spreading outwards across the country. Cargill noted that 'Jamaica in 1955 had come a long way from the outpost of empire of 1935. Increasing numbers of black or coloured people were in high positions of all kinds.' At the same time, there was an upsurge of literature, theatre and the visual arts that celebrated black courage, strength and beauty. The popularity of hair-straightening and skin-bleaching products – promoted through demonstrations by the 'House of Issa' – began slowly to decline. Painters, playwrights and novelists stressed the need for self-reliance and self-confidence, underlining that black Jamaicans were worthy material for art. In Port Maria, the literary Quill and Ink Club, led by Rupert Meikle, had the motto 'Po'[or] thing, but mine own is better than fine raiment.'

Norman Manley always argued that 'political awakening must and always goes hand in hand with cultural growth'. And as what he called 'the dead hand of colonialism' was gradually lifted during the 1950s, so 'a freedom of spirit was released and the desert flowered'. In turn, nationalist poets and writers such as Roger Mais, Una Marson, John Hearne, Victor Stafford Reid, George Campbell, Archie Lindo and Evon Blake influenced and gave confidence to the politicians in the new House of Representatives, who now demanded that control of finance and local government be in elected hands. In 1957, the old imperial Executive Council was abolished in favour of a council of elected ministers. It was another firm step towards independence – now the British held power over only foreign policy and defence.

For Morris Cargill, writing in the *Gleaner*, it was as much about psychology as politics: 'The umbilicus which attached us so sadly to Mother England was as much a fantasy as a reality and had to be cut.' The 'need for independence', he continued, 'the need to cut ourselves away from a deadening childishness was, and is, a profound psychological need'.

Ironically, the same year as Norman Manley's ground-breaking election in 1955 saw an anniversary – 300 years of British rule of Jamaica. To help mark the occasion, the island was blessed with a visit from Princess Margaret, in whose name an edict was issued making it clear that Her Royal Highness would not dance with black Jamaicans. Coward thought this stupid: 'Jamaica is a coloured island and if members of our Royal Family visit it they should be told to overcome prejudice.' Sir Hugh Foot describes it as the only order from London in his career that he entirely ignored.

The Princess's visit was a great success. The only complaint recorded by *Public Opinion* from poor black Jamaicans was that she had not spent more time with them. Bustamante was reportedly 'dead gone on' the Princess. Even Michael Manley, son of Norman and Edna and later Jamaica's most controversial prime minister, wrote in his newspaper column for *Public Opinion* that she was 'a very young woman of rare charm'. Edna Manley thought differently, however, concluding from her meeting with the Princess that 'whatever the magic that attaches to a throne it belongs to the past'. But she was in a minority among Jamaicans. As an American reporter wrote, 'The populace would dearly love to see the pretty Princess appointed as the first Governor-General of the new West Indies Federation.' So in spite of all the changes, it seemed that the 'bamboozle' still worked in Jamaica. Nonetheless, when Fleming returned Bond to the island in *Dr No* two years later, he would portray a very different country from the Jamaica of just a few years earlier.

1956
From Russia, with Love

'Doesn't do to get mixed up with neurotic women in this business. They hang on your gun-arm, if you know what I mean.'

M to Bond, *From Russia, with Love*

The following year's Goldeneye sojourn once again caused furious rows. Ann was determined that Caspar should accompany them, but Ian was adamant that he should stay in England: in the end, Ann herself refused to come. Instead, she used the time to check into a health farm, Enton Hall in Surrey, ostensibly for treatment for fibrosis, but also to help wean her off the barbiturates to which she had become addicted. So, for the first time since their marriage, Ian was on his own at Goldeneye.

This year's book, in terms of reviews and sales, was his best so far. *From Russia, with Love* would remain the novel Fleming was most proud of. Here he returns with great gusto to the Cold War, loading the narrative with insider details on intelligence practices, including references to recent events. The villains are again the Soviets who, the head of SMERSH declares, 'continue to forge everywhere stealthily ahead – revolution in Morocco, arms to Egypt ... trouble in Cyprus, riots in Turkey, strikes in England, great political gains in France'. Their leaders have been visiting 'India and the East and blackguard[ing] the English'.

The Russians only understand the stick, Bond tells us later, but in Britain 'the trouble today is that carrots for all are the fashion. At home and abroad. We don't show teeth any more – only gums.'

But there is one bastion left. At the meeting of SMERSH near the beginning of the novel – in a chapter titled 'The Moguls of Death' – the various strengths and weaknesses of the West's secret services are discussed in an effort to target the best with a 'conspicuous act of terrorism'. The summary is delivered by General Vozdvishensky, to whom Fleming gives impeccable authority: he is a 'professional spy to his fingertips' with a fine war record against Germany and Japan. The smaller countries don't have the resources, the General says. Italy and Spain are too focused on the Mediterranean; the French services have been thoroughly 'penetrated' (although Mathis from *Casino Royale* gets a good mention). The Americans 'have the biggest and richest service among our enemies', but 'have no understanding of the work … [they] try to do everything with money', But 'England is a different matter altogether.'

'Their agents are good,' General Vozdvishensky says. 'They pay them little money – only a thousand or two thousand roubles a month – but they serve with devotion. Yet these agents have no special privileges in England, no relief from taxation and no special shops such as we have, from which they can buy cheap goods. Their social standing abroad is not high, and their wives have to pass as the wives of secretaries. They are rarely awarded a decoration until they retire. And yet these men and women continue to do this dangerous work. It is curious. It is perhaps the Public School and University tradition. The love of adventure.'

It is this 'spirit of adventure' that has built the Empire and that is now the great hope of Britain 'punching above its weight'. The Service

Goldeneye today. The trees planted by Ian Fleming have grown to maturity but the banana groves that once surrounded the property are long gone.

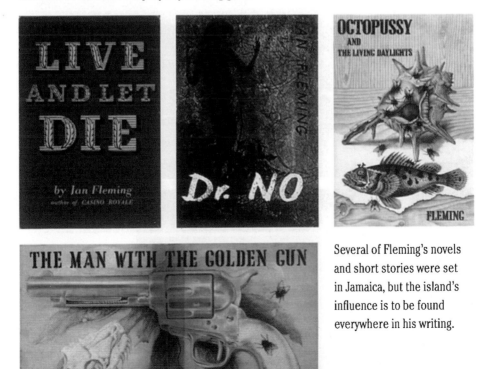

Several of Fleming's novels and short stories were set in Jamaica, but the island's influence is to be found everywhere in his writing.

LEFT: Kingston's premier hotel, Myrtle Bank, photographed for a postcard in the late 1940s. The hotel was rebuilt after the earthquake of 1907, but was destroyed by fire in 1966.

ABOVE: Ian entertains two ladies off the Goldeneye beach.

LEFT: Newly-elected Senator John Kennedy, on a visit in January 1953, poses outside Sunset Lodge, the hotel that launched the jet-set in Jamaica.

Coward and friends on the Sunset Lodge beach. From left to right: Graham Payn, Noël Coward, John C. Wilson, Princess Natasha Paley and Joyce Carey.

Ann on her first visit to Goldeneye, with her chaperone, the Duchess of Westminster, in the background.

A view over Port Maria harbour from Noël Coward's house, Firefly, showing Cabrita Island, the inspiration for Mr Big's Isle of Surprise in *Live and Let Die*.

The beautiful Streamertail hummingbird, or 'Doctor Bird'.

Although in decline by the time Fleming built Goldeneye in St Mary, the banana business was still the most important economic activity in the Oracabessa area.

ABOVE: Lucian Freud visited Goldeneye in 1953 and spent much of his time painting in a nearby banana grove. He had produced this portrait of Ann three years earlier.

LEFT: Ian and Ann at their wedding in Port Maria. Ian later wrote that the prospect of marriage had filled him with 'terror and mental fidgets'.

LEFT: Montego Bay, 1953: Katherine Hepburn with her partner Irene Selznick, one of the north coast's many high-profile gay partnerships. In 1955 Ann wrote to her brother from Goldeneye, 'We are the only heterosexual household for 50 square miles.'

ABOVE: The private beach at Jamaica Inn. Some black Jamaicans found their depiction on tourist postcards offensive.

LEFT: The Tower Isle hotel swimming pool where Barrington Roper taught Caspar Fleming to swim.

Blanche and Ian on the beach at Goldeneye in 1958.

The staff who continued working at Goldeneye. From left: Miss Myrtle, Violet Cummings and Ramsay Dacosta.

Chris Blackwell with Ursula Andress at the Ferry Inn during the shooting of *Dr. No* in 1962. In the background can be seen director Terence Young and Sean Connery.

Connery with a young fan. A fellow cast member remembers him being 'very modest and bit bemused by the whole thing.'

Blanche, Sean and Noël.

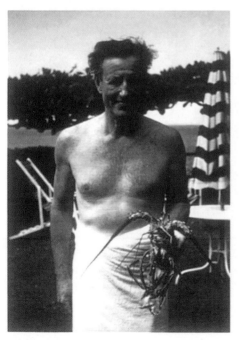

1964: a tired-looking Ian shows off his latest catch.

Roger Moore visiting Goldeneye in December 1972 during the filming of *Live and Let Die*.

still has the global reach that used to characterise British power before the Empire started to decline; its operatives are self-reliant, piratical perhaps, but vigorous, a million miles from what Fleming calls the 'featherbedded' modern youth of the Welfare State era. Later in the same novel, Bond reflects that the Russians have 'all the money and equipment in the world, while the Secret Service put against them a handful of adventurous, underpaid men'. In the non-fiction *Diamond Smugglers*, published the same year, Fleming tells us that John Blaize is one of 'Britain's best secret agents' because of his 'taste for adventure and a romantic streak'.

So it is in the Secret Services that Fleming sees preserved – perhaps uniquely – everything he cherished about his country.

John Le Carré is, of course, a very different writer from Fleming. Characters like Smiley and Leamas – the central figure in Le Carré's 1963 breakthrough novel *The Spy Who Came in from the Cold* – can even be seen as 'anti-Bonds', sharing none of his glamour, casual sadism, sense of purpose and self-assurance. But in a 1989 interview, Le Carré, when asked why he returned to work for the Secret Service, replied: 'In my quest for a moral institution I believed that somewhere in the heart of the brotherhood of intelligence the key was to be found to our identity, to our collective desires and our destiny ... I grew up in the decline of the tradition of the Empire, and I believe I considered our secret intelligence service to be the last church of this Empire theology.'

Indeed, in *A Perfect Spy*, Le Carré's most autobiographical creation, we are told that Pym 'loved the firm ... He adored its rough, uncomprehending trust in him, its misuse of him, its tweedy bear-hugs, flawed romanticism and cock-eyed integrity.' In *The Man with the Golden Gun*, Bond similarly reflects on M: 'He's a romantic at heart like all the silly bastards who get mixed up with the Service.' For both very different writers, the Secret Service represents the last bastion of what used to be great about Britain.

In *From Russia, with Love*, SMERSH are looking to target someone from the ranks of the British Secret Service 'who is admired and whose ignominious destruction would cause dismay. Myths are built on heroic deeds and heroic people. Have they no such men?' Of course they do; Bond, who has 'at least twice frustrated the operations of SMERSH', is selected for assassination.

Led by the repulsive Rosa Klebb, with a plan concocted by a Russian chess master, the agent of Bond's destruction is to be Red Grant, 'the result of a midnight union between a German professional weight-lifter and a Southern Irish waitress'. Named after Fleming's favourite boatman on the Rio Grande banana rafts, 'a cheerful, voluble giant of villainous aspect', Red Grant is 'an advanced manic depressive' who works for the Russians because he admires 'their brutality, their carelessness of human life, and their guile'. Part of his extensive training has been in incitement among 'the colonial peoples, the negroes'.

Thanks to a visit Fleming had made in June 1955 to Istanbul to cover a meeting of Interpol for the *Sunday Times*, Bond has a well-observed and exciting new setting. And in Istanbul he meets the 'shrewd pirate' Darko Kerim, who runs Station T brilliantly on a shoestring and shares Bond's nostalgia for the Second World War – 'the excitement and turmoil of the hot war'. (Kerim's office has a portrait of the Queen and borrowed, it seems, from Fleming's wedding: 'Cecil Beaton's war-time photograph of Winston Churchill looking up from his desk in the Cabinet Offices like a contemptuous bulldog'.)

Typically, the plot of *From Russia, with Love* has some cracks, but Fleming keeps the action moving fast enough for the reader to skim over them. The climax takes place on the Orient Express, where Bond faces what seems like certain death at the hands of Grant, who warns him: 'Careful, old man. No tricks. No Bulldog Drummond stuff will get you out of this one.' Of course, Bond and Fleming have the last laugh because the Bulldog Drummond stuff with Grant's bullet hitting Bond's cigarette case works just fine.

*

The distant separation during the time of writing *From Russia, with Love* caused both Ann and Ian to write fondly to each other and, for Ann, a change in heart about Goldeneye. 'I love scratching away with my paintbrush while Ian hammers out pornography next door,' she wrote to Evelyn Waugh. 'Very sad without you,' Ian wrote to Ann soon after his arrival. 'Today started book. Got two conches but no fun as you weren't there and sea *crawling* with lobster … It's a wonderful place and I can't sell it but you must be here. It belongs to you and you're stupid not to come here. You must get rid of your fear of things. Your fears of things are as bad as my fears of people. (5th gin and tonic and goodnight my love and come if you possibly can) I love you only in the world,' he finished the letter.

Ann replied that she was missing 'our wonderful lives at Goldeneye'. 'I have thought of the bean soup and the clucking bird and of your typewriter and the drunken Scrabble, and I don't believe you realized how much I wanted to come and how much I mind you being alone there. I hope you won't learn to be happy there without me.' Ian replied: 'I wish I could start again and wipe out the black patches in these four years but you can never know how desperately difficult I found it all.'

Ian relented and decided that next year Caspar should come out at last to the house. So down on his beach he built a mini-rock pool where the child could safely play, and also directed the construction of a gazebo on a spot at the extreme end of his property overlooking Oracabessa. Here, he planned to escape from his family to write.

On the aeroplane over from New York, Ian had met Truman Capote, who fascinated him with stories of his recent trip to the Soviet Union. Two weeks later, Capote, having telegrammed, turned up at Goldeneye 'hustling and twittering along with his tiny face crushed under a Russian Commissar's uniform hat'. He had hated Round Hill where he was staying, and he needed somewhere to write his series of articles for the *New Yorker* about Russia – which would become his first book-length work of non-fiction, *The Muses Are Heard*, published that same year.

'Can you imagine a more incongruous playmate for me?' Ian wrote to Ann, but 'he's a fascinating character and we really get on very well'. Ann was most amused, writing back: 'I do love the thought of you and Truman resting together. Goldeneye was the last heterosexual household. What will its reputation be now!'

Ian took Capote to meet Noël Coward at Firefly, his recently completed house up on Look-Out Hill. This was to be Coward's writing retreat when the guests at Blue Harbour became too much of a disruption. It was a modest, 1930s-style one-storey, one-bedroom construction, with a large slit window similar to those at Goldeneye. Morris Cargill called it 'another ugly house ... I thought it was dreadful, but funnily enough, Noël ... didn't seem to have much in the way of taste either in his furniture or in his houses ... He shared this with Ian Fleming. Neither of them had any good taste at all.' The house was later improved with the removal of the crazy-paving-style cladding on the exterior, and still boasts a sensational view over Port Maria harbour.

According to Fleming, who was used to Coward ribbing him about the downsides of Goldeneye, the heavy rain had been hard on Coward's new abode: 'His Firefly house is near-disaster,' he reported to Ann. 'The rain pours into it from every angle and even through the stone walls so that the rooms are running with damp.' Coward was living there on his own, which necessitated his secretary Cole Lesley spending 'half the day running up and down in the car with ice and hot dishes of quiche Lorraine! A crazy set-up.'

Ian had other guests, including his American publisher, but most social time was spent with Coward and his circle. On one occasion, Noël, Ian and Graham Payn stayed at an old, falling-down villa on Negril beach for a few days: 'nothing but buggers all around me', Ian

Firefly today, now a shrine to Coward and his circle's love for Jamaica.

wrote to Ann. For Ian, it was research for a series of articles about Jamaica for the *Sunday Times*. He described the bay at Negril as 'the most beautiful I have seen in the world … the classic back-drop of Stevenson and Stacpoole [authors of *Robinson Crusoe* and *The Blue Lagoon* respectively]'. A large part of the attraction was the unspoilt, undeveloped nature of the spot. But he predicted, accurately as it turned out, that 'one dreadful day this remote corner of Jamaica will be as famous a sunshine holiday-resort as any in the world'.

Also to gather material for his articles, there was a trip with Payn, Cole Lesley and Cargill's wife Barbara to the Blue Mountains looking for rare birds. Fleming described it as being dragged somewhat unwillingly from 'the soft enchantments of the tropic reed and the sun-baked sand of my pirate's cove' to ride uncomfortably on donkeys up the mountain.

Most importantly for his life in Jamaica, however, it was on this stay that Fleming met Blanche Blackwell. The previous year, she had received a summons from her family. Her father had died in 1946

Graham Payn, Ian, and Morris Cargill's wife Barbara in the Blue Mountains. Fleming described it as 'the most intoxicating landscape I have ever seen'.

and now her mother was finding running the family businesses overly onerous. Unless Blanche could come back to Jamaica and help out, they would have to sell the St Mary banana plantations.

Blanche was enjoying England, particularly the hunting and horse racing, but she reluctantly packed up her life there and headed back to the island with her son, Chris. There she divided her time between the Terra Nova mansion in Kingston and a cottage called Bolt on the Wentworth north-coast banana estate that she decided to rebuild.

Here she found herself a close neighbour of Noël Coward, who had bought the land for both Blue Harbour and Firefly from Blanche's brother Roy. 'I thought I should be polite and invite him for a drink,' Blanche remembered. 'I was quite sure he would put me off. When

he accepted I was frightened stiff; what do you say to a man like that?'
But when Coward came up the steps, they simply clicked: 'there was
an instant recognition; it was as though we had known each other all
our lives'. Thereafter Blanche would remain one of Coward's closest
Jamaica friends.

Blanche had known Ian's friend Ivar Bryce since the 1930s. He,
like Coward, loved her combination of demureness and spirit. 'She is
joyful,' Bryce wrote of Blanche, 'her peals of laughter can banish any
despondent thoughts.'

It was towards the end of Fleming's 1956 stay in Jamaica that he and
Blanche met at last, at a dinner party given by Charles and Mildred
D'Costa, at whose lavish Kingston home Ann and Ian had stayed
before picking up her father, stepmother and Lucian Freud two years
previously. Blanche didn't like Charles, but accepted the invitation
as Mildred was a bridge-playing friend. She took along her current
house guests, the former Governor of Jamaica, Sir Arthur Richards,
and his wife.

Ian clearly found the whole thing utterly ghastly. At one point
he called Richards' wife a 'silly bitch', rude even for him. His first
words to Blanche were little better: talk turned to the burgeoning
homosexual community on the north coast – both male and female –
and Blanche told Fleming that her family owned extensive land there.
Fleming retorted: 'You're not another lesbian, are you?'

Blanche, though offended, had been warned about Fleming, and
was nonetheless a little bit intrigued. Her son Chris says that his
mother 'Loved the English. She was strictly into expats.' She was also
taken by Ian's 'blue eyes and coal black hair' and his 'rugged vitality'.
There was instant physical attraction on his part as well. Previously
Ann had asked Ivar Bryce not to tell her what Ian got up to without her,
unless he was 'near a middle-aged Jewess'. Ian later said that his ideal
woman was not the pert-bottomed Bond girl but someone who was
'thirtyish, Jewish, a companion who wouldn't need education in the

arts of love. She would aim to please, have firm flesh and kind eyes.' (In *Dr No*, Honeychile Rider's 'behind' is described as 'almost as firm and rounded as a boy's'. Noël Coward wrote to Ian, 'I know we are all becoming progressively more broadminded nowadays but really, old chap, what could you have been thinking of.' Tatiana Romanov in *From Russia, with Love* had a 'behind that jutted out like a man's'.)

Blanche had been very exclusively raised and was impeccably polite and well-mannered, but at the same time she was not above playing up to the West Indian Creole stereotype of unashamed sensuality. At over a hundred years old, she remains today a curious mix of the expected formality of her age and class but also a lively, adventurous spirit who frequently breaks off talking with the exclamation 'I'm very strange! I'm a wild animal, you know!' This was an alluring combination for Fleming – the Jamaican cocktail of 'disciplined exoticism' that had done so much to shape the Bond novels.

After the party, Fleming sent Blanche a telegram saying he wanted to see her again. She invited him to dinner, but then had to retract when the Richardses refused to have anything to do with him. Eventually a new arrangement was made: 'I had this party, with two friends, just the four of us,' says Blanche. Fleming was 'quite different' this time, 'completely charming'. A few days later, he stayed with her in Kingston, and she helped him buy a scooter and toy train for Caspar. In letters to Ann, he played down their time together, writing that Blanche would be 'quite a pleasant neighbour'.

When she had returned to Jamaica, Blanche had found her old riding haunts on the north coast so built up that, as she puts it, she 'took to the sea'. Her guide was Barrington Roper, a local fisherman who had represented Jamaica at international swimming competitions and now worked as a lifeguard at Tower Isle Hotel. He was also an expert spear fisher, catching snapper, barracuda and parrotfish and then selling them door to door, at Bolt and Blue Harbour among other places. He taught Blanche about the pleasures and dangers of the ocean, including how to deter barracuda attacks by 'showing no fear'. She became a huge enthusiast, and was delighted when Ian invited her to snorkel at Goldeneye. She had known the land when it was still a racecourse, as she and Joe Blackwell had owned a string of racehorses before the war, and it was now the nearest beach to her house at Bolt.

According to Bryce, Blanche was 'a fine swimmer', able 'to plunge into the depths in search of trigger fish and octopuses with skill of a

Fleming with Barrington Roper and a large barracuda.

high degree'. Of course, this was a passion she shared with Ian. She also brought Barrington Roper to meet Ian, and thereafter he too became a regular presence at Goldeneye. He remembers diving for shells with Fleming, and how he would sometimes drop by on his way back from Tower Isle, and talk for hours about 'fish and underwater things', a subject Ian would never tire of. Sometimes he would stay for dinner. 'We became friends,' he says.

Barrington Roper has been incorrectly attributed as inspiration for Fleming's Quarrel character. In fact he did not meet Fleming until after Quarrel's first outing in *Live and Let Die*. Nonetheless, like Quarrel with Bond, Roper now showed Ian, Blanche, Noël and all their respective guests 'the ways of the reef'. He was such a reassuring presence that some of Ian's 'friends from England', he remembers, 'sometimes they wouldn't go out to the reef unless I was with them'.

With Blanche now spending so much time at Goldeneye (and offering to keep an eye on it in Ian's absence in return for swimming rights on the beach), there were inevitable rumours that they were having an affair. Blanche was horrified, and rode up to Firefly to berate Coward for spreading the incorrect gossip. Ian had tried it on, she told Noël, but she had rejected his advances. Coward as ever was intrigued by his friends' romances, and was already writing a play, *Volcano*, about Ian, Blanche and Ann.

Also returned to Jamaica with Blanche was her eighteen-year-old son Chris, who would have an important role to play in the story of Bond and Goldeneye. He had been born in England, but grew up in Jamaica. Partly because he was sickly – suffering very badly from asthma – his childhood was almost as isolated and solitary as that of his mother in the 1920s. At one point he had an English nanny, remembered by Chris as 'kinda cruel', and a tutor flown out from England (who was so ineffectual that Chris could hardly read or write at seven). He 'never saw anyone', and the only friends he remembers are the Kirkwoods' daughter Roberta, and the Foot children. 'The only

Messing about in the water with Blanche Blackwell.

people I spent any time with were the black staff,' he says. 'There were more than twenty for the huge house, with land, horses, gardens … All the pictures I have of that time are of them. There are no pictures with other children. I'd line them up, like school photos and take their picture. I was still the little Lord Fauntleroy but I really got to know them, and became friends with them. I cared for them, and I think they cared for me a bit, although there was still a huge natural divide.'

In 1945, Chris had been taken to England and put into a Catholic school, where he spent most of his time in the sanatorium. After that, he attended Harrow School, but left before completing his A levels.

He always considered himself Jamaican, and that his future was to be in Jamaica. Before he left England, he had secured himself a job as an ADC to Sir Hugh Foot. So he was now living at King's House, which he loved. He adored Sir Hugh, and enjoyed the excitement of the time when 'Bustamante and Manley and all the top politicians and people, who were going to take over Jamaica, were coming to King's House all the time. He was very good with them. They all really loved Hugh Foot.' Chris remembers also the excitement of visiting

Goldeneye and hearing Fleming and Coward in mid verbal joust. Fleming made a good impression on him. 'In those days children were seen and not heard,' he says, 'but Fleming always talked to me as an adult. There was a coldness to him, but he would open up and talk to me.'

After a short trip with Ivar Bryce to Inagua in the Bahamas, Fleming returned to England on 22 March to find Ann in much better health. At Enton Hall she had lost nearly five pounds and was now 'free from pain'. Fleming, however, was suffering from sciatica and a heavy cold, and checked himself in to the same sanatorium. Though it would provide useful material for the scenes at 'Shrublands' in *Thunderball*, it was of little use for his health, partly because he would not stick to the regime. He went to see Dr Beal soon afterwards, who noted that 'He complains of greater exhaustion than is natural in a man of his age.' Beal suggested a better diet and advised against any cigarettes or alcohol. Fleming cut down to fifty Morlands a day, and switched to bourbon, but his stepson Raymond remembers noticing that he was still 'drinking a great deal'. There then followed a return of his agonising kidney stones, which necessitated a stay in the London Clinic and large quantities of morphine.

Almost all Fleming's efforts to make Bond a more rounded character involved putting more of himself into his creation. And so, for the first time, readers would begin to see Fleming's declining health and vitality leaking into Bond. In the first four books, he is fit and vigorous: in *Casino Royale*, the doctor treating his torture injuries tells him that few men could have survived them; in *Live and Let Die*, he is 'strong and compact and confident'; in *Moonraker*, he is the best shot in the service; in *Diamonds are Forever*, his medical shows 'he is in pretty good shape'. But in *From Russia, with Love*, Bond has a new physical and mental ennui. The chapter 'The Soft Life', originally titled 'The Boredom of Bond', begins, 'The blubbery arms of the soft life had Bond round the neck and they were slowly strangling him. He was a man of war and when, for a long period, there was no war, his spirit went into decline.' Now he is 'restless and indecisive'. Action, however, has its own dangers, and we hear that, for assassins like Bond, eventually 'The soul sickens of it ... A germ of death enters his body and eats into him like a canker. Melancholy and drink take him, and a dreadful lassitude which brings a glaze to the eyes and slows up movements.'

An antidote for this lethargy is found in the character of Kerim. 'I drink and smoke too much,' he tells Bond. 'I am greedy for life. I do too much of everything all the time. Suddenly one day my heart will fail. The Iron Crab will get me as it got my father. But I am not afraid of The Crab. At least I shall have died from an honourable disease. Perhaps they will put on my tombstone "This Man Died from Living Too Much".' For Fleming, this had also become the thinking behind his refusal to stop smoking or meaningfully reduce his alcohol intake. Copying a phrase from another writer, he wrote in his notebook: 'Death is like any untamed animal. He respects a scornful eye.'

Fleming was also suffering from The Boredom of Bond. That summer he wrote to Raymond Chandler, 'My muse is in a bad way ... I am getting fed up with Bond and it has been very difficult to make him go through his tawdry tricks.' He decided to add a final twist to the very end of the new book – Rosa Klebb kicks Bond with her poisoned shoe dagger. *From Russia, with Love* thus ends: 'Bond pivoted slowly on his heel and crashed headlong to the wine-red floor.' Fleming leaves us hanging, not knowing whether Bond is dead or alive.

While Fleming moped, Ann was becoming ever more social, and her dinners more frequent and high-powered. One boasted the Leader of the Opposition, Hugh Gaitskell, Randolph Churchill and Robert Boothby, an influential Tory politician and broadcaster. She had a strong rapport with the 'gentle and loving' Labour leader, and soon afterwards the two of them began going dancing together at the Café Royal, nightclubbing with Lucian Freud and Francis Bacon or staying with Ann's aristocratic friends in the country. 'Gaitskell is a changed man,' Ann wrote to Beaverbrook. 'All he wants is wine, women and song.'

In the autumn, Ann and Gaitskell started an affair that would last until his death in 1963, meeting for trysts at the house of Anthony Crosland. Trade unionist figures disapproved of the way in which Ann Fleming 'showed him the pleasures of upper class frivolity', but for her this was part of the challenge and the fun. In November, she wrote to Evelyn Waugh: 'Mr Gaitskell came to lunch … He had never seen cocktails with mint in them or seen a magnum of champagne, he was very happy. I lied and told him that all the upper classes were beautiful and intelligent and he must not allow his vermin to destroy them.'

In the meantime, Ian had been conducting an affair with Lord Beaverbrook's granddaughter Lady Jeanne Campbell, then in her twenties. It seems that he was the first to stray since his and Ann's marriage, but, as Blanche Blackwell remembers, he was furious about Ann's infidelity.

Before Ian's next visit to Jamaica, Goldeneye, through an extraordinary and somewhat ironic set of circumstances, was to become famous.

In July that year, President of Egypt Gamal Abdel Nasser had nationalised the Suez Canal. Britain's government led by Sir Anthony Eden responded by planning a joint attack with Israel and France to regain control of the waterway and remove Nasser from power, at the same time, it was hoped, dealing a blow to the region's Arab nationalism and Soviet influence.

The whole operation was dressed up as a peacemaking intervention by Britain and France to separate Israeli and Egyptian forces, though this was quickly seen as a sham. It was, as Eisenhower would comment, going to war 'in the mid-Victorian style', a throwback to the days of high imperialism.

A bad-tempered television debate on 31 October, featuring the popular historian A. J. P. Taylor, Lord Boothby and Michael Foot, demonstrated how divided the country was. On the same day, as British bombers hit Cairo, Hugh Gaitskell told the House of Commons that it was 'an act of disastrous folly whose tragic consequences we shall regret for years. Yes, all of us will regret it, because it will have done irreparable harm to the prestige and reputation of our country.'

Lord Beaverbrook's *Daily Express* was supportive, declaring that Eden was acting 'to safeguard the life of the British Empire'. The Prime Minister himself believed that unless they met the challenge of Nasser, 'Britain would become another Netherlands'. But because Eden suspected that the United States was out 'to replace the British Empire', he made the fatal mistake of not 'consulting the Americans', and now President Eisenhower led the widespread condemnation of the attack, even voting with the Soviets and against Britain and France in the UN. He also blocked Britain's access to the International Monetary Fund until she withdrew her troops, and refused to provide the oil to replace supplies interrupted from the Middle East; ministers feared a disastrous run on the pound.

With most of the Commonwealth refusing to provide support, Eden broke, calling a ceasefire on 6 November, even as troops were still landing. It was a stunning humiliation, a demonstration to the world that the British Empire was now 'toothless, immoral and anachronistic'. The Deputy Cabinet Secretary judged the crisis 'the psychological watershed, the moment when it became apparent that Britain was no longer capable of being a great imperial power'. Sir Anthony Nutting, who resigned from his position as Foreign Minister over the attack, called it the 'dying convulsion of British Imperialism'. Conservative opinion also saw it as ending the hopes of the Commonwealth as a 'military or economic bloc' and a huge boost for anti-colonial movements all around the British Empire.

After Suez, there could be no more doubts about the way the Empire was going. Colonialism was more than ever a dirty word. 'Empire Day' became 'Commonwealth Day' in Britain, and four years later, the UN passed resolution 1514, which recognised that 'the peoples of the world ardently desire the end of colonialism in all its manifestations'.

Noël Coward, who had now sold his homes in England and was dividing his time between Jamaica, Bermuda and Switzerland, saw Suez as the end of 'good old imperialism' and the 'British Empire, a great and wonderful social, economic and even spiritual experiment'. The decision to 'knock Nasser for six was a good one', he wrote to a friend at the end of November. The real mistake, he believed, was withdrawing troops from the Canal Zone in the first place. This had been due, he wrote, to 'our usual misguided passion to prove to the Americans and the rest of the world what wonderful guys we were. We just let go our hold as we have done, with disastrous results, in so many other parts of the world.'

Coward had recently become Britain's first high-profile tax exile, prompting a backlash, but for him, London had become as grey as Moscow, and the British beyond saving: 'We've lost our will to work, lost our sense of industry, lost our sense of pride in our heritage and above all lost our inherent conviction that we are a great race.' Fleming was similarly appalled by the disaster. In a letter to his Jamaica friend Sir William Stephenson, he wrote: 'In the whole of modern history I can't think of a comparable shambles created by any single country.'

Eden himself now became erratic and apocalyptic, and his health, which had been very poor for a number of years, deteriorated rapidly. On 21 November, Downing Street announced that he was 'suffering from the effects of severe overstrain. On the advice of his doctors he has cancelled his immediate public engagements.' The following day, the news came out: with exquisite irony, Eden had chosen to recover at Goldeneye, the birthplace of the imperial hero Bond, the 'one-man Suez task force'.

Predictably, there were digs about the 'Sunshine Trip' and accusations that the captain was deserting a sinking ship. Randolph Churchill waded in, drawing a parallel between Suez and the Battle of Stalingrad, saying that not even Hitler had wintered in Jamaica. The *Daily Mirror* ran a competition on how best to solve the Suez crisis, with the first prize being a three-week holiday for two in Jamaica.

Ian was delighted; Ann less so. She had told her friend Clarissa Eden about Goldeneye, which was how the idea for the trip had formed, but now she was worried that the Edens would find the house horribly uncomfortable and primitive. As she was not officially supposed to know about the Edens' plans, it was only when Clarissa confided in her forty-eight hours before departure that she was able to warn her of Goldeneye's drawbacks. 'She seemed disconcerted,' Ann wrote to Waugh, 'to hear that if one wished a bath one had to give two days' notice, and that I did not know if there was a dentist on the island and that all the doctors were black. I warned her that shoes must be worn while bathing, and that the reef abounded with scorpion fish, barracuda and urchins … The plumbing is not good at the moment, after plugs are pulled noises of hunting horns are heard for at least twenty minutes … I think Torquay and a sun-ray lamp would have been more peaceful and more patriotic.'

Ian, on the other hand, was thrilled at the publicity he would get for his rental property, and enjoyed the cloak-and-dagger nature of the arrangement. The Colonial Secretary, Alan Lennox-Boyd, had originally phoned Ann to ask if the house was free for himself, although he swore her to secrecy. A few days later, Lennox-Boyd summoned Fleming to the Foreign Office to tell him in person that it was to be for the Prime Minister. There was even a cover for the meeting – talking about a book project. Still not allowed to tell anyone, Fleming sent a telegram to Anthony Lahoud in Jamaica saying that 'three important friends' were coming to stay for three weeks. Violet should get extra staff, he instructed, and the house be prepared. When he received back

No. 17,575 · THURSDAY NOVEMBER 22 1956 3a.m. forecast: Early frost; cold Price 2d.

'SEVEN SEAS' PLANE IS STANDING BY AT LONDON AIRPORT
Lady Eden goes with him : Holiday for three weeks : They'll stay in seaside house

EDEN: SUNSHINE TRIP

Off to Jamaica tomorrow: he stays in charge

Express Political Correspondent DEREK MARKS

SIR ANTHONY EDEN, suffering from "severe overstrain," is flying to Jamaica tomorrow for three weeks' rest in the sun. Lady Eden will go with him.

THE BEST SALESMEN IN BRITAIN

GOLDENEYE: A white house with no phone —but a garden leading to the sea

A BATTALION MOVES OUT TO SHOW 'GOOD FAITH'

Rush-hour chase

MOLOTOV MOVES —BUT IS IT UP OR DOWN?

By STEPHEN CONSTANT

Eden's borrowing of Goldeneye made Ian Fleming front page news for the first time.

a rather relaxed-sounding 'Everything is ok Lahoud', he telegraphed again asking that uniforms be found for the staff and that Lahoud should be 'prepared for considerable publicity'.

Once the news was out, Fleming sent another telegram to Violet. 'The Commander told me someone is coming,' she recalled, and that 'I would be surprised. I would see a lot of excitement. But I must be calm. Because although he is Prime Minster, he is just the next man. I must not let them get me off my nerve.'

The press were intrigued by Goldeneye and its dashing owner. On 22 November, the *Daily Express* led its front page with two pictures, one of Ann and Ian, the other of Goldeneye. Ann, letting the side down a bit, was quoted in the accompanying article: 'It's a small house with a nice garden leading on to the sea … It's no luxury place. The Edens will have to rough it.' She then went on, rather spitefully, 'We lent the house to Noël Coward seven years ago after he had a colossal flop in New York.' The next day, she wrote to Waugh: 'yesterday's *Daily Express* will mean a permanent breach with Noël Coward'.

At Goldeneye itself, there was a rush of activity. Blanche Blackwell had been told about the mysterious telegrams by Lahoud, and as she happened to be back in Kingston later the same day, she asked at King's House. Here she was given the recently received news that the Prime Minister was coming to Goldeneye. Together with Foot's private secretary and his wife, and her Lindo sister-in-law, Blanche rushed back to Oracabessa to attempt to get the place in shape. Six extra men were quickly gathered to help gardener Felix Barriffe tidy up the outside, where, the *Gleaner* reported the day before Eden's arrival, 'the hibiscus was in full bloom and the poinsettias were adding their scarlet quota'. Blanche remembers doing what she could inside. Fleming later teased her that he had conjured up a picture of her 'punching up my faded cushions and putting cut glass vases of flowers beside the detectives' beds'.

Harry George, the Bahamas-born chef from King's House, was driven over to draw up menus and organise supplies, while two telephone lines were installed in the living room and the new gazebo was commandeered as a communication centre and office, with typewriters and emergency telephones. New maids and a valet were taken on and dispatch riders lined up to buzz over the island between Kingston and Oracabessa several times a day.

Lady Foot suggested that Violet might make way for staff from King's House, but she was having none of it, replying, 'No, Lady, I obey my Commander.' When Lady Foot tried to convince her that the Queen herself would want this arrangement, Violet remained adamant: 'I respect the Queen but I obey the Commander.'

Noël, who had played and sung at the Edens' house during the war, rushed off to Kingston to buy a huge basket of Earl Grey tea, caviar, cutlets, champagne and foie gras paté – 'Anything I could see in fact that might mitigate the horrors I knew the poor dears were in for.'

The Edens landed on Saturday 24 November to be greeted at Kingston airport by a calypso band singing 'Jamaica the Garden of Eden welcomes Britain's Sir Anthony Eden'. Sir Hugh Foot and his wife Sylvia accompanied them to Goldeneye. The next day, Blanche received a telephone call from Violet: there had been some confusion over who was doing what and there was no lunch for the Edens. Blanche was eating with Coward and had to pack the food up quickly and send it over to Goldeneye. Thereafter she was the first call to sort out any small problems, to the chagrin of the agent Lahoud.

Over the next few days, Coward, Brownlow and Bryce all offered hospitality, but it was declined. The extent of the Edens' sociability was hosting a lunch for the Foots and Blanche. 'A complete inertia has overcome us,' Clarissa Eden wrote to Ann after a week. 'We are blissfully happy and it is everything we had hoped for but far more beautiful. We haven't been outside the gates so far.' There was a trip to Antonio's emporium in Falmouth, where Eden bought a pair of willow-pattern shorts, but for almost all of their three-week stay, the large white Cadillac, lent by Prime Minister Norman Manley, remained unused as they kept to the house and beach. Eden did not take to the snorkelling. As Clarissa reported to Ann, 'After one claustrophobic splash, Anthony had absolutely refused to put his head under water, so he swims up and down in the deep bit, occasionally crashing himself into a reef of coral. I am obsessed by the fishes, and now swim about with a wet towel tied to my back on account of bad sunburn.'

One reason for the seclusion was that the property was soon surrounded by journalists and photographers from the English press. They even rented boats to capture shots of the Edens on the beach. The tiniest rumours were published, including the news that a doctor had visited during the night. (In fact, the local doctor Lenworth Jacobs was only giving some aspirin to Clarissa.) The finger of blame for this leak was pointed at Anthony Lahoud, who then had his police pass rescinded. When Ian heard about this, he immediately contacted Downing Street and King's House to have his man's honour restored.

Coward had his ear to the ground for information about the ailing Prime Minister. For his part, he thought it very curious that Eden was at Goldeneye while 'the Egyptians and the Arabs and the Israelis and the Iranians and the Syrians and the Russians are frigging away in the Middle East'. In a letter to a friend, he reported 'fairly well authenticated rumours that [Eden] has wakened in the night screaming several times and sent for the guard. This of course might be accounted for by the acute discomfort of Ian's bed and the coloured prints of snakes and octopuses that festoon the peeling walls.'

Eden at Goldeneye, with Sir Hugh Foot on his left, bids farewell to the great and good of Oracabessa. He is shaking hands with W. E. White, owner of the local bakery.

Towards the end of the three weeks, Coward received a note from Clarissa thanking him for the 'goodies' and saying she was feeling much better, although her husband was 'rather fretting at being out of England!' And well he might. During Eden's absence, Macmillan and Butler were plotting his downfall, while the *Spectator* commented on 7 December, 'Jamaica has done more damage than Suez to Sir Anthony's standing in his party at Westminster.' So the Edens returned to London 'to find everyone looking at us with very thoughtful eyes', as Clarissa wrote in her diary. Three weeks later, Sir Anthony Eden was ousted, with poor health given as the excuse. For Eden, Goldeneye had been a political and public relations disaster.

Not so for Ian Fleming. The use of his house had brought him to the attention of a much larger public than his books had hitherto done, and it was the beginning of a run of good fortune for both him and his Bond creation.

There was a more oblique and subtle benefit as well. The Suez disaster had ended Britain's imperial pretensions. Even the thickest-skinned nostalgist could no longer deny the country's second-class status. But this would make the escapism of Fleming's stories, in which, behind the scenes, Britain in the figure of super-agent 007 still bestrides the globe, more popular than ever. The world of Bond was rapidly becoming a place where the nation could congregate around a vision that denied Britain's disappointing new reality.

1957
Jamaica Under Threat – Dr No

I feel horribly insecure, like this house when the mountain rumbles and the walls tremble, scared of what might happen next.

Adela, in *Volcano*

Before Ian returned to Jamaica at the beginning of 1957, Coward had completed his play *Volcano*.

An unflinching examination of marital breakdown, it is set on Coward's Jamaica stand-in, Samolo, where Melissa Littleton arrives suddenly, having been alerted that her husband Guy is having an affair with a local widow and plantation owner called Adela Shelley. Several people recur from Coward's other Samolo stories, and, as in the novel *Pomp and Circumstance*, there are two very obvious Ian and Ann characters. There's also a similarly obvious new arrival: Blanche.

The jealous wife Melissa shares Ann's fear of flying, her renown as a society hostess and her difficulty with getting on with other women. She doesn't like the rigours of the tropics and is described by various others as 'hectic', 'brittle' and 'scratchy'.

Her errant husband Guy speaks in nautical metaphors and spends all his time in Samolo spearing fish. He has a spartan house with uncomfortable furniture and a 'vast living-room that throws the whole house out of balance'. His wife complains that he considers the island 'his own private bachelor paradise'. He is immensely attractive, but has a 'sex ego too strongly developed, too greedy; it demands constant attention like a child banging its spoon on the table'.

The Adela/Blanche character is the most sympathetically portrayed of the three. A widow in her forties who runs a profitable plantation – bananas, coconuts, sugar – she is well liked by her friends, self-reliant, 'steady' and dignified, but with a heart as 'lively as a cricket'. We learn that she had become accustomed to being on her own but the previous year had met Guy and they had fallen in love while swimming and snorkelling together. Guy's wife Melissa is used to her husband's casual indiscretions but flies out to Samolo to check out Adela, who 'might have been just that exception'.

At their meeting, tensions are high, with everyone drinking strong spirits heavily, as they do relentlessly throughout the play. Melissa thanks Adela for 'how kind' she was 'to him when he was out here on his own last year'. Adela now feels guilty and foolish.

The atmosphere gets even heavier as the volcano in the background – seen by some as the characters' buried anger, by others as the coming of independence – gets louder and threatens their night-time outing to see the dawn from its summit. Guy then seduces a much younger married woman who is also part of the group. This sidesteps the stand-off between the Ann and Blanche characters and turns both of them against him.

Melissa responds by threatening divorce, clearly not for the first time. Guy replies: 'You knew perfectly well when you married me what I was like. You knew that I was temperamentally incapable of remaining faithful for long to any one person. I never tried to deceive you about it, in fact I told you so myself, and you settled for it … I am what I am and I'm too old a dog to change my ways … Are you going to pretend that you've been strictly faithful to me in the last few years?' he adds. 'No. I'm not going to pretend anything,' says Melissa. 'I'm not even going to pretend that there's any hope.'

The fault is laid at the failure of the 'physical passion we had for each other when we were first married'. This, Guy says, 'never lasts, you know that as well as I do, we've often discussed it'. Now they only stay together, 'jog along', for the sake of their child, a young, rather difficult son. At the same time, Melissa admits that she is tied to Guy, whatever his behaviour. 'Yes. I do love him,' she says. 'And I accept I always shall. I can't help myself. I have no illusions about him. I don't admire him or even respect him. But there it is. He was my choice and I'm stuck with it. Nobody can explain that sort of thing can they. It's far beyond reason and common sense.'

For Adela, the arrival of Melissa together with Guy's latest escapade on the volcano turns her against her former lover. 'You have an exaggerated view of your own personal charm,' she tells him witheringly. Earlier she announces that she no longer loves him: 'I thought I did for a little – but not any more.' When, right at the end of the play, he brings her shells as a peace offering, she smashes them on the stage as the final curtain comes down.

Before the end of 1956, Coward approached his Jamaica friend Katharine Hepburn to play the lead, Adela, and sent the play to his long-time theatrical producer 'Binkie' Beaumont. Both rejected it. Beaumont may well have considered that the drama's very overt discussion of sex might have gone down badly with Coward's now middle-aged audience, or even fallen foul of the censors of the Lord Chamberlain's office. In addition, although a dissection of marriage every bit as probing and ruthless as *Private Lives*, *Volcano* was far from Coward's best work.

The play remained unperformed until 2012, when after a brief regional tour it arrived in London. But the production struggled with the material: the colonial setting was jarring, with the locals portrayed, if at all, as unreliable, untruthful and hysterical. The only humour was at the expense of the servants and their 'funny' way of speaking English. Reviews were unkind and the run was short.

Blanche Blackwell and Ann's daughter Fionn, now good friends, both saw the play soon after it opened. Fionn found it 'not terribly good', but Blanche insists she enjoyed it, although she claims that the Adela character is nothing like her: much more articulate and forceful.

Blanche's version of the story told in *Volcano* is not so different from the play, apart from the ending. (In fact, Coward also wrote a different ending, in which the Blanche character accepted Guy's advances.) Ian and Blanche had indeed become very close that first winter in 1956 while swimming, hunting and dodging barracudas on Goldeneye's reef, but Blanche denies that they became lovers that year.

In January 1957, however, Ian arrived in Jamaica alone with the news that Ann, in a burst of post-health-club positivity, had 'renewed her marriage vows', but then within days had started her affair with Gaitskell, to Fleming's fury. Blanche says this made her less inclined to continue to resist Ian's persistent advances, and to suppress her own attraction to him. By this time, she had another suitor in Jamaica, and marriage had been discussed, but Ian now insisted she drop him and Blanche agreed.

Two days later, Ann and her party arrived. Ian had come by air, but because of Ann's fear of flying, she had taken the boat, along with four-year-old Caspar, his nanny, Joan Sillick, and Ann's twenty-four-year-old son Raymond O'Neill.

It was a 'horrific' journey, Ann wrote to Evelyn Waugh from Goldeneye. For eight of the eleven days at sea, there had been a 'full gale'. Nanny Sillick suffered from 'seasickness, rheumatism and neuralgia', meaning that Ann had to entertain her sons. Caspar woke at six each morning, while Raymond insisted on being taken to the nightclub each evening. 'I remained mobile on Dramamine and gin … in a stupor of fear and dope,' Ann wrote. Everyone on the boat was 'old and ugly'.

It was Raymond's first visit to the tropics, and he was enchanted by Jamaica and Goldeneye. *Time* magazine the following year would describe it as Fleming's 'luxurious Jamaican residence', but Raymond remembers it from that time as being still 'extremely primitive, the simplest house I'd ever been in. But it didn't matter – you spent all your time in bathing trunks. I love nature so I spent most of the time in the sea.' Everyone had a swim in the morning, 'then spent a lot of time in the sunken garden reading. Hummingbirds were buzzing all around you, and the doctor birds with their long tails – it was an absolute paradise.'

The snorkelling was a highlight, and they often went out further afield in the little inflatable boat and would eat for supper the fish they had caught that day. An octopus found living very near the beach was befriended and christened 'Pussy'. Ann had one setback: she thought she saw a shark and in a panic put her foot on to a rock, which 'happened to be the home of a moray eel. Grabbed her by the ankle. Her whole leg swelled up.'

At night, Raymond remembers, because there was no glass in the windows, 'the most amazing wildlife flew in. Enormous moths flapped in, landed on the wall and then were consumed by lizards, also on the wall. I loved it because you were really in the bush.'

Caspar had inherited his father's interest in nature, and was wildly excited when he saw a scorpion, but most of the time, while Ann painted, wrote letters or read, Raymond swam and Ian hammered out *Dr No* in his new gazebo, the little boy was looked after by the nanny. On a couple of occasions, Ann took him to the Tower Isle Hotel swimming pool, where Barrington Roper gave him swimming lessons. When he was not writing, Fleming undertook to teach his son the Latin names for the fish on the reef. Housekeeper Violet, who at this time had two maids working under her at the house, adored Caspar. 'He's a fine little boy and I hope his mother brings him to Jamaica again,' she said. 'He and I got along just fine.'

There was a certain amount of social life, Raymond remembers, but it really only 'revolved around Blanche and Noël Coward and Noël Coward's friends, of which there were a large number around'. On one occasion, Ian sent Raymond to Blue Harbour in the Austin saloon car kept at Goldeneye to collect 'Noël-y and Coley, Binkie and Perry' (John Perry, 'Binkie' Beaumont's partner). He also ran errands into Port Maria, and stayed a night in Kingston with Blanche at Terra Nova. On another occasion, he was sent to visit Bolt and shown round the banana estate by Blanche and the plantation manager. But 'real' Jamaica, or Jamaicans other than staff, was largely ignored. It was, he says looking back, life 'in a little bubble'.

Raymond was very fond of Ian. They had a shared love of motor cars (Raymond had hurtled round the roads of Kent to help research the timings for the car journeys in *Moonraker*); Ian was, he says, a 'far better step-father than Lord Rothermere', but he believes Ian and his mother 'should never have married. He was a bachelor at heart. Ladies were for a short time.'

Like almost everyone, he got on well with Blanche, but did not entirely miss the awkward tension that her presence in the Fleming–Coward circle was causing. Even before leaving England, Ann had been rather put out to hear from Clarissa Eden how wonderfully helpful 'someone called Blanche Blackwell' had been during their stay. Once in Jamaica, she was irked by the evidence of Blanche's sprucing up of Goldeneye for the Eden visit, and by her popularity in their little circle. Ann could see that she had a serious rival. Nonetheless, after only four weeks, she and the rest of the family boarded the ship back to England, leaving Ian alone once more.

According to Blanche, this was when they became lovers. They spent much of his last two weeks in Jamaica together. In a sign that their relationship had reached the stage of affectionate teasing, Ian called the 'aged' guano tanker in *Dr No* the *Blanche*. 'She was a tomboy kind of girl, really,' Chris Blackwell says of his mother. 'Somebody ready to go swimming, climb a mountain. His wife was not like that at all. She liked her society more.' Ian found Blanche easy and relaxed company, very different from Ann. Blanche says that with her, Ian did not need to make any effort. If he was rude, she just ignored it. 'One of the most important things he said to me,' she remembers, 'was if you don't have anything to say, for God's sake don't say it.' Blanche didn't mind this at all: 'He was a charming, handsome, gifted man,' she says, 'exceptionally manly and definitely not for domesticating.'

Blanche introduced Ian to her favourite book, Frank Cundall's *Historic Jamaica*. Published in 1915, it describes, parish by parish, buildings and monuments surviving from the 'glory days' of the sugar empire. It is a remarkable work of scholarship, but even in the 1950s old-fashioned. No mention is made of the horrors of slavery in Jamaica, and multiple slave-owner Sir Charles Price is described as a 'truly great man'. (In *Dr No*, Bond reads the *Handbook of the British West Indies*, published in 1926 and much in the same vein.) Blanche,

Ian and Blanche at Bolt, her house close to Goldeneye in St. Mary.

perhaps more at home in a sanitised, romantic, even heroic Jamaican imperial past than in the complex reality of the time, had undertaken to visit every site listed in Cundall's book, and now recruited Ian to accompany her.

Ian also stayed with Blanche in Kingston, and spent a weekend with her and her friend Anne Carr in the Cayman Islands. This would give him material for another *Sunday Times* article. Because they had not booked in advance, on the first night the three had to share a room. According to Blanche, Ian took a sleeping pill and snored loudly, driving her to bunk down in the mosquito-ridden hallway. The ostensible purpose of the trip was to collect shells, but in this the Caymans were a huge disappointment. 'It was the most ghastly sea bottom I had ever explored,' Fleming wrote. He was clear as to who was to blame: 'the American way of life, which has Grand Cayman in its grip, had penetrated the surrounding sea. Everywhere there was refuse.'

To Ann, Ian described the trip as 'very chaste and proper ... Blanche jabbers and the other is v dull and cold', but then slightly ruined it by adding, 'Wished you didn't mind aeroplanes. We miss so many adventures.'

Ostensibly Ian was staying on in Jamaica to finish his latest book. After *From Russia, with Love*, he had been unsure whether he had another Bond book in him. Part of his lack of momentum had been the disappointments over selling film rights for his existing Bond books. Television rights to *Casino Royale* had been sold to CBS, who in October 1954 had broadcast an hour-long show with an American 'Jimmy Bond', helped by a British Felix Leiter, but the show is deservedly forgotten. At one point Peter Lorre, the actor playing Le Chiffre, is seen to get up after his 'death' and walk off to his dressing room. *Casino Royale* film rights had been sold for $6,000 in March the following year, but nothing had happened thereafter. With £3,000 of the money Fleming bought himself a Ford Thunderbird, described by Ann as 'above our price range and below our age range' (she now started called Ian 'Thunderbird' in letters to her friends). There had also been interest in the other stories, but nothing had come of it. It was frustrating, as Fleming clearly saw Bond as a film property – much later, he would write, 'You don't make a great deal of money from royalties ... but if you sell film rights, you do very well.'

In the summer of 1956, however, Fleming had been approached by Henry Morgenthau III, a rich film producer who had been in contact with the Jamaican government about developing a movie industry on the island, starting with a series of films for American television. Ian offered to write a treatment for a half-hour television series, based on Bond but with the central character called Commander Jamaica, later changed to Commander James Gunn.

The combination of the freedom from Bond, and the Jamaica setting – a 'home fixture' – reinvigorated Fleming. A storyline emerged that saw Commander Gunn battle with a sinister international spy of German-Chinese extraction. Fleming suggested locations around Goldeneye, and even put forward some local people for roles in the filming: Cousins, his shark-fishing accomplice, 'would be an excellent labour boss and general fixer'; Barrington Roper, 'the Caribbean overarm swimming champion', had 'a slightly Chinese cast of countenance and a good deadpan face'. He even suggested one of his favourite Jamaican calypsos as a theme tune.

The TV show came to nothing, but Fleming found that he suddenly had a fresh and inventive new Bond story ready to go. *Dr No* would, of course, be the story that launched the Bond film franchise and, along with *From Russia, with Love, Live and Let Die* and *Thunderball*, is one of Fleming's finest novels. It is also one of the most fantastical, gothic and melodramatic; and at times frankly, even knowingly, over the top. Responding to later criticism, Fleming would declare: '*Dr No* was very cardboardy and need not have been ... The trouble is that it is much more fun to think up fantastical situations and mix Bond up in them.'

It is this sense of Fleming's enjoyment of the story, and in particular its Jamaican setting, that is the real strength of *Dr No*. It also provides a fascinating take on Fleming's attitude to the changes taking place in Jamaica, and by implication in the wider empire post-Suez.

The novel boasts one of Fleming's most memorable villains. Dr No, half German, half Chinese, is hugely tall, has steel pincers for hands and looks like 'a giant venomous worm wrapped in grey tinfoil'. His particular interest is the human body's ability to withstand pain. He has effectively annexed a portion of offshore Jamaica, ostensibly for the extraction of guano (in which Bryce's family had made their fortune), but actually for the establishment of a secret radar station that can send American missiles from the nearby test base on the British Turks Island off-target. This allows him to collect the prototype rockets and sell them to the Russians or, failing that, the Chinese. He has a captive plantation-style workforce made up of devilish half-breeds – 'Chigroes', half Chinese, half negro.

Owing more than a little to Fleming's boyhood reading of Dr Fu Manchu, Dr No blends the threat of the 'Yellow Peril' and of the Mau Mau. But his base of Crab Key, thirty miles off the north coast of Jamaica, has already been partly 'annexed' by the Americans, in the shape of the Audubon Society, who want to protect a colony of Roseate Spoonbill birds. This leads to pressure from the United States on the British authorities to investigate Dr No.

After the disappearance of the local Secret Service agent, Bond, having recovered from his poisoning after all, is sent to Jamaica in large part as a rest cure, 'something easy to start with … a bit of a breather'. As in *Live and Let Die*, 'Dr Jamaica' is highly effective in this regard. At the fictional 'Blue Hills' hotel, Bond 'was welcomed with deference because his reservation had been made by King's House'. Here he 'took off his London clothes … washed his hair to remove the last dirt of big-city life. Then he pulled on a pair of Sea Island cotton shorts and, with sensual pleasure at the warm soft air on his nakedness, unpacked his things and rang for the waiter.'

Elsewhere, the Jamaica of *Dr No* is a similarly 'traditional' one – the Jamaica drawn in *Live and Let Die*, and written about by Fleming back in 1947 in his *Horizon* article. It is a backward, unchanged place of sensuality, deference, colourful history, physical beauty and warm melancholy. Flying in over the island, Bond admires the 'azure and milk of the inshore shoals', and the 'scattered dice of small-holdings' in the high mountains of the interior, where 'the setting sun flashed gold on the bright worms of tumbling rivers and streams. "Xaymaca" the Arawak Indians had called it – "The Land of Hills and Rivers." Bond's heart lifted with the beauty of one of the most fertile islands in the world.' Driving over the mountains, Bond likewise enjoys scenes unchanged 'for two hundred years or more', and even imagines that he 'smelled the dung of the mule train in which he would have been riding over from Port Royal to visit the garrison at Morgan's Harbour in 1750'. Elsewhere, he wallows in the 'melancholy of the tropical dusk'.

The distinctly old-fashioned figure of Quarrel makes another appearance, of course, with his unquestioning loyalty, childishness and superstition. Quarrel navigates his small canoe to Crab Key by 'instinct', and is backward enough, like most of the other blacks, to believe in the story about a dragon defending the island.

Bond's love interest, Honeychile Rider, encountered gathering shells on Crab Key, is depicted as similarly 'innocent'. Like Solitaire from *Live and Let Die*, she is a Creole beauty raised in the melancholy ruins of a Great House. As she explains to Bond, 'The Riders were one of the old Jamaica families. The first one had been given the Beau Desert lands by Cromwell for having been one of the people who signed King Charles's death warrant. He built the Great House and my family lived in it on and off ever since. But then sugar collapsed and I suppose the place was badly run, and by the time my father inherited it there was nothing but debts – mortgages and things like that.' The house was sold off, but Honeychile continued to live in the cellar, eating Jamaican food and looked after by a devoted black nanny. Bond finds himself 'lost in the picture of the little flaxen-haired girl pattering about the ruins'. Honeychile believes in 'duppies' and is 'naturally' sensuous. The book ends with a clinch and a Creole cliché: 'She had no inhibitions. They were two loving animals. It was natural. She had no shame.'

In *Dr No*, Bond is specifically defending Jamaica. So he is fulfilling his role as defined earlier by Felix Leiter: 'protecting the security of the British Empire'. There is a possibility that if Dr No is not stopped, one of the mis-guided missiles could hit Kingston. But there are other threats to the colony, both obvious and subtle, as the fascinating opening pages establish.

The novel starts with the sun setting 'punctually' over Richmond Road, uptown Kingston, Jamaica, welcomed by the 'zing and tinkle' of crickets and tree frogs in the 'fine gardens'. The wide street contains the large homes, withdrawn from the road, of the colony's white elite – top civil servants, bank managers and company directors. Everything is quiet, 'an empty stage'. Inside the houses, the man, back from work punctually at five, is having a shower or discussing the day with his wife. At half past six, the 'street would come to life again with the cocktail traffic'.

It is Jamaica's Park Avenue, Fleming tells us, 'its Kensington Palace Gardens, its Avenue D'Iéna', and at its top 'lie the grounds of King's House, where the Governor and Commander-in-Chief of Jamaica lives with his family. In Jamaica, no road could have a finer ending.'

Fleming's eye, having gazed seemingly adoringly in the direction of King's House, the centre of British power, now focuses in on the top intersection, where a 'substantial two-storey house' with pillared entrance stands among tennis courts and sprinkler-fed lawns. This is the 'social Mecca of Kingston', Queen's Club, and an accurate description of a real place, the Liguanea Club. Here are gathered, as 'most evenings', a bridge four representing colonial power – a brigadier in charge of the British armed forces in the Caribbean, 'Kingston's leading criminal lawyer', a senior professor from the university and our old friend from *Live and Let Die*, the dashingly naval-looking John Strangways, 'the local representative of the British Secret Service'. All are obviously British, with their 'blast you's and 'damned nuisance's, and white – in contrast, we are informed, the steward is 'coloured'.

Suddenly we come to the point: all this is under mortal threat. 'Such stubborn retreats' as Queen's Club, Fleming writes, 'will not long survive in modern Jamaica. One day it will have its windows smashed and perhaps be burned to the ground.'

It is a shocking and fascinating aside, calling to mind not just Evelyn Waugh's letter from two years previously – 'Perhaps they will massacre the whites one day...' – but also the deep fear that haunted the white community from the first days of slavery. It explodes a bomb under the scene just set. Certainly it makes us look back on the preceding four paragraphs of the book. There we can now see the tiny warning signs: the predictable, deadening routine; the gardens 'too trim' and slightly fake, with 'the finest trees and flowers from the Botanical Gardens'. Although Richmond Road may be withdrawn from the 'hot and vulgar sprawl of Kingston', it is there 'where its residents earn their money'. The street may be the 'best' and have the 'best' people, but the quotation marks are Fleming's. In all, it is complacent, flabby, shallow, drifting. The reference to the glory of King's House will, of course, prove ironic.

And what are the attractions of Queen's Club to its members? It is 'well run, well staffed and [has] the finest cuisine and cellar in the Caribbean' – this is civilisation as expressed by good staff, food and wine, with perhaps even a hint that such pleasures have blunted the effectiveness of the white elite. Certainly its days are numbered: it is, Fleming tells us, 'a useful place to find in a sub-tropical island', but only 'for the time being'.

Then comes the actual violence: the murder of Strangways by the 'three blind beggars'. In part, it is Strangways' 'iron routine', at once an expression of his commendable meticulousness and his lack of excitement and energy, that proves his downfall, as it allows 'the enemy' to plan his death. 'Unfortunately, strict patterns of behavior can be deadly if they are read by an enemy,' Fleming notes. But there is also a hint that the divide between white and black, rich and poor is a contributing factor. The beggars 'would not have been incongruous in Kingston, where there are many diseased people on the streets, but, in this quiet rich empty street, they made an unpleasant impression'.

Black threat is even clearer in the murder of the significantly named and sexually attractive Mary Trueblood, Strangways' assistant, a scene Fleming describes with lascivious relish: 'A man stood in the doorway. It wasn't Strangways. It was a big Negro with yellowish skin and slanting eyes. There was a gun in his hand. It ended in a thick black cylinder. Mary Trueblood opened her mouth to scream. The man smiled broadly. Slowly, lovingly, he lifted the gun and shot her three times in and around the left breast.' The subtext does not need spelling out.

But then, having invoked the spectre of black revolution in Jamaica with his comments about Queen's Club being burnt to the ground, and the murder of Mary Trueblood, Fleming backs away. Soon after his arrival in Jamaica, Bond meets Pleydell-Smith, the Colonial Secretary, who has recently read up about Bond's adventures in Jamaica in *Live and Let Die*. 'Splendid show. What a lark!' he says. 'I wish you'd start another bonfire like that here. Stir the place up a bit. All they think of nowadays is Federation and their bloody self-importance. Self-determination indeed! They can't even run a bus service. And the colour problem! My dear chap, there's far more colour problem between the straight-haired and the crinkly-haired Jamaicans than there is between me and my black cook.'

Although the authority of Pleydell-Smith is slightly undermined by the fact that he has failed to notice that his new secretary, Miss Taro, is a spy, he is described by Fleming as young and energetic, with 'bright, boyish eyes'. Bond takes to him immediately: 'Bond grinned at him. This was more like it. He had found an ally, and an intelligent one at that.' The Jamaica Pleydell-Smith describes is certainly a more anxious place for the colonial authorities than that of *Live and Let Die* four years previously because of the blacks' 'self-importance' – Bond notes on arrival that the immigration official is 'Negro' – but this threat is depicted as weakened by their incompetence (the bus service) and division (the colour problem).

Bond and Pleydell-Smith go for lunch at Queen's Club, where the latter 'delves well below the surface of the prosperous peaceful island the world knows'. In a comment that again calls to mind Evelyn Waugh's, Pleydell-Smith explains to Bond that 'The Jamaican is a kindly, lazy man with the virtues and vices of a child. He lives on a very rich island but he doesn't get rich from it. He doesn't know how to and he's too lazy.' Having run through the other constituent parts of the population – the English, who 'take a fat cut and leave', the Portuguese Jews ('snobs'), Syrians and Indians – he gets to the Chinese (in real life the bugbear of Sir Hugh Foot and generally unpopular because of their commercial success and exclusivity). They are 'solid, compact, discreet – the most powerful clique in Jamaica. They've got the bakeries and the laundries and the best food stores. They keep to themselves and keep their strain pure ... Not that they don't take the black girls when they want them. You can see the result all over Kingston – Chigroes – Chinese Negroes and Negresses. The Chigroes are a tough, forgotten race. They look down on the Negroes and the Chinese look down on them. One day they may become a nuisance. They've got some of the intelligence of the Chinese and most of the vices of the black man. The police have a lot of trouble with them.'

It is 'Chigroes' – an expression that seems to be the invention of Fleming – who carry out the murders of Strangways and Trueblood and act as overseers on Crab Key. But they are only operating on behalf of Dr No. It is still the outsider who represents the greatest threat to Jamaica in the novel. Furthermore, Dr No has achieved his wealth and therefore his power thanks to his success as a gangster in New York. So there is a suggestion that it is the crime-ridden nature of American society that, in the end, threatens Jamaica, as well as the fact that the British have allowed American missiles to be stationed on their territory near the island.

More than anything, though, it is the British themselves who are to blame. It was the Jamaican imperial government who sold Dr No the island in the first place for the tempting sum of £10,000. Furthermore, the complacency of the elite residents of Richmond Road is nothing compared to what Bond finds at King's House. Leaks from a spy in the centre of British power on the island twice threaten Bond's life – the poisoned fruit and the centipede in his bed. Foot – a 'great success' – has left (he would in real life leave in late 1957 to try to sort out the difficulties in Cyprus), and the acting Governor, dressed in 'an inappropriate wing collar and spotted bow tie', is a time-server who keeps trying to close the Strangways case to avoid trouble – 'all he wants is to retire and get some directorships in the City', Bond is told by a friend in the Colonial Office. (So offended were the colonial authorities by their depiction in the novel that in 1962 they refused permission to film *Dr No* inside King's House.) The acting Governor even wants to shut down the Secret Service office in Jamaica, having 'every confidence in our police', earlier dismissed by M as only understanding 'sex and machete fights', and seen as unsuccessful in investigating Strangways' disappearance.

Nonetheless, the novel makes clear that this imperial weakness is not unique or specific to Jamaica. Britain's responsibilities are shown to be widespread – in the radio calls from stations around the globe, and in M's comment 'There were plenty of other worries waiting

A parade in Kingston with a jokey effigy of the Governor Sir Hugh Foot. Chief Minister
Norman Manley and his wife Edna stand to the right of the saluting base.

to be coped with round the world' – but there are simply not the
resources to make good on these commitments. Bond notes M's
concerns about the 'slim funds of the Secret Service', and how M
had been unsuccessfully 'trying for years to get the Treasury to give
him an Auster [a light aircraft] for the Caribbean station'. Yet, more
than financial, it is viewed as a failure of hardiness and purpose: M
complains at the beginning of the novel, 'Nowadays, softness was
everywhere.'

In April 1957, Fleming travelled to Tangier to interview John
Collard, an English solicitor who had worked for the Internal
Diamond Security Organisation, established to reduce diamond
smuggling from Sierra Leone and elsewhere. The result was a series

of articles for the *Sunday Times*, collected into a book, *The Diamond Smugglers*, which would echo and amplify many of the themes of *Dr No*. Fleming has great fun 'Bondifying' the whole thing, changing Collard into a 'famous spy', giving him a pseudonym, John Blaize, with Bond's initials, and even allowing him Bond's (and Fleming's) golf handicap of nine. But he is also fascinated by Blaize's comments about Liberia and Sierra Leone, in which he is 'scathing about Liberia … The first Negro State [*sic*], and Utopia in the imagination of coloured peoples all over the world, and if this was going to be the pattern of Negro emancipation Blaize didn't hold out much hope for the future of Ghana and the Federation of the West Indies.' He 'despised many of the comic opera Negroes in official positions, but he thought even less of the white men who backed them and often incited them in their venality'.

For Blaize, Sierra Leone is an imperial possession gone totally wrong, with corruption and squalor everywhere, leading to rioting and 'a complete collapse of law and authority throughout the whole of a British colony nearly as big as Ireland'. He believes that only prompt action by a handful of men on the ground with 'guts' prevented European families being 'hacked to death'. And again, the fault is not just with the Africans, but with 'drift, weak local government and ignorance in Whitehall'. He concludes, like M, that, 'We've got bits and pieces of territory all around the world, and not enough money and enthusiasm to go around.'

No one can accuse Bond of 'softness' or a lack of enthusiasm. In *Dr No*, through bravery and initiative, he survives a tortuous journey past electric shocks, a red-hot zinc tube, huge spiders, then a captive giant squid, defeated with his improvised weapons. Dr No himself perishes, buried in guano. There is wider hope, too, at the end, when the brigadier in command of the Caribbean Defence Force takes prompt action. He is a 'modern young soldier', 'unimpressed by relics from the Edwardian era of Colonial Governors, whom he

collectively referred to as "feather-hatted fuddy-duddies"'. A modern
navy warship, HMS *Narvik* (flagship of the British Task Force for
the atomic bomb tests in Monte Bello Islands in 1952), is on station
to be sent to Crab Key. Perhaps, *Dr No* suggests, the empire is not
entirely moribund after all. Best of all, for Bond and Fleming,
resolution is achieved without any help from the Americans, who, in
a way, caused the problems in the first place. And yet, stepping back,
the overriding picture is of imperial decline, a feeling not entirely
washed away by the therapeutic, fantastical heroism of Bond.

1958-60
Goldfinger; For Your Eyes Only; Thunderball

The man from the Central Intelligence Agency was due in by Pan American at 1.15. Bond hoped he wouldn't be a muscle-bound ex-college man with a crew-cut and a desire to show up the incompetence of the British, the backwardness of their little colony.

Thunderball

Six weeks after Fleming's return from Jamaica, *From Russia, with Love* was published by Cape in hardback. It came wrapped in what would be an award-winning jacket by a new designer, Richard Chopping, featuring the embrace of a gun and a rose. It was also serialised and heavily pushed in Beaverbrook's *Daily Express* from 1 April, a week before publication. (From July the following year, *Express* support would also include a strip cartoon of Bond's latest adventures. Bond was on a roll.)

Fleming's previous novel, *Diamonds are Forever*, the first to be serialised by the *Express*, had sold well, but *From Russia, with Love*

238

was the breakthrough, the first emphatically on the best-seller lists. The timing of publication was good, against the backdrop of rising Cold War tensions. An advertising campaign played on Eden's visit to Goldeneye. Reviewers were impressed as well, the *TLS* calling it Fleming's 'tautest, most exciting and most brilliant tale'. Bond, the paper declared, was 'the intellectual's Mike Hammer'. Raymond Chandler commented that Fleming's public would now 'never let him go'.

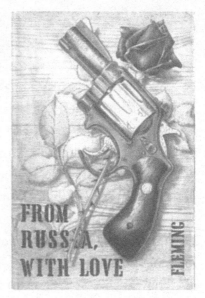

From the outset, Fleming had been described by reviewers as 'Peter Cheyney for the carriage trade' – a thriller writer for educated, knowing, even 'intellectual' readers. But beginning in April 1955 with *Casino Royale*, the books were now appearing as paperbacks with ever-increasing commercial success. The year after the publication of *From Russia, with Love*, Fleming explained to a US TV company: 'In hard covers my books are written for and appeal principally to an "A" readership, but they have all been reprinted in paperbacks, both in England and in America and it appears that the "B" and "C" classes find them equally readable.' So readable, in fact, that the Bond books are credited with bringing the American paperback revolution to Britain. Fleming's paperback publisher, Pan, would later affirm that no fewer than ten of the first eighteen million-selling UK paperbacks were Bond novels.

All these factors combined to make Fleming a new literary superstar. So much so that when *Dr No* was published a year later, the inevitable backlash occurred. Suddenly he was noticed, and important enough to be shot down. First off the blocks was literary critic Bernard

Bergonzi, who deplored the relish with which violence was described at a 'horror-comic level', and wrote that 'Fleming rarely rises above the glossy prose of the advertising copywriter.' Further missing the point about Fleming's cleverly updated jingoism and imperial nostalgia, Bergonzi compared Bond unfavourably to the Buchan heroes, who were 'more virtuous, and deserved their ultimate victory. Much of this patriotic ethic now seems impossibly priggish and even hysterical.' He was closer to the truth when he wrote: 'His fantasies of upper class life can only be a desire to compensate for the rigours of existence in a welfare state.'

Next came Paul Johnson in the *New Statesman*, who described Fleming as 'the owner of Goldeneye, a house made famous by Sir Anthony Eden's Retreat from Suez'. In a review headlined: 'Sex, Snobbery and Sadism', he declared that *Dr No* was the 'nastiest book I have ever read', but acknowledged that because of the novels' popularity, 'here was a social phenomenon of some importance'. Writing about the 'dual Bond-Fleming personality', it all got quite personal. 'There are three basic ingredients in *Dr No*,' he went on, 'all unhealthy, all thoroughly English: the sadism of a schoolboy bully, the mechanical, two-dimensional sex-longings of a frustrated adolescent, and the crude, snob-cravings of a suburban adult.' Worse still, it was 'very second-rate snobbery … not even the snobbery of a proper snob – it's the snobbery of an expense-account man'.

Of course, Fleming enjoyed the success of *From Russia, With Love*, but he had returned from Jamaica and his time alone with Blanche to find Ann understandably suspicious and resentful. Blanche had got into the habit of visiting England every summer with her mother, and Ann took the opportunity to invite her for lunch at Victoria Square, along with a coterie of friends, including Paddy Leigh-Fermor and Peter Quennell. Ann, who could be prone to 'flick-knife remarks', did her best to make Blanche feel uncomfortable, introducing her to all and sundry as 'Ian's mistress'. In the awkward silence that followed,

Blanche responded quietly: 'Ann, that's an unfair attack.' Blanche disliked Ann's intellectual friends as much as Ian did. 'They were talking so much,' she remembered. 'At that party I felt it was a whole lot of children frightened of the dark.'

Through the rest of the year, Ann and Ian's relationship continued to deteriorate, which didn't go unnoticed by her family. Her brother Hugo, who had never liked Ian, wrote to his other sister Mary Rose: 'Ian is a subtle bitch and in fact married to no one but himself ... Esmond was a come down from [O'Neill] – but Ian was really falling through the floor. And I believe [Ann] has really suffered with him – as one must being married to a person who really exists only for themselves – and who is neurotic and verbally violent into the bargain.'

In fact, Ian was immensely depressed about his failing marriage. In December, he and Ann had a 'clear-the-air' lunch at Scott's. This achieved nothing except the decision that they would spend their winters apart. On 16 December, Ian scribbled in his notebook: 'One of the great sadnesses is the failure to make someone happy.'

So Ian was on his own at Goldeneye again in January 1958 to write the new book, *Goldfinger*. He had 'arrived in a tempest' and the weather had remained poor: 'torrential winds and rain', as he reported to Ann in the first of a series of anguished letters. 'Thank God for the book, at which I hammer away in between bathing in the rain and sweating around the garden in a mackintosh ... The sofas were covered with the stains of rat shit as it appears the servants have used the house as their own since I left. Paint peeling off the eaves, chips and cracks all over the floor and not one bottle of marmalade or preserves ...' Then, after completing the 'sitrep', Fleming ended the letter: 'I can't write about other things. My nerves are still jangling like church bells and I am completely demoralized by the past month. I think silence will do us both good and let things heal.'

There was no Noël Coward and entourage this time, as he was acting in his *Nude with Violin* in California, but Blanche was ever-present. Soon a routine was established. She had now almost finished the rebuilding of Bolt and was spending most of her time there. 'I used to come down to swim at twelve o'clock, when he had more or less finished writing, and that's when we would go on the reef,' she says.

'He was strict with himself,' she remembers. 'Because he always had the shutters closed near his desk he didn't know when I arrived but as soon as he found out I was there, then he came down.' The two became closer than ever. Blanche found Ian 'very unhappy, in a terrible state of depression. I was able to give him a certain amount of happiness. I felt terribly sorry for him.'

When Fleming's friends the Pitmans arrived for a short stay, Blanche acted the hostess, taking the family off on long excursions along the coast or into the mountains while Ian worked. Later she would write to them in England, saying, 'Someone should keep an eye on Ian.' 'She was really in love with Ian Fleming,' says Blanche's son Chris. 'He was the love of her life. She saw her role as looking after him.'

While Ian was in Jamaica, Ann had checked in once more to the Enton Hall health farm in another effort to get herself off the pills. Soon the combination of productive work and the ministrations of Blanche and 'Doctor Jamaica' had mellowed Ian once more into a sympathetic husband. 'I'm terribly worried about your health,' he wrote in late January, 'and I pray that Enton's prison walls have mended your darling heart and somehow got you off this tragic switchback of pills which I implore you to stop... They are a way of life which is killing you ... You've no idea how they change you – first the febrile, almost hysterical gaiety and then those terrible snores that seem to come from the tomb! ... My darlingest darlingest love get well.'

At the end of his stay, with the writing of *Goldfinger* completed, Ian took the chance to go with Blanche on a trip to Pedro Cays, small islands sixty miles off the south coast. Blanche had signed up to help with a mission there to collect insect, fish and bird samples for the Jamaica Institute. She remembers that the crew were inexperienced and the yacht almost entirely without charts. After a roundabout route they eventually found the Cays, where, to Ian's horror, the scientists tipped the Indian poison curare into the sea in an effort to capture a specimen of a particular fish.

At the end of Fleming's trip, refurbishment work at Bolt was still under way and so Blanche was invited to stay rent-free at Goldeneye in his absence. She paid her way by having the house painted, improving various comforts, and planting in the garden. Her old friend Errol Flynn also came to stay and worked on his autobiography. (Flynn was by now in a very bad way, 'a floating, boozy bum', according to David Niven. He would be dead the next year at the age of just fifty.) As a parting gift on her return to her home, Blanche presented Goldeneye with a small wooden coracle, which Ian christened Octopussy.

Goldfinger is the longest and densest of the Bond novels. It went straight to the top of the best-seller charts and was well reviewed, the *Observer* commenting under the headline 'Sophisticated Sapper' that Fleming, 'even with his forked tongue sticking right through his cheek … remains manically readable'. As in *Diamonds are Forever*, Bond in *Goldfinger* is on an economic mission. Britain is suffering from a currency crisis and high bank rate because the villain, Auric Goldfinger, is smuggling out gold, 'the foundation of our international credit'. As during the recent Suez Crisis, the Americans are unwilling to help.

Goldfinger, 'a misshapen short man with red hair and a bizarre face', is the richest man in England, but not actually English, of course, and his international headquarters is in the badlands of the Caribbean, in Nassau. He is part of the international super-rich, a class Fleming of course knew from Jamaica's smartest hotels and whom he increasingly disliked (in Miami, he speculates, his hotel bill would have used up his year's salary in just three weeks). Goldfinger's allies are Germans and Koreans, 'the cruellest, most ruthless people in the world'. Like Sir Hugo Drax, Goldfinger cheats at cards, and like Spang from *Diamonds are Forever*, he doesn't drink or smoke – he's not to be trusted on either count.

Bond gets the better of his enemy twice – in Miami and on the golf course – but then, in a possibly fatal plot flaw, Goldfinger makes the mistake of employing Bond to help in his plan, with the aid of American gangsters, to rob Fort Knox and hand the gold over to SMERSH in the form of a waiting Soviet cruiser. 'It was modern piracy with all the old-time trimmings,' Bond muses. 'Goldfinger was sacking Fort Knox as Bloody Morgan had sacked Panama.'

So Bond once more comes to the aid of the Americans on American soil, and although they are grateful, he is left dissatisfied after Goldfinger escapes. 'Who in America cared about the Bank of England's gold?' he asks himself. 'Who cared that two English girls had been murdered in the course of this business? Who really minded that Goldfinger was still at liberty now that America's bullion was safe again?' Bond wonders in a passage that seethes with post-Suez resentment at the United States.

For Ian, the 1958 trip was perhaps the most cocooned of any he made to Jamaica. With Ann absent, there was no pressure to go to any parties, and there was no Coward dropping in with his friends. Nonetheless, outside the Goldeneye bubble, there were significant events taking place for Fleming's Jamaica.

Sir Kenneth Blackburne, previously governor of the Leeward Islands, had been appointed as Foot's replacement in Jamaica, but now the post had little to do with the day-to-day running of the country, which was firmly in the hands of elected Prime Minister Norman Manley. There had been some significant achievements: the national income of Jamaica had more than doubled from 1952 to 1958, and

A scene from Kingston's Kings Street in 1961.

exports increased by 250 per cent in value. In the same period, industrial output by value quadrupled, in all producing an annual growth rate of 8 per cent. Manley would retain power in the election of 1959, increasing his party's share of the vote and its majority.

But at the same time, the huge promise of the PNP's victory in 1955 had not been met. Expectations had risen faster than tangible wealth, and the population had grown even more than the economy. Land reform had failed and industrial development had degenerated into going cap-in-hand to foreign investors with ever-increasing inducements. Manley was forced to admit that the rich had got richer, but the poor poorer.

Against this backdrop, on 3 January 1958, two days before Fleming's flight touched down at Montego Bay, the West Indies Federation came into being. Its capital was in Trinidad and its first prime minister was Barbadian Grantley Adams. As part of the post-Suez rush to decolonise and disengage with those parts of the Empire that were unprofitable, it was planned in Britain that the Federation should achieve independence as a dominion within four or five years. The American consul in Trinidad made an accurate assessment: he reported to Washington that British support for the Federation had two aims: '(1) To impress the United Nations with its eagerness to grant self-government and independence to its colonial dependencies; and more important, (2) to rid itself of the continuing financial drain of supporting an area which is dependent upon grants and development aid.'

The Americans were watching closely. 'As colonial ties with Britain are loosened,' one United States newspaper opined, 'the possibilities for lucrative trade will increase with the development of the islands … American influence, too could help the new-born federation towards the stable democratic government now lacking among some of its Caribbean neighbors.'

As early as the 1947 Montego Bay conference, federation had seemed inevitable. But in the intervening years, enthusiasm for the project had ebbed away as scepticism grew in all quarters about the viability of the plan. It was a blow when Belize (then British Honduras) and Guyana (British Guiana) refused to join: it was hoped that these largely empty territories would have provided scope for immigration from the disastrously overpopulated islands. At the same time, distrust had worsened between the British and the local Caribbean governments. By the time it was launched, both sides had shown their reluctance to confer significant authority on the federal government. Instead, national governments and the British Governor-General would pull the strings.

Colonial Secretary Lennox-Boyd had virtually promised the position of Governor-General of the new Federation to Sir Hugh Foot, who remained hugely popular in Jamaica. But instead it was decided by Prime Minister Harold Macmillan that the new man was to be Patrick Buchan-Hepburn, 1st Baron Hailes, a former personal secretary to

Winston Churchill and chief whip for the Conservative Party, recently appointed Knight Grand Cross of the Order of the British Empire. No one was consulted in the West Indies, where Hailes was almost unknown. The American embassy in London reported the prevailing opinion across the political spectrum that 'his lack of distinction ... was not particularly complimentary to the new Federation'. Instead, 'it gave the appearance of a political deal', a sinecure. Morris Cargill described Hailes as 'a bird-brain. His attention span was about ten seconds.'

At Hailes's inauguration, Manley complained about Britain's 'parsimonious attitude towards this new Federation'. Frequent requests for loans had been turned down, causing an editorial in the *Jamaica Times* to lament: 'In the Commonwealth and Empire, in the way of loyalty and belief in a straight British future, few other territories can today equal the West Indies in sincerity. Yet we are the people that Britain, it appears, has chosen to leave to swim if we can, or sink if we can't.'

Fleming was certainly among those who, like Sir Hugh Foot, believed that Britain should support its former overseas possessions even after independence. So when, in April, he travelled to the Seychelles to write a series of articles for the *Sunday Times*, he first contacted Lennox-Boyd at the Colonial Office, offering to help promote tourism there in return for letters of introduction and travel advice. 'Having visited Jamaica for twelve years for my holidays,' he wrote, 'it is very much a bee in my bonnet that English people should become empire-minded for their holidays, and I shall encourage this idea in all my articles.'

The purpose of Fleming's trip was to report on a treasure-hunting project that was searching for a supposed hoard worth around £120,000 hidden by Olivier Levasseur, an eighteenth-century French pirate. But this proved to be a dead end, and Fleming found the place full of retired colonels, the 'flotsam and jetsam of our receding empire'.

In a letter back to England, he crossed out 'Government House, Seychelles' on the headed paper and wrote in 'State of Decay'.

The trip did, however, provide the setting for one of Bond's adventures in the book of short stories Fleming would write the following winter at Goldeneye. In 'The Hildebrand Rarity', Bond is sent to the Seychelles to give an independent view on the notion of situating a naval base there, as there was trouble in the Maldives, 'Communists creeping in from Ceylon. Strikes, sabotage – the usual picture.'

His mission completed, Bond is at a loose end. Then, as an 'underwater ace' (the story opens with Bond hunting a deadly stingray with his 'Champion harpoon-gun'), he is invited to go along on a specimen hunt with an American hotel-owning millionaire, Milton Krest, who has the 'finest damned yacht in the Indian Ocean'. Krest is gathering fish samples for the Smithsonian, but only as a tax dodge. Drawing on his experience of specimen hunting in Pedro Cays with Blanche the previous year, Fleming shows Bond appalled and disgusted when Krest tips poison on to the lovingly described reef in order to collect his target, a fish known as the Hildebrand Rarity.

Krest, who although American is of German ancestry, is an obnoxious drunk who uses a dried stingray tail to beat his beautiful English wife. He delights in patronising his guests. To Bond he declares, 'there were only three great powers – America, Russia and China. That was the big poker game, and no other country had either

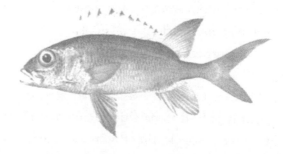

The fictional 'Hildebrand Rarity', according to Milton Krest, was from the squirrel-fish family (right) but 'bright pink with black transverse stripes.' Squirrel fish spines are often venomous as well as sharp.

the chips or the cards to come into it. Occasionally some pleasant little country ... like England would be lent some money so that they could take a hand with the grown-ups. But that was just being polite like one sometimes had to be – to a chum in one's club who'd gone broke.'

Krest gets his comeuppance, of course, but his view of Britain as third rate, in decline and imperial retreat, is an ever more pressing concern of Fleming. The following year, he undertook a world tour for a series of articles for the *Sunday Times* under the heading 'Thrilling Cities', which would be collected and published in 1963. 'A trip around the world, however hasty,' he wrote, 'brings home all too vividly the fantastically rapid contraction of our influence, commercial and cultural, over half the globe ... it was a source of constant depression to observe how little of our own influence was left ... our trading posts are everywhere in retreat.' Instead, in the 'Orient', 'where we did so much of the pioneering', 'Americans, and American culture, communications and trade have almost a monopoly'.

'Can this contraction be halted or even reversed?' Fleming asks. Only if, perhaps emulating Bond, 'the spirit of adventure which opened the Orient to us can be rekindled and our youth can heave itself off its featherbed and stream out and off across the world again'.

In the West Indian stories in the *For Your Eyes Only* collection, there is also a palpable sense of decline and retreat. In 'Quantum of Solace', the Bahamas are tired and dull: 'the winter visitors and the residents who had houses on the island talked of nothing but their money, their diseases and their servant problems,' Bond complains. The Governor had 'filled the minor posts for thirty years while the Empire crumbled around him'. In the title story, the estate of Fleming's exemplary Jamaicans, the Havelocks, is portrayed as a rare island of efficiency amid general rack and ruin.

The story opens with an introduction full of fondness for the flowers and birds of Jamaica. Then Colonel Havelock looks up from his copy of the *Gleaner* to comment on the situation in nearby Cuba: 'It looks to me as if [President] Batista will be on the run soon. Castro's keeping up the pressure pretty well.' Later in the story, we discover that the man behind the Havelocks' killers, von Hammerstein, is an ex-Nazi who worked as Batista's head of counterintelligence. We also learn from M that Bond's investigations won't get anywhere with 'the Batista people, but we've got a good man with the other side – with this chap Castro'. This was a time when Fidel Castro seemed very much the lesser of two dictatorial evils. After the US withdrew support and even recognition for Batista's regime in December 1958, he fled on 1 January 1959; US–Castro relations did not begin to sour until the spring of 1960.

(In 'Quantum of Solace', Bond is in the Bahamas to stop a shipment of arms to the Cuban rebels: 'He hadn't wanted to do the job. If anything, his sympathies were with the rebels, but the Government had a big export programme with Cuba in exchange for taking more Cuban sugar than they wanted, a minor condition of the deal was that Britain should not give aid or comfort to the Cuban rebels.')

However, the result of the revolutionary turmoil was that a lot of Batista cronies – 'crooks and gangsters' – were trying to get their 'funk money' out of Cuba. In 'For Your Eyes Only', von Hammerstein has taken a liking to the Havelocks' Jamaica estate, and in a scene that is amongst Fleming's most powerful and affecting, they are killed when they refuse to sell.

Fleming writes in an interesting subtext. It was, of course, widely known that the Batista regime had for a long time been propped up by the United States government and corporate interests, as well as cooperating closely with the American Mafia. So although the hitmen in the story are Cuban, and their boss German, they carry Pan American holdalls stuffed with 'solid wads of American money'. Havelock tells them, 'I do not share the popular thirst for American dollars.' When they make their escape from Jamaica, Fleming makes a point of informing us that their boat flies the Stars and Stripes. Once again, he implies that the threat to Jamaica comes in a roundabout way from the United States, a society, he declares in *Thrilling Cities*, riddled with 'criminality'.

The Havelocks had been friends of M – he was best man at their wedding – and Bond agrees to take on this mission of private revenge, recasting it as 'protecting the security of the British empire': 'If foreign gangsters find they can get away with this kind of thing, they'll decide the English are as soft as some other people seem to think we are … They had declared and waged war against British people on British soil.'

In the course of tracking down and killing von Hammerstein, Bond encounters the Havelocks' daughter, Judy. She is one of Bond's favourites, another very un-Ann-like and even Blanche-like Creole: 'wild and rather animal … good hard English stock spiced with the hot peppers of a tropical childhood … Bond thought she was wonderful.'

There is one very unusual short story in the collection. 'Quantum of Solace' only features Bond as a framing device for a tale narrated by the Governor of the Bahamas about marital infidelity that gives a chilling glimpse into Ian and Ann's relationship around this time. It is based on a story that Blanche told Ian about a Jamaican couple (as 'payment', he gave her a Cartier watch). 'She was a very lovely woman,' says Blanche. 'He was a very unattractive little man. And she was having a terrific love affair.'

In real life, the man was a police inspector, but here Fleming makes him a colonial civil servant, Philip Masters. After Fettes and Oxford, Masters is sent by the government to Nigeria, where 'he was lenient and humane towards the Nigerians, which came as quite a surprise to them'. Although 'shy and rather uncouth', Masters meets and marries an air hostess, Rhoda. When he is posted to Bermuda, Rhoda starts an affair and, rather like Molly Huggins with Robert Kirkwood, 'didn't make the smallest attempt to soften the blow or hide the affair in any way … poor Masters was wearing the biggest pair of horns that had ever been seen in the Colony.'

Masters is then posted to Washington for five months, and Rhoda, ditched by her lover, prepares to be reconciled with her husband. But when he comes back, he tells her that they will divorce in a year, and in the meantime, he has split the house into two sections. He will never speak to her in private, although they will continue to appear as a couple in public. A year later, Masters returns to England, leaving his wife penniless and with debts, an act of cruelty that he would have been incapable of a few years before.

'When all kindness has gone, when one person obviously and sincerely doesn't care if the other is alive or dead, then it's just no good,' explains the Governor. This was when the Quantum of Solace stood at zero. 'It's extraordinary how much people can hurt each other,' says Bond.

Fleming travelled to Jamaica alone again at the beginning of 1959, but then pushed hard for Ann to come and join him, adding that he was impressed with Blanche's improvements to Goldeneye. Ann was not quite ready to cede to her rival proprietary rights in Jamaica and flew out a few weeks later. The trip was not a success, with Ian failing to hide his great affection for Blanche (in the summer of the previous year he had tried to persuade her to join him in New York to 'snatch what we can', although she had declined).

On her return to London, Ann received a letter from Peter Quennell that gives some indication of the anguish she had suffered whilst away. Blanche was not a 'formidable rival', he wrote. 'It's tragic, nevertheless, that she should have cast a shadow over your visit and dimmed the goldenness of Goldeneye! How tiresome of the Commander to let her bother you.' He went on to explain that Ian's 'gallant escapades' were only his way of shoring up his 'often badly-battered ego', more affected by her and her friends' disdain for

Blanche and Ann on the Goldeneye window ledge, with Ian between them. Much later, Ann told a friend, 'Men suffer from not knowing what or whom they want.'

his novels 'than you have ever quite suspected'. Thus he was in need of 'the classical "little woman", whose big eyes reflect only trust and love and admiration'.

For Ian's winter trip the following year, Ann, pumped full of tranquillisers for the flight, came along with reinforcements: Caspar, on only his second trip to his father's Jamaica house, Caspar's governess, Mona Potterton, and later in the month, Ann's own lover Hugh Gaitskell made an appearance. The result was a mixture of farce and tragedy.

Caspar, now aged seven, was clearly a precociously intelligent little boy, interested in everything. Ann's daughter Fionn, who remembers him with immense affection, describes how he was always treated as an adult, and seemed as a result far older than his years. In Coward's play *Volcano*, the Ann character Melissa calls her son a 'little monster', but blames herself: 'I'm not the mother type. I say the wrong things.' Her son is like his father 'inside and out', she says: 'He's got Nanny and me and my sister exactly where he wants us. He's started young, taking women for granted.'

Violet, now the leader of a house staff of five at Goldeneye – an extra cook, Miss Elfreda Ricketts, a maid, Luna Smith, a laundress, Rena Oliphant, and an errand boy, Leaford Williams – remained a huge fan of Caspar. But most others depict him as highly difficult, with Evelyn Waugh describing him as 'a very obstreperous child, grossly pampered'. Fleming himself complained to Ann: 'I am nauseated by his bad manners which you seem to tolerate so indulgently.'

On her arrival at Goldeneye, Ann discovered that Blanche had been working hard on the garden, and promptly ripped out all the new plants and threw them over the cliff into the sea. John Gielgud, who was staying with Noël Coward, came over for lunch. He found Ann 'wizened, and gossipy … I felt they were on the verge of a frightful row.' Gielgud also met Blanche shortly afterwards, describing her as 'Noël's new cicerone and apparently Ian's mistress, a very rich widow with a toothy smile and Joyce Grenfell voice.' By now, Ann was referring to Blanche as 'Thunderbird's Jamaican wife'.

The weather was again terrible. 'We have endured six days of rain and gales,' Ann wrote to Evelyn Waugh on 26 January. 'The sofa and sheets are all sopping, sticky damp and the ill-fitting shutters drip all day: the rivers belch yellow water and coconut husks into the sea in widening circles of bile and filth, the dainty beach is piled high with refuse, and landslides block all the roads.'

In the meantime, the highly efficient and prim governess was getting on Fleming's nerves. She had arrived in a 'pleated bonnet', causing Ian to give Ann a pound and say, 'Take her to buy a straw hat, and forbid any raffia decorations.' When she took too long in the one rather primitive bathroom, he banged on the door, shouting, 'Lights out, Miss Potterton!'

Hugh Gaitskell had become very adept at 'coincidentally' being in the same place as Ann (just as Ian had done when Ann was married to Rothermere). A couple of weeks into the trip, he turned up for a few days' 'fact-finding mission' in Jamaica, much to the displeasure of his political party, who warned that the 'Eden Goldeneye legend' would make their leader the butt of silly jokes. Ann took him rafting on the Rio Grande, but the river was in spate, causing him to be thrown into the water: 'He disappeared for several minutes, and we were about to form a human chain when he rolled onto the shore like an amiable hippo.'

By now, the English press had cottoned on to the affair, and there followed a game of cat-and-mouse, with the local *Express* stringer emerging as the most consistent pest, to the extent that at one point Ann was driven to send a telegram to Beaverbrook to call him off. While she was doing so at the post office in Oracabessa, Gaitskell, or 'Heavenly' as Ann had taken to calling him, waited in his car in a discreet side street. But he was spotted there by the *Express* man, at which point he panicked and sped off along the coast road to Port Maria.

From Johnson's hardware store, Gaitskell telephoned Morris Cargill, who had been appointed his chaperone, to come and collect him. He had some of Ann's belongings in his car that needed to be returned to Goldeneye. Cargill arrived to find the Leader of the Opposition hiding behind a keg of nails. Gaitskell concealed himself in the back of Cargill's pick-up truck, and when they reached the house, he jumped out and hid behind some bushes. Here Ann found him and took him back to his hotel. By this point, Ian had had enough and took himself off to Bolt to see Blanche. It was all a huge mess.

'Not at all nice there,' Ann reported to Evelyn Waugh when she returned to England. To her friend Diana Cooper she wrote: 'The gold's out of Goldeneye. I wish I did not remain in love with Ian – isn't it odd?'

Still, the book that would come out of all this chaos was one of Fleming's very best.

Thunderball had begun its complicated gestation in the autumn of 1958, when Ivar Bryce introduced Fleming to a young film producer called Kevin McClory. McClory wanted to make a James Bond film, but from a new, specially written story featuring plenty of underwater scenes. Together with an experienced English scriptwriter, Jack Whittingham, and Ian's American friend Ernie Cuneo, Fleming and McClory worked on a number of ideas that eventually produced a plot in which the villains steal two nuclear bombs and then use them to blackmail the US and UK governments. Unfortunately, the film would go the way of other earlier aborted Bond TV and movie projects, but in the meantime Fleming wrote the 'novel of the film', failing to credit the others for their input. This would lead to a long and protracted legal case that significantly contributed to his poor health.

Thunderball's most significant departure was the abandonment of SMERSH and the Cold War. They had provided the 'motivation' for all the Bond villains so far, with the exception of the American gangsters of *Diamonds are Forever* (and possibly Dr No, who was prepared to sell his captured rockets to the Chinese if they outbid the Soviets). Instead, there is a new villainous organisation, SPECTRE, 'The Special Executive for Counterintelligence, Terrorism, Revenge and Extortion', manned by a potpourri of off-the-shelf baddies: ex-Gestapo, crime syndicates including the Mafia, drugs barons and former spies now freelance. The manuscript shows that the 'R' had originally stood for 'Revolution', but this was changed, making SPECTRE entirely unbothered by political or ideological motivation.

Curiously, near the beginning of the book, Bond reflects that 'with the Cold War wearing off, it was not like the old days'. It has been suggested that Fleming believed that by the time his new book was published, this would indeed be the case; but that hope would have been extraordinarily misplaced, with the Berlin stand-off, the Bay of Pigs and the Cuban missile crisis just around the corner.

Another explanation for the intriguing move from SMERSH to SPECTRE is that Fleming felt that to put a British agent in the front line against the Russians, leading the battle against 'Redland', would have now, post-Suez, tested the credulity of his readers. But, to be frank, the ludicrous SPECTRE tested that credulity far more. Or it may have been, as Bond explains, that the British security forces now had their hands full dealing with the rapid retreat from empire and, as such, did not have the resources to fight the Cold War as well. In *Thunderball*, Felix Leiter comments that 'Peace [is] bustin' out all over.' But Bond replies that for his country, 'There always seems to be something boiling up somewhere ... Cyprus, Kenya, Suez.'

Or perhaps Fleming was simply sickened by the Cold War and the bad in both sides. There is an early hint of this in *Moonraker*, when M implies that the United States is as dangerously bellicose as the Soviet Union. Similarly, in *Thrilling Cities*, there is a surprising moment during Fleming's piece on East Berlin when he quotes an experienced 'independent operator' in the spy 'game' who suggests that the Western way may not be the best way: to intelligent East Germans, his informant says, the success of the Soviet Union in round one of the Space Race, which had triggered the 'Sputnik Crisis' in the US, had made a big impression. 'The future with Communism looks just as good, if not better, than life in Europe and America. Such people are not attracted to democratic chaos,' he tells Fleming. 'They are quite sure they are on the winning side ... Why should they exchange these solid things for the trashy "comforts" of the West?' In *Thunderball*, the moment of most seriousness comes from the much-admired commander of the US nuclear submarine, who admits to being 'terrified by the whole business. Got a wife and two children ... These atomic weapons are just too damned dangerous.' In early 1963, Fleming was interviewed by the Jamaica *Gleaner* and asked about nuclear disarmament: 'I am all for it,' he replied. 'The two big poker players, America and Russia are evenly poised and the bluff and double bluff going on all the time is above my head. I hope it will all settle down in the end as I expect the two powers are so evenly matched, they will finally decide to call the game off and we shall all be able to settle down and not worry about it any more.'

Maybe Fleming's decision to exclude the Cold War and SMERSH from *Thunderball* was a curious combination of all these contradictory explanations. Most importantly, SPECTRE is fantastical, gothic and melodramatic, even fun: the culmination of all the self-deprecatory remarks Fleming made about Bond being 'adolescent pillow-fantasy'; the result of Ann and her circle's many derogatory comments about how juvenile his books were; an acknowledgment about what he now knew his readers wanted; the logical culmination of all those knowing asides. In *Thunderball*, Leiter points out, 'Planes with atom bombs don't get stolen in real life'; on another occasion, Bond laughs: 'It's a damned good sequence for a comic strip.' This self-awareness and silliness, a daydream on a Jamaican beach rather than the grim reality of, say, Le Carré's seedy safe houses with their instant coffee, is the fatal flaw of the Bond books as serious spy fiction, but their greatest strength as enduring British cultural properties.

The leader of SPECTRE is Ernst Stavro Blofeld. The purity of his apolitical villainy, combined with his recurrence in two further novels, made him Bond's Moriarty, the best known and even best loved of all the Fleming villains. He is, of course, a physical freak, a non-smoker and non-drinker and of mixed race, born of a Polish father and Greek mother.

Together with an arresting new villain, *Thunderball*'s setting and plot allowed Fleming to play to his Jamaica-inspired strengths. The many underwater scenes are superb, including a gripping night-time mission across a rubbish-strewn harbour, the horror of the downed aircraft – the 'squirming, red-eyed catacomb' – where octopuses are feasting on the decaying bodies of the crew, and the epic botched ambush at the end.

SPECTRE has chosen the lawless, free-wheeling space of the Caribbean in which to operate, where their scheme is headed by Blofeld's number two, Emilio Largo, described as 'an adventurer, a predator on the herd. Two hundred years before, he would have been a pirate – not one of the jolly ones of the story books, but a man like Blackbeard, a bloodstained cut-throat who scythed his way through people towards gold.' His cover story is that with the help of a pirate's map, he is searching for treasure, 'a sunken galleon thickly overgrown with coral'. For here, Fleming tells us, used to be 'the haunt of every famous pirate in the Western Atlantic'. At the end of the underwater fight, the men return with wounds 'that looked as if they belonged to the days of the pirates'. It's all told with swashbuckling relish.

The same year as *Thunderball* was written, Fleming lent Goldeneye to writer Graham Greene, in the hope that he in return would provide an introduction for a new omnibus edition of Bond. Blanche helped look after the guests, although she didn't like Greene. He was 'obsessed by drugs', she says. 'I asked him if he'd ever tried ganja and quick as a flash, he said he'd like to, although he said he'd never taken drugs in his life. Which I think was a big, blackhearted lie!' Blanche asked her overseer to bring some over to Goldeneye. 'He wanted me to stay and watch how he reacted. Why should I? I left him to it. I went home to bed.'

Greene and his mistress also had a falling-out with Violet, accusing her of drinking their whisky and overcharging for groceries from Port Maria. Violet responded that they had soiled their sheets, and the odd tot of whisky was to steel herself to wash them. To Greene's fury,

Fleming sided with Violet as his code demanded; the introduction for the omnibus edition would not be forthcoming.

But a far better endorsement was round the corner. On his way back from Jamaica in March 1960, Ian flew to Washington, where he visited his friend 'Oatsie' Leiter. Oatsie was an old friend of the Kennedys from her youth in South Carolina. She had introduced Jack Kennedy to his first Bond book, *Casino Royale,* when he had been ill in bed in Newport, Rhode Island, five years earlier. In 1957, his wife, Jacqueline, had given a copy of *From Russia, with Love* to the head of the CIA, Allen Dulles, saying: 'Here is a book you should have, Mr Director.' From then on, it became a tradition that Dulles and Jack Kennedy would exchange copies of Bond novels as they appeared, Dulles adding notes in the margins. He later commented that 'The modern spy could not permit himself to become the target of luscious dames … I fear that James Bond in real life would have had a thick dossier in the Kremlin after his first exploit, and would not have survived the second.'

'Oatsie' was going to the Kennedys' for dinner that night, and after lunch she was driving Ian along Georgetown's P Street in her white Chrysler when she saw the couple out walking. She stopped the car and asked them if she could bring a visitor to dinner with them that evening. 'Who's that?' asked Jack Kennedy politely. She introduced the two men. 'Mr Ian Fleming – Senator Kennedy.' Kennedy studied Fleming for a moment and said as they shook hands, 'James Bond? But, of course, by all means – do please come.'

Fleming had the *Thunderball* manuscript in his suitcase at the time, in which the United States' vulnerable southern flank is threatened with nuclear weapons. As the captain of the US submarine remarks: 'any one of these little sandy cays around here could hold the whole of the United States to ransom'. Over dinner, Kennedy asked Fleming what James Bond would do to get rid of Fidel Castro, who had come to power in Cuba the year before, and the previous month had signed a deal to ship part of his country's sugar crop to the Soviet Union in exchange for a loan of $20 million in convertible currency and $80 million worth of Soviet goods.

Fleming, clearly on top form, turned the whole thing into a joke, explaining that Bond would drop leaflets saying that the fallout from American nuclear tests provoked a strange reaction in men with facial hair, reducing them to sexual impotence. All the famous 'bearded ones' of the uprising would immediately shave off their beards, and the revolution would be over. (Ian's own views on Cuba and Castro were probably close to those expressed by Scaramanga in *The Man with the Golden Gun*: 'If the Americans once let up on their propaganda and needling and so forth, perhaps even make a friendly gesture or two, all the steam'll go out of the little man.')

The next day, Allen Dulles heard of Fleming's suggestion and unsuccessfully tried to set up a meeting with him; Ian was already on his way home. But Dulles might have taken it seriously. In *Red Heat: Conspiracy, Murder and the Cold War in the Caribbean*, Alex von Tunzelmann adds a coda to her telling of the Fleming–Kennedy dinner: 'Shortly afterwards, the CIA agent David Atlee Phillips remembered being told of a box of cigars, impregnated with a strong depilatory, that would be given to Fidel and would make his beard – indeed all his body hair – fall out. The agency also developed a thallium powder, which could be dusted on his shoes to the same effect.' Writing about Ian just after his death, Dulles confessed that he was 'always interested in the novel and secret "gadgetry" Fleming described', and having read about the homing device in *Goldfinger*, 'put my people in CIA to work on this as a serious project'.

Fleming worked the Kennedy connection hard, sending all his later books to Jack, his brother Robert and their sister Eunice Shriver. JFK was intrigued by Fleming, often asking the *Sunday Times* correspondent in Washington, Fleming's friend Henry Brandon, for news of him. 'Kennedy was fascinated by the line dividing Ian's real life from the fantasy life that went into his books,' Brandon explained. 'He often asked me how such an intelligent, mature, urbane sort of man could have such an element of odd imagining in his make-up.' When a few years later Ann met Bobby Kennedy at a dinner, she found him 'obsessed by Ian's books'.

Jack Kennedy would have an immense impact on Ian's career. Fleming's books had so far sold respectably in the United States, but not on the same level as in Britain. Then on 17 March 1961, *Life* magazine ran a piece on the President's favourite books. In ninth place, just above Stendhal's *Scarlet and Black*, was *From Russia, with Love* by Ian Fleming. It is hard to overestimate the importance of the article. From that moment, the Bond boom in the United States began.

The magazine publication was quickly exploited with a major push from Fleming's US paperback publisher. One campaign, run a few months after the Bay of Pigs debacle, read: 'INCREASE IN TENSION'. It showed a picture of the White House, with a single upstairs light burning, an arrow pointing to it labelled 'You can bet on it he's reading one of these Ian Fleming thrillers.' Thereafter Fleming became the best-selling thriller writer in America.

But just as huge commercial success came his way, Fleming's James Bond lifestyle – the Morland cigarettes and the cocktails – well and truly caught up with him. For the remaining few years of Fleming's life, Bond would hit new height after new height, while his creator's health and well-being went into freefall.

1961-2

The Spy Who Loved Me; On Her Majesty's Secret Service

There were moments, as he grew older, when with his heavy eyelids and mixed look of determination and abstraction, his face looked like the sculptured mask of melancholy.

William Plomer on Ian Fleming

Thunderball's heroine, Domino Vitali, named after another rare Caribbean bird, is everything Bond could wish for in a woman: she is beautiful and spirited in a slightly damaged way; she loves scuba diving and has romantic dreams about the Royal Navy; and, Bond notices approvingly, she 'drives like a man'. But what provides him with his excuse for meeting her is her smoking habit.

Domino is in a Nassau tobacconist's asking for cigarettes that taste so disgusting they will help her stop smoking. Bond makes his move. 'I'm the world's authority on giving up smoking,' he tells her. 'I do it constantly. You're lucky I happen to be handy.' They then go to a bar, where her idea of a 'soft' drink is a double Bloody Mary.

The beginning of the novel sees Bond suffering from his drinking, waking hung-over from a night that included eleven whiskies. 'When he coughed – smoking too much goes with drinking too much and doubles the hangover – a cloud of small luminous black spots swam across his vision ... Bond swallowed down two Phensics and reached for the Enos.' He has 'that nagging sense of morning guilt that one is slowly wrecking one's body'. Later that day, he meets M, who reads part of his latest medical report: 'Despite many previous warnings, he admits to smoking sixty cigarettes a day ... the officer's average daily consumption of alcohol is in the region of half a bottle of spirits.'

M sends him to Shrublands health farm to dry out. The scenes there, where Bond is prodded, weighed and checked, show that Fleming was now clearly a man in the grip of the doctors. The previous year he had given up his *Sunday Times* job (although he was kept on a retainer of £1,000 a year), but the removal of this burden failed to improve his health. Ann's letters from the summer and autumn of 1960 include several references to his new weakness, breathlessness and high blood pressure. In September, he spent a week at a 'liver cure resort' in Brittany.

At the beginning of 1961, Ann and Ian flew to Jamaica and Ian arrived suffering from bronchitis. 'Ian had a high fever and was fearfully cross,' Ann reported to Evelyn Waugh. 'Happily Noël Coward came to call and proved himself a Florence Nightingale, changing Thunderbird's sopping pajamas, turning the mattress, and fetching him iced drinks. Noël has always found T-B fearfully attractive and jumped at the opportunity to handle him. While Noël fetched ice cubes from the Frigidaire T-B's language was something horrible, he blamed me for exposing him to homosexual approaches.'

In his diary, Coward reported a depressing scene: 'Annie looking exhausted and strained', Ian 'scarlet and sweating in a sopping bed and in a hellish temper. Their connubial situation is rocky ... My personal opinion is that although he is still fond of Annie, the physical side of

Alec Guinness in the pool at Blue Harbour, where he stayed en route to Cuba to film 'Our Man in Havana'. He found the atmosphere at Coward's house 'too flamboyantly camp.' He would also later complain of valuables pilfered from his room.

it, in him, has worn away. It is extraordinary how many of my friends delight in torturing one another.'

Part of the conflict involved Jamaica, now hated by Ann, Coward wrote, but still loved by Ian. She wanted him to sell Goldeneye to help pay for the renovations to a huge new house she planned to buy – Sevenhampton near Swindon – but Ian refused to do so. (In the event, the money was found from elsewhere.)

Ann was not alone in her new dislike. Coward himself wrote to a friend at the end of 1960 that he had 'taken against Jamaica in a big way ... the once peaceful island is full of noises – noises of tourists and noises of underlying discontent. All wages and prices have risen astronomically. The roads are, mostly, in a dreadful state and the whole atmosphere has changed.'

In 1960, tourist arrivals topped a quarter of a million for the first time (in 1950, there had been 1,650 hotel beds on the island; by 1962, there were over 7,000). And it was in the main a different sort of tourist, less wealthy and arriving all year round. Jamaica was no longer the exclusive preserve of the super-rich, to the disappointment of people like Sir William Stephenson, who now sold his house on the island. In 1960, John Pringle offloaded Round

Hill; soon afterwards, Beaverbrook sold Cromarty. It seemed an era was coming to an end.

Part of this change, of course, was the Jamaicans' new assertiveness as independence loomed. Coward's American friend and fellow expatriate Marion Simmons complained: 'Jamaica's going to go to the dogs. Why do they need independence? We wouldn't have the British discipline and sense of order. It's going to be chaos. It's time to leave Jamaica.' Writing to Waugh in the winter of 1961, Ann reported an ugly incident: 'Lord Brownlow imported a farm manageress, a maiden of fifty summers weighing fourteen stone, she gave a peremptory order to a sugar cane worker who promptly raped her, she took her riding breeches to the local doctor for analysis and also her person; a tremendous hue and cry is in progress but she has failed to identify the villain amongst a parade of Perry's slaves; Perry is very ill as a result.' Coward wrote that his 'trust' in Jamaica was gone, and in early 1961 put Blue Harbour on the market. 'I owe Jamaica much happiness and peace and enjoyment,' he wrote, 'and I know now beyond a shadow of a doubt that all that is over.'

The Spy Who Loved Me, the book Fleming wrote during his visit in 1961 despite his health, is utterly different from every other Bond story. For a start, it is narrated by a woman, a young Canadian, and Bond himself does not even appear until the last third of the novel.

The story opens with Vivienne Michel – named after a Jamaican neighbour of Fleming – running away from England, 'from drabness, fustiness, snobbery, the claustrophobia of close horizons' and from her 'sequence of untidy, unattractive love affairs'. These are described in unglamorous, realistic detail: her first is with a public-school rotter who tries to take her virginity in the box of the Windsor cinema (where Fleming claimed to have lost his). Then comes Kurt, a German who steers her away from what he calls 'The Anarchic Syndrome', which he defines as 'smoking and drinking, phenobarbital, jazz, promiscuous sleeping-about, fast cars, slimming, Negroes and their new republics, homosexuality, the abolition of the death penalty and a host of other deviations'. He pays for her to have an abortion.

Vivienne ends up in northern New York State at a small motel among pine trees. Surveying herself in the mirror, she notices that her skin has changed – 'from the grimy sallowness that had been the badge of my London life to the snap and colour and sparkle of living out of doors'. More than anything, she enjoys being alone.

She is left in charge of the motel, but gangsters arrive to burn it down with her inside as part of an insurance scam. Vivienne is then rescued by the arrival of Bond, at which point Fleming returns to his more familiar ground of shootouts and seduction.

It is Fleming's most sexually explicit work, and although this misfires badly in parts, he does try to go beyond Bond's usual cartoon-strip seduction. Sex gives the narrator Vivienne both her best and worst moments. She is by some way Fleming's most realised and credible female character, and in this sense, and in the anti-heroic tone of the story, it is his most ambitious and literary novel. Although the villains have comic-book characteristics, including their names – Sluggsy and Horror – they are far more credible than the freakish megalomaniacs that had become such an important 'ingredient' of the earlier novels. 'I tried to break away from my usual formula,' he explained on *Desert Island Discs* two years later. 'It took quite a beating from the critics.'

Noël Coward thought that the book 'started brilliantly' but 'as usual' went too far. Ivar Bryce, however, described it as 'the single lamentable lapse in the quality of his work'. Like Bryce, few reviewers cared to try a new recipe when they were enjoying the old one so much.

The press were withering. The *Telegraph* exclaimed: 'Oh Dear Oh Dear Oh Dear.' One critic described it 'as if Mickey Spillane had tried to gatecrash his way into the Romantic Novelists' Association'. The realistic detail was 'dreary'; where was 'the High-Stakes Gambling

Scene, the Meal-Ordering scene, the Torture Scene … ?' lamented *Time* magazine.

Fleming was so horrified and embarrassed by his experiment's reception that he told his publishers to stop all further editions of *The Spy Who Loved Me* and refused to allow a paperback to be sold. Ann, who by the time of publication in April 1962 was busy doing up Sevenhampton, wrote to Waugh that she was 'doing my best to reverse this foolish gesture because of the yellow silk for the drawing-room walls'. She was now calling the money from the Bond books 'our pornography fund'. (After Fleming's death, Ann would allow a paperback edition to be published, which sold more than half a million copies in its first six months.)

On his return to England, Fleming found himself embroiled in a laborious court case around the publication of *Thunderball*. It was stressful, exhausting and infuriating. The following month, while attending the monthly *Sunday Times* conference on 12 April, he suddenly went very quiet and pale. His friend Dennis Hamilton, later editor of the paper, noticed something was badly wrong, and helped Fleming out of the room and into a car to the London Clinic.

Still only fifty-two years old, Fleming had suffered a major heart attack. He was lucky to be alive. He would remain in the clinic for a month; Blanche, who was in London with her mother, visited and ran errands – much to Ann's displeasure. After that, he was sent to a south-coast hotel to convalesce. Here he used the time to write up a children's story he had created for Caspar – *Chitty-Chitty-Bang-Bang*.

Slowly, he recovered, writing to his American publisher: 'I am glad to say that while the iron crab made quite a sharp pass at me, he missed with the major claw.' But he was never quite the same again: as 'the claws of "the iron crab" tightened around his heart, he seemed slowly to abandon life', Peter Quennell later wrote. 'Words reached him; he listened and replied; but one felt he was listening from a certain distance. Meanwhile courageous, defiant, aloof, he dismissed all chances of recovery that his doctors offered him, and refused to give up alcohol and tobacco, which had become his only sensory pleasures.' (At Shrublands on a healthy regime, Bond had worried that he was 'losing the vices that were so much part of his ruthless, cruel, fundamentally tough character'.)

And so, in Fleming's next novel, *On Her Majesty's Secret Service*, we find Bond more than ever staggering from drink to drink. Near the beginning of the book, his 'plan for the evening' consists of two double vodka and tonics, then two more, 'and then, slightly drunk, go to bed with half a grain of Seconal', a barbiturate. 'Encouraged by the prospect of this cosy self-anaesthesia, Bond brusquely kicked his problems under the carpet of his consciousness.' The next morning at the airport, he has moved on to 'a double brandy and ginger ale'. His urine, which he uses as 'invisible ink', indicates 'a super-abundancy of alcohol in the blood-stream'. At one point, we learn, 'Bond was aching for a drink', and he tells his heroine Tracy that he needs three drinks to her one. She complains later that 'all he thinks about is drink'. And so on. Moreover, Bond is still 'chain-smoking', and is often tired,

Fleming writing *On Her Majesty's Secret Service* at the red bullet-wood desk in his now favourite spot in his bedroom. He had bought a gold-plated typewriter after finishing *Casino Royale*, but didn't take it to Jamaica.

sometimes breathless, and using alcohol to perk himself up as well as relax him. Of course, we would now call this a fairly chronic case of alcoholism, and the reality of that was now even dawning on Fleming.

This new novel, written at Goldeneye in January and February 1962, was a return to the classic Bond formula, and a reprise of Blofeld, whom Bond is hunting at the beginning of the story. He is so frustrated by his lack of success that he even drafts a letter of resignation to give to M, but before he delivers it, he meets Contessa 'Tracy' di Vicenzo, suicidal daughter of a crime boss, Marc-Ange Draco. Draco, another of Fleming's likeable pirates, gives Bond information on Blofeld's whereabouts. Impersonating an officer from the College of Arms, Bond meets Blofeld at his mountaintop lair, where Blofeld is infecting impressionable young women with diseases to carry back to Britain. The plot is foiled, but Blofeld escapes again, having killed Tracy just hours after her marriage to Bond.

On Her Majesty's Secret Service was considered by Bond film script-writer Richard Maibaum to be 'by the far the best novel [Fleming] ever wrote'. Its great strengths are the set-piece ski chase (which would become a stock ingredient of the films), the attack on the alpine redoubt, and also the real tenderness with which Fleming writes about Bond's feelings for Tracy. It would become the most successful Bond novel to date, selling over 70,000 hardback copies in the UK in the first year, and topping the US best-seller chart for over six months. The *Observer* newspaper also considered it the best Bond for a while: 'It is better plotted and retains its insane grip until the end.' An American reviewer in the *Los Angeles Times* saw the book's success as a reaction against 'the 20th century vogue of realism and naturalism', exactly what Fleming had so unsuccessfully attempted with his previous book. 'With Fleming,' the reviewer went on, 'we do not merely accept the willing suspension of disbelief, we yearn for it, we hunger for it.'

In *Thunderball*, Bond had come once more to the rescue of the United States; in *On Her Majesty's Secret Service*, the threat is to Britain alone. But it is a country in palpable retreat. We hear about 'the miracle of the latest German export figures'; at the College of Arms, they are busy working on flags, stamps and medals for 'the new African States'. Bond spends Christmas Day with his beloved M, who regales him with naval stories, 'all true and it was all about a great Navy that was no more and a great breed of officers and seamen that would never be seen again'.

As had become customary, the 1962 trip to Goldeneye saw Ann leave Jamaica well ahead of Ian. Soon after she got home, she received a jaunty letter from him saying he was cheerful and well. She replied at length, expressing her upset at his evident preference for Blanche over her. He had phoned Blanche the moment he arrived, and now she was 'an adjunct of life in Jamaica'. 'I fear that since the rise of James Bond you do not care for a personality that in any way can compete with yours,' Ann suggested. 'No doubt there is more adulation to be had at [Bolt], and you refuse to see that it is an impossible situation for me. However, you have now two weeks for adulation ... no doubt that is why you wanted me to go ... Your personality has greatly changed with success, Bond and bad health – this is a *general* opinion ... If you were well and we were both younger our marriage would be over,' she ended. 'But I love you and want to look after you, and grind my teeth when you smoke ...'

Part of Ann's fury was at what she called Ian's 'patronage' of Blanche's family. He had helped get her son Chris Blackwell a job on a new film being shot in Jamaica. Fleming had long seen his hero, James Bond, as a movie property. Now, at last, it was happening. The filming of *Dr No*, starring Sean Connery, was under way.

In December 1960, Harry Saltzman, a Canadian film producer based in London who had worked on a number of critically acclaimed 'kitchen-sink' dramas, had taken a six-month option on all the Bond books. But he had failed to raise money, and with time running out went into partnership with Albert 'Cubby' Broccoli, formerly a Hollywood agent, but more recently a London-based film producer. Broccoli had tried unsuccessfully for the same option in 1958. The idea to film Bond had been in the back of his mind for some time. 'James Bond appealed to me on several levels,' he later wrote. 'Fleming's fictional character offered exciting scope for all the basics in screen entertainment: a virile and resourceful hero, exotic locations, the ingenious apparatus of espionage, and sex on a fairly sophisticated level.' Broccoli had worked with director Terence Young, designer Ken Adam and scriptwriter Richard Maibaum, all of whom would be vital to the Bond films' success.

Saltzman and Broccoli set up Eon Productions, and started to look for backers. They originally planned *Thunderball* as the first film, but the McClory injunction stopped that and they opted for *Dr No*, partly on account of its exotic Jamaican location. Work started on the script, with one early version having Dr No as a monkey (the scriptwriters thought Fleming's Dr No 'a ludicrous character, Fu Manchu with hooks'). At another time, the plan was for the villain to be an arms dealer planning to blow up the Panama Canal. Fleming himself demanded no input on the script, but Broccoli insisted: 'It's got to be the way the book is.'

'Ian attended several of our meetings well before the picture started,' Broccoli later wrote. 'It was good having him around. His whole persona, the way he held his cigarette, his laid-back style, that certain arrogance, was pure James Bond.'

In the end, the scripwriters made Dr No a member of SPECTRE, various new characters were invented, and the more over-the-top elements at the end of the novel – including the fight with the giant squid – were discarded. As in the book, Bond is helping out the Americans, but US influence is much stronger in the film. Having been issued with an American gun, he flies via New York on Pan Am to find Felix Leiter, who does not appear in the book, already in Jamaica and on the case. Nonetheless, Leiter knows this is British territory, commenting, 'Limeys can be pretty touchy about trespassing.' For his part, Bond tells the American: 'It's my beat.'

Eon Productions had several rejections from distributors, but in June 1961, they secured the backing of United Artists. The budget for the film was set at $1 million. Fleming was to get $50,000 on signature, then $100,000 per film plus 5 per cent of the 'producers' profits'. He arranged for this money to go directly into a trust fund for Caspar.

As soon as the deal was done, director Terence Young, designer Ken Adam and the two producers headed to Jamaica to look for locations. This 'beautiful island', said Broccoli, 'had everything we were looking for'. On Fleming's recommendation, Chris Blackwell was taken on as location manager and general local fixer. He had given up the ADC job at King's House on Foot's departure in 1957 and then spent a short time in London studying to be an accountant, but he had hated it and soon returned to Jamaica. There he had worked in various jobs and was currently running the Ferry Inn, halfway between Kingston and Spanish Town. His great love, though, was Jamaican music, and he had set up Island Records in July 1959. Fleming hoped that Blackwell would bring some of this expertise to the film.

The casting of James Bond was, of course, crucial. Fleming had always thought of David Niven in the role. The producers sounded out Cary Grant, but he was too expensive and refused to commit to a series of films; James Mason would only do two, and thought the books 'all rather a load of nonsense'; Roger Moore was busy doing television; both Patrick McGoohan and James Fox refused the role because of religious scruples.

Almost making a virtue out of a necessity, an unknown Scottish actor, Sean Connery, was selected, mainly on the strength of his sex appeal, and the fact that he looked a lot like the *Express* cartoon-script Bond. When casting had been discussed for a stillborn US TV project a few years before, Fleming had suggested that there should be no 'stage Englishness ... no monocles, moustaches, bowler hats

Fleming and Sean Connery during the filming of *Dr No* in Jamaica. After initial doubts about his suitability, Fleming was converted when he invited Connery to dinner at the Savoy and a young female guest pronounced him extremely attractive.

or bobbies, or other "Limey" gimmicks. There should be no blatant English slang, a minimum of public school ties and accents.' Even so, he was worried that the working-class Scot Connery might not have the panache for his hero. Connery later commented: 'I never got introduced to Fleming until I was into the movie – but I know he was not that happy with me as a choice. He called me, or told somebody, that I was an over-developed stuntman ... But when I did eventually meet him he was very interesting, erudite and a snob – a real snob. But his company was very good for a limited time.'

Connery's Bond would be different to that of the books, in which he only reads *The Times* newspaper and complains about 'the cheap self-assertiveness of young labour since the war'. Connery, at thirty-one, was younger, tougher and somehow more modern and classless. Interestingly, Fleming would later comment that he was 'not quite the idea I had of Bond, but he would be if I wrote the books over again'. In an interview with *Playboy* magazine conducted after two Connery films had been released, Fleming even reinvented Bond to the extent of suggesting that his politics were 'a little bit left of centre'.

An idea was floated to ask Noël Coward to play Dr No. 'The character required brains, sophistication and a kind of Machiavellian wit,' wrote Broccoli later. 'Ian thought it was a brilliant idea. I did, too. Since I didn't know Coward and Ian did, I asked him to cable our offer to Noël in Jamaica. He did so, and received a swift response by telegram: "Dear Ian, The answer to your suggestion is No ... No ... No ... No! Thank you. Love, Noël."'

The bulk of the cast and crew flew out on a chartered Britannia 312, arriving in Jamaica on Sunday 14 January. Connery and a handful of others had come out the previous week and set up camp at New Kingston's Courtleigh Manor Hotel on Trafalgar Road. Originally a private house lived in by, amongst others, the Swedish consul, it had become a hotel by 1948. As well as providing accommodation, it would also be used for a handful of scenes in the film.

Filming began two days later at Kingston's Palisadoes airport, witnessed by a reporter from the *Gleaner*: 'If the first day's shooting was any indication of the quality of the finished product,' he wrote, 'DR NO promises to be a slapdash and rather regrettable picture.' Apparently there were continuity problems: an extra carrying a large suitcase and coat over his arm 'soon got much too tired of toting them around. And it was as hot as blazes.' So in a scene filmed later but shown immediately after, he is holding only a hat. 'What I have heard of the dialogue is appalling,' the *Gleaner* writer added.

After the first day of filming, the film's top brass retreated to Chris Blackwell's Ferry Inn. There the *Gleaner* man spoke to two of the extras, who were having dinner. '"Never again," said one extra – one of Jamaica's most highly-paid models. "We've been at it since eight o'clock this morning, and do you know what they paid us? Thirty shillings!"' The *Gleaner* called this 'a pittance'. '£5 a day and a free luncheon would be modest enough.' The two extras 'certainly wouldn't be reporting on the set tomorrow'.

By later Bond standards, the budget for *Dr No* was modest, and every effort was made to save money. This included using as many locals as possible, even if they were not experienced actors. On director Terence Young's first visit to Jamaica the summer before, he had been very taken by the young woman who worked at the BWIA check-in desk. This was twenty-three-year-old Marguerite Le Wars, who earlier in the year had won the Miss Jamaica pageant, securing herself the prize of a Ford Anglia car. She did not take him seriously, but when Young returned to Jamaica for the filming, he asked again, and as she had done some stage acting and television commercial work, she agreed to go along for an audition that afternoon at the Courtleigh Manor Hotel.

Young wanted her to play Miss Taro, the King's House secretary secretly working for Dr No, but she refused as it involved 'kissing a strange man' and her parents would be horrified. So instead she was cast as the photographer who tries to take Bond's picture at the airport and during the scene in Morgan's Harbour bar.

Filming the bridge-playing scene at the Liguanea Club was helped by casting its manager Colonel Burton as one of the four players. In the same way, Dolores Keator played Strangways' secretary Mary Trueblood; according to Young, she 'got the job because she owned the house and she allowed us to use it [to film her scene]!'

Other locals included the parts of Pleydell-Smith, Jones the chauffeur (Reggie Carter, who was brother-in-law of Marguerite Le Wars), the three blind beggars (one of whom was a dentist), bar manager Puss-Feller (Lester Prendagast, who in real life owned the Glass Bucket club in Kingston), and sundry guards, hotel receptionists and waiters. None were required to do any of the filming in England. Of the forty-four featured roles, nineteen were locals.

Strangways, the first character to be killed in a Bond film, was played by Timothy Moxon, who had done some stage acting in

England but who now worked in Jamaica as a pilot of crop-spraying aircraft. He had known Terence Young in London and happened to be sitting in the Courtleigh Manor Hotel. Young said, 'I've got a small part you can do at the beginning.' Moxon thanked him and asked about the little-known actor playing the lead. Young replied, 'Sean's got this terrible Scottish accent, but I think he's going to make it.' Moxon was paid just over a hundred pounds for his two days' work.

Moxon lived in Oracabessa and had already met Fleming in a supermarket there and been invited to Goldeneye, which he found very 'bare-boned and austere'. He wasn't impressed that everyone there called Fleming 'the Commander', as he 'didn't do a tremendous amount during the Second World War but he did gain the title of Commander and lived on it' (Moxon himself had flown bombing raids over Germany). But, as Moxon explained just before he died, 'over time our friendship grew. He was a good man at lifting the elbow. He knew how to put away the booze, but I found him charming.' According to Moxon, Fleming was 'not wildly impressed with the Dr No movie' and hadn't even realised that Moxon had appeared in it. 'He didn't talk about it, he preferred to discuss things like swimming and scuba diving.'

While the film crew were based in Kingston, as well as at the Courtleigh Manor, scenes were shot in downtown Kingston (the three blind beggars at the beginning of the film), at Morgan's Harbour bar out on the Palisadoes, on the cement company road up Wareika Hills and at Dolores Keator's house on Kinsale Avenue off Jacks Hill Road.

Then, at the end of the month, the production moved to Jamaica's north coast, with the crew split between the Carib Ocho Rios Hotel and the Sans Souci – both of which are still in operation today. A Sans Souci villa doubled as Miss Taro's house, where Professor Dent was shot. The Reynolds bauxite pier at Ocho Rios served as Crab Key's docks. Fleming had advised on locations near Goldeneye, and seems

Filming *Dr No*. So tight was the budget that between takes it was producer Cubby Broccoli himself who raked the sand clear of footprints.

to have persuaded his friend Lord Brownlow to open up his mansion as the interior of King's House, where the crew was not allowed to film. Fleming also recommended for the scene in which Bond first meets Honey Rider the stunning Laughing Waters beach, access to which was owned by a friend of his. Honey, Bond and Quarrel wash themselves in Dunn's River Falls near Ocho Rios, now one of Jamaica's most popular tourist attractions, and then are filmed in the White River, St Ann, nearby, where the three hide using improvised snorkels. The final location shoots were at Vanzie salt marsh near Falmouth, a mosquito-infested wasteland where Dr No's 'dragon' captures Bond and Honey and kills Quarrel.

Chris Blackwell did his best to get his musician friends jobs as grips and gofers, and also introduced the film's music supremo Monty Norman to Byron Lee and the Dragonaires, the veteran ensemble who had played at Jamaica's north-coast hotels and at Kingston's nightclubs since the mid fifties. Their manager Ronnie Nasralla, charged with providing the musicians for the Morgan's Harbour bar scene, says he interviewed others to play, including Bob Marley, who was turned down as he was 'very untidy and crude'. But somewhat inevitably the job went to Byron Lee's group. As the band's guitarist Rupert Bent recalled, 'We were the number one band in Jamaica at the time, in fact, in the Caribbean. There was no one else to turn to when the people were making the film.' Byron Lee himself is seen in the film playing the bass guitar in 'Jump Up'. Ernest Raglin would provide extra guitar for the final sound, and another Jamaican legend, Count Prince Miller, does his trademark dance. As it turned out, the film would provide a great international showcase for Jamaican and, more generally, West Indian music.

Chris Blackwell loved the whole experience, describing the filming as 'a riot'. Each day, undeveloped film and soundtrack was put on a plane to London, processed overnight then sent back. Inevitably, there were setbacks. Saltzman wrote from Jamaica: 'The biggest problem is the "manana" attitude of the local people and the fact they do not keep their promises to their contracts ... we have been gulled and taken in due to the complete and utter inefficiency of the locals.' Thunderstorms and other problems with weather also meant that more filming than had originally been planned needed to be done back in England. Running along Laughing Waters beach, Ursula Andress jagged her leg on a piece of coral. As she arrived in Jamaica a week or so after the rest of the cast, she was far too white-skinned to play her role as a Creole local, so each day had to rise early to strip naked and be covered from head to foot in fake tan. She recalled how, while this was going on, a breakfast tray would be brought in. And then another, as members of the crew took the opportunity to feast their eyes on the sight. Sometimes there would be up to twenty breakfast trays in her room before the tanning job was done. The solution to her coral wound, which refused to heal, was to plaster on more of the fake tan.

During the filming at Laughing Waters, Fleming took the opportunity to visit the set. With him was Ann, the ever-present Peter Quennell and the poet Stephen Spender, who was staying at Goldeneye while in Jamaica lecturing for the British Council.

'They were shooting a beach scene,' Ann reported to Evelyn Waugh, 'the hero and heroine cowering behind a ridge of sand to escape death from a machine gun mounted on a deep-sea fishing craft borrowed from a neighbouring hotel and manned by communist negroes. The sand ridge was planted with French letters full of explosive – by magic mechanism they blew up the sand in little puffs. The machine gun gave mild pops but I was assured it will be improved on the sound track; all this endeavor was wasted because unluckily a detachment of the American Navy entered the bay in speed launches and buggered it all up ... they told us they were on French leave from Cuba and were in search of drink and women.' Terence Young says that the Fleming group appeared out of nowhere and threatened to ruin the take. He shouted at them, 'Lie down you bastards!' He shot the scene and then forgot all about them. Half an hour later someone asked, 'What happened to those geezers on the beach?' Someone was sent to find them; they were still lying down as instructed.

Ian became a regular visitor to the set, and invited cast members to dinner at Goldeneye. Ursula Andress remembers that she spent more time with Fleming than with the film's producers. Fleming was clearly smitten, name-checking Andress in the book he was writing at the time, *On Her Majesty's Secret Service* – 'that beautiful girl with the long fair hair at the big table, that is Ursula Andress, the film star'. She also met Noël Coward, another visitor to the set: 'Together they were a joy to be with,' she remembered, 'two great personalities with a sense of humour; witty and interesting. It was my big discovery in Jamaica – Ian Fleming and Noël Coward.'

No one was sure whether they were making a hit or a turkey. Most believed the latter. But Chris Blackwell remembers the turning point:

Fleming and Andress in Jamaica, getting to know each other over a few drinks.

when the crew sat down in the Cove cinema in Ocho Rios to watch the rushes of Ursula Andress' emergence from the sea at the beautiful Laughing Waters beach. Then, he says, they knew they had something (and of course, bikini sales would sky-rocket).

The *Gleaner* had also changed its mind, declaring, 'Filming has brought employment and publicity to Jamaica. Mr Fleming is becoming a kind of one-man national asset.' The writer went on: 'Perhaps most important of all, many of us have seen the leading lady, Miss Ursula Andress, in a bikini: a sight as sensational and perhaps even more stimulating than such natural splendours as Niagara Falls and the Grand Canyon combined.'

Although none of the cast and crew could have expected it, the film would provide Jamaica with its greatest international exposure to date. So what version of Jamaica is shown?

Chris Blackwell says it was an 'accurate' portrayal of Jamaica at the time. Marguerite Le Wars, who acted in *Dr No*, says it was 'fairly accurate, though a large chunk of Jamaica was omitted'. The film opens with the three blind beggars crossing the road heading north along the east side of what is now St William Grant Park, named after a 1930s labour leader, but then called Victoria Park. The background shows a modern scene with buses, cars and electricity and telephone pylons and wires. At the end of the shot, the statue of Queen Victoria appears on their left. The next shot is on the north side of the park, which puts the colonial-style Ward Theatre in the background. Then, although they are in theory heading north to New Kingston, where the club is located, they are seen walking south along King Street to the waterfront. This enables the viewer to see a ship in the harbour, but also, on their right, the statue of Sir Charles Metcalfe, British Governor of Jamaica 1839–42 (this has now been moved to St William Grant Park and replaced with a large copy of Edna Manley's 'Negro Aroused'). So in a way, the men are on a walking tour of colonial statues!

Much of the portrayal of Jamaica as 'imperial' is, of course, much less subtle. The next stop is Queen's Club, clearly a bastion of white colonial rule. After the murder of Mary Trueblood, we are shown Whitehall and the Houses of Parliament in London, then the Secret Service headquarters, with radio operators receiving signals in an efficient way from all around the Empire. King's House is seen, with a prominent Union Jack flying from the flagpole, and uniformed guards in white tunics, including a Gurkha-style soldier with a rifle with bayonet fixed. Inside, there is a portrait of the Queen amidst the lavish furnishings, and a military official in Raj-style khaki shorts.

It is a touristic portrayal as well, with the beautiful beaches and the picturesque local women with huge loads on their heads. Apart from Quarrel, as subservient a character as in the book, most of the other locals are entertainers or waiters. In addition, as in Fleming's stories, Jamaica is a place of romantic adventure and dangerous mystery. Nowhere is there a hint that this outpost of empire will be independent before the film is even released.

The Federation of the West Indies, launched with a marked lack of enthusiasm back in January 1958, had struggled from the outset.

Everything proposed at a federal level, particularly taxation and freedom of movement, was opposed by island populations who saw each other in competition for foreign markets and investment. Two of the region's most brilliant politicians – Jamaica's Norman Manley and Trinidad's Eric Williams – declined to take on federal leadership responsibility, instead choosing to concentrate on their home constituencies. When in 1960 Bustamante declared his JLP party opposed to federation, Prime Minister Manley called a national referendum. In September 1961, with a low turnout that reflected voter apathy, this delivered a narrow majority in favour of Jamaican withdrawal. Without the organisation's most populous member, the federation experiment was over. As Eric Williams declared, 'One from ten leaves nought.'

The British government immediately agreed to start negotiations with Jamaica for separate independent statehood. An independence constitution was drafted and approved by the Jamaica Legislature by January the following year. On 1 February 1962, talks began at Lancaster House in London. By the 9th, an agreement had been signed and the date of independence set for 6 August. An election in April to decide who would lead the new country saw Bustamante capitalise on his referendum victory, winning by twenty-six seats to nineteen.

The larger post-imperial 'federation', the British Commonwealth, was also looking increasingly stillborn. The *Gleaner* reported that as the number of members increased, with colonies becoming independent at a fast rate, 'the bonds uniting the Commonwealth have been substantially weakened'. In Jamaica, there was still considerable loyalty and affection towards what had been planned as the Commonwealth's glue – the British royal family. The same article reported local delight that the sister of the monarch, Princess Margaret, was set to 'be the centrepiece' of the independence ceremonies. But there were concerns that Britain would join the European Common Market, threatening preferential deals on importing tropical produce. The issue of free movement of labour that had bedevilled the West Indies Federation also struck a blow at the Commonwealth. After years of trying, in April 1962 the Conservative Party in Britain passed the Commonwealth Immigrants Act, effectively ending mass Jamaican immigration to the United Kingdom. (Immigration to America had been restricted back in 1952.) The image of Britain as the 'mother country' had depended to a considerable extent on free entry. As one historian of the Commonwealth has written: 'a mother who shuts the door is no mother'.

Labour leader Hugh Gaitskell called the Act 'cruel and blatant anti-colour legislation' (although many Labour MPs supported it). Fleming's golfing companion Sir Jock Campbell, the boss of Booker's, which had huge sugar interests in Guyana and elsewhere in the Caribbean, responded with a letter to *The Times*: 'More than anywhere else in the old colonial empire, the West Indies are what we made them. Consciences cannot be cleared by a judicious and tidy withdrawal from sovereignty. We brought the Negro slave and the indentured Indian to the West Indies, and it was we who started the West Indies on their present course. Already, to the great majority of West Indians, the Commonwealth Immigrants Act has seemed like a repudiation of the consequences of our actions.'

Preparations in Jamaica for independence continued nonetheless. On 21 April, at the Queen's Official Birthday Parade at Up Park Camp, the men of the Royal Hampshire Regiment, the last of a long line of British troops garrisoned in Jamaica, marched symbolically through the ranks of the newly formed Jamaica Regiment and left the island.

Two days before the set date of midnight on 5 August 1962, the *Gleaner* reported: 'All over the island there is now tip-toe expectancy, a breathlessness that will increase with each passing moment until the appointed hour is reached and Jamaica shall at last call her soul her own.' The following day, the paper, noting that there had been 'a virtual explosion of new nations in Africa in the past two years', concluded that 'the era of colonialism is coming to an end'. By now, Trinidad and Tobago had a date for independence as well: 31 August.

On 1 August, in London, Ann Fleming was entertaining the Duke and Duchess of Devonshire (the Duchess was the youngest of the Mitford sisters). In his capacity as Parliamentary Under-Secretary for Commonwealth Relations, the Duke was flying out the next day to 'celebrate the independence of Jamaica'. He was grumbling that Margaret's consort Armstrong-Jones 'had twelve attendants and he was not allowed a valet' and that 'the Joneses had two thirds of the airplane private'. Ann warned them that 'five white tie occasions in the hurricane season will not be much fun', but she 'cheered them all up with dazzling descriptions of Charles da Costa and Ian's black wife'.

After an eighteen-hour flight via the Azores, the royal party arrived on the morning of 3 August and drove, the *Gleaner* reported, into 'a Kingston gaily bedecked with flags and bunting in the national colours

Princess Margaret, representing the Queen at the celebrations of August 1962. Between 1960 and 1964, sixteen other British colonies also gained independence.

of black, gold and green and resplendent in coats of paint that have been splashed on public buildings, commercial houses and private homes in a clean-up and paint-up campaign actively carried out over the past months'.

At a string of public events, the Princess was cheered by huge crowds. Pathé News reported: 'They rejoiced, not that they were parting from Britain – they are firm adherents of the crown – but because Jamaica stood on the threshold of independence.'

Lady Fiona Aird, who was the Princess's lady-in-waiting, remembers 'the most amazing, tremendous reception'. Margaret, she says, loved Jamaica for its 'sun, sea, and the joyfulness of their spirit', but adds that the royal party was largely protected from any dealings with ordinary Jamaicans. There was a certain amount of sadness within the royal party that Jamaica was becoming independent – it felt like 'the end of an era' – but the Princess was 'very pragmatic about what had to happen'. Apart from the heat, the only irritating factor was the US Vice President Lyndon Johnson, who as the representative of the US President thought himself the most important person there. In addition, there were several occasions when his motorcade passed along the streets about half a mile ahead of that of the Princess. According to Lady Aird, to the royal party's annoyance he was announcing through a loudspeaker: 'Now you're going to be free at last! The colonial oppressor is vanquished!'

Meanwhile, celebrations were occurring all over the island, including folk singing, dramatic presentations, regattas, bonfire parties, beauty pageants and donkey races. In Oracabessa, it was 'Boat Races, Swimming Races, Dress Parade, Quadrille Dances, Grease Pole, Eating Race, Domino Tournament'. According to local resident Pearl Flynn, the 'Eating Race' involved watermelons and flour dumplings. She remembers 'Street dancing, dancing all over, parties. Church bells were ringing.' In the national stadium on 5 August, there were speeches, march-pasts, songs and fireworks. Strangways actor Timothy Moxon, in his Cessna crop-sprayer, was part of a fly-past in pouring rain. The climax came at midnight, when 20,000 people saw the Union flag lowered and the black, green and gold of independent Jamaica raised. For Pearl Flynn, watching on television, this was a great moment. 'I felt good, elated,' she says. 'I always loved Jamaica, I was always fighting for my rights. So many promises were made, we all felt elated.'

On 7 August came the opening of the first session of the new Jamaica parliament, attended by dignitaries including Lyndon Johnson, a papal envoy and a number of leaders of the newly independent African nations. First came a message from the Queen, read by Princess Margaret, in which warm mention was made of Britain's 'bonds of friendship' and 'more than three hundred years of close association with the island and her people'. Some found the portrayal of British rule as benevolent somewhat extraordinary, and the failure of the speech to make any mention of Jamaica's role in achieving its own independence was criticised. Leader of the Opposition Norman Manley, when he spoke, did acknowledge that Jamaicans had had a hand in their own freedom: the 'men who in the past and through all our history strove to keep alight the torch of freedom in this country. No one will name them today but this House is in very deed their memorial.'

Timothy Moxon's daughter, Judi Moxon Zakka, remembers that 'at the time of Jamaican independence people were very excited and filled with anticipation. It was a huge step into the future, the shackles of colonialism would be finally thrown off. Jamaica would be free of its European oppressors.' Before the end of the year, there was a new Governor-General – a black Jamaican, Sir Clifford Campbell – and Jamaica had become the 109th member of the United Nations.

Veteran journalist Morris Cargill, Fleming's close friend, wrote two years later: 'A people who have managed so successfully the transition to self-government from beginnings which were so corrupting and destructive to human decency are, it seems to me, capable of almost anything if given even the smallest chance.' At the same time, he noted that per capita income in Jamaica in 1963 was £140, more than most African and Asian countries, and higher even than Portugal. The greatest challenge, in his opinion, was population growth. Already at 370 people per square mile, density was among the highest in the western hemisphere.

Norman Manley had declared before independence that Jamaica would stay aligned to the West and look for even closer ties with the United States. Bustamante went further, announcing as he arrived at La Guardia airport in New York: 'Jamaica stands between Castro and the Panama Canal.' 'We are pro-American,' he said later, 'we are anti-communist. We have nothing to do with Cuba or any communist country. We belong to the West.'

From New York, Bustamante flew to London for meetings with British officials, and to ask for loans; not 'as beggars', but as the *Gleaner*'s correspondent reported: 'In asking for economic aid Sir Alexander will back his case with moral and political reasons. He says that the Colonial Office has ruled Jamaica as a colony for 300 years and left a legacy of unemployment they have the duty to help clear up.' In the event, Jamaica got a lot less from Britain than it asked for and felt entitled to.

The Jamaican coat of arms from imperial days was retained, but with a new motto: 'Out of Many, One People'. As Norman Manley had declared in February 1962, 'The right road will have us all walk together – black, white, and brown – in peace and harmony, united because we are citizens of one land.' When British Prime Minister Harold Macmillan had toured the Caribbean in March the previous year, he had praised the West Indies as an example to the rest of the Commonwealth as a place where multiracial society worked.

Nonetheless, soon after independence, some of the richer whites started moving themselves and their money out of the country. Among them, somewhat surprisingly, was Chris Blackwell, who relocated his still-fledgling Island Records business to England. 'I thought in 1962, in view of my complexion, I'd be better off in England than in Jamaica,' he says. 'Jamaica had just become independent and every problem was considered to be associated with white folk and previous colonial oppression. It's a changed situation. People who had no money, no influence, they say they were oppressed by the British … they want to get theirs now. Finally it's their time.'

Just before independence, Ann and Ian had been invited by Terence Young to a private room at the Travellers' Club for their first viewing of the new film. Other guests included the Duke and Duchess of Bedford, Lord and Lady Bessborough and Peter Quennell. The Flemings took along their staff – Mr and Mrs Crickmere – as well as 'Nanny, old Caspar and all the Miss Lambtons'. 'It was an abominable occasion,' Ann reported to Evelyn Waugh. The children 'were very restive, and I feared Mrs Crickmere might give notice and no more coconut soup; luckily she found the film "quite gripping". I wish I had, for our fortune depends on it. There were howls of laughter when the tarantula walks up James Bond's body: it was a close-up of a spider on a piece of anatomy too small to be an arm.'

The general public, however, was much less sniffy. Three days later, just two weeks before the Cuban missile crisis, the film went on general release in 110 cinemas across the UK. In all but seven, it broke box office records. It would go on to be one of the biggest hits of the 1962–3 season and gross £60 million worldwide.

Book sales went through the roof. *Dr No* sold 1.5 million copies within seven months of the release of the film. In 1961, the Bond books had sold a highly respectable 670,000 copies in paperback in Britain; by the end of 1963, the figure was 4,468,000. The same year saw the release of *From Russia, with Love*, with twice *Dr No*'s budget; the third film, *Goldfinger*, was also in production, with a £3 million budget. Bond seemed unstoppable.

1963-4
You Only Live Twice;
The Man with the Golden Gun

I don't want yachts, race-horses or a Rolls-Royce. I want my family and friends and good health and to have a small treadmill with a temperature of 80 degrees in the shade and in the sea to come to every year for two months. And to be able to work there and look at the flowers and fish, and somehow to give pleasure, whether innocent or illicit, to people in their millions.

Fleming on Goldeneye, 1964

A few weeks before the preview screening of *Dr No*, Ann and Ian had experienced one of their worst ever rows. On the surface it was about nine-year-old Caspar. Ian complained: 'Watching his character deteriorate under your laissez-faire depresses me beyond words, because I see him not being casually spoiled now but spoilt when it comes to facing the world ...' Beneath this was Ian's fury at Ann's relationship with Hugh Gaitskell, who had suddenly fallen ill – Ann made little effort to hide her deep concern for him. Ian complained that he was 'jealous and lonely' and, in case she had forgotten, he was ill too.

Getting nowhere with the 'stale' arguments, Ian suddenly decided he needed to go to Jamaica. On the BOAC flight to New York, he scribbled a note to Ann: 'In the present twilight we are hurting each other to an extent that makes life hardly bearable.' All his efforts to make her happy, he said, were answered by 'a string of complaints. When I want to do the things I enjoy, as this sudden trip to Jamaica, that is also a cause for complaint. You have had to get another man for a dinner-party! ... can you wonder that I'm fed up to the teeth? But for my love for you and Caspar I would welcome the freedom which you threaten me with.' He was exhausted, he said, and needed to 'regain some spirit, which, though you haven't noticed it, is slipping out of me through my boots'. From New York, he cabled Blanche to meet him at Goldeneye for a 'honeymoon'. He told her he was leaving his wife.

Blanche as ever was on hand with undemanding adoration and kindness. 'He was sick and so miserable in his marriage,' she says. 'I looked after him. Jamaica and me: we could have kept him alive.' But after only a week, a cable arrived from Ann saying she was dangerously ill. Fleming delayed, but Blanche persuaded him he had to return to her bedside. Ann recovered from what turned out to be a minor operation, but the marriage remained exhausting and trying for them both.

During the time he did manage to spend in Jamaica, however, Fleming wrote what Blanche calls his most autobiographical story. 'Octopussy', like 'Quantum of Solace', is not really about Bond. Instead the focus is on Dexter Smythe, a golf-loving retired special operative who after the war, seeking to escape bad weather, austerity and the Labour government back home, moves with his wife Mary to Jamaica.

Many years later, Bond arrives at Wavelets, Smythe's north-shore house (with stairs to a beach and reef), to investigate an old crime.

The body of a ski instructor and mountain guide has been found in the Alps. It turns out that Major Smythe, in the course of tracking down Nazi records and hideouts at the end of the war, had stumbled on a cache of gold. He had killed the guide who helped him reach it, and then smuggled the bullion to Jamaica, where he'd done a deal with Chinese traders in Kingston to sell it off gradually. Bond skilfully gets Smythe to confess, then hints that it might be better all round if the Major dies before being taken back to Britain for trial. In the event, Smythe goes out on the reef, where he is killed by a combination of a scorpion fish – 'far more dangerous than barracuda or shark' – and his reef pet, Octopussy.

But this is really a story about alcoholism. For their first years in Jamaica, the Smythes enjoy an 'endless round of parties', 'cheap drinks' and 'lazy, sunshiny days'. They both put on weight. Then he has a heart attack and is told to cut down on his cigarettes and alcohol. 'At first Mary Smythe tried to be firm with him; then, when he took to secret drinking and to a life of petty lies and evasions, she tried to back-pedal on her attempts to control his self-indulgence. But she was too late. She had already become the symbol of the janitor to Major Smythe and he took to avoiding her. She berated him with not loving her any more and, when the resultant bickering became too much for her simple nature, she became a sleeping-pill addict.' After a flaming row, Mary takes an overdose 'just to show him', but it kills her.

The story opens two years later. Smythe, like Fleming, is in his early fifties. He is slightly bald and his belly sags; he is now just 'the remains of a once brave and resourceful officer and of a handsome man who had made easy sexual conquests all his military life'. Although with the help of 'a discreet support belt behind an immaculate cumberbund, he was still a fine figure of a man at a cocktail party or dinner on the North Shore', he 'had nothing but contempt for the international riff-raff with whom he consorted'.

He has now suffered a second heart attack and 'it was a mystery to his friends and neighbours why, in defiance of the two ounces of whisky and ten cigarettes a day to which his doctor had rationed him, he persisted in smoking like a chimney and going to bed drunk, if amiably drunk, every night'. He takes pills to go to sleep and more pills in the morning to deal with his hangover. On the day Bond arrives, Smythe has started drinking at 10.30 a.m.: brandy and ginger ale – what Fleming calls 'the drunkard's drink'. (This is also Bond's choice in *On Her Majesty's Secret Service,* and Fleming's, too, when he was interviewed by a magazine the following year.) By half past eleven, Smythe is lighting his twentieth cigarette of the day.

'Dexter Smythe had arrived at the frontier of the death-wish,' Fleming explains. 'General disgust with himself had eroded his once hard core into dust.' Only one thing in his life keeps him from swallowing 'the bottle of barbiturates he had easily acquired from a local doctor'. 'The lifeline that kept him clinging to the edge of the cliff' was 'the birds and insects and fish that inhabited the five acres of Wavelets, its beach and coral reef beyond. The fish were his particular favourites.' With his snorkel and Pirelli mask, he spends all his time 'stirring up the sand and rocks for the bottom feeders', 'breaking up sea eggs and urchins for the small carnivores', and bringing out 'scraps of offal for the larger ones'. 'He knew them all intimately, "loved" them and believed that they loved him in return.'

Six months later, in January 1963, Ian was back in Jamaica, and after the filming of *Dr No* found himself something of a local celebrity. The *Gleaner* sent a reporter to Goldeneye to interview him. 'When you see "Doctor No" you will be proud of the Jamaican actors,' Fleming pronounced, claiming that he had urged the directors to use as many locals as possible. When asked if he would write another book with a Jamaican setting, 'he said with a chuckle, "I can't go on plugging

Jamaica like this or my public will think I have shares in the Jamaican Travel business.'" (He did, however, manage a plug for Jamaican cigars in his current book, *You Only Live Twice*.) He was then asked to comment on one of the ever-present issues in Jamaica – race and colour. 'That is rather getting into the realms of politics,' he replied, 'but I am very happy the way things are going, the way we are becoming what we basically are – brothers. As far as I am concerned, the colour problem does not exist.'

The interviewer found the main room of Goldeneye 'loaded with spear fishing and underwater diving equipment'. But according to Ann, Ian, although 'far better here', was 'alas, unable to prowl the reef'.

Ann herself had suffered a series of blows. Ian had continued to take every opportunity to see Blanche – on one occasion in New York, another in Austria and several times in England. More seriously, Ann's brother Hugo was very ill, and her sister Mary Rose had lost her long-running battle with alcoholism. Two days before Christmas, she was found by one of her children dead in her bed, having drunk, on an empty stomach, the best part of a bottle of brandy. Ann wrote to Evelyn Waugh that Mary Rose had had 'no contact with the present and death was a merciful relief'. Then 'Heavenly' Hugh Gaitskell was taken into hospital, having suffered a collapse. Ann was desperate to visit him, but also did not want to upset his wife, Dora. In the meantime, Ian's latest visit to his own doctor had produced the information that he had at most five years to live. After agonising over the decision, Ann elected to go with Ian to Jamaica. Gaitskell died on 18 January. Soon afterwards, Ann wrote from Goldeneye to Clarissa Eden: 'I mind very much more than I could have imagined.'

Somewhat unsurprisingly, given the circumstances, the 1963 visit saw the production of one of Fleming's darkest and strangest books.

In mid November 1962, Fleming had travelled to Japan to research *You Only Live Twice*. As ever, he was curious about everything. Visiting

Mikimoto's Island, he had alarmed one of the young girls diving for pearls by gently rubbing her shoulder. 'You must touch to get the precise texture of wet feminine skin,' he explained.

Since the murder of his wife at the end of the previous novel, Bond has gone into a severe decline. Even a month off in Jamaica after Tracy's death hasn't helped. 'He's going slowly to pieces,' M tells Sir James Malony, the Secret Service's nerve specialist. 'Late at the office. Skimps his work. Makes mistakes. He's drinking too much …' ('It was three thirty,' Bond tells himself at the beginning of the book. 'Only two more hours to go before his next drink!') Bond has bungled his last two missions and is facing the sack. Malony replies that Bond has admitted to him that 'all the zest had gone. That he wasn't interested in his job any more, or even in his life.' He then suggests that as Bond is a 'patriotic sort of chap', an especially difficult and important mission might help him 'forget his personal troubles'.

So Bond is sent to Japan on a diplomatic mission to persuade Tiger Tanaka, the head of the Japanese secret service, to reinstate an arrangement to share intelligence. To save money, the British had been closing down operations in the Pacific, relying instead on the CIA. But high-profile defections and arrests for treason had made the Americans wary of passing on secrets. (While Fleming was still writing the book, the news broke of the defection of Kim Philby.) Britain is 'a now more or less valueless ally – an ally now openly regarded in Washington as of little more account than Belgium or Italy'. M comments about Tiger Tanaka, 'He probably doesn't think much of us. People don't these days.'

When Bond raises the purpose of his mission Tanaka taunts him: 'You have not only lost a great Empire, you have seemed almost anxious to throw it away with both hands … when you apparently sought to arrest this slide into impotence at Suez, you succeeded only in stage-managing one of the most pitiful bungles in the history of the world, if not the worst. Further, your governments have shown themselves successively incapable of ruling and have handed over effective control of the country to the trade unions, who appear to be dedicated to the principle of doing less and less work for more money. This feather-bedding, this shirking of an honest day's work, is sapping at ever-increasing speed the moral fibre of the British, a quality the world once so much admired. In its place we now see a vacuous, aimless horde … whining at the weather and the declining fortunes of the country, and wallowing nostalgically in gossip about the doings of the Royal Family.'

'The liberation of our Colonies may have gone too fast, but we still climb Everest and beat plenty of the world at plenty of sports and win Nobel Prizes,' Bond replies, somewhat lamely.

To prove that Englishmen are still to be reckoned with, Tanaka challenges Bond to kill Dr Guntram Shatterhand, who is luring Japanese people to his bizarre castle of death to commit suicide with the help of his collection of poisonous plants, fish and snakes. Shatterhand turns out to be Blofeld, and Bond is on a mission of revenge.

Of course, the more Britain faded, the more outstanding and exemplary Bond became, the individual bucking the trend. The *New York Times*, reviewing the book, noted that 'Bond's mission is aimed at restoring Britain's pre-World War II place among the powers of the world. And on that subject, above all others, Ian Fleming's novels are endlessly, bitterly eloquent.'

But Bond himself is not immune from decline. When out diving for shells with the novel's love interest, Kissy Suzuki, his joints crack and 'he had to admit to himself that his lungs were in a terrible state'. While hiding in a shed in Blofeld's 'garden of death', the urge to smoke gets so strong that he puts his life in danger to have a cigarette.

The completion of his mission leaves Bond with a severe blow to the head that causes amnesia. Kissy doesn't tell him about what he earlier called his 'dark and dirty life', and they enjoy an idyllic time living simply and fishing. (M assumes he is dead and writes his obituary.) The undemanding lover and simple life cannot help but remind us of Blanche and Goldeneye. But then something triggers a memory, and Bond is dragged back to the 'real world'.

You Only Live Twice is overburdened with the travelogue material Fleming had gathered on his trips to Japan, and reviewers complained that 'some of the old snap seems to be gone'. Although it was perhaps Fleming's weakest novel, it was also the most successful so far for his publishers, Jonathan Cape, when, after the success of the first two films, it was published in March 1964 with pre-orders topping 62,000 copies.

It is the least revised of any of the completed novels, an indication of Fleming's fading energy. In mid 1963, a friend noted that he 'looked like death, time-worn and gaunt'. But, she later commented, 'Ian always was a death-wish Charlie.' (In *You Only Live Twice*, Tanaka describes Bond's hard-drinking Australian friend Dikko Henderson as 'a man who lives as if he were going to die tomorrow. This is a correct way to live.') Nonetheless, in May Fleming flew to Istanbul for the filming of *From Russia, with Love*, and in the summer travelled in Europe. At the premiere of the second Bond film in October 1963, he took his doctor along with him in case of emergencies.

The following month, the McClory case over *Thunderball* reopened. Ann joked in a letter to Evelyn Waugh that it was good for Ian as he could not smoke in court and was only able to take an hour for 'a simple' lunch. But it was draining, and the pains in his chest and his hypertension were getting worse. After a couple of weeks, Ivar Bryce settled with McClory out of court as he could see the case was worsening his friend's health still further.

A month later, Bryce suggested that he and a Chicago friend join Ian at Goldeneye in January 'for a last bachelor visit'. Ian replied, 'Your vastly welcome decision was vastly welcome.'

One of the last photographs of Fleming at Goldeneye on his beloved beach.

'The weather and the island were at their best,' Bryce remembered of his last stay at Goldeneye. 'Ian, although showing signs of deep fatigue to me, seemed to be gaining in strength and tranquility.' 'For old times' sake', they went rafting on the Rio Grande and, on another occasion, drove up to Bellevue, where Fleming's Jamaican adventure had begun. It had been sold by Bryce's ex-wife to the Roman Catholic Church, which had turned it into a seminary. (The ghost remained, however, and when an exorcism attempt failed, the Church sold up.)

Bryce remembered Fleming taking great trouble over the rock in the middle of the bay off the beach at Goldeneye, building a strange pot-like affair on it for a palm. He christened it 'Fleming's last erection'. In Ann's absence, Blanche played the hostess, taking the other men on trips when Ian wanted to work. 'Her acquaintance gave Ian much delight and solace in his later years and I was glad to see it,' Bryce wrote, but he also noted that with Ian's new book, 'He was in trouble with his plot. The fecund mind was not so fertile with ideas.'

Housekeeper Violet Cummings, when interviewed shortly after Fleming's death, remembered noticing that the rigid writing regime was now a thing of the past. 'The last time the Commander came,' she said, 'he took longer in bed in the morning. He used to have a dip at seven, then shower, then breakfast. Now he stay in bed to eight. But I was not too worried. I just felt as if he was resting his brains a little ... We all knew about his heart condition but he never mentioned it and of course we didn't either.'

For what would turn out to be his last novel, *The Man with the Golden Gun*, Fleming returned Bond 'home' to Jamaica, now, of course, independent. The story starts with Bond back in London, having been brainwashed by the KGB after his adventure in Japan, and attempting to kill M. The attack with cyanide is foiled and M reacts by deciding, once Bond is cured, to send him to the West Indies to assassinate Scaramanga, the hitman of the book's title and 'possibly the fastest gun in the world'. Scaramanga frequently works for the Cuban and Soviet secret services, and has recently been responsible for the deaths of a number of British agents in the Caribbean. The Chief of Staff protests: 'But that's suicide, sir! Even 007 could never take him.' M's view is that 'in exchange for the happenings of that morning, in expiation of them, Bond must prove himself at his old skills. If he failed, well, it would be a death for which he would be honoured.' 'It was better,' M said, 'that Bond fall on the battlefield.'

As ever, Bond is soothed and reinvigorated by Jamaica, swimming in the mornings and 'letting the scented air, a compound of sea and trees, breathe over his body, naked save for the underpants' while listening to 'cicadas singing from the lignum vitae tree'. He is trying again, somewhat unsuccessfully, to cut down on his smoking and drinking – he 'felt guilty that this was his third double'. Soon his eyes have lost their previous 'dull and lacklustre' look. Jamaica also evokes fond memories of 'his many assignments and many adventures on the island': 'Beau Desert and Honeychile Rider ...

James Bond smiled to himself as the dusty pictures flicked across his brain.' For him, Jamaica was 'the oldest and most romantic of former British possessions'.

Bond's search for Scaramanga leads him to Jamaica's south coast, 'not as beautiful as the north'. At Savanna-la-Mar, there are fishermen's canoes pulled up on the beach, and the small shop where he buys cigarettes smells of spices. He is later told that Savanna-la-Mar is 'like sort of old Jamaica. Like it must have been in the old days. Everyone's friends with each other. Help each other when they have trouble.' (In one of his 1956 *Sunday Times* articles, Fleming had described being met by people in the mountains 'with those warm, wide smiles that "progress" is so rapidly wiping off the face of modern Jamaica'.)

His destination is a brothel at 3½ Love Lane, a building in the kind of romantic decline that Fleming loved about Jamaica: it has seen better days, 'perhaps as the private house of a merchant', but 'the ginger-bead tracery beneath the eaves was broken in places and there was hardly a scrap of paint left on the jalousies ... the patch of "yard" bordering the street was inhabited by a clutch of vulturine-necked chickens that pecked at nothing and three skeletal Jamaican black-and-tan mongrels'. Beauty is provided by a lignum vitae tree in full blue blossom, and a pretty girl on a rocking chair in the tree's 'delicious black shade'. She is 'an octoroon, pretty as, in Bond's imagination, the word octoroon suggested'.

As planned, Bond meets Scaramanga at the brothel, and succeeds in being taken on as his temporary personal assistant (a repeat of the shaky plot device in *Goldfinger*). He then learns that Scaramanga is involved in a tourism development at Negril ('the Thunderbird Hotel'), with investors from the American Mafia and the KGB. The group is involved in a number of schemes, which amount to a rather thrown-together medley of plots.

As Mary Goodnight, Bond's former secretary now posted to Jamaica, explains, the West Indian Sugar Company at Frome near Savanna-la-Mar has been having problems with Rastafarians, 'cane burning and other small sabotage – mostly with thermite bombs brought in from Cuba'. This is being organised by Castro in an attempt to raise the price of his country's sugar crop. It turns out that Scaramanga is supplying the Rastafarians with ganja in exchange for 'plenty fires and trouble on the cane lands'. The ganja comes from Scaramanga's growers in 'Maroon Country'. The KGB man also wants to smuggle huge quantities to the United States to corrupt American youth. The 'group' makes money from the drugs and from speculating in sugar futures. Meanwhile, the Russian agent is organising sabotage of the island's bauxite industry.

A lot of this information is garnered thanks to Felix Leiter and a fellow CIA operative, who is pretending to be an electrical engineer while bugging the meeting room of the hotel. The CIA, it seems, is already on to Scaramanga and the group of villains, and is operating in Jamaica without comment, unlike in *Live and Let Die* and *Dr No*, when Jamaica was definitely Bond's territory.

Scaramanga also suggests that they seek to open casinos in Jamaica, explaining that a few years earlier the mobsters kicked out of Havana had tried the same thing, but 'overplayed the slush fund approach'. A combination of the Church, the opposition party and 'the old women' put a stop to it. Now, he says, 'things have changed. Different party in power, bit of a tourist slump last year, and a certain Minister has been in touch with me. Says the climate's changed. Independence has come along and they've got out from behind the skirts of Aunty England. Want to show that Jamaica's with it. Got oomph and all that.'

For the benefit of the KGB agent, Scaramanga spells out the political advantages of Jamaica allowing gambling: 'It'll almost certainly lead to trouble. The locals'll want to play – they're terrific gamblers here. There'll be incidents. Coloured people'll be turned away from the doors for one reason or another. Then the Opposition party'll get hold of that and raise hell about colour bars and so on … It can all add up to a fine stink. The atmosphere's too damn peaceful round here. This'll be a cheap way of raising plenty of hell. That's what your people want, isn't it? Give the islands the hot foot one after another?'

So there is a very new threat to independent Jamaica from a desire for self-promotion and 'modernity' (the book ends with Bond noting the 'traffic tearing up and down the Kingston roads' and then news of a 'multiple crash at Halfway Tree'), and from the fallout from the Cuban revolution, in terms of both American gangsters looking for a new playground, and 'Redland' looking to duplicate the establishment of a communist regime in the United States' back yard. Still, there is also a curious timelessness about the threat. As in all the Fleming novels, the West Indies is a lawless, pirate-infested space. Scaramanga declares, 'I guess you could call the Caribbean a pretty small pool. But there's good pickin's to be had from it.' Bond also speculates about the 'hot money drifting around the Caribbean' and at one point even invokes the 'redcoats' of the eighteenth century. The references to the Maroons and rebellious blacks causing cane fires could have come from a melodrama by Herbert de Lisser or Hugh Edwards.

The Man with the Golden Gun would not be published until after Fleming's death. As a result, reviewers were on the whole polite, but most found it confusing, muddled and, with the exception of the detail about Jamaica, a great disappointment. It was clearly an unfinished work. His publishers at Cape were worried enough to ask Kingsley Amis to try to tidy it up, although his suggestions were not used. It was, in all, a sad end to Fleming's career.

Halfway through writing, Ian suddenly found he really wanted Ann in Jamaica with him. A new telephone had been installed at Goldeneye and he used it to badger her to come out. She was his 'solace', he said. Ann herself was not in the best of health, but on 30 January, on a 'perfect spring day', she 'reluctantly' boarded an aircraft at London airport and flew to Kingston.

Almost immediately, she regretted it. She arrived in a 'tropical thunderstorm', and the weather remained oppressively damp and humid. 'There are great grey bags of cloud overhead,' she wrote to Evelyn Waugh four days later, 'no oxygen, dreadful humidity inducing even more dreadful lethargy … These conditions make Thunderbird very ill.' To Clarissa Eden she wrote a week later: 'I *loathe* the tropics, can only think of this glorious early English spring and the burgeoning bulbs at Sevenhampton.' But she knew Ian needed her, so she was stuck in what she called 'this gilded prison' until mid March.

Ann reported that Fleming was now able to write for only an hour a day. 'It is painful to see Ian struggle to give birth to Bond,' she wrote

Ann, Ian and Violet's helper Miss Myrtle. Fleming had been told to stop smoking and drinking. Ann's anguish is clearly visible.

to her brother. Adding to the exhaustion was something that she had never quite realised: 'the hysterical success of Bond'. In London, fan mail and press requests and other business had gone to Ian's office, but now they were deluged. A local woman was taken on as a secretary to help with the mail, but there was a stream of journalists and film crews arriving to do interviews and take pictures. The *Gleaner* gave a special lunch for Ian. 'It never stops,' Ann wrote. In letters home, she started calling him 'Beatle Bond'.

Ann was also appalled by the inauguration at nearby Ocho Rios of a new 'Bunny Club' by an 'obscene American publication called Playboy'. Even closer to home, next to the garden gate of Goldeneye, a new petrol station had established an 'infernal machine called a "sound system". It relays calypso from 9 p.m. to 3 a.m. Special favourite being a syncopated version of "Three Blind Mice".' (This had become a hit for Island Records after its use at the beginning of the *Dr No* film.)

Funnily enough, Ian does not seem to have minded the new sound system. In *The Man with the Golden Gun*, Bond enjoys 'the softness of the night, the fact that the "Sound System" was now playing a good recording of one of his favourites, "After You've Gone"'.

He did, however, share Ann's distaste for the direction Jamaican tourism was taking. In *The Man with the Golden Gun*, Bond complains that Kingston airport has sacrificed volume for comfort and is selling 'piles of over-decorated native ware'. The 'big tax concessions that Jamaica gave' have attracted the likes of Scaramanga to the tourism business. At his hotel, unfinished areas are 'mock-ups', covered up with curtains and other essential props, and the dining room is hastily turned into 'a tropical jungle' with potted plants. It is all tacky, hollow and fake. Surveying the swamp at the edge of the property, Bond speculates, 'If the hotel got off the ground ... there would be native boatmen, suitably attired as Arawak Indians, a landing from which the guests could view the "tropical jungle" for an extra ten dollars on the bill.'

As elsewhere, particularly *Thunderball* and *Thrilling Cities*, Fleming also shows his dislike for the homogenised 'Americanisation' that came with the tourist business, with its air conditioning and 'grim, impersonal' rooms and 'conventional cruise ship' dinner that would be the same all over the world.

At Goldeneye, there was one set of guests they were amused to meet, however. The ornithologist James Bond and his wife turned up unannounced. Fleming gave them lunch and pronounced them 'a charming couple who are amused by the whole joke'. For Ann, they were the exception. 'It's been an epic year for bores, mostly retired naval officers with letters of introduction,' she wrote.

Goldeneye had provided Ann and Ian with the very best moments of their time together: the early, stolen holidays when they were so in love they forgot discretion; their shared love of the reef and the wildlife; their wedding in Port Maria. But now it provided what must have been one of the worst, partly because of the latest 'epic bores'.

As Ann explained in a long, distraught letter to Peter Quennell, they had already been arguing when a couple of guests arrived for lunch. 'Ian was as bored as me, and retreated to his siesta at 2.25.' But no one could find the guests' driver, so Ann was forced to make small talk for another hour and a half. Then she discovered that Ian had accepted an invitation to their hotel, Frenchman's Cove, the following evening for a 'Jamaican Beach Barbecue' and a stay over. That night, 'post-whisky', there was another huge row, culminating in Ian shouting at Ann: 'Fuck off! Go home at once. You spoil everything. Do you expect me to look at your face every evening? You're a monumental bore.' 'The scene produced hypertension, tears, and screaming claustrophobia – how does one leave Goldeneye at midnight? No friends to go to, not enough money,' Ann wrote to Quennell. Distraught, she packed, got out her winter coat, found her passport and tickets and prepared to leave. Then loud noises of partying and people letting off guns started coming from Oracabessa.

So instead of departing, she drank some more, took some pills and passed out.

The following night at Frenchman's Cove was little better. Ann pleaded a fever and avoided the beach barbecue. She was awoken in their room by the noise of their host 'briskly driving the Commander home – he was in no condition to drive himself ... in a very slurred voice he repetitively complained of the impossibility of getting a drink ... finally he fell into a noisy drunken sleep'.

Bond's obituary in *You Only Live Twice* ends with a note from his secretary Mary Goodnight in which she suggests an epitaph that reflects his philosophy: 'I shall not waste my days in trying to prolong them.' Winston Stona, a young Jamaican who would play the policeman in the film *The Harder They Come*, met Ian in 1964 at Morris Cargill's house. He remembered Fleming asking for caviar on toast, washed down with vodka. 'He gave the impression of not being able to get out of bed without a bottle of vodka,' Stona remembered. 'I guess he drowned himself.' In his notebook at this time, Fleming scribbled: 'I've always had one foot not wanting to leave the cradle, and the other in a hurry to get to the grave, which has made for an uncomfortable existence.'

Yet in spite of her anger, Ann still felt sorry for him: 'Poor broken Commander,' she wrote at the end of her letter to Quennell.

Back in England in the spring of 1964, friends remember Fleming as a 'gloomy, fragile figure' walking by the lake at Sevenhampton, glass of whisky in hand. At Easter, after playing golf in the rain, he was hospitalised with blood clots on his lungs. His chest pains, the 'Iron Crab', worsened in spite of heavy medication. In June, on her fifty-first birthday, Ann wrote from Sevenhampton to Evelyn Waugh: 'nothing nice or funny is happening'.

On 24 July, Eve Fleming died. Ian would not be talked out of attending his mother's funeral in Oxfordshire. His friend William Plomer wrote early the following year: 'When his health was no longer good, it was impossible to imagine him settling down to the existence of a prudent invalid obsessed with trying to make it last as long as possible. I think he knew he had, as they say, "had it".' Ian's friend Alan Ross found him at this time 'very shaky, his normally brick-red complexion the dry mauve of a paper flower'.

On 8 August, Ann wrote to her son-in-law John Morgan and daughter Fionn, who had just had their first baby: 'Ian's life from now on hangs on a thread. Such recovery as he could make depends on his self-control with cigarettes and alcohol. The doctor spent Bank Holiday with us, and was able to witness the sad change that ill health and drugs can bring. Poor Ian nags at me specially and then Caspar all the time. It ends all fun and is anguish to be with one one loves who is very mentally changed and fearfully unhappy – poor old tiger.'

Nevertheless, feeling in better spirits that summer, Ian was determined to attend the committee meeting of the Royal St George Golf Club near Sandwich. He was thrilled at the prospect of being nominated as club captain for the following year. He travelled down, taking in a lunch with Blanche in London. On 11 August, he had lunch at the club, and then dinner with Ann at the nearby Guildford Hotel. Shortly after eating, he collapsed and an ambulance was called to take him to the Canterbury Hospital. He had suffered a massive haemorrhage and died at 1.30 in the morning. It was his son's twelfth birthday.

The news of Ian Fleming's death at the age of only fifty-six was reported by the Jamaica *Gleaner* the following day, 13 August. A subsequent article two days later, probably written by his friend Morris Cargill, described him as 'a great friend of Jamaica ... wherever he went, he sang the praises of Jamaica; and through his books, films and articles he did more perhaps than any other single person to give our country extensive and favourable publicity abroad'.

Ann would never return to Goldeneye. Apart from anything else, she had not liked what she had seen of the new post-imperial Jamaica on the 1964 trip; the old deference was gone. 'Independence has not improved the island,' she had written to Evelyn Waugh. 'They have cancelled all the porters at airports, instead fascist black police rock with laughter while elderly exhausted white tourists feebly try to move their baggage to the customs table, where aggressive Negro customs officials enjoy themselves hugely by a minute examination of underclothes, displaying the curiosity of the savage in clocks or trinkets.' Later the same month, she had reported that 'The Brownlows are very unpopular. He in permanent sulk: the Government want to run a teeny road over a small corner of his property, and are not interested in his threats to leave the island.'

Noël Coward, who had failed to sell his Blue Harbour house, was also furious with the customs officers who refused to allow him to import half a dozen of his records to give to friends. Around this time, he wrote his short story 'Solali', a return to Samolo, his fictionalised Jamaica. It is very different in tone to the innocent Samolo of *Pomp and Circumstance*. The Samolans have changed. 'Although by nature gentle, indolent and well disposed towards their white-skinned overlords, concealed beneath their eternally smiling friendliness is a strain of cruelty,' he writes. The story ends with a gruesome double murder.

Fleming's last pronouncements on independent Jamaica were rather different. In his final novel, *The Man with the Golden Gun*, Bond enjoys the unchanged parts of Jamaica, which remain delightfully old-fashioned, ramshackle and eccentric, and the local use of old terms like 'chains and perches' (proper 'Imperial' measurements).

Apart from the cartoon-villainous Rastas, for most of the novel Jamaicans only appear as sex workers, musicians or hotel staff, happy to do Bond's bidding for rum or money, as in the distasteful scene when he organises an orgy and striptease for Scaramanga's cronies (which he later regrets). It never seems to occur to either the British or Americans to involve local authorities in their investigations on Jamaican soil. It is striking in the book how the people in authority

Bond encounters are actually still British. The boss of the sugar operation in Frome and the owner of the hotel in Morgan's Harbour are not only both English but, even better, ex-naval intelligence!

At the hospital, where Bond is recovering from his final battle with Scaramanga, the senior doctor, although Jamaican, is a 'graduate from Edinburgh'. The matron is 'a kindly dragon on loan from King Edward VII's', a private London hospital. It is they who display competence and authority while the nurse, presumably locally trained, 'is allowed to listen' and 'excited by all this high-level talk' before returning 'to her copy of *Ebony*'.

During his last trip to Jamaica in 1964, Fleming planned with his friend Morris Cargill a book called *Ian Fleming Introduces Jamaica*. His contribution starts by describing how, during the eighteen years he had been coming 'regularly as clockwork' to Goldeneye, 'Jamaica has grown from a child into an adult'. Still, the Jamaican characters in the novel he was writing at the time remain, like Quarrel, childlike. The local police constable who arrives on the scene after the final gun battle is a figure of fun with his 'extremely smart' uniform and 'dignified gait'. Leiter has explained to him 'that a good man was after a bad man in the swamp'. The policeman can only write 'in a laborious hand'.

The 'comedy' continues when the Jamaican Commissioner of Police, 'resplendent in his black uniform with silver insignia', and the judge of the Supreme Court, 'in full regalia', arrive at Bond's bedside to carry out a judicial inquiry into what has happened. They are both full of what is assumed to be misplaced self-importance. Much to Bond's amusement, what they are after is in fact a rewriting of events so as to preserve the dignity of their nation. So the wording requested includes the fictions that the Jamaican police knew all about Scaramanga's doings and were consulted about action against them, and that Bond and the CIA were 'Jamaica-controlled'. Amid much nodding and winking, this is all agreed to and the foreigners are given the 'Jamaican Police Medal for gallant and meritorious services to the

Independent State of Jamaica'. The message, of course, is that the whole thing – including real agency on the part of the local authorities, real independence – is a sham.

Earlier in the novel, there is a very striking affirmation by Bond: 'For all her new-found "Independence", he would bet his bottom dollar that the statue of Queen Victoria in the centre of Kingston had not been destroyed or removed to a museum as similar relics of an historic infancy had been in the resurgent African states.' The quotation marks are highly significant. For Fleming, it's almost as if he's in denial: independence is not real, only a sweet given to a child.

This dismissal of independence in *The Man with the Golden Gun* is in stark contrast to the edginess of *Dr No*, where we read the prediction that 'Such stubborn retreats [as Queen's club] will not long survive in modern Jamaica. One day it will have its windows smashed and perhaps be burned to the ground.' Perhaps the brickbat of 'independence' has, in Fleming's opinion, actually reaffirmed the status quo (just as in the *Horizon* article of 1947 he predicted that the 'liberality and wisdom of our present policy will take the edge off passions').

In the event, Ian was only able to write the first few pages of *Ian Fleming Introduces Jamaica*. They would be his last and perhaps fondest and most sentimental words on Jamaica. He acknowledges that there have been changes: 'She had gained her Independence and Membership of the United Nations, bauxite and tourism have changed her economy ...' But at the same time, nothing has changed: 'The people are just the same, always laughing and bawling each other out, singing the old banana songs as they load the fruit into the ships, getting drunk on rum when the ship has sailed, sneaking an illicit whiff of ganja, or an equally illicit visit to the obeahman when they are ill or in trouble, driving motor cars like lunatics, behaving like zanies at the cricket matches and the races, making the night hideous with the "Sound System" on pay night, and all the while moving gracefully and lazily through the day and fearing the "rolling calf" at night.'

This seems like a return to the Jamaica he outlined back in 1947 with his article in *Horizon* magazine, where politicians fighting for independence are 'gorgeously flamboyant' but no more troublesome than insect bites, where 'a touch of the zany persists' and where Jamaica's gruesome history of slavery and rebellion becomes romantic tales of pirates and picturesque Maroons.

The West Indies has always inspired fantasy, from the search for El Dorado, to *Robinson Crusoe*, to 'Boy's Own' pirate stories, to the Edenic paradise of the tourist brochures. From this fertile soil, and impossible without it, came imperial hero James Bond.

Goldeneye Since Fleming

'I loved him and am angry with him for dying but I see his point,' Noël Coward told John Pearson in what appears to have been a well-oiled encounter in the Dorchester Hotel in London in May 1965. In his diary, Coward had written: 'It is a horrid but expected sadness. He went on smoking and drinking in spite of all warnings ... He has been a good and charming friend to me ever since I have known him ... I loved him and he loved me.'

Coward did not leave Jamaica as he had planned around Independence, but got used to the changes under way and recovered his enthusiasm for the country. In February 1965, he hosted a lunch for the Queen Mother at Firefly. Blanche was among the small group of guests. For the two staunch royalists, it was a thrilling occasion. Noël described the Queen Mother as 'gayer and more enchanting than ever'.

Coward died at Firefly in 1973 and is buried there. By this time he had at last been knighted and his reputation had enjoyed a renaissance. His properties were left to Graham Payn and Cole Lesley. They gave Firefly to the Jamaican government, and it is preserved as Coward left it. On the walls are photographs, now faded by the sun into a pale sepia, of visitors Sophia Loren, Peter Ustinov, Charlie Chaplin, Maggie Smith, Richard Burton and James Mason. Blue Harbour is now owned by an American family and can be rented out. The cottages still have electrical fittings from the 1940s and smell of damp and disuse. It is hard to imagine that the royalty of Hollywood stayed in them. But it is still a beautiful and private spot, with cool breezes coming off the sea, the sound of which is ever present.

According to Mark Amory, who became part of Ann Fleming's circle in the later years of her life and would edit her letters, 'It is hard to exaggerate the importance of the death of Ian Fleming to Ann. He was the love of her life and now he was gone.' He personally remembers Ann as 'quite intimidating. Very Funny. Quick, with great integrity. A glamorous, forceful, entertaining person.' Certainly her letters remain sparkling and witty.

Caspar grew up a gifted child, bookish and with a passionate interest in archaeology, but also wilful and even cruel. Raymond O'Neill remembers that he was 'potentially brilliant' but that 'he gave my mother a terrible time'. Apart from losing, at a vulnerable age, the

At Lord O'Neill's wedding to Georgina Douglas-Scott on 10 June 1963. From left: Caspar, Francis Grey, Joan Sillick, Ann and Ian.

father he idolised, it was complicated being the son of the creator of James Bond. Ann had reported Caspar saying when he was eleven that he would never marry, as 'he was not so oversexed as James Bond'. At prep school, the connection had earned him considerable cachet, and he had traded his father's signature and Bond bits and pieces. The year after his father's death, he went on to Eton, where, according to Raymond, 'because the Bond thing was taking off, he was a hero'. However, he was already needing pills to help him sleep, and then got involved with recreational drugs. Mark Amory remembers him as 'an extraordinary figure, astonishingly sophisticated and a charming boy. But you didn't have to be very perceptive to see that things were not right.'

Caspar also became obsessed with guns. When a loaded revolver was found in his room at Eton, the police were called and he was expelled. He worked hard and got to Oxford, but did not complete his degree. By now, according to his frantically worried mother, he was 'talking all the trendy nonsense of his generation, anti-materialism and all sorts of nonsense'. Ann was determined that her son should become a politician, a career to which he was wildly unsuited.

When he reached the age of twenty-one, in August 1973, Caspar came into a large inheritance from his father. According to his girlfriend since Oxford, Rachel Fletcher, he bought a 'ridiculous' flat on Church Street, Chelsea, 'with one huge room' he never got round to decorating. Here, there always seemed to be hangers-on, some who brought drugs with them. He had also inherited Goldeneye, which had been rented out to family friends. In August the following year, by which stage, according to Rachel Fletcher, he was 'in a very bad way', he went to Jamaica for the first time since his trip in 1960. With him was his cousin, Hugo's daughter Frances Charteris. She remembers Goldeneye as 'a magical place, though then in some disrepair'. Both Violet and Blanche were delighted to see Caspar, but he was losing his battle with depression. After about a week, he took an overdose and

Ann in later life. In one letter she complained of 'permanent nervous gastritis from misery of last years.'

swam out to sea from the beach at Goldeneye in an attempt to take his own life. He was rescued by a local fisherman and then Blanche managed to call a helicopter to take him to hospital in Kingston.

Now diagnosed as a severe depressive, Caspar was given psychiatric treatment including electric shock therapy, and was in and out of institutions until, on 2 October 1975, he killed himself with another overdose.

As Mark Amory writes, 'This was a blow so stunning that some of her friends thought that Ann, in her turn, might never recover. She had for some time been using alcohol as a calculated weapon in her struggle against the blacker side of her life and she continued to do so ... then, with a remarkable effort of will, she gave it up and took full control of her life once more.' She would die of cancer in 1981 at the age of sixty-eight. The friend who gave her memorial address said that 'In naval terms she was something of a privateer. She would move into a calm lagoon where barques and frigates were careening peacefully and suddenly let off a broadside. The calm vanished, ripples spread across the waters, the whole harbour became animated, galvanized, expectant.'

In late 1972, Bond returned to Jamaica. It was fitting that just as the island had hosted Sean Connery's first performance in the title role, so the filming of *Live and Let Die* in Jamaica should see Roger Moore's debut as Bond. The movie was shot at the Ruins restaurant, the Green Grotto caves, in Montego Bay, Runaway Bay, Falmouth and at Rose Hall. The bridge that shears off the top of the double-decker bus is at Johnson Town, near Lucea. Roger Moore remembers arriving to be welcomed by 'searing heat and a calypso steel band'. The cast and crew stayed for two weeks at the Sans Souci Hotel in Ocho Rios, described by the leading lady, Jane Seymour, as the most beautiful

she had ever seen: 'I just remember the music and the warmth and the beautiful beaches. It was just so exotic and glorious.'

There were difficulties. Frequent power cuts played havoc with the schedule, and Moore remembers the groans of the crew as they lugged hundreds of yards of cable and heavy lamps in the ninety-degree heat. When Gloria Hendry, the actress playing Rosie Carver, had to lie dead on the grass, she was

Roger Moore meets Violet Cummings at Goldeneye, December 1972.

'eaten by ants'. Roy Stewart, Quarrel Jr, although Jamaican-born, suffered in the heat. He had not been back for twenty years and could not believe the changes that had taken place over that time.

The villain's name came from the real-life Ross Kananga, owner of a crocodile farm found in the east of the island by production designer Syd Cain and chosen as the location of one of the film's most famous scenes. 'Production and construction noise has driven all the crocs and alligators to ground,' Moore reported. 'Ross Kananga, the alligator specialist and handler, is busy digging them out of the mud where they have buried themselves. I have sent him word not to bother on my account.'

One of the extras was Karen Schleifer, niece of Marion Simmons, who now lived in her aunt's house, Glory Be. She remembers one evening at the Sans Souci when filming had finished chatting to members of the crew. 'So where is the famous Goldeneye?' they asked her. When she replied that it was just up the coast, they asked to be taken for a look to pay homage to where it had all begun. Later during the filming, Roger Moore visited the house as well. He says he felt 'a great sense of awe, and was quite humbled to think everything started within those simple rooms with the first Bond book'.

Goldeneye was put on the market by the Fleming family soon after Caspar's death. Blanche Blackwell still kept an eye on the place and swam off the beach. In 1976, Chris Blackwell took Bob Marley there for a look around. 'I'd just paid him seventy thousand pounds in royalties,' says Chris. 'I talked Bob into buying Goldeneye – he said he would always let my mother swim there. But then he got cold feet, said it was too posh, so the next year, when I was flush again, I bought it myself. I thought of living there, but I never did – I just went there sometimes, swam there sometimes, let friends and family stay there sometimes. It was a house I used as an entertaining place.'

At one point it looked like Goldeneye would be sold to a Canadian millionaire, who planned to build a lift down to the beach. Instead Blanche Blackwell persuaded her son Chris to buy the property.

In 1989, Blackwell sold Island Records to Polygram, a deal that allowed him to invest in films and hotels and which eventually led to the development of Goldeneye as a high-end resort. In a tradition started by Sir Anthony Eden, guests are today encouraged to plant trees on behalf of the Oracabessa Foundation, which supports local sports and schools and has recently started a project to undo the damage caused to Fleming's beloved reef by pollution and overfishing. These guests have included film stars, ex-American presidents, models and

In 1956, the Edens planted a Santa Maria tree as a memento of their stay. Later visitors following the tradition include Michael Caine, Bill Clinton, Harrison Ford, Sir Richard Branson, Marianne Faithful, Naomi Campbell, River Phoenix, Yoko Ono and Princess Margaret.

musicians. (Sting wrote 'Every Breath You Take' at Goldeneye; U2 wrote the theme tune to the *GoldenEye* film here.) It is as close as Jamaica now gets to the glory days of Sunset Lodge and Round Hill in the late forties and early fifties. A nearby airstrip has been renamed 'Ian Fleming International Airport', and Goldeneye plays host to film and other creative festivals.

Tourism is now the key business for Jamaica, outstripped in foreign earnings only by remittances from the huge Jamaican diaspora in North America, the UK and elsewhere. The bauxite industry on the island, undercut by cheaper sources, particularly in Australia, is largely in mothballs.

In the 1970s, the PNP government of Michael Manley, Norman and Edna's son, moved the country sharply to the left, ending its alignment with the West, and under a programme of 'democratic socialism' sought to nationalise industry and banks. Manley explained his thinking in an interview with a US television station in 1977: 'There are tremendous social pressures in Jamaica. Jamaica, like almost all countries that had a long colonial experience, is a product of that experience and reflected at the time of independence sharp class divisions, a very small and highly privileged elite, who were really the beneficiaries of colonialism and that imperialist process of exploitation, tremendous poverty, dangerous gaps between the haves and the have-nots; all those are colonial legacies and all those are charged with social tension. A lot of what we have tried to do as a government is to address those problems.'

The experiment led to a further mass exodus of professional Jamaicans, a withdrawal of US support and credit, and the return in 1980, in an election marred by severe violence, of a right-wing administration. When Manley returned to government later in the decade, he was far more pragmatic. However, inequalities and divisions remain deep in Jamaica.

This has led many towards a very Fleming-like romanticisation of the imperial past. Pearl Flynn comments: 'We were looking forward to a better Jamaica, more jobs and so on, but people weren't satisfied. We would have been better off without independence.' Chris Blackwell concedes: 'If you speak to most older Jamaicans, they will probably say that things were better before.' His mother Blanche declared that independence was 'the worst thing that could have happened to Jamaicans – they were simply not ready for it'. Others see the Manley experiment of the 1970s as a much-needed effort to wrest the country's wealth and assets from a tiny elite who, along with foreign interests, arguably still control most of Jamaica. When, in 2005, he was asked about Jamaica at the time of filming *Dr No*, Timothy Moxon, who played Strangways, responded: 'That wasn't altogether a completely happy time. People were selected for jobs because of their colour and it was very Jim Crow, really. We're going through a difficult time at the moment but I'm a great believer that Jamaica will come out on top again, as it always has done in the past. However, I don't think Coward or Fleming would have cared for it much at the moment.'

At the time of Fleming's death, his books had sold thirty million copies and been translated into eighteen languages. Within two years, after the success of the *Goldfinger* and *Thunderball* films, sales had nearly doubled. The films were the dominant British movies of the 1960s and exported an image of Britain that was enjoyed globally, as all-pervasive as the Beatles (whose first album came out in 1962, the year of the first Bond film). The books remain popular, and the films go from strength to strength, spawning a host of impersonators and parodies as well as taking over $5 billion dollars at the box office.

Their success cannot be put down to the car chases, jeopardy, beautiful people and exotic locations. Plenty of other films and books have done this without sharing Bond's gargantuan success. Bond, like his creator, is in many ways pretty unlikeable. So why has he survived?

The defining moment of all the films comes in 1977's *The Spy Who Loved Me*. Roger Moore, in an outrageous yellow 'onesie', is being chased on skis by a host of villains. He is heading towards a huge drop. Still the baddies come; Bond is hopelessly outnumbered. The music rises in pitch, then abruptly cuts off as Bond skis straight over the edge of a cliff and hangs in the sky, tumbling downwards in slow motion. Seconds pass. Then, suddenly, a parachute opens. A Union Jack parachute. And the theme music roars back in celebration.

The audience, holding its breath, lets out a huge cheer. Then laughs. It is exciting and funny. Gripping but ridiculous. We are laughing at ourselves, and celebrating that self-consciousness. Americans call it one of the great moments of British humour.

Just as the books don't take themselves too seriously, with Fleming forever reminding us that we are reading a 'comic book' and that what the imperial hero calls home is now a country in sharp decline, so the films have continued this sense of fun and national self-deprecation. This can be seen in the very first film, *Dr No*, described by a reviewer at the time as 'full of submerged self-parody'. Bond expresses our complicated relationship with our past, and our empire – at once a little bit proud, a little bit ashamed, and forever aware that our 'greatest days' are behind us.

It is this complexity, born in the Jamaica of Fleming's time, that gives continued life to James Bond and projects an image of Britishness that makes us likeable to ourselves, and to the rest of the world – who no doubt enjoyed the appearance of Bond in the Olympic opening ceremony almost as much as we did.

Acknowledgements

So many thanks due for this book!

First to two complete gentlemen, Fleming biographers John Pearson and Andrew Lycett. Rather than be annoyed by my blundering into their territory, they have been unfailingly enthusiastic and helpful, providing leads, unpublished notes and interviews, putting up with my constant questions and much more. I am greatly indebted to their books for their outstanding research, detail and insight. Both biographies are highly recommended.

Although my greatest debt is to Lycett and Pearson, I have also found other work by writers on Bond extremely useful, in particular Simon Winder, David Cannadine, Raymond Benson, James Black, Jon Gilbert, Ben Macintyre and Henry Chancellor. Mark Amory, both in person and in his book of Ann Fleming's letters, has had large input into this work.

I am also greatly indebted to Ian's extended family who agreed to be interviewed, provided contacts and gave expert feedback on my ideas about Ian and Jamaica. In particular thanks are due to Kate Grimond, Fionn Morgan, Lucy Williams and Lord O'Neill. I would also like to thank all at Ian Fleming Publications for their support.

I am especially grateful to Blanche Blackwell, for putting up with hours of interviews with great patience and kindness. Likewise her son Chris Blackwell, who opened a lot of doors for me in Jamaica and has supported this project from the outset. Special thanks as well to Mark Painter, who undertook a lot of picture research for this book, and to Suzette Newman.

I am grateful to everyone else who agreed to be interviewed for this book, who gave advice and encouragement, suggested leads or photographs or read and commented on early drafts. These include, from Jamaica: Cathy Aquart; Christopher Barnes, MD of the *Gleaner*; Dr Dalea M. Bean, UWI; Valerie Facey; George Faria; the late Patrice Wymore Flynn; Pearl Flynn; Pauline Forbes-Lewis of BITU; Marguerite Gordon (neé Le Wars); Jonathan Gosse; Olivia Grange-Walker; Ahon Gray; Ann Hodges; Donald Lindo; Kyle Mais, manager of the Jamaica Inn; Dr John McDowell; George Meikle; Ray Miles, Snr.; Donnalee Minott; Andrew Roblin; Sheree Roden of the *Gleaner* photograph archive; Barrington Roper; Karen and Ronnie Schleifer; Paul Slater; Kathy Snipper of Island Outpost; Winston Stona; Douglas Waite; Anthony and Jean Watson; Michael 'Von' White and Judi Moxon Zakka.

And from elsewhere: Lady Fiona Aird; Raymond Benson; Hannah Barbara Blake; Barbara Broccoli; Alan Brodie and all at the Noël Coward estate; Professor Barbara Bush; Frances Charteris; Ajay Chowdhury; John Cork; Julian Drinkall; Professor Mike Faber; Rachel Fletcher; Benjamin Foot; Professor Robert Hill; Mark Holford; Geoff Lucas; Sir Roger Moore; Mark O'Connell; Steve Oxenrider; Sheila Parker; Hal W. Peat; Lee Pfeiffer; Anne and Paul Swain; Ian Thomson; Alex Von Tunzelmann and Calder Walton.

A special thank you to the late, much missed Sally Ford, at whose Welsh hill farm much of this was written and, more importantly, where she provided a magical place for several generations of my family.

I have been blessed with a brilliant publishing team at Hutchinson, in particular Sarah Rigby, my hugely talented, supportive and hard-working editor. I am grateful to everyone at Hutchinson and Windmill for their efforts on behalf of this and my other books, as well as Jane Selley for her expert copy-edit, Mandy Greenfield for her meticulous proof-read, Chris Bell for the detailed index and Richard Carr for his superb design. As before, I was lucky to have the brilliant Martin Brown draw the map for this book.

My agent Julian Alexander has, as always, provided expert advice and warm encouragement. I am also indebted to my US agent George Lucas and publisher Pegasus Books for their support for this project.

Last, but by no means least, love and thanks to Hannah and our family, to Ollie, Tom and Milly, who have watched a lot of Bond films with me over the past few years and with good grace put up with my long absences researching this book and long distraction writing.

Picture and Quotation Credits

Integrated Pictures

1. Bellevue, 1835. From *Nature & On Stone* by J.B. Kidd. Public Domain.
2. Fleming boys with their mother. Courtesy of Lord O'Neill.
3. Young Fleming © The Ian Fleming Estate.
4. Map of Jamaica, 1752. Library of Congress.
5. Goldeneye from the sea. Private Collection.
6. Molly Huggins. Time & Life Pictures/Getty Images.
7. Whites Wharf, Oracabessa. Photographer: Eric B. White. Courtesy Richard 'Von' White.
8. Fleming and Ivar Bryce. The Orion Publishing Group, London.
9. Fleming at the back bedroom of Goldeneye. Getty Images.
10. Fleming eating a sea urchin. Courtesy Island Trading Archive.
11. Errol Flynn. Time & Life Pictures/Getty Images.
12. Molly Huggins presiding over a mass wedding. Time & Life Pictures/Getty Images.
13. Norman Manley. Courtesy of the National Library of Jamaica.
14. Alexander Bustamante. Courtesy Bustamante Industrial Trade Union.
15. Lady Rothermere and Lady Huggins. Time & Life Pictures/Getty Images.
16. Ann on the beach. Courtesy of Aitken Alexander.
17. Ian and Ann on the rock. Courtesy of Aitken Alexander.
18. Garden and sea from inside Goldeneye. Courtesy Island Trading Archive.
19. Rafting on the Rio Grande. Courtesy Island Trading Archive.
20. Marilyn Monroe and Arthur Miller. Courtesy Jamaica Inn.
21. Noël Coward. © Estate of Noël Coward by permission of Alan Brodie Representation Ltd. www.alanbrodie.com.
22. Evon Blake. Courtesy of the National Library of Jamaica.
23. Fleming at the Traveller's Tree. Private Collection.
24. American military power. Time & Life Pictures/Getty Images.
25. Governor Sir Hugh Foot. Crown copyright. Centre of Information, National Archives.
26. Gathering at Blue Harbour. Courtesy of the Cecil Beaton Studio Archive at Sotheby's.
27. Port Royal and Kingston Harbour, 1782. Library of Congress.
28. A Jamaican Maroon. Public Domain.
29. The Sunken Garden. © Estate of Noël Coward by permission of Alan Brodie Representation Ltd. www.alanbrodie.com.

30. Ian and Ann with Caspar. Courtesy of the Cecil Beaton Studio Archive at Sotheby's.
31. *Casino Royale*. Courtesy Random House Archives.
32. 'Churchill to visit Jamaica'. *Gleaner*, 27 December 1952.
33. Winston Churchill. © TopFoto.
34. Fleming and a local fan. © The Gleaner Company Ltd.
35. Negril. Courtesy of the National Library of Jamaica.
36. Queen and Prince Philip. Popperfoto/Getty Images.
37. Fleming and Felix Barriffe. Courtesy Island Trading Archive.
38. Fleming at the main window. © Bradley Smith/CORBIS.
39. Firefly. Courtesy of the author.
40. Blue Mountains. © Estate of Noël Coward by permission of Alan Brodie Representation Ltd. www.alanbrodie.com.
41. Fleming with Barrington Roper. Courtesy Island Trading Archive.
42. Fleming in the water. Private Collection.
43. 'Eden: Sunshine Trip'. © Express Newspapers/Express Syndication.
44. Anthony Eden. Photographer: Eric B. White. Courtesy Richard 'Von' White.
45. Fleming and Blanche Blackwell. Courtesy Island Trading Archive.
46. Effigy of the Governor Sir Hugh Foot. Used with permission of Benjamin Foot.
47. *From Russia, with Love*. Courtesy Random House Archives.
48. Kingston's Kings Street, 1961. Crown Copyright. Centre of Information, National Archives.
49. Squirrel fish. NOAA Central Library Historical Fisheries Collection.
50. Fleming, Blanche and Ann. Courtesy Island Trading Archive.
51. Alec Guinness. Courtesy Island Trading Archive.
52. Fleming writing *On Her Majesty's Secret Service*. © TopFoto.
53. Fleming and Sean Connery. Photographer Bert Cann *Dr No* © 1962 Danjaq, LLC and United Artists Corporation. All rights reserved.
54. Filming *Dr No*. Photographer Bert Cann *Dr No* © 1962 Danjaq, LLC and United Artists Corporation. All rights reserved.
55. Fleming and Ursula Andress. © Bettmann/CORBIS.
56. Princess Margaret. Paris Match via Getty Images.
57. Fleming on his beach. Getty Images.
58. Ann, Fleming and Miss Myrtle. © National Portrait Gallery, London.
59. Caspar, Francis Grey, Joan Sillick, Ann and Fleming. Courtesy of Fionn Morgan.
60. Ann in later life. Photograph by Michael Astor; courtesy of the Hon. Judy Astor.
61. Roger Moore and Violet Cummings. David Steen/Scopefeatures.com.
62. 'For Sale or Rent' sign. Courtesy Island Trading Archive.
63. Planters. Island Outpost Images/© David Yellen/© Adrian Boot.

Colour Pictures

1. Goldeneye today. Island Outpost Images/© Peter Brown.
2. *Live and Let Die*; *Dr No*; *Octopussy*; *The Man with the Golden Gun*. Courtesy Random House Archives.
3. Myrtle Bank. Courtesy Hutchinson.
4. Fleming on the water. Courtesy Island Trading Archive.
5. John Kennedy. Getty Images.
6. Coward and friends. Getty Images.
7. Ann on her first visit. Courtesy Lord O'Neill.
8. Port Maria harbour. Island Outpost Images.
9. Vervain hummingbird. Courtesy Runesm/Creative Commons.
10. Banana carrier. Courtesy of the National Library of Jamaica.
11. 'Portrait of Mrs Ian Fleming', 1950. Private Collection/© The Lucian Freud Archive/Bridgeman Images.
12. Fleming and Ann on their wedding day. Courtesy Lord O'Neill.
13. Katherine Hepburn and Irene Selznick. Getty Images.
14. Jamaica Inn. Courtesy Island Trading Archive.
15. Tower Isle. Courtesy Island Trading Archive.
16. Blanche and Fleming. Courtesy Island Trading Archive.
17. Goldeneye staff. Island Outpost Images/© Adrian Boot.
18. Chris Blackwell and Ursula Andress. Courtesy Island Trading Archive.
19. Sean Connery and a young fan. Photographer Bunny Yeager *Dr No* © 1962 Danjaq, LLC and United Artists Corporation. All rights reserved.
20. Blanche, Sean and Noël. © Estate of Noël Coward by permission of Alan Brodie Representation Ltd. www.alanbrodie.com.
21. Fleming and his catch. Courtesy Island Trading Archive.
22. Roger Moore. David Steen/Scopefeatures.com.

Quotations

Reproduced with permission of Ian Fleming Publications Ltd, London:

Casino Royale Copyright © Ian Fleming Publications Ltd 1953; *Live And Let Die* Copyright © Ian Fleming Publications Ltd 1954; *Moonraker* Copyright © Ian Fleming Publications Ltd 1955; *Diamonds are Forever* Copyright © Ian Fleming Publications Ltd 1956; *From Russia, with Love* Copyright © Ian Fleming Publications Ltd 1957; *The Diamond Smugglers* Copyright © Ian Fleming Publications Ltd 1957; *Dr No* Copyright © Ian Fleming Publications Ltd 1958; *Goldfinger* Copyright © Ian Fleming Publications Ltd 1959; *For Your Eyes Only* Copyright © Ian Fleming Publications Ltd 1960; *Thunderball* Copyright © Ian Fleming Publications Ltd 1961; *The Spy Who Loved Me*

Notes

Abbreviations

Diamonds are Forever (*DF*)
Dr No (*DN*)
From Russia, with Love (*RWL*)
Goldfinger (*GF*)
Live and Let Die (*LLD*)
Moonraker (*MR*)
On Her Majesty's Secret Service (*MSS*)
Quantum of Solace: The Complete James Bond Short Stories (*SS*)
The Diamond Smugglers (*DS*)
The Man with the Golden Gun (*MGG*)
The Spy Who Loved Me (*SLM*)
Thrilling Cities (*TC*)
Thunderball (*TB*)
You Only Live Twice (YLT)

The Noël Coward Diaries (*NC Diary*)
The Letters of Noël Coward (*NC Letters*)
Pomp & Circumstance (*P&C*)

Cecil Beaton (CB)
Ann Charteris/Rothermere/Fleming (AF)
Hugo Charteris (HC)
Virginia Charteris (VC)
Lady Diana Cooper (DC)
Ian Fleming (IF)

Epigraph

viii: 'My own life has been turned upside down': Cargill ed., *Ian Fleming Introduces Jamaica*, 11.

1943: Fleming and Jamaica – First Contact

1: the very same journey that will one day be replicated..., *LLD*, (Penguin Classics Omnibus ed. 2003), 204.

2: 'pelting with rain …', *You Only Live Once*, Bryce, 69.

2: 'resembled a river bed …', Bryce, 70.

3: 'It was definitely haunted,' Blanche Blackwell interview, 13 March 2012.

4: 'foods with more variety …', Bryce, 71.

4: 'really dreadful', Ibid.

4: 'Ivar, I have made a great decision …', Bryce, 72.

5: 'is how much of Ian they retain …', Pearson, *The Life of Ian Fleming*, (Aurum ed. 2003), 6.

6: 'In Jamaica Ian seemed perfectly at home …', Quennell, *The Wanton Chase*, 152.

7: 'rather melancholic …', Fleming interview, *Playboy*, December 1964.

7: 'If I have to make a choice, I would rather catch no salmon …', Amory ed., *The Letters of Ann Fleming*, 53.

7: the Royal Hawaiian Serenaders, *TC*, (Vintage 2013 ed.), 87.

8: 'quite a frightening woman', Lucy Williams interview, 9 July 2013.

9: 'The fact that I was so much happier when I was alone …', *SLM*, (Vintage ed. 2012), 6.

9: 'his inmost self strongly fortified', William Plomer, 'Ian Fleming Remembered', *Encounter*, January 1965, vol. xxiv, no.1.

10: 'the English upper crust …', Robert Harling, *Vogue*, November 1963.'self-consuming.', obituary by Donald McLachlan, *Sunday Telegraph*, quoted in Lycett, *Ian Fleming*, 443.

10: 'Bryce had laid his hands on a second-hand Douglas motorbike' …, Bryce, 3.

11: 'He ought to make an excellent soldier…', Pearson, 31.

11: 'having fun with the local Heidis …', Lewis, *Cyril Connolly: a Life*, 297.

11: 'have a powerful weakness for young Englishmen', *TC*, 192.

11: 'irresistible to women.', Pearson, 46.

11: 'a promise of something dashing …', Plomer, *Encounter*.

12: 'a series of appealing nymphs …', Bryce, 101.

12: 'countless neurotic patients had disappeared …', *YLT*, (Vintage ed. 2012), 22.

12: 'happy and electrically alive', Bryce, 47.

13: 'I left Berlin without regret …', *TC*, 177.

13: 'handsome and moody creature', Amory, 35.

13: 'Godlike but unapproachable.', Pearson, 211.

14: 'None of us had any affection …', AF to HC, December 1950, Amory, 95.

14: 'a slim, dark, handsome, highly strung …', Harling, *Vogue*.

14: 'I thought Ian original and entertaining', Pearson, 212.

14: 'I knew instinctively it would be fatal …', Amory, 41.

14: 'cads and bounders', Amory, 32.

15: 'the night before I married Esmond …', Amory, 42.

15: 'affluent pre-War style', Quennell, *Wanton Chase*, 105.

15: 'that little rat Attlee', Quennell, *Wanton Chase*, 107.

15: 'stimulating *inspiratrice*', Quennell, *Wanton Chase*, 58.

15: 'not a man of single aspect', Plomer, *Encounter*.

15: 'a brilliant and witty talker …', Allen Dulles, 'Our Spy-Boss Who Loved Bond', *Life*, 28 August 1966.

15: 'conveyed the sense of being alone …', Plomer, *Encounter*.

1946: Oracabessa and 'Old Jamaica'

16: 'Mr Luttrell's house was left empty …', Jean Rhys, *Wide Sargasso Sea*, 18.

16: 'Ten acres or so, away from towns …', Pearson, 159.

16: 'an old gentleman …', Bryce, 76.

16: 'a little place with good swimming and an island.', Pearson notes from his

Jamaica trip, 1965, Manuscripts Department, Lilly Library Pearson, J. Mss.

18: 'handful of heartbreakingly relaxed sounding words', Winder, *The Man Who Saved Britain*, 143.

20: 'steady zing of the crickets ...', *DN*, (Penguin Classics Omnibus ed. 2002), 239.

20: 'no glass in the windows, only good old Jamaica jalousies.':, *Gleaner*, 20 September 1964.

20: 'so that the birds could fly through ...', *Gleaner*, 10 February 1963.

21: 'modern – a squat elongated box without ornament.', *RWL*, (Penguin Classics Omnibus ed. 2002), 6.

21: 'a small army of men, women, children, and donkeys ...', *Sunspots*, unpublished memoir by Marion Simmons, 15–16.

21: 'insignificant and small', Bryce, 79.

21: 'often hiss like vipers ...', *Ian Fleming Introduces Jamaica*, 13.

22: 'extremely uncomfortable dining table ...', Bryce, 50.

22: 'That was a bit of a job', Pearson notes.

22: 'infinitely practical and direct ...', Bryce, 80,

22: 'It had cost £7000 ...', Huggins, *Too Much to Tell*, 103.

22: 'the finest house in the island.', Montgomery Hyde, *The Quiet Canadian*, 238.

23: 'That young whippersnapper!', Pearson, 171.

24: 'as if the sky were a glass ceiling ...', Thompson, *An Eye for the Tropics*, 27.

24: 'stories of pirates and desperadoes ...', Mitchell, *In My Stride*, 139.

25: 'hail and icy sleet', *DN*, 219.

25: 'velvet heat', *DN*, 237.

25: 'Prince's Club, in the foothills above Kingston ...', *SS*, (Penguin ed. 2002), 209.

25: 'those generously red-splashed maps ...', Mitchell, *The Spice of Life*, 19.

25: 'bled pretty thin by a couple of World Wars.', *YLT*, 109.

26: 'an occasional man going off to his precipitous smallholding ...', *DN*, 267.

26: 'We absorbed the doctrine that white was virtue ...', Sherlock, *Manley*, 24.

27: 'the social life of the upper classes ...', Cargill, *A Selection of his Writings in the Gleaner*, 34.

27: 'very reserved and even unfriendly', *West Indian Review*, 9 September 1950, vol. 2, no.19, 13.

27: 'an unimaginative man ...', *Spotlight* August 1950, 16.

27: 'she was the one that really registered.', Chris Blackwell interview, 8 July 2013.

28: 'an ugly, squat, grey cement building.', Huggins, 79.

28: 'much of it brought out from England in the old days ...', Huggins, 84.

28: 'We rather startled Jamaica in the early days ...', Huggins, 82.

28: 'sadly neglected', Huggins, 129.

28: 'there seemed to be a great deal of poverty ...', Huggins, 49.

28: 'the Jamaican plantocracy ...', Huggins, 110.

28: 'the sugar workers were very badly paid ...', Huggins, 59.

28: 'and there were a great many pathetic ones asking for money ...', Huggins, 81.

28–9: 'I realized very quickly that what Jamaican women needed …', Huggins, 109.

29: 'every three or four years' , Huggins, 4.

29: 'I suppose I fell in love with Jamaica …', Huggins, 109,

30: 'Nothing like Lady Molly Huggins ever happened …', *Life*, 24 April 1950.

30: 'The handsome young men …', *West Indian Review*, 9 September 1950, vol. 2, no.19.

31: 'senior staff of the Frome sugar estates.', *MGG*, (Pan ed. 1966), 57.

32: 'one of the island's most desirable properties', Hakewill, *A Picturesque Tour* n.p.

32: 'a very fine piece of water …', Edward Long, *A History of Jamaica*, 1744, 2:76.

32: 'production in Jamaica slumped…' , Deere, *The History of Sugar*, vol.1, 199.

32: 'sugar plantations shrank from more than 500 to just 77.', Thomson, *The Dead Yard*, 49.

32: 'Trinity's output halved …', Higman, *Jamaica Surveyed*, 118.

33: 'ruined slaves' quarters, ruined sugar-grinding houses …', Richard Hughes, *High Wind in Jamaica*, 1.

33: 'through three centuries …', *SS*, 35.

33: 'a thousand acres of cattle-tick …', *SS*, 33.

34: 'vibrant, colourful characters', interview filmed for Oracabessa oral history project, 1997.

34: 'sleazy, brilliantly lit wharves …' , Ross, *Through the Caribbean*, 129.

35: 'work night and day to make any money …', Oracabessa oral history project, 1997.

1947: The Bachelor Party

36: 'He knew, deep down, that love from Mary Goodnight …', *MGG*, 191.

36: 'DaCosta remembers him waving to the boys …' , Ramsay Dacosta interview, 3 July 2012.

37: 'Cool as hell …' , Raymond Benson interview, 11 February 2014.

38: 'a cubist arrangement of concrete surfaces …', Bryce, 80.

38: 'beautiful married blonde from Bermuda', Lycett, 174.

38: 'a million fragments of damaged cotton goods …', Bryce, 85.

39: 'The Colonel will be delighted to receive you, sir …', Bryce, 102.

40: 'All writers possessed of any energy …', Amis, *The James Bond Dossier*, 115.

40: 'Every exploration and every dive …', Bryce, 84–5.

40: 'There are so many things which would make you giggle here …', IF to AF, 26 January 1947, Amory, 55.

41: 'small blackamore troubles …', IF to AF, 26 January 1947, Amory, 55.

41: 'coping with staff.', 'How to Write a Thriller', *Books and Bookmen*, May 1963.

41: 'They require exact instructions …', Fleming, 'Where Shall John Go? XIII – Jamaica', *Horizon*, vol. 16, no.96, December 1947.

41: 'Jamaican servants, for all their charm …', *MGG*, 94.

41: 'One of those superlative human beings …', Bryce, 84.

41: 'The Commander was the best man I ever met …', *Gleaner*, 20 September 1964.

42: 'conch gumbo and fried octopus tentacles with tartare sauce …' , Pearson, 171.

42: 'Too many of the English and American wives …', *TC*, 16–17.

42: 'a passport into the lower strata of coloured life …', *DN*, 239.

42: 'My neighbours, both coloured and white …', *Horizon*.

44: 'she really preferred women to men.', Huggins, 144.

44: 'the last word in comfort and luxury …', Sunset Lodge brochure.

44: 'huge bonfire on the beach …', IF to AF, 26 January 1947, Amory, 56.

44: 'When they found Jamaica, they found it so beautiful …', Blanche Blackwell interview, 16 February 2012.

45: 'By 1938 visitor numbers had grown …' , Taylor, *To Hell with Paradise,* 155.

45: 'Here they come', *Gleaner*, 29 January 1948.

45: 'We want taking out of ourselves …', Chancellor, *James Bond: the Man and his World,* 169.

46: 'I've always thought that if I ever married …', *SS*, 77.

46: 'sun is always shining in my books …', Fleming, 'How to write a Thriller', *Books and Bookmen*, May 1963.

47: 'After four days of storm …', Flynn, *Wicked Ways,* 307.

48: 'According to his widow, Patrice …', Patrice Wymore Flynn interview, 8 July 2012.

48: 'She hadn't wanted to see me …', Flynn, *Wicked Ways,* 309.

49: 'gorgeous god …', *Sunday Times*, 7 October 2012.

49: 'I just wasn't allowed to know any black people …', Blanche Blackwell interview, 16 February 2012.

50: 'a very handsome man …', Chris Blackwell interview, 8 July 2013.

50: 'pretentious and full of himself', Patrice Wymore Flynn interview, 8 July 2012.

50: 'For God's sake! That's the worst insult you can pay a man.', *RWL*, 144.

51: 'Yes, I'm fucking them both.', Lycett, 164.

51: 'everything starts wrong and goes on wrong …', Ibid.

51: 'an admiring sugar planter's daughter', Ann Diary fragment, Amory, 60.

51: 'His days of fame …', Huggins, 87.

51: 'If the moral standard of the women can be raised …', *West Indian Review*, 9 September 1950, vol. 2, no.19, 15.

51: 'came in cars, on mules, donkeys and horses.', Huggins, 117.

52: 'the Continental attitude', Huggins, 150.

52: 'nymphomaniac', Blanche Blackwell interview, 17 April 2013.

52: 'the love of the people of Jamaica for me.', Huggins, 150.

53: '2000 different varieties of flowers', *Horizon*.

53: 'The most beautiful bird in Jamaica …', *SS*, 32.

54: 'some of the most beautiful scenery in the world.', *LLD*, 271.

54: 'the most beautiful large island in the world.', Pearson, 172.

54: 'you drop down, often through a cathedral of bamboo …', *Horizon*.

54: 'a description that Fleming would reuse ...' , *LDD*, 271.

55: 'dictatorship of white supremacy', Beckles, *Britain's Black Debt*, 3.

55: 'the children have yaws on their legs ...', Pringle, *Waters of the West*, 45.

56: 'ugly' past ...', Norman Manley's introduction to omnibus, Roger Mais novels, Jonathan Cape, 1966, vol. v.

57: 'The Empire and British rule rest on a carefully nurtured sense of inferiority ...', Sherlock, *Manley* 160, 27.

57: 'nurture a sense of inferiority in the masses', *Public Opinion*, 29 May 1943.

57: 'Each Jamaican was a smoldering little volcano ...', *Spotlight*, August 1950, vol. 11, no.8, 11.

57: 'revolution because of class resentment', Pringle, *Waters of the West*, 105.

58: 'make our Colonies in the Caribbean good examples ...', Fraser, *Ambivalent Anti-Colonialism*, 74.

58: 'We want bread!', Chris Blackwell interview, 8 July 2013.

58: 'I shall never forget the rich people ...', Edna Manley Diary, 28 December 1944, 23.

59: 'had caused more harm than good ...', Roberts, *Jamaica: the Portrait of an Island*, 245.

59: 'must have been sent out by the Colonial Office ...', *Public Opinion*, 8 March 1944.

1948: Lady Rothermere

61: 'Bond knew that he was very close to being in love with her.', *DF*, (Vintage ed. 2012), 249.

61: 'They'd just had the mother and father of all rows ...', Lycett, 176.

61: 'I loved being whipped by you ...', Lycett, 179,

63: 'at typical tropical sunset hour.', Ann Diary fragment, Amory, 60.

64: 'Ian always complained that flowers gave him headaches ...' , Pearson, 165.

65: 'used to leave in a small boat to fish ...', Vickers, ed. *Cocktails and Laughter*, 99.

66: 'determined assaults on her virtue.', *MR*, (Penguin Omnibus ed. 2003), 326–7.

66: 'strangely uncomfortable.', Vickers, ed. *Cocktails and Laughter*, 99.

67: 'If you burden yourself with the big-town malaises ...', Pearson, 172.

67: 'I did love it all ...', AF to IF, February 1948, Amory, 68.

67: 'a sort of Beau Brummel of the islands.', 65.

68: 'whirling and snapping in the water ...', *LLD*, 290.

68: 'terrible snuffling grunt ...', *LLD*, 260.

68: 'a horrible grunting scrunch', *LLD*, 313.

68: 'tied up good and firm ...', Pearson, 176.

68: 'I do hope the remoteness of Goldeneye ...', AF to IF, February 1948, Amory, 65.

68: 'It would be an interesting feat to be faithful ...', AF to IF, 13 February 1948, Amory, 66.

68: 'steadfast as a rock', Lycett, 182.

69: 'might serve as a model for new houses in the tropics ...', Leigh Fermor, *The Traveller's Tree*, 360.

70: 'extraordinary book', *LLD*, 158.

70: 'Commander Fleming Gives Modest ...', *Gleaner*, 6 March 1948.

70: 'accepting her duties cheerfully.', AF to EW, 15 July 1948, Amory, 69.

70: 'The spell was cast and held ...', Hoare, *Noël Coward*, 342.

71: 'It is quite perfect ...', Payn & Morley ed., *NC Diary*, 24 March 1948, 107.

72: 'Behind the house are banana plantations ...', Day ed., *NC Letters*, 540.

72: 'and all sorts of tropical deliciousness.', *NC Letters*, 546.

72: 'I am now a property owner in Jamaica ...', *NC Diary*, 25 April 1948, 108.

72: 'grown over with orchids', *NC Letters*, 546.

72: 'Somebody's suddenly gone and bought that ghastly Blue Harbour hotel.', *SS*, 33.

73: 'as if he were a distinguished member of the opposite sex ...', Quennell quoted in Hoare, *Noël Coward*, 388.

72: 'was always subtly understanding ...', Quennell, *Wanton Chase*, 151.

74: 'a bloody good thing but far too late.', *NC Diary*, 30 January 1948, 103.

74: 'taxation, controls and certain features ...', Fleming, 'If I Were Prime Minister', *Spectator*, 9 October 1959.

74: 'an irrelevant survival ...', Morley, *The Private Lives of Noël and Gertie*, 270.

74: 'a reaffirmation of Britain's continued great-power status ...', Cannadine, *Churchill's Shadow*, 280–1.

74: 'a one-man Suez task force.', Durgnat, *A Mirror for England*, 153.

74: 'benevolent to the point of indifference', Quennell, *Wanton Chase*, 161–2.

75: 'My darling, there was morphia and pain ...': AF to IF, undated 1948, Amory, 70

75: 'making a fuss of her ...', AF to IF, undated 1948, Amory, 71.

1949: Noël and Ian, Samolo and Jamaica

77: 'Empire, family life and the Conservative Party', Lycett, 192.

77: 'The house is entrancing ...', *NC Diary*, 3 February 1949, 123.

77: 'As you glide down this river ...', Flynn, *Wicked Ways*, 333.

78: 'Strong Bak Soup' , *Sunday Times*, 9 January 1955.

78: 'enchantingly languid ...', Ibid.

78: 'and was vastly entertaining all the way.', *NC diary*, 20 February 1949, 124.

78: 'scandal with a local Bustamante ...', *NC Diary*, 6 April 1949, 125.

79: 'a personality like a battering ram.', Coward, *P&C*, 78.

79: 'They sing from morning till night ...', Coward, 'South Sea Bubble', *Play Parade*, vi, 117.

79: 'industrious and enthusiastic, but ...', *P&C*, 26.

79: 'nip a breadfruit off a tree ...', Coward, 'South Sea Bubble', *Play Parade* vi, 129.

80: 'With that race, that place, that title …', Barringer, *Art and the British Empire*, 183.

80: 'There is a great deal of sex …', *P&C*, 16.

80: 'shopping for silk pyjamas.' , Huggins, 42.

80: 'most amusing rhyme about my second daughter, Cherry.', Huggins, 89.

80: 'happy and contented under British rule for so many years …', Coward, 'South Sea Bubble', *Play Parade* vi, 117.

81: 'After the last war British imperialism was too weak …', *Public Opinion*, 28 January 1950.

81: 'old fashioned Noël Coward …', Lesley, *The Life of Noël Coward*, 287.

81: 'Tourism has brought the island undreamed of prosperity …', *P&C*, 44.

81: 'This coast is being bought up like mad', *NC Letters*, 546.

81: 'rash of millionaire hotels', *DN*, 236.

81: 'the wealthier members of the plantocracy …', *P&C*, 51.

82: 'undoubtedly the most fashionable resort …', Chapman, *Pleasure Island*, 158.

82: 'In a cool elevation overlooking the sea', advertisement in *West Indian Review*, September 1950.

82: 'on top of the cliff, with a breath-taking view of the Caribbean …', Chapman, *Pleasure Island*, 152–3.

82: 'of England's powerful Kemsley Press', Chapman, *Pleasure Island*, 138.

82: 'Mr F., being Italian, has excellent manners …', Simmons, *Sunspots*, 48.

84: 'Costing a quarter of a million pounds …' , Issa, *Mr Jamaica*, 92.

84: 'In 1951, Jamaica played host to nearly 100,000 visitors …' , Taylor, *To Hell with Paradise*, 160.

85: 'twin-dieseled Chriscraft motorboat', *SS*, 41.

86: 'naked on Noël's …', Hoare, *Noël Coward*, 399.

86: 'Cargill himself complains he lost his girlfriend …', Cargill, *Jamaica Farewell*, 57.

86: 'By day you idle on a beach …', Waugh, *Notes from the Sugar Islands*, 203.

86: 'The atmosphere is a compound of Wall Street …', Leigh Fermor, *The Traveller's Tree*, 362.

86: 'Quite quite horrid …', *NC Letters*, 543.

87: 'an epidemic of homosexuality', *Public Opinion*, 28 May 1938.

87: 'there is hardly a lissom chambermaid …', *P&C*, 52.

87: 'evil example … sybaritic torpor …', Taylor, *To Hell with Paradise*, 195–6.

87: 'The labourers will not work for economical wages …', 'Jamaica the Beautiful', Dr. Josiah Oldfield, *Spotlight*, August 1950, 6.

88: 'a colour bar that is non-existent in law …', Leigh Fermor, *The Traveller's Tree*, 345.

88: 'That's how we keep out the niggers …', Morris Cargill interview filmed for Oracabessa oral history project, 1997.

88: 'in some barred by means of adroit subterfuges.', Roberts, *Jamaica: the Portrait of an Island,* 188

89: 'Call the police. Call the army ...', quoted in Thompson, *An Eye for the Tropics,* 204.

89: 'Tourists were people with money ...', Douglas Waite interview, 21 June 2013.

89: 'We saw water, electricity, motor cars ...', Ramsay Dacosta interview, 3 July 2012.

89: 'with homes of their own ...', *Gleaner,* 24 June 1949.

90: 'in a blaze of Jamaican publicity ...', *NC Letters,* 546.

91: 'spends all his time doing underwater fishing ...', *P&C,* 59.

91: 'bleak, overmasculine barrack', *P&C,* 119.

91–2: 'find himself caught up in an over-social marriage ...', *P&C,* 172.

92: 'I've funked everything these last few days ...', IF to AF, 20 February 1949, Amory, 77–9.

92: 'I have doubts about their happiness ...', *NC Letters,* 10 July 1949, 130.

1950: Doctor Jamaica

93: 'Up to forty, girls cost nothing ...', *DF,* 270–1

93: 'the most healthy life I could wish to live.', *Ian Fleming Introduces Jamaica,* 12.

95: 'On with your Aqua Lung ...', *P&C,* 214.

95: 'If Noël has a problem ...', Elaine Stritch to NC, 6 August 1963, *NC Letters,* 682.

95: 'Everything is unbelievably lovely.', *NC Diary,* 15 December 1949, 137.

95: 'It has been a lovely holiday ...', *NC Diary,* 22 April 1952, 191.

95: 'this place has a strange and very potent magic for me ...', *NC Letters,* 674.

96: 'healing, beneficial and inspiring.', AF to HC, 1 February 1952, Amory, 105.

96: 'Here there is peace and that wonderful vacuum ...', IF to AF, 20 January 1958, Amory, 213.

96: 'I suppose it is the peace and silence ...', *Ian Fleming Introduces Jamaica,* 12.

96: 'Always took life strangely hard, except in Jamaica.', Quennell, *Wanton Chase,* 154.

97: 'Fleming is at his mellow best.', Harling, *Vogue.*

97: 'very charming, attractive character ...', Chris Blackwell interview, 8 July 2013.

97: 'the parasites will have him within a day or two.', Lycett, 198.

97: 'The gold and black tiger's eye was on him ...', *TB,* (Vintage ed. 2012), 237.

98: 'It is easy to enjoy the orchids and the hummingbirds ...', Fleming, 'Pleasure Islands?', *Spectator,* 4 July 1952.

98: 'I am still grateful for the gentle ministrations ...', Olivier, *Confessions of an Actor,* 185.

98: 'Do you know that when you said that to me …', AF to IF, February 1950, Amory, 79.

98: 'stressed-concrete jungle', *LLD*, 144.

99: 'such matters as radio and weapons …', *RWL*, 37.

99: 'of 'excellent' 'manufacture', *RWL*, 20.

99: 'their total unpreparedness to rule the world …', Lycett, 164.

99: 'continual homeopathic doses of Anti-Americanism.', Introduction to *Casino Royale, Live and Let Die, Moonraker,* (Penguin ed., 2003), xii.

100: 'biggest business, bigger than steel …', *DF*, 25.

100: 'after washing the filth …', *TC*, 108.

100: 'ghastly', *DF*, 178.

100: 'the hysterical pursuit of money', *TC*, 133.

100: 'one of the grimmest suburbs …', *TC*, 120.

100: 'society that fails to establish …', *TC*, 97.

100: 'It's your territory.', *LLD*, 166.

100: 'because the place is British territory.', *DN*, 235.

100: 'Bond was glad to be on his way …', *LLD*, 262.

100: 'You see, it belongs to an American now …', *LLD*, 268.

100-101: 'a trace of an American accent', *DN*, 338.

101: 'millionaires in beach clothes', *P&C*, 76.

101: 'islands of the West Indies …', Willis J. Abbot, *Panama and the Canal,* (Syndicate Publishing Company, London, 1913), 15.

102: 'The American invasion', Huggins, 56.

103: 'were equaled only in the most sociologically retarded …', Thompson, *An Eye for the Tropics,* 238–9.

103: 'threatened the undoing of the British Empire.', *Spotlight*, December 1953.

104: 'the delegation made it plain …', Fraser, *Ambivalent Anti-Colonialism,* 113.

104: 'I was in New York …', *Gleaner*, 3 August 1948.

105: 'Jamaica has the largest bauxite deposits …', *Spectator*, 4 July 1952.

105: 'You fear the moral "dégringolade" of the tropics …', *Horizon*.

106: 'wanted to get the hell away from King's House …', *DN*, 399.

106: 'though our political views differed.', Huggins, 138.

106: 'though I don't think she really approved of me …', Huggins, 107.

107: 'I'll be damned.', *Gleaner*, February 1950.

107–8: 'We were proud to be nonconformists and Roundheads …', *New York Times*, 7 September 1990.

108: 'dapper' and 'well-bred', *Spotlight*, August 1950, 19.

108: 'charming, likable, infinitely clever person.', Edna Manley Diaries, 14 November 1953, 46.

109: 'Quite nice, really, but a bit sticky.': Coward, 'South Sea Bubble', *Play Parade,* vi, 117.

109: 'true-blue conservative', *P&C*, 223.

109: 'an ardent socialist in his earlier years.', Ibid.

109: 'When I was governor of Jamaica ...', Foot, *Empire into Commonwealth*, 8.

109: 'advancing at an accelerating rate ...', Foot, *Start*, 120.

1951: 'Disciplined Exoticism'

110: 'What I endeavour to aim at ...', 'How to Write a Thriller'.

110: 'more than any other woman', IF to AF, February 1950, Amory, 80–1.

110: 'static emotional state', AF to HC, 18 August 1950, Amory, 93.

111: 'Christmas without Ian seems a bleak affair ...', AF to HC, 2 November 1950, Amory, 94.

111: 'Cecil was tremendously brave ...', AF to DC, 10 February 1951, Amory, 96.

111: 'something reptilian about him.', Fionn Morgan interview, 24 January 2013.

113: 'a genuine coral reef 18th century-print wreck ...', AF to DC, 10 February 1951, Amory, 97.

113: 'got off with women because he could not get on with them.', Amory, 37.

113: 'the extremely unfeeling use to which he put his great attractions', Quennell, *Wanton*, 152.

114: 'stories of battles, tornados ...', *MSS*, (Vintage ed. 2012), 257.

114: 'gave you the impression of being in a battleship in harbour.', *MR*, 346.

114: 'a keen sailor's face, with the clear, sharp sailor's eyes', Ibid.

115: 'the sort of aquiline good looks that are associated ...', *LLD*, 265.

115: ' with 'what almost amounted to the "Nelson Touch", *YLT*, 271.

116: 'divers barbarous acts', Parker, *The Sugar Barons*, 141.

116: 'debauched wild blades', Parker, *The Sugar Barons*, 177.

116: 'the buccaneers of Port Royal ...', Mitchell, *The Spice of Life*, 51.

117: 'four-penny horrors', *Playboy* interview.

117: 'doubtless stuffed with pirate treasure ...', *Horizon*.

117: 'I wouldn't love you if you weren't a pirate', *MSS*, 323.

117: 'piratical.', *CR*, 40,

117: 'the slightly piratical air ...', Lycett, 371.

117: 'greedy boisterous pirate.', *SS*, 132.

117: 'exuberant shrewd pirate.', *RWL*, 108.

117: 'All history is sex and violence.', Fleming on Desert Island Discs, 1963.

118: 'known, the map says, by the name of Look Behind.', *Horizon*.

119: 'supersonic John Buchan.', *Listener*, 23 April 1953.

120: 'seeing the West Indies in their last rip-roaring days ...', Hugh Edwards, Introduction to *All Night at Mr Staneyhursts*, (Jonathan Cape, London, 1964), xvii.

120: 'exaggeration and things larger than life.', *Playboy* interview.

120: 'hot-blooded sadism and slaves set in the 1850s.', *Horizon*.

121: 'the stews of Kingston', *Horizon*.

122: 'Some things have happened recently ...', *Sunspots*, 60.

122: 'The thing is to let the blacks know I *have* a pistol', Pearson, 194.

122: 'for defence against the Blackamoors.', Pearson, 319.

122: 'most law abiding and God-fearing …', *Horizon*.

123: 'luscious clash of ostentation and restraint': introduction to Penguin ed., vii.

213: 'What I endeavour to aim at …', 'How to write a Thriller'.

1952: *Casino Royale*

124: Then he slept, and with the warmth and humour …', *CR*, 10.

124: 'the easiest way', AF to HC and VC, January 1952, Amory, 102.

124: 'We are of course totally unsuited …', IF to HC, 23 February 1952, Amory, 106.

125: 'You might get too irritated …', IF to AF, February 1949, Amory, 78.

125: 'quite a step for him …': AF to HC and VC, 15 March 1952, Amory, 111.

125: 'BOAC, with its Stratocruiser …', *Gleaner*, 6 May 1952.

126: 'I watched the banks for new flowers …', Ann's Diary 1952, Amory, 109.

127: 'Dine with Ian and Annie …', *NC Diary*, 16 February 1952, 189.

127: 'should be used as a cabaret and not as a guest …', AF to CB, 29 February 1952, Amory, 106–7.

127: 'rather a tense period in our lives.', Pearson, 224ff.

128: 'This morning Ian started to type a book …', undated Ann diary, Amory, 108.

129: 'the house runs away with money all through the year.', Pearson, 196.

130: 'These blithering women …', *CR*, 75.

130: 'the lengthy approaches to a seduction bored him …', *CR*, 112.

130: 'brutally ravaged', *CR*, 34.

130: 'People are islands …', *CR*, 121.

130: 'wasn't very anxious to start …', Pearson, 224.

130: 'main thing is to write fast …', *Playboy* interview.

131: 'an important fifth column …', *CR*, 10.

131: 'efficient organ of Soviet vengeance', *CR*, 12.

131: 'Jamaican plantocrat …', *CR*, 19.

131: a 'taciturn man who was head of the picture desk …', *CR*, 7.

131: 'Charles DaSilva of Chaffery's, Kingston', *CR*, 19.

131: 'What is more natural than that you should pick up a pretty girl …', *CR*, 23.

132: 'excited by her beauty', *CR*, 28.

132: 'They're stupid, but obedient …', *CR*, 23.

132: 'like an octopus under a rock.', *CR*, 65.

132: 'a ridiculous pleasure in what I eat and drink.', *CR*, 43.

132: 'bowled out.', *CR*, 22.

132: 'the old days of the hero getting a crack over the head …', Desert Island Discs.

133: 'who had probably had plenty of money ...', *CR*, 52.

133: 'a mixture of taciturnity and passion.', *CR*, 112.

133: 'I don't think Bond has ever been melted ...', *CR*, 29.

133: 'like all harsh, cold men, he was easily tipped over into sentiment.', *CR*, 180.

133: 'ironical, brutal and cold', *CR*, 10.

133: 'Bond lit his seventieth cigarette ...', *CR*, 9.

134: 'passion for speed, his taste for mechanical devices ...', Quennell, *Wanton Chase*, 157.

134: 'probably a mixture of Mediterranean with Prussian or Polish strains', *CR*, 14.

134: 'moist yellowish skin ...' , *CR*, 90.

134: 'large sexual appetite.', *CR*, 15.

134: 'lip-smacking descriptions', *CR*, 32.

134: 'three measures of Gordon's ...', *CR*, 36.

135: 'Although he seemed to talk quite openly about his duties in Paris ...', *CR*, 38.

135: 'Marshall Aid.', *CR*, 61.

135: 'That envelope was the most wonderful thing ...', *CR*, 69.

136: 'this country right or wrong business is getting a little out of date', *CR*, 102.

135: 'Washington's pretty sick we're not running the show...', *CR*, 37.

136: 'History is moving pretty quickly these days ...', *CR*, 102.

137: 'one of the highlights of the north coast season', *Gleaner*, 29 February 1952.

137: 'It is frighteningly agreeable.', AF to HC and VC, 15 March 1952, Amory, 110.

137: 'a marvelous honeymoon ...', IF to VC and HC, 23 February 1952, Amory, 106.

138: 'I shall wear long elbow gloves and give the bride away ...', *NC Letters*, 573.

138: 'We took our duties very seriously ...', Lesley, *The Life of Noël Coward*, 310.

138: 'an enormous oleograph of Churchill ...', Pearson, 208.

138: 'a slimy green wedding cake ...', Pearson notes, interview with NC, 22 May 1965, Manuscripts Department, Lilly Library Pearson J. Mss.

139: 'Surely one doesn't dedicate books of this sort to people.', Chancellor, *James Bond: the Man and his World*, 237.

139: 'tubes performing every physical function.', AF to HC, 3 September 1952, Amory, 120.

139: 'You have been wonderfully brave ...', IF to AF, August 1952, Amory, 119.

140: 'as he considers himself responsible for the whole thing.', AF to CB, 2 September 1952, Amory, 119.

141: 'The game of Red Indians is over ...', *CR*, 86–7.

141: 'been reading too many novels of suspense ...', *DN*, 353–4

141: 'looked like a gangster in a horror-comic.', *DF*, 129.

141: 'I could hardly believe it ...', *SLM*, 143.

141: 'the stuff of an adventure-strip ...', *SS*, 100.

141: 'the best new thriller writer since Eric Ambler.', *Sunday Times*, 3 May 1963.

141: 'Ian Fleming has discovered the secret of narrative art ...', Chancellor, *James Bond: the Man and his World*, 25.

142: 'Ian's thriller starts well but ends as the most disgusting thing ...', Lycett, 244.

142: 'the Doctor Birds are waiting in the Crown of Thorns bushes ...', Lycett, 236.

1953: The First Jamaica Novel – *Live and Let Die*

143: 'Caribbean reality resembles ...' , Gabriel García Márquez interview in *Paris Review*, no.82, Winter 1981.

143: 'This island is no stranger to distinguished visitors ...', *Gleaner*, 29 December 1952.

144: 'work on his memoirs', *Gleaner*, 12 January 1953.

144: 'The doctors have advised me not to swim ...', Mitchell, *Spice of Life*, 123.

145: 'He selected the exact spot and went to work with a spade ...', Mitchell, *Spice of Life*, 118.

145: 'Great British Empire.', *Gleaner*, 19 May 1953.

146: 'Britons made them feel like the uninvited they were ...', *Spotlight*, December 1953.

146: 'in 1955, the figure would reach seventeen thousand ...' , Hart, *The End of Empire*, 341.

146: 'magpie society and that would never do', James Winton, 'The Black experience in the Twentieth Century' in Philip D. Morgan and Sean Hawkins eds., *Black Experience and the Empire*, (OUP, Oxford, 2004), 370.

146: 'Keep Britain White.', Ibid, 371.

146: 'made no reference whatever to any of my political relatives', Foot, *Start in Freedom*, 124.

147: 'the Communist movement in Jamaica', Public Records Office, CO O859/425 File SSD 176/01, July–August 1953.

148: 'fanatical opponent of communist.', Foot, *Start*, 136.

148: 'Bustamante called for Communism to be banned by law ...' , *Gleaner*, 29 November 1952.

149: 'shouts, screams and threats ...', *Public Opinion*, 2 June 1952.

149: 'when the Communist headquarters in Cuba ...', *LLD*, 270.

150: 'a cloak of verdure', Bryce, 80.

150: 'She was wearing brief shorts ...', AF to EW, 3 April 1953, Amory, 126.

150: 'seemed to derive pleasure out of seeing them bow and scrape ...', Bret, *Errol Flynn Gentleman Hellraiser*, 212.

151: 'Where there is a party, the Commander make his Poor Man's Thing.', Pearson notes

151: 'rich influential Portuguese Jews.', Amory, 124.

152: 'the world's bloodiest boy ...', Lewis, *Cyril Connolly: a Life,* 142–3.

152: 'three black slaves', AF to HC, 2 March 1953, Amory, 124.

151: 'She asked me to one of those marvelous parties ...', Grieg, *Breakfast with Lucian,* 105.

152: 'ghastly', Grieg, *Breakfast with Lucian,* 106.

152: 'Palms wave – waves ripple ...', Amory, 125.

152: 'I am still sitting in almost the same place ...', Amory, 125.

153: 'evening was totally ruined', AF to EW, 3 April 1953, Amory, 126.

153: 'Papa is very happy ...' AF to HC, 2 March 1953, Amory, 125.

153: 'lurid meller ...', *New York Times,* 10 April 1955.

153: 'adventure', *LLD,* 212.

153: 'like the bad man in a film ...', *LLD,* 239.

154: 'Sort of damsel in distress? Good show!', *LLD,* 278.

154: 'half negro and half French': *LLD,* 154.

154: 'grey-black, taut and shining ...', *LLD,* 185.

154: 'raving megalomaniac', *LLD,* 194.

154: 'one of the most valuable treasure troves in history', *LLD,* 152.

154: 'Bloody Morgan, the pirate', *LLD,* 150.

154: 'of countless raids on Hispaniola ...', *LLD,* 266.

154: 'a face born to command ...', *LLD,* 213.

154: 'a lonely childhood on some great decaying plantation ...', *LLD,* 191.

154: 'the most dreadful spirit in the whole of Voodooism', *LLD,* 218.

155: 'it took him minutes to forget the atmosphere ...', *LLD,* 161.

155: 'She herself considers her 'second sight' to be genuine ...' , *LLD,* 211.

155: 'half-belief in them', *LLD,* 218.

155: 'the extraordinary power of her intuitions.', *LLD,* 236.

155: 'Local black magic (obea) is scarce and dull ...', *Horizon.*

155: 'the secret heart of the tropics ...', *LLD,* 217.

155: 'rather intrigued by fortune-telling ...', *TC,* 59.

156: 'strong feel of the supernatural in the air', Chris Blackwell interview, 23 June 2013.

156: 'the shadowy form of a woman', Huggins, 93.

156: 'read most of the books on Voodoo ...', *LLD,* 218.

156: 'accepted through all the lower strata of the negro world ...', *LLD,* 156.

156: 'the sixth sense of fish, of birds, of negroes.', *LLD,* 217.

157: are 'clumsy black apes', *LLD,* 188.

157: 'negro bodies', *LLD,* 179.

157: 'The "paper tiger" hero, James Bond ...', Eldridge Cleaver, *Soul on Ice,* (Jonathan Cape, London, 1969), 80.

157: 'the usual German chip on the shoulder.', *MR,* 386.

157: 'an unquenchable thirst for the bizarre ...', *YLT,* 174.

157: 'bums with monogrammed shirts ...', *DF*, 24–5.

157: 'a bastard race, sly, stupid and ill-bred.', *DF*, 6.

157: 'hysterical', *DN*, 215.

158: 'all foreigners are pestilential', Lycett, 282.

158: 'they were trespassing. They just weren't wanted', *LLD*, 175.

158: 'Fortunately I like the negroes ...', *LLD*, 170.

158: 'Bond had a natural affection for coloured people.', *DF*, 144.

158: 'lashed his revolver into the centre of the negro's huge belly.', *DF*, 151.

159: 'I didn't like those two men in hoods ...', *DF*, 168.

159: 'spellbound', *LLD*, 177.

159: 'Seems they're interested in much the same things ...', *LLD*, 174.

159: 'sour sweet smell', *LLD*, 178.

159: 'probably the most powerful negro criminal in the world ...', *LLD*, 153.

159: 'shrewd', *LLD*, 148.

159: 'The negro races are just beginning ...', *LLD*, 153.

160: 'In the history of negro emancipation ...', *LLD*, 302.

160: 'a taut, exciting, intelligent and extremely sophisticated who-dunnit', *Gleaner*, 8 September 1954.

160: 'Surely one is not being over-sensitive at the implied condescension ...', *Gleaner*, 30 September 1956.

160: 'learned about living amongst, and appreciating, coloured people ...', *Ian Fleming Introduces Jamaica*, 12.

161: 'whereas Ian was a gregarious person ...', Robert F. Moss 'James Bond's Jamaica', *Signature*, January 1983, 39.

161: 'full of goodwill and cheerfulness and humour.', Fleming, 'Pleasure Islands?', *Spectator*, 4 July 1952.

161: 'integrated', Olivia Grange interview, 21 April 2014.

161: 'It was like the South of France ...', Chris Blackwell interview, 8 July 2013.

161: 'natural affection', DN, 397.

162: 'a good man to act as your factotum ...', *LLD*, 269.

162: 'Bond liked him immediately.', *LLD*, 270.

162: 'pirate of Morgan's time.', *DN*, 238.

162: 'spatulate nose and the pale palms of his hands were negroid', *LLD*, 270.

162: 'warm grey eyes.', *LLD*, 284.

162: 'have somehow managed to keep their bloodstream ...', *Sunday Times*, 7 April 1957.

162: 'reverence for superstition and instincts ...', *DN*, 396–7.

162: 'there was no desire to please ...', *LLD*, 270.

163: 'follow Bond unquestioningly.', *DN*, 318.

163: 'the most beautiful beach he had ever seen ...', *LLD*, 273.

163: 'succulent meals of fish and eggs and vegetables.', *LLD*, 274–5.

164: 'Bond was sunburned and hard ...', *LLD*, 277.

164: 'glad to be back …', *LLD*, 270.

165: 'grim suburbs of Philadelphia showing their sores, like beggars', *LLD*, 215.

165: 'gloomy silent withered forests of Florida', *LLD*, 228.

165: 'gleaming moonlit foothills of the Blue Mountain …', *LLD*, 264.

165: 'paw-paw with a slice of green lime …', *LLD*, 270.

165: 'Anglo-American snarls to disentangle', *LLD*, 204.

165: 'a first printing of 7,500 …' , Pearson, 296.

166: 'How wincingly well Mr Fleming writes.', Lycett, 255.

166: 'the most interesting recent recruit …', *TLS*, 30 April 1954.

166: 'It is an unashamed thriller …', Chancellor, *James Bond: the Man and his World*, 43.

1954-5: *Moonraker, Diamonds are Forever*

167: 'Most marriages don't add two people together …', *DF*, 260.

167: 'She now corrals the people she finds interesting …', Beaton, *The Strenuous Years*, 174–5.

168: 'The noise in there …', Amory, 129.

168: 'gilded cage.', Lycett, 236.

168: 'The Flemings' life together deteriorated …', Vickers, ed. *Cocktails and Laughter*, 99.

168: 'He couldn't cope at all', Lycett, 241.

169: 'We may have been accused of having been paternalistic …', Foot, *Race Relations*, 5.

170: 'a most loyal supporter of the Crown', Huggins, 104.

170: 'The Queen was like Lord you know …', Pearl Flynn interview, 21 June 2013.

170: 'There was total respect for the head of state …', Douglas Waite interview, 21 June 2013.

170: 'the character and stability to carry the role …', Edna Manley Diary, 15 December 1953, 47.

172: 'He was a great friend of my mother's …', Salewicz, *Firefly*, 41.

172: 'with their mimic high life …', Pringle, *Waters of the West*, 89–90.

172: 'By 1956, there were 1,350.' , Taylor, *To Hell with Paradise*, 164.

173: 'regarded it as a tourist trap', Bryce, 88

173: 'Montego was horrible as usual …', *NC Diary*, February 1957, 346.

173: 'crazily inflated tourist boom …', *Sunday Times*, 28 March 1954.

173: 'Rather odd that in Jamaica …', *Gleaner*, 18 May 1938.

173: 'fast international set', *MSS*, 57.

173: 'sunburned men in England …', *MR*, 332.

173: 'British atmosphere.', *Oakland Tribune*, 15 November 1953.

174: 'There are no "America. Go Home!" signs on this island …', *Charleston Gazette*, 13 April 1957.

174: 'success stories in the tourist industry of Jamaica …', *Gleaner*, 27 September 1955.

174: 'doubling between 1951 and 1959 to nearly 200,000 …', Taylor, *To Hell with Paradise,* 160.

174: 'The American who comes here …', Thompson, *An Eye for the Tropics,* 239–40.

174: 'invested in local property', *DS,* (Vintage ed. 2013), 85.

175: 'usually three of four a week …', *P&C,* 91.

175: 'Lady Rothermere's Fan' Fionn Morgan, 'Beautiful, Dandified Detachment', *Spectator,* 12 December 2008.

175: 'neither a wild bohemian nor a rampant homosexual.', Quennell, *Wanton,* 146.

175: 'I must admit …', Quennell, *Wanton,* 157.

175: 'a natural melancholic …', Quennell, *Wanton,* 153.

175: 'The Puritan and the Jesuit …', *MR,* 332.

176: 'dew was glittering …', Quennell, *Sign,* 112–13.

177: 'The Caribbean night falls …', Quennell, *Sign,* 117.

177: 'worked and played according to a prearranged schedule …', Quennell *Wanton,* 154.

177: 'Another peculiarity of the place …', Pearson, 170.

178: 'genial Caribbean squire', *Vogue,* November 1963.

178: 'far closer to the life of some self-absorbed eighteenth-century original …', Pearson, 168.

179: 'awoke the authoritarian', AF to Clarissa Churchill, later Eden, 3 March 1952, Amory, 108.

179: 'Everybody understood that his work came first …', *Gleaner*, 20 September 1964.

179: 'evidently enjoyed his work', Quennell, *Wanton,* 152.

179: 'with a fierce intensity.', Harling, *Vogue.*

179: 'By 24 February, he had written 30,000 words …' , Lycett, 255.

179: 'a raving paranoiac', *MR,* 381.

179: 'loud-mouthed and ostentatious', *MR,* 334.

180: 'Useless, idle, decadent fools …', *MR,* 481.

180: 'white scribbles in the sky.', *MR,* 430.

180: 'where Caesar had first landed …', *MR,* 430–1.

180: 'the best in the world.', *MR,* 360.

180: 'the Palace … the softly beating heart of London.', *MR,* 457, 506.

181: 'of course I have the affectionate reverence for Sir Winston Churchill …', Fleming, 'If I Were Prime Minister', *Spectator*, 9 October 1959.

181: 'two virtues, patriotism and courage.' , *Playboy* interview.

181: 'The boy stood on the burning deck …', *MR,* 489.

181: 'Height: 5ft 7. Weight: 9 Stone …', *MR,* 394.

181: 'Noël brought a Mainbocher …', AF to HC, January 1954, Amory, 135.

182: 'making love, with a rather cold passion …', *MR*, 328.

182: 'Marriage and children and a home were out of the question …', *MR*, 326.

182: 'What's the alternative? …', *MR*, 505.

182: 'prairie fire of fear, intolerance and hatred …', *Sunday Times*, 22 November 1953.

182: 'What's [M] so worried about?', *DF*, 24.

182: 'Seems that most of what they call "gem" diamonds …', *DF*, 19

183: 'One's almost ashamed of it being an English possession …', *DS*, 82.

183: 'won't be much help to us, I'm afraid.', *DF*, 21.

183: 'pick Britain's chestnuts out of the fire.', *DF*, 58.

184: 'a poor substitute for the product of Scotland.', *DF*, 90.

184: 'hit Bond's face like a fist.', *DF*, 172.

184: 'Bond wishfully dreams he is back in Jamaica', *DF*, 228.

184: 'ghastly glitter', *DF*, 178.

184: 'Now the hoodlums don't run liquor …', *DF*, 170.

184: 'Maybe you can strike a blow …', *DF*, 214.

184: 'the great safe black British belly', *DF*, 252.

184: 'the extra exotic touch of the negroes', *DF*, 125.

184: 'He had been a stage-gangster …', *DF*, 241.

184: 'Mike Hammer routine …', *DF*, 71.

184: 'That was quite an exit …', *DF*, 232.

185: 'heart-sinking', 'How to write a Thriller'.

185: 'I baked a fresh cake in Jamaica …', Pearson, 305ff.

185: 'As early as 1955 …', Quennell, *Wanton*, 155.

185: 'Mr Fleming is splendid …', advert in *The Times*, 28 April 1955.

185: 'It is utterly disgraceful …', Benson, *James Bond Bedside Companion*, 11.

185: 'disappointment.', *TLS*, 20 May 1955.

185: 'weakest book, a heavily padded story.', *TLS*, 27 April 1956.

186: 'they had all the time in the world', *DF*, 98.

186: 'Bond knew that he was very close to being in love with her.', *DF*, 249.

186: 'handing round canapés …', *DF*, 262–3.

186: '*Live and Let Die* has the wind under its tail …', Bryce, 103–4.

186: 'These dreadful Bond books.', Harling, *Vogue*.

186: 'It is the best he has done yet …', *NC Diary*, 23 January 1955.

187: 'The Commander was suffering greatly …', Fionn Morgan, *Spectator*, 12 December 2008.

187: 'with great reluctance', AF to HC, 14 February 1955, Amory, 150.

188: 'a very interesting man. A very nice man …', Morris Cargill interview.

188: 'polishing up horror comic number four', AF to Joan Raynor and Patrick Leigh Fermor, 27 March 1955, Amory, 153.

188: 'a peaceful and appreciative guest …', AF to HC, 14 February 1955, Amory, 150.

188: 'Goldeneye was delightful ...', Lycett, 267.

188: 'hated each other', Mark Amory interview, 27 September 2013.

188: 'Evelyn wore blue silk pyjamas ...', AF to Joan Rayner and Patrick Leigh Fermor, 27 March 1955, Amory, 153.

189: 'I have watched him, a cigar in his mouth ...', Quennell, *Sign,* 240–1.

189: 'Jamaica is an odd island ...', EW to Auberon Waugh, 27 January 1955, *The Letters of Evelyn Waugh,* ed. Amory, 438.

190: 'The Moscow Trojan horse has arrived in Jamaica ...', *Gleaner,* 12 March 1954.

190: 'but the Caribbean was ignored.', Andrew, *The KGB and the World,* 28.

191: as 'always more skillful as a national psychiatrist than as a politician.', *Gleaner,* 1 September 1954.

191: 'We have to stop being colonials and start being Jamaicans ...', Sherlock, *Manley,* 10.

192: 'I don't see why me and the telephone operator ...', Pearl Flynn interview, 21 June 2013.

192: 'Jamaica in 1955 had come a long way ...', Cargill interview.

192: 'House of Issa', *Gleaner,* 6 October 1951.

192: 'political awakening must and always goes hand in hand ...', quoted in Arnold, *A History of Literature in the Caribbean,* 336.

193: 'the dead hand of colonialism', Manley, Introduction to *Three Novels of Roger Mais,* (Jonathan Cape, London, 1966).

193: 'The umbilicus which attached...' , *Gleaner,* 1 September 1954.

193: 'Jamaica is a coloured island ...', *NC Diary,* 15 January 1955, 254.

193: 'The only complaint ...' , *Public Opinion,* 24 February 1955.

193: 'dead gone on' the Princess ... , *Daily Herald,* Texas, 18 April 1957.

194: 'whatever the magic that attaches to a throne ...', Edna Manley Diary, 2 April 1955, 48.

194: 'The populace would dearly love to see the pretty Princess ...', *Daily Herald,* Texas, 18 April 1957.

1956: *From Russia, with Love*

195: 'Doesn't do to get mixed up with neurotic women ...', *RWL,* 85.

195: 'the novel Fleming was most proud of.', Blanche Blackwell interview, 16 February 2012.

195: 'continue to forge everywhere stealthily ahead ...', *RWL,* 30.

196: 'the trouble today is that carrots for all are the fashion ...', *RWL,* 141.

196: 'conspicuous act of terrorism', *RWL,* 29.

197: 'featherbedded', *TC,* 146.

197: 'all the money and equipment ...', *RWL,* 123.

197: 'taste for adventure ...', *DS,* 41.

197: 'In my quest for a moral institution ...', *New York Review of Books,* 6 June 2013.

197: 'loved the firm …', Le Carré, *Perfect Spy,* 621.

197: 'He's a romantic at heart …', *MGG*, 186.

198: 'who is admired and whose ignominious destruction …', *RWL*, 38–9.

198: 'the result of a midnight union …', *RWL*, 1.

198: 'a cheerful, voluble giant of villainous aspect', *Sunday Times,* 9 January 1955.

198: 'their brutality, their carelessness …', *RWL*, 16.

198: 'the colonial peoples, the negroes.', *RWL*, 23.

198: 'the excitement and turmoil of the hot war.', *RWL*, 176.

198: 'Cecil Beaton's war-time photograph of Winston Churchill …', *RWL*, 101.

198: 'Careful, old man. No tricks …', *RWL*, 190.

199: 'I love scratching away with my paintbrush …', AF to EW, 13 January 1956, Amory, 172–3.

199: 'Very sad without you …', IF to AF, January 1956, Amory, 173.

199: 'our wonderful lives at Goldeneye …', AF to IF, 25 January 1956, Amory, 174.

200: 'Can you imagine a more incongruous playmate …', AF to IF, 16 February 1962, Amory, 176.

200: 'another ugly house …', Hoare, *Noël Coward,* 421.

200: 'His Firefly house is near-disaster …', IF to AF, 11 February 1956, Amory, 175.

201: 'the most beautiful I have seen in the world …', *Sunday Times,* 1 April 1956.

201: 'the soft enchantments of the tropic reed …', *Sunday Times,* 8 April 1956.

202: 'the most intoxicating landscape …' , Ibid.

202: 'I thought I should be polite and invite him for a drink …', Ranston, *Lindo Legacy,* 121.

203: 'She is joyful …', Bryce, 135.

203: 'You're not another lesbian, are you?', Blanche Blackwell interview, 13 March 2012.

203: 'Loved the English ….', Chris Blackwell interview, 8 July 2013.

203: 'near a middle-aged Jewess.', Lycett, 285.

203: 'thirtyish, Jewish …', Lycett, 178.

204: 'almost as firm and rounded as a boy's.', *DN*, 276.

204: 'behind that jutted out like a man's …', *RWL*, 58.

204: 'I'm very strange!', Blanche Blackwell interview, 16 February 2012.

204: 'completely charming', Blanche Blackwell interview, 13 March 2012.

204: 'quite a pleasant neighbour.', Lycett, 285.

204: 'took to the sea.', Blanche Blackwell interview, 16 February 2012.

205: 'a fine swimmer', Bryce, 135.

206: 'We became friends', Barrington Roper interview, 23 August 2013.

206: 'never saw anyone …', Chris Blackwell interview, 22 January 2014.

208: 'free from pain', AF to DC, 24 January 1956, Amory 171.

208: 'He complains of greater exhaustion …', Pearson 335.

208: 'drinking a great deal', Raymond O'Neill interview, 13 May 2013.

208: 'few men could have survived it.' , *CR*, 97.

208: 'strong and compact and confident', *LLD*, 170.

208: 'the best shot in the service.', *MR*, 37.

208: 'he is in pretty good shape.', *DF*, 18.

208-209: 'The blubbery arms of the soft life ...', *RWL*, 77.

209: is 'restless and indecisive.', *RWL*, 82.

209: 'The soul sickens of it ...', *RWL*, 22.

209: 'I drink and smoke too much ...', *RWL*, 112.

209: 'My muse is in a bad way ...', Lycett, 291–2.

209: 'He decided to add a final twist ...' , Griswold, *Ian Fleming's James Bond*, 197.

209: 'Bond pivoted slowly ...', *RWL*, 208.

209: 'One boasted the leader of the Opposition ...' , AF to EW, 4 April 1956, Amory, 182.

209: 'gentle and loving', Brivati, *Hugh Gaitskell*, 246.

210: 'showed him the pleasures of upper class frivolity', Thorpe, *Eden*, 441.

210: 'Mr Gaitskell came to lunch ...', AF to EW, 24 November 1956, Amory, 189.

210: 'he was furious about Ann's infidelity.', Blanche Blackwell interview, 17 April 2013.

211: 'to safeguard the life of the British Empire.', *Daily Express*, 1 November 1956.

211: 'consulting the Americans', Brendon, *The Decline and Fall of the British Empire*, 505.

211: 'toothless, immoral and anachronistic', Cannadine, *Churchill's Shadow*, 269.

211: 'the psychological watershed ...', Brendon, *The Decline and Fall of the British Empire*, 504.

212: 'good old imperialism', *NC Letters*, 29 November 1956, 626–8.

212: 'In the whole of modern history ...', Pearson, 349.

213: 'Sunshine Trip', Thorpe, *Eden*, 535.

213: 'The *Daily Mirror* ran a competition ...' , Brivati, *Hugh Gaitskell*, 284.

213: 'She seemed disconcerted ...', AF to EW, 24 November 1956, Amory, 188–9.

214: 'The Commander told me someone is coming ...', Pearson notes.

215: 'yesterday's *Daily Express* will mean a permanent breach ...', AF to EW, 24 November 1956, Amory, 189.

215: 'the hibiscus was in full bloom ...', *Gleaner*, 24 November 1956.

215: 'punching up my faded cushions ...', Pearson, 349.

215: 'No, Lady, I obey my Commander.', Pearson, 348.

215: who had played and sung at the Edens' house during the war ... , Thorpe, *Eden*, 330.

215: 'Anything I could see in fact that might mitigate the horrors ...', Pearson, 348.

216: 'Jamaica the Garden of Eden ...', Thorpe, *Eden*, 535.

216: 'A complete inertia has overcome us ...', CE to AF, Lycett, 305.

217: 'Fairly well authenticated rumours ...', *NC Letters*, 626.

218: 'rather fretting at being out of England!', Ibid.

218: 'to find everyone looking at us with very thoughtful eyes', Thorpe, *Eden,* 544.

1957: Jamaica Under Threat – *Dr No*

219: 'I feel horribly insecure ...', 'Volcano' unpublished script, Act 1:Scene 2:33

220: 'vast living-room ...', 'Volcano', 1:1:15.

220: 'his own private bachelor paradise.', 'Volcano', 1:1:21.

220: 'sex ego too strongly developed ...', 'Volcano', 2:2:36.

220: 'lively as a cricket.', 'Volcano', 1:1:5.

220: 'might have been just that exception.', 'Volcano', 2:2:37.

221: 'No. I'm not going to pretend anything ...', 'Volcano', 1:2:41.

221: 'physical passion we had for each other ...', 'Volcano', 1:2:42.

221: 'Yes. I do love him ...', 'Volcano', 2:2:40.

222: 'seasickness, rheumatism and neuralgia ...', AF to EW, 19 January 1957, Amory, 191–2.

223: 'luxurious Jamaican residence', *Time,* 5 May 1958.

223: 'extremely primitive ...', Raymond O'Neill interview, 13 May 2013.

223: 'An octopus was found ...' , 'My Friend the Octopus', *Sunday Times,* 24 March 1957.

223: 'the most amazing wildlife flew in ...', Raymond O'Neill interview, 13 May 2013.

223: 'wildly excited when he saw a scorpion.' , Fionn Morgan interview, 24 January 2013.

223: 'He's a fine little boy ...', *Gleaner,* 20 September 1964.

224: 'Noël-y and Coley, Binkie and Perry.', Raymond O'Neill interview, 13 May 2013.

224: 'She was a tomboy kind of girl, really,', Chris Blackwell interview, 8 July 2013.

225: 'One of the most important things he said to me ...', Blanche Blackwell interview, 13 March 2012.

225: 'He was a charming, handsome, gifted man ...', Thomson, *Dead Yard,* 233.

225: 'truly great man.', Cundall, *Historic Jamaica,* 260.

226: 'It was the most ghastly sea bottom I had ever explored ...', *Sunday Times,* 7 April 1957.

226: 'Wished you didn't mind aeroplanes ...', Lycett, 309.

227: 'You don't make a great deal of money from royalties ...', 'How to Write a Thriller'.

227: 'would be an excellent labour boss and general fixer', Lycett, 297.

227: '*Dr No* was very cardboardy and need not have been ...', Chancellor, *James Bond: the Man and his World,* 111.

228: 'something easy to start with ...', DN, 221.

228: 'was welcomed with deference because his reservation ...', DN, 241.

229: 'the setting sun flashed gold on the bright worms of tumbling rivers ...', DN, 236.

229: 'smelled the dung of the mule train …', *DN*, 267.

229: 'melancholy of the tropical dusk.', *DN*, 271.

229: 'The Riders were one of the old Jamaica families …', *DN*, 303.

230: 'She had no inhibitions …', *DN*, 402.

230: 'protecting the security of the British Empire', *DF*, 88.

230: 'its Kensington Palace Gardens, its Avenue D'Iéna …', *DN*, 211.

231: the steward is 'coloured.', *DN*, 213.

231: 'well run, well staffed …', *DN*, 212.

232: 'Unfortunately, strict patterns of behavior can be deadly …', *DN*, 214.

232: 'would not have been incongruous in Kingston …', *DN*, 213.

232: 'Splendid show. What a lark!', *DN*, 252–3.

233: 'Bond grinned at him. This was more like it …', *DN*, 253.

233: the immigration official is 'Negro', *DN*, 237.

233: 'delves well below the surface …', *DN*, 257.

234: 'an inappropriate wing collar and spotted bow tie', *DN*, 250.

234: 'sex and machete fights', *DN*, 230.

234: 'There were plenty of other worries …', *DN*, 231.

235: 'slim funds of the Secret Service', *DN*, 235.

235: trying for years to get the Treasury …', *DN*, 234.

235: 'Nowadays, softness was everywhere.', *DN*, 222.

236: 'scathing about Liberia … The first Negro State …', *DS*, 104.

236: 'drift, weak local government …', *DS*, 106.

236: 'unimpressed by relics from the Edwardian era …', *DN*, 395.

1958-60: *Goldfinger*; *For Your Eyes Only*; *Thunderball*

238: 'The man from the Central Intelligence Agency …', *TB*, 168.

239: 'tautest, most exciting and most brilliant tale.', *TLS*, 12 April 1957.

239: 'Peter Cheyney for the carriage trade', Chancellor, *James Bond: the Man and his World*, 43.

239: 'In hard covers my books are written for …', Pearson, 355.

240: 'Fleming rarely rises above the glossy prose …', *The Twentieth Century*, March 1958.

240: 'Sex, Snobbery and Sadism', *New Statesman*, 5 April 1958.

240: 'flick-knife remarks', Harling, *Vogue*.

241: 'At that party I felt it was a whole lot of children …', Blanche Blackwell interview, 13 March 2012.

241: 'Ian is a subtle bitch …', Lycett, 314–15.

241: 'One of the great sadnesses is the failure to make someone happy.', Lycett, 323.

241: 'arrived in a tempest …', IF to AF, January 1958, Amory, 211–12.

242: 'I used to come down to swim at twelve o'clock …', Blanche Blackwell interview, 17 April 2013.

242: 'She was really in love with Ian Fleming ...', Chris Blackwell interview, 8 July 2013.

242: 'I'm terribly worried about your health ...', IF to AF, 20 January 1958, Amory, 213.

243: 'a floating, boozy bum', David Niven, *Bring on the Empty Horses*, (Hamish Hamilton, London, 1975), 123.

243: 'even with his forked tongue sticking right through his cheek ...', *Observer*, 22 March 1959.

243: 'the foundation of our international credit', GF, (Penguin omnibus ed. 2002), 451.

244: 'the cruellest, most ruthless people in the world.', GF, 512.

244: 'It was modern piracy ...', GF, 590.

244: 'Who in America cared ...', GF, 610.

245: an annual growth rate of eight per cent. , Wallace, *The British Caribbean*, 129–30.

245: Manley was forced to admit that the rich had got richer, but the poor poorer., Sewell, *Culture and Decolonization*, 116.

246: '(1) To impress the United Nations ...', Fraser, *Ambivalent Anti-Colonialism*, 140–1.

246: 'As colonial ties with Britain are loosened ...', *Portsmouth Herald*, 1 May 1958.

247: 'a bird-brain. His attention span was about ten seconds.', Cargill, *Jamaica Farewell*, 160.

247: 'In the Commonwealth and Empire ...', David Killingray ed., *The West Indies (British Documents on the End of Empire)*, (The Stationery Office, London, 1999), 210.

247: 'Having visited Jamaica for twelve years ...', Lycett, 319.

247: 'flotsam and jetsam of our receding empire', Lycett, 335.

248: 'Communists creeping in from Ceylon ...', SS, 148.

248: 'underwater ace', SS, 147.

248: 'Champion harpoon-gun', SS, 144.

248: 'finest damned yacht in the Indian Ocean.', SS, 146

248: 'there were only three great powers ...', SS, 170.

249: 'A trip around the world ...', TC, 145–6.

249: 'the winter visitors and the residents ...', SS, 77.

249: 'filled the minor posts for thirty years ...', SS, 79.

250: 'It looks to me as if [President] Batista will be on the run soon ...', SS, 33.

250: 'the Batista people, but we've got a good man ...', SS, 44.

250: 'He hadn't wanted to do the job ...', SS, 78.

251: riddled with 'criminality.', TC, 97.

251: 'protecting the security of the British empire', DF, 88.

251: 'If foreign gangsters find they can get away with this kind of thing ...', SS, 47

251: 'They had declared and waged war ...': SS, 69

251: 'wild and rather animal ...': *SS*, 62–7

251: 'She was a very lovely woman ...', Blanche Blackwell interview, 16 February 2012.

251: 'she didn't make the smallest attempt ...', *SS*, 88–9.

252: 'When all kindness has gone ...', *SS*, 92–3.

252: 'It's extraordinary how much people can hurt each other ...', *SS*, 98.

252: 'snatch what we can', Lycett, 337.

252: 'It's tragic, nevertheless, that she should have cast a shadow ...', Lycett, 345.

253: 'Men suffer from not knowing ...' , Amory, 395.

254: 'I'm not the mother type ...', 'Volcano', 2:1:2.

254: 'a very obstreperous child, grossly pampered.', Amory, 158.

254: 'I am nauseated by his bad manners ...', IF to AF, undated, Amory, 296.

254: 'wizened, and gossipy ...', *Gielgud's Letters*, ed. Richard Mangan, (Weidenfeld & Nicolson, London, 2004), 258.

254: 'We have endured six days of rain and gales ...', EF to AW, 26 January 1960, Amory, 249.

255: 'Not at all nice there,', AF to EW, 26 March 1960, Amory, 252.

255-256: 'The gold's out of Goldeneye ...', Lycett, 364.

256: 'The Special Executive for Counterintelligence ...', *TB*, 69.

256: 'with the Cold War wearing off ...', *TB*, 91.

257: 'Peace [is] bustin' out all over.', *TB*, 209.

257: 'independent operator' in the spy 'game', *TC*, 173.

257: 'terrified by the whole business ...', *TB*, 296.

258: 'The two big poker players ...', *Gleaner*, 10 February 1963.

258: Planes with atom bombs don't get stolen ...', *TB*, 178.

258: mixed race, born of a Polish father and Greek mother., *TB*, 61.

259: 'an adventurer, a predator on the herd ...', *TB*, 135.

259: 'a sunken galleon thickly overgrown with coral.', *TB*, 144.

259: 'the haunt of every famous pirate ...', *TB*, 160.

259: 'that looked as if they belonged to the days of the pirates.', *TB*, 351–2.

259: "I asked him if he'd ever tried ganja ...', *Sunday Times* interview, 7 October 2012.

259: 'He wanted me to stay and watch ...', Blanche Blackwell interview, 13 March 2012.

260: 'The modern spy could not permit himself ...', Dulles, 'Our Spy-Boss Who Loved Bond', *Life*, 28 August 1966.

260: any one of these little sandy cays ...', *TB*, 296.

261: in exchange for a loan of $20m in convertible currency ... ,.Von Tunzelmann, *Red Heat*, 187–9.

261: 'If the Americans once let up ...', *MGG*, 142.

261: 'Shortly afterwards, the CIA agent David Atlee Phillips ...', Von Tunzelmann, *Red Heat*, 207.

261: 'put my people in CIA to work on this …', Dulles, 'Our Spy-Boss Who Loved Bond', *Life*, 28 August 1966.

262: 'obsessed by Ian's books', AF to CE, 16 February 1964, Amory, 336.

262: the President's favourite books … , Hugh Sidey, 'The President's Voracious Reading Habits', *Life*, 17 March 1961.

1961–2: *The Spy Who Loved Me; On Her Majesty's Secret Service*

263: 'There were moments …', Plomer, *Encounter*.

263: 'I'm the world's authority on giving up smoking …', *TB*, 154–161.

264: 'that nagging sense of morning guilt …', *TB*, 1–2.

264: 'Ian had a high fever and was fearfully cross …', AF to EW, 4 February 1961, Amory, 278

264: 'Annie looking exhausted …', *NC Diary*, 29 January 1961, 463.

265: 'taken against Jamaica in a big way …', *NC Letters*, 23 December 1960, 673.

265: 'Jamaica's going to go to the dogs …', Karen Schleifer interview, 21 June 2013.

265: 'Lord Brownlow imported a farm manageress …', AF to EW, 4 February 1961, Amory, 279.

266: 'from drabness, fustiness, snobbery …', *SLM*, 3.

266: 'smoking and drinking, phenobarbital …', *SLM* ,67.

266: 'from the grimy sallowness that had been the badge of my London life ….', *SLM*, 4.

267: 'started brilliantly', *NC Diary*, 8 April 1962, 503.

267: 'The single lamentable lapse …', Bryce, 105.

267: 'dreary' chancellor… , *James Bond: the Man and his World*, 187.

267: 'the High-Stakes Gambling Scene …', *Time*, 13 April 1962.

267: 'doing my best to reverse this foolish gesture …', AF to EW, 20 April 1962, Amory, 306.

267: 'our pornography fund.', letter to EW, 2 August 1962, Amory, 314.

268: 'I am glad to say that while the iron crab …', Pearson, 391.

268: 'the claws of "the iron crab" tightened around his heart …', Quennell, *Wanton Chase*, 156.

268: 'losing the vices that were so much part of his ruthless …', *TB*, 45.

268: 'and then, slightly drunk, go to bed …', *MSS*, 101.

269: 'a super-abundancy of alcohol in the blood-stream.', *MSS*, 248.

269: 'Bond was aching for a drink', *MSS*, 256.

269: he needs three drinks to her one., *MSS*, 327.

269: 'chain-smoking', *MSS*, 45.

270: 'by the far the best novel …', *Cinema Retro* Magazine, 'Movie Classics Special Edition', no.4, 22.

270: selling over 70,000 hardback copies … , Benson, *James Bond Bedside Companion*, 24.

270: 'It is better plotted and retains its insane grip ...', *Observer*, 31 March 1963.

270: 'the 20th century vogue of realism ...', *LA Times*, 25 August 1963.

270: 'the miracle of the latest German export figures', *MSS*, 323.

270: 'the new African States.', *MSS*, 113.

270: 'all true and it was all about a great Navy ...', *MSS*, 257.

271: Broccoli had tried unsuccessfully for the same option ... , Broccoli, *Snow Melts*, 126.

272: 'a ludicrous character, Fu Manchu with hooks.', Tashchen, 31.

272: 'Ian attended several of our meetings ...', Broccoli, *Snow Melts*, 159.

273: 'had everything we were looking for.', Broccoli, *Snow Melts*, 174.

273: Patrick McGoohan and James Fox refused the role ..., Duncan, *The James Bond Archives*, 32.

273: 'stage Englishness ... no monocles, moustaches, bowler hats ...', Broccoli, *Snow Melts*, 159.

273: 'I never got introduced to Fleming ...', BBC Scene by Scene, quoted in *Cinema Retro*, 'Movie Classics Special Edition', 132.

274: 'the cheap self-assertiveness of young labour since the war.', *TB*, 12.

274: 'not quite the idea I had of Bond ...', Michael Denning, 'Licensed to Look', in Lindner, ed. *The James Bond Phenomenon*, 58

275: 'Dear Ian, The answer to your suggestion is No... No...', Duncan, *The James Bond Archives*, 34.

275: 'If the first day's shooting was any indication ...', *Gleaner*, 17 January 1962.

276: 'kissing a strange man', Marguerite Gordon interview, 21 January 2014.

276: 'got the job because she owned the house ...', *Cinema Retro*.

277: 'Sean's got this terrible Scottish accent ...', Moxon unpublished memoir.

277: 'didn't do a tremendous amount during the Second World War ...', interview by Lee Pfeiffer, *Cinema Retro*, 31.

278: 'very untidy and crude', *Cinema Retro*, 50.

279: 'a riot', Chris Blackwell interview, 22 January 2012.

279: 'The biggest problem is the "manana" attitude ...', Draxin, *A Bond for Bond*, 58–9.

280: 'They were shooting a beach scene ...', AF to EW, 17 February 1962, Amory, 297–8.

280: 'that beautiful girl with the long fair hair ...', *MSS*, 155.

280: 'Together they were a joy to be with ...', *Cinema Retro*, 124.

281: 'Filming has brought employment and publicity ...', *Gleaner*, 20 February 1962.

284: 'a mother who shuts the door is no mother.', Miller, *Survey of Commonwealth Affairs*, 341.

284: 'More than anywhere else in the old colonial empire ...', Wallace, *The British Caribbean*, 217.

284: 'All over the island there is now tip-toe expectancy ...', *Gleaner*, 4 August 1962.

285: 'had twelve attendants and he was not allowed a valet', AF to EW, 2 August 1962, Amory, 315.

285: 'a Kingston gaily bedecked with flags ...', *Gleaner*, 3 August 1962.

285: 'the most amazing, tremendous reception.', Fiona Aird interview, 20 February 2014.

286: 'Boat Races, Swimming Races, Dress Parade ...', *Gleaner*, 2 August 1962.

287: 'I felt good, elated ...', Pearl Flynn interview, 21 June 2013.

287: 'at the time of Jamaican independence ...', Judi Moxon Zakka interview, 18 January 2014.

287: 'A people who have managed so successfully ...', *Ian Fleming Introduces Jamaica*, 32.

288: 'Jamaica stands between Castro and the Panama Canal.', *Gleaner*, 30 June 1962.

288: 'In asking for economic aid ...', *Gleaner*, 2 July 1962.

288: 'The right road will have us all walk to ...', *Gleaner*, 2 February 1962.

288–9: 'I thought in 1962, in view of my complexion ...', Chris Blackwell interview, 22 January 2014.

289: 'It was an abominable occasion ...', AF to EW, 2 August 1962, Amory, 315.

289: *Dr No* sold 1.5 million copies ... , Black, *The Politics of James Bond,* 96.

289: in 1963 the figure was 4,468,000. , Lindner ed., *The James Bond Phenomenon,* 17.

1963–4: *You Only Live Twice; The Man With The Golden Gun*

290: Quote from IF, 64 radio interview by Rene MacColl.

290: 'Watching his character deteriorate ...', IF to AF, undated 1962, Amory, 296.

291: 'In the present twilight we are hurting each other ...', IF to AF, undated 1962, Amory, 296.

291: 'regain some spirit, which, though you haven't noticed it ...', IF to AF, no date, Amory, 303–4.

291: 'I looked after him. Jamaica and me: we could have kept him alive.', Blanche Blackwell interview, 17 April 2013.

292: 'far more dangerous than barracuda or shark', *SS*, 188.

293: 'it was a mystery to his friends ...', *SS*, 185.

293: 'When you see "Doctor No" ...', *Gleaner*, 10 February 1963.

294: 'she had no contact with the present ...', AF to EW, 1 January 63, Amory, 320.

295: 'You must touch to get the precise texture ...', Lycett, 412.

295: 'Late at the office ...', *YLT*, 19.

295: 'It was three thirty ...', *YLT*, 27.

295: 'patriotic sort of chap', *YLT*, 23.

295: 'He probably doesn't think much of us ...', *YLT*, 36.

295: a now more or less valueless ally ...', *YLT*, 66.

295: 'You have not only lost a great Empire ...', *YLT*, 108–9

296: 'Bond's mission is aimed at ...', *New York Times*, 22 August 1964.

296: 'he had to admit to himself that his lungs were in a terrible state.', YLT, 195–6.

297: 'some of the old snap seems to be gone.', *The Times*, 19 March 1964.

297: 'Ian always was a death-wish Charlie.', Lycett, 422.

297: 'a man who lives as if he were going to die tomorrow ...', *YLT*, 63.

297: he could not smoke in court ... , AF to EW, 6 December 1963, Amory, 331.

297: 'Your vastly welcome decision was vastly welcome.', Bryce, 134.

298: 'The weather and the island were at their best ...', Bryce, 136.

299: 'The last time the Commander came ...', *Gleaner*, 20 September 1964.

299: 'But that's suicide, sir!', *MGG*, 27.

299: 'letting the scented air ...', *MGG*, 82.

299: 'dull and lacklustre', *MGG*, 94.

299: 'Beau Desert and Honeychile Rider ...', *MGG*, 45.

300: 'not as beautiful as the north ...', *MGG*, 57.

300: 'like sort of old Jamaica ...', *MGG*, 62–3.

300: 'with those warm, wide smiles ...', *Sunday Times*, 8 April 1956.

300: 'perhaps as the private house of a merchant ...', *MGG*, 59.

300: 'The Thunderbird Hotel', *MGG*, 51.

301: 'Maroon Country', *MGG*, 137.

301: 'overplayed the slush fund approach.', *MGG*, 138–40.

301: 'It'll almost certainly lead to trouble ...', *MGG*, 140.

303: 'no oxygen, dreadful humidity ...', EW from AF, 4 February 1964, Amory, 333.

303: 'I *loathe* the tropics ...', AF to CE, 16 February 1964, Amory, 335–6.

303: 'this gilded prison', AF to Frances Donaldson, 16 February 1964, Amory, 334–5.

303: 'It is painful to see Ian struggle ...', AF to HC, 17 February 1964, Amory, 336–7.

304: 'obscene American publication called Playboy.', AF to EW, 22 February 1964, Amory, 338.

304: 'piles of over-decorated native ware.', *MGG*, 42.

304: 'big tax concessions that Jamaica gave', *MGG*, 86.

304: If the hotel got off the ground ...', *MGG*, 87.

305: 'Ian was as bored as me ...', AF to Peter Quennell, 5 March 1964, Amory, 339.

306: 'I shall not waste my days in trying to prolong them.', *YLT*, 273.

306: 'He gave the impression of not being able to get out of bed ...', Winston Stona interview, 23 June 2013.

306: 'I've always had one foot ...', Chancellor, *James Bond: the Man and his World*, 231.

306: 'gloomy, fragile figure', Lycett, 437.

306: 'nothing nice or funny is happening.', AF to EW, 19 June 1964, Amory, 342.

306: 'When his health was no longer good ...', Plomer, *Encounter*.

307: 'very shaky, his normally brick-red complexion ...', Ross, *Coastwise Lights*, 197.

307: 'Ian's life from now on hangs on a thread ...', AF to John and Fionn Morgan, 8 August 1964, Amory, 349.

307: 'a great friend of Jamaica ...', *Gleaner*, 15 August 64.

308: Independence has not improved the island ...', AF to EW, 4 February 1964, Amory, 333.

308: 'The Brownlows are very unpopular ...', AF to EW, 22 February 1964, Amory, 338.

308: 'Although by nature gentle, indolent ...', Coward, *Complete Short Stories*, 32.

309: 'graduate from Edinburgh.', *MGG*, 172.

309: 'regularly as clockwork', *Ian Fleming Introduces Jamaica*, 11.

309: 'that a good man was after a bad man in the swamp.', *MGG*, 172–3.

310: 'For all her new-found "Independence" ...', *MGG*, 45.

310: 'She had gained her Independence ...', *Ian Fleming Introduces Jamaica*, 11.

Epilogue: Goldeneye Since Fleming

312: 'I loved him and am angry with him ...', Pearson notes, NC interview, 22 May 1965. Manuscripts Department, Lilly Library Pearson J. Mss.

313: 'It is hard to exaggerate the importance of the death of Ian Fleming to Ann ...', Amory, 353.

313: 'quite intimidating. Very funny ...', Mark Amory interview, 27 September 2013.

313: 'potentially brilliant', Raymond O'Neill interview, 13 May 2013.

314: 'he was not so oversexed as James Bond.', AF to EW, 12 March 1963, Amory, 323.

314: 'an extraordinary figure ...', Mark Amory interview, 27 September 2013.

314: 'talking all the trendy nonsense ...', AF to Clarissa Avon, 27 February 1969, Amory, 393.

314: 'According to his girlfriend since Oxford, Rachel Fletcher ...', Rachel Fletcher interview, 31 March 2014.

314: 'A magical place ...', Frances Charteris interview, 12 April 2014.

315: 'Permanent nervous gastritis ...' , AF to Leigh Fermor, 24 October 1976, Amory, 416.

315: 'This was a blow so stunning ...', Amory, 353.

316: 'In naval terms she was something of a privateer ...', Huth, *Well-Remembered Friends*, 78.

316: 'searing heat and a calypso steel band.', Moore, *Roger Moore as James Bond*, 62.

316: 'I just remember the music and the warmth ...', Duncan, *The James Bond Archives*, 226.

317: 'Ross Kananga, the alligator specialist and handler ...', Moore, *Roger Moore as James Bond*, 43.

317: 'a great sense of awe ...', Roger Moore email interview, 17 February 2014.

317: 'I'd just paid him seventy thousand pounds ...', Chris Blackwell interview, 23 June 2013.

320: 'We were looking forward to a better Jamaica ...', Pearl Flynn interview, 21 June 2013.

320: 'If you speak to most older Jamaicans ...', Chris Blackwell interview, 8 July 2013.

320: 'the worst thing that could have happened to Jamaicans ...', Thomson, *Dead Yard*, 233.

320: 'That wasn't altogether a completely happy time ...', *Cinema Retro*.

321: 'full of submerged self-parody.', *Observer*, 8 October 1962.

Select Bibliography

Ian Fleming (all Jonathan Cape, London)

Fiction

Casino Royale, 1953
Live and Let Die, 1954
Moonraker, 1955
Diamonds are Forever, 1956
From Russia, with Love, 1957
Dr No, 1958
Goldfinger, 1959
For Your Eyes Only, 1960
Thunderball (based on a film treatment by K. McClory, J. Whittingham and Ian Fleming), 1961
The Spy Who Loved Me, 1962
On Her Majesty's Secret Service, 1963
You Only Live Twice, 1964
Chitty-Chitty-Bang-Bang, 1964
The Man with the Golden Gun, 1965
Octopussy, 1966

Non-Fiction

The Diamond Smugglers, 1957
Thrilling Cities, 1963

Secondary Works

Abrahams, Isaac. *Jamaica: an Island Mosaic*. London: HMSO, 1957
Amis, Kingsley. *The James Bond Dossier*. London: Jonathan Cape, 1965
Amory, Mark, ed. *The Letters of Ann Fleming*. London: Collins Harvill, 1985
Amory, Mark, ed. *The Letters of Evelyn Waugh*. London: Weidenfeld & Nicolson, 1980
Andrew, Christopher and Mitrokhin, Vasili, *The KGB and the World: The Mitrokhin Archive II*. London: Allen Lane, 2005
Arnold, James A., ed. *A History of Literature in the Caribbean*. Vol. 2 Philadelphia: John Benjamins Publishing Company, 2001
Atkins, John. *The British Spy Novel*. London: John Calder, 1984

Barringer, T. J., Quilley, Geoff and Fordham, Douglas, ed. *Art and the British Empire*. Manchester: Manchester University Press, 2007

Beaton, Cecil. *The Strenuous Years: Diaries 1948–53*. London: Weidenfeld & Nicolson, 1980

Beckles, Hilary. *Britain's Black Debt*. Kingston: University of the West Indies Press, 2013

Bennett, Tony and Woollacott, Janet. *Bond and Beyond: the Political Career of a Popular Hero*. Basingstoke: Macmillan Education, 1987

Benson, Raymond. *James Bond Bedside Companion*. London: Boxtree, 1988

Black, Clinton V. *The History of Jamaica*. Kingston: Longman Caribbean, 1988

Black, James. *The Politics of James Bond*. Westport, CT: Greenwood Publishing, 2000

Boyd, Ann S. *The Devil with James Bond*. Westport, CT: Greenwood Publishing, 1967

Brendon, Piers. *The Decline and Fall of the British Empire, 1781–1997*. London: Jonathan Cape, 2007

Bret, David. *Errol Flynn: Gentleman Hellraiser*. London: JR Books, 2009

Brivati, Brian. *Hugh Gaitskell*. London: Richard Cohen Books, 1996

Broccoli, Albert R. *When the Snow Melts: the Autobiography of Cubby Broccoli*. London: Boxtree, 1998

Bryce, Ivar. *You Only Live Once*. London: Weidenfeld & Nicolson, 1975

Del Buono, Oreste and Eco, Umberto, ed. *The Bond Affair*. London: Macmillan, 1965

Cannadine, David. *In Churchill's Shadow: Confronting the Past in Modern Britain*. London: Allen Lane, 2002

Cargill, Morris, ed. *Ian Fleming Introduces Jamaica*. London: André Deutsch, 1965

Cargill, Morris. *Jamaica Farewell*. Secaucus, NJ: Lyle Stuart, 1978

Cargill, Morris. *A Selection of his Writings in the Gleaner 1952–1985*. Kingston: Topical Publishers, 1987

Carlton, David. *Eden: A Biography*. London: Allen Lane, 1981

Chancellor, Henry. *James Bond: the Man and his World*. London: John Murray, 2005

Chapman, Esther, ed. *Jamaica, 1955*. London: Chantrey Publications, 1954

Chapman, Esther. *Development in Jamaica*. Kingston: Arawak Press, 1954

Chapman, James. *Licence to Thrill: A Cultural History of the James Bond Films*. New York: I. B. Tauris, 1999

Comentale, Edward P., Watt, Stephen and Willman, Skip, ed. *Ian Fleming and James Bond: the Cultural Politics of 007*. Bloomington, IN: Indiana University Press, 2005

Cooper, Artemis, ed. *Mr Wu and Mrs Stitch: the Letters of Evelyn Waugh and Diana Cooper*. London: Hodder & Stoughton, 1991

Coward, Noël. *The Complete Short Stories*. London: Methuen, 1985

Coward, Noël. *Play Parade*. 6 vols. London: William Heinemann, 1934–62

Coward, Noël. *Pomp and Circumstance*. London: William Heinemann, 1960

Cundall, Frank. *Historic Jamaica*. Kingston: Institute of Jamaica, 1915

Darwin, John. *Britain and Decolonisation*. London: Macmillan, 1988

Day, Barry, ed. *The Letters of Noël Coward*. London: Methuen, 2007

Deerre, Noel. *The History of Sugar*. 2 vols. London: Chapman & Hall, 1949–50

Draxin, Charles. *A Bond for Bond: Film Finances and Dr No*. London: Film Finances, 2011

Duncan, Paul, ed. *The James Bond Archives*, London: Taschen 2012

Durgnat, Raymond. *A Mirror for England: British Movies from Austerity to Affluence*. London: Faber and Faber, 1970

Fermor, Patrick Leigh. *The Traveller's Tree*. London: John Murray, 1950

Flynn, Errol. *My Wicked Wicked Ways*. London: Heinemann, 1960

Foot, Sir Hugh. *Empire into Commonwealth*. London: Liberal Publication Department, 1961

Foot, Sir Hugh. *A Start in Freedom*. London: Hodder & Stoughton, 1964

Foot, Sir Hugh. *Race Relations in the British Commonwealth and the United Nations*. Cambridge: Cambridge University Press, 1967

Fraser, Cary. *Ambivalent Anti-Colonialism: The United States and the Genesis of West Indian Independence, 1940–1964*. Connecticut: Cary Greenwood Press, 1994

Gilbert, Jon. *Ian Fleming: The Bibliography*. London: Queen Anne's Press, 2012

Greig, Geordie. *Breakfast with Lucian*. London: Jonathan Cape, 2013

Griswold, John. *Ian Fleming's James Bond: Annotations and Chronologies for Ian Fleming's Bond Stories*. Bloomington, IN: AuthorHouse, 2006

Grose, Peter. *Gentleman Spy: The Life of Allen Dulles*. London: André Deutsch, 1995

Hakewill, James. *A Picturesque Tour of the Island of Jamaica*. London, 1825

Hart, Richard. *The End of Empire*. Kingston: Arawak Publications, 2006

Hart, Richard. *Time for a Change*. Kingston: Arawak Publications, 2004

Henriques, Louis Fernando M. *Family and Colour in Jamaica*. London: Eyre & Spottiswoode, 1953

Higman, B. W. *Jamaica Surveyed*. Kingston: University of the West Indies Press, 1988

Hoare, Philip. *Noël Coward: A Biography*. London: Sinclair-Stevenson, 1995

Huggins, Molly. *Too Much to Tell*. London: Heinemann, 1967

Hugill, Antony. *Sugar and All That: A History of Tate and Lyle*. London: Gentry Books, 1978

Hulme, Peter. *Colonial Encounters: Europe and the Native Caribbean, 1492–1797*. London: Methuen, 1986

Huth, Angela, ed. *Well-Remembered Friends: Eulogies on Celebrated Lives*. London: John Murray, 2004

Issa, Suzanne. *Mr Jamaica: Abe Issa*. Kingston, 1994

Kerr, Madeline. *Personality and Conflict in Jamaica*. London: Collins, 1963

Lesley, Cole. *The Life of Noël Coward*. London: Jonathan Cape, 1976

Lewis, Jeremy. *Cyril Connolly: a Life*. London: Jonathan Cape, 1997

Lindner, Christoph, ed. *The James Bond Phenomenon: A Critical Reader*. Manchester: Manchester University Press, 2009

Lycett, Andrew. *Ian Fleming*. London: Weidenfeld & Nicolson, 1995

Macintyre, Ben. *For Your Eyes Only: Ian Fleming & James Bond*. London: Bloomsbury, 2008

Martin, L. Emile. *Reflections on Jamaica's Tourism*. Montego Bay, 1994

Mawby, Spencer. *Ordering Independence: the End of Empire in the Anglophone Caribbean, 1947–69*. London: Palgrave Macmillan, 2012

McCormick, Donald. *17F: The Life of Ian Fleming*. London: Peter Owen, 1993

McIntyre, W. David. *The Significance of the Commonwealth, 1965–90*. Basingstoke: Macmillan Academic and Professional, 1991

Meikle, George. *In Praise of Jamaica*. Kingston, 2011

Miller, J. D. B. *Survey of Commonwealth Affairs*. London: OUP, 1974

Mitchell, Sir Harold. *In My Stride*. London: Chambers, 1951

Mitchell, Sir Harold. *The Spice of Life*. London: Bodley Head, 1974

Montgomery Hyde, H. *The Quiet Canadian: The Secret Service Story of Sir William Stevenson*. London: Hamish Hamilton, 1962

Moore, Roger. *Roger Moore as James Bond*. London: Pan Books, 1973

Morley, Sheridan. *The Private Lives of Noël and Gertie*. London: Oberon, 1999

O'Connell, Mark. *Catching Bullets: Memoirs of a Bond Fan*. Droxford: Splendid Books, 2012

Olivier, Laurence. *Confessions of an Actor*. London: Weidenfeld & Nicolson, 1982

Payn, Graham and Morley, Sheridan, ed. *The Noël Coward Diaries*. London: Weidenfeld & Nicolson, 1982

Pearson, John. *The Life of Ian Fleming*. London: Jonathan Cape, 1966

Pfeiffer, Lee and Worrall, Dave. *The Essential Bond: the Authorized Guide to the World of 007*. London: Boxtree, 1998

Pringle, Kenneth. *Waters of the West*. London: G. Allen & Unwin, 1938

Quennell, Peter. *The Sign of the Fish*. London: Collins, 1960

Quennell, Peter. *The Wanton Chase*. London: Collins, 1980

Rankin, Nicholas. *Ian Fleming's Commandos: The Story of 30 Assault Unit in WWII*. London: Faber and Faber, 2011

Ranston, Jackie. *The Lindo Legacy*. London: Toucan Books, 2000

Read, Piers Paul. *Alec Guinness*. London: Simon & Schuster, 2003

Roberts, W. Adolphe. *Jamaica: the Portrait of an Island*. New York: Coward-McCann, 1955

Ross, Alan. *Coastwise Lights*. London: Collins Harvill, 1990

Ross, Alan. *Through the Caribbean: The MCC Tour of the West Indies, 1959–1960*. London: Hamish Hamilton, 1960

Salewicz, Chris and Boot, Adrian. *Firefly: Noël Coward in Jamaica*. London: Victor Gollancz, 1999

Sewell, Sharon Catherine. *Culture and Decolonization in the British West Indies: Literature and Politics, 1930–80*. Proquest, 2007

Sherlock, Philip. *Norman Manley*. London: Macmillan, 1980

Sherlock, Philip and Bennett, Hazel. *The Story of the Jamaican People*. Kingston: Ian Randle, 1998

Starkey, Lycurgus Monroe. *James Bond: His World of Values*. New York: Lutterworth Press, 1967

Taylor, Frank. *To Hell with Paradise: A History of the Jamaican Tourist Industry*. Pittsburgh: University of Pittsburgh Press, 1993

Thompson, Krista A., ed. *An Eye for the Tropics: Tourism, Photography, and Framing the Caribbean Picturesque*. Durham, NC: Duke University Press, 2006

Thomson, Ian. *The Dead Yard: Tales of Modern Jamaica*. London: Faber and Faber, 2009

Thorpe, D. R. *Eden*. London: Chatto & Windus, 2003

Turner, Louis. *The Golden Hordes: International Tourism and the Pleasure Periphery*. London: Constable, 1975

Vickers, Hugo, ed. *Cocktails and Laughter: The Albums of Loelia Lindsay*. London: Hamish Hamilton, 1983

Von Tunzelmann, Alex. *Red Heat: Conspiracy, Murder and the Cold War in the Caribbean*. London: Simon & Schuster, 2011

Wallace, Elisabeth. *The British Caribbean: from the Decline of Colonialism to the End of Federation*. Toronto: University of Toronto Press, 1977

Warner, Keith Q. *On Location: Cinema and Film in the Anglophone Caribbean*. London: Macmillan Educational, 2000

Waugh, Alec. *The Sugar Islands*. London: Cassell, 1958

Winder, Simon. *The Man Who Saved Britain*. London: Picador, 2006

Index

Italicised numbers refer to pictures or their captions.